Charlotte R. Peck

from

Ann Bayard Ketterer

COMMON
WEEDS
OF
THE UNITED
STATES

COMMON
WEEDS
OF
THE UNITED
STATES

Prepared by the Agricultural Research Service of the

United States Department of Agriculture

Dover Publications, Inc.

New York

Published in Canada by General Publishing Company, Ltd., 30 Lesmill Road, Don Mills, Toronto, Ontario.

Published in the United Kingdom by Constable and Company, Ltd., 10 Orange Street, London WC 2.

This Dover edition, first published in 1971, is an unabridged and unaltered republication of the work originally published by the United States Department of Agriculture (Govt. Printing Office) in 1970 under the title *Selected Weeds of the United States*.

International Standard Book Number: 0-486-20504-5
Library of Congress Catalog Card Number: 70-152417

Manufactured in the United States of America
Dover Publications, Inc.
180 Varick Street
New York, N. Y. 10014

CONTENTS

INTRODUCTION

Plant species are considered weeds when they interfere with man's activities or his welfare. Such plants grow where they are not wanted. They reduce yield and quality of crop and forage species; they make roadsides, utility rights-of-way, and landscape plantings unsightly; they poison livestock and man either directly or as allergens; they clog lakes, irrigation ditches, and drainageways; and they reduce the availability of fish and wildlife. Weeds thrive in close association with man and his domesticated plants and animals.

Losses caused by weeds exceed losses caused by any other class of agricultural pests. Losses in developed countries in the temperate zones, where efficient methods of weed control have been developed, range from 10 to 15 percent of the total value of agricultural and forest products. Losses from weeds are greater in tropical regions. Here, half or more of the total effort of farming may be devoted to combating invading vegetation.

The life duration of the different weeds is not uniform. Many weeds are annual or winter annual; some are biennial; and many are perennial. Also, any particular species may have both annual and winter annual forms, or annual and biennial, or biennial and perennial. We still have much to learn about life duration of weeds. Investigations of this type are complicated by the influences of climate, disease organisms, insects, and other factors.

Annuals complete their life cycles within one year. Annuals have no means of survival from one year to the next except by seeds, although some spread, as purslane, by the rooting of prostrate stems or stem segments. Winter annuals germinate in the fall and pass through one winter as seedlings or rosettes; biennials germinate in the spring or early summer and

survive the winter as rosettes. Both winter annuals and biennials complete their life cycles after producing seed in the second year. Control measures for these groups of weeds thus include the prevention of seed production by destroying the weeds before flowering and the encouragement of germination by cultural practices. This latter reduces the reservoir of seed in the soil.

Simple perennials persist for more than 2 years. Since these weeds have no means of spreading other than by seeds, they may be treated much as annuals or biennials, but deeper root cutting may be necessary to eliminate them.

More difficult weeds to control are the creeping or persistent perennials spreading by means of seed, underground lateral roots, rhizomes, aboveground stolons, and stems that root upon contact with the soil (layering). It is apparent that in spite of the application of severe control measures, many of these weeds are able not only to survive but also to increase through lateral spread. Control depends on prevention of seed production and destruction of shoots and roots.

Since 1945 the use of herbicides in agriculture has expanded remarkably. Use of these chemicals has revolutionized weed control practices; in fact, no other innovation in the history of agriculture has been accepted so rapidly and widely as the use of chemical weed killers. Such herbicides have been devised for many control purposes and we expect that even more effective and more specific herbicides will be discovered in the future.

In spite of the successful application of herbicides to control weeds, other methods continue to be important. Very frequently, a combination of tillage and application of herbicides to weeds in a crop will be more effective than either method alone. Also, because some weeds respond only slightly, if at all, to herbicides and some crops are more sensitive to herbicides than the weeds themselves, mechanical methods of control must be used. Herbicidal

[1] Descriptions and distribution maps by Clyde F. Reed, *research botanist* and *plant explorer*, Crops Research Division, Agricultural Research Service, and drawings by Regina O. Hughes, *scientific illustrator*, Crops Research Division, Agricultural Research Service.

sprays are not persistently effective in reclaiming grassland or in removing weeds from lawns if soil fertility is too low or drainage too poor for vigorous growth of grasses and clover. Under such conditions, either fertilization or drainage, or both, are also required to enable the grasses and clover to compete more successfully with weed and shrub seedlings, even after herbicide has been applied. Also, grazing often has to be adjusted to prevent deterioration of the grassland.

Control methods are developing so rapidly that recommendations are soon out of date. Also, recommendations for weed control vary from one area to another. For these reasons, we omitted recommendations on control in this publication. These will be found in other publications that are more easily kept current.

Methods of weed control are determined by the specific weed species to be controlled. Therefore, the first step in deciding how to solve a weed problem is to correctly identify the weed species. It is for this purpose that this handbook has been prepared. This information will be useful to research workers, weed specialists, agricultural extension agents, and others interested in weeds and their control. This handbook will help to identify some of the more common and important weeds infesting lawns, gardens, crops, pastures, ponds, and other areas.

Handbooks such as this can only assist in identification; much effort has to be made by the person identifying the weeds. The great number of weed species, the variability within a single species, and the problems attendant on recognizing weeds in different stages of growth, all make identification difficult. In addition, this handbook does not describe all the weeds that may be found. Because few people will be able to identify all the weeds growing on their land, their only recourse is to send specimens of the unknown weeds to the county agent or to the weed specialist at the agricultural college at the State university.

Too frequently, people send specimens for identification without first taking proper care in collecting and packaging. The material arrives at its destination in such poor condition that it cannot be identified. The sender should collect the best possible material, preferably with flowers, seed-bearing parts, and part of the underground system. Lack of a complete plant, however, should not deter anyone from sending a specimen. Unless the material is to be mailed promptly, it should be dried between papers and cardboards placed under some heavy object. The packaging should be adequate to insure safe arrival. When several plants are submitted, each specimen should bear a numbered tag corresponding to duplicates kept by the sender. Notes on habit, history of infestation, and place and habitat of the collection are valuable for identification and sometimes give information useful in giving advice for control.

This handbook illustrates and describes many of the important weeds in the United States and it indicates their geographical distribution in this country. In 1848, the species of plants considered as weeds was about 10 percent of the species known in the United States; today, over 50 percent of our flora is made up of species that are considered undesirable by some segment of our society. Most of our weeds have been introduced, either accidentally or intentionally. A few of our native species have become more common weeds because of man's activities and because of his modern means of transportation.

The 224 species of weeds included in this handbook were selected by weed scientists largely from the composite list of 1,775 weeds published by the Weed Science Society of America in *WEEDS* 14: 347–386, 1966. Those selected are some of the prevalent weeds in croplands, grazing lands, noncroplands, and aquatic sites.

The scientific and common names of weeds used in this publication also generally are those of the Weed Science Society of America. In a few cases, changes in scientific name were made after extensive study.

The general organization of the families in this book follows the evolutionary order. It begins with the simplest plants (*Chara*) and the ferns and fern allies, and proceeds through the monocots and dicots to the Compositae. Within each family the genera and species are arranged alphabetically according to the scientific name. Occasionally synonyms are given, especially those appearing in various current flora and weed lists. The common name suggested in *WEEDS* is given first (and should be the one used), and then additional common names are given sometimes. No attempt is made to give complete scientific synonomy or a complete list of common names.

DESCRIPTIONS AND MAPS

The descriptions and maps in this publication have been prepared and compiled from regional, State, and local publications on flora of the United States.

The maps give only a general approximation of the area in which a plant may be considered a weed, because weeds come and go in a region and because detailed information often has not been available. The denser hatching on the maps indicates an area where the weed is of great economic importance. After the original maps were made, they were submitted to groups of weed scientists for review and suggestions. Insofar as possible, the suggestions are incorporated in the final maps. Even so, the exact boundaries of weed distribution are often questionable. For instance, it is not likely that weed distribution boundaries and State lines would often coincide; nevertheless, in many maps, such distributions are indicated.

The descriptions are semitechnical, with the terminology simplified wherever possible. A glossary of technical terms will be found on page 449. Some of the terms are illustrated for clarity on pages 446–448. Where a plant characteristic is found in only one species (as in *Chara*, where many technical terms apply to algae only), that characteristic is identified in the description and not in the glossary. Most confusing is the use of the words "fruit" and "seed" by the laymen because their meaning differs from that used by botanists. For example, a corn "seed" or "grain" is really a "caryopsis." A caryopsis is a particular kind of fruit.

All measurements in this publication are in the metric system and pertain to the life size of plants.

The time of year indicates when the species is in flower, unless otherwise indicated as a fruiting range. In any particular region the dates of flowering may be earlier or later than indicated.

DRAWINGS

The drawings of the species of weeds illustrated in this book have been prepared from herbarium specimens. Herbarium specimens for this work were loaned to us by the National Arboretum, the U.S. National Herbarium, and the Reed Herbarium.

A habit sketch and magnified areas of leaves, stems, flowers, fruits, and seeds are included for the species illustrated. Size of parts illustrated relative to life size of plants varies according to the part being shown; some are less than life size, others are magnified. Relative size is shown in the legend. The structures of some species discussed are illustrated here for the first time in a manual of this type.

CHARACEAE

Chara vulgaris L.

CHARA

Perennial aquatic herb (Fig. 1); *Plants* monoecious, moderately to heavily encrusted, rarely unencrusted; *Stems* 5–60 (occasionally 100) cm. long, moderately slender to stout, 0.2–1.1 mm. in diameter, the internodes 1–3 times as long as the branchlets, up to 4 (rarely 10) cm. long; *Cortex* essentially 2-layered, furrowed, equal-sided or lumpy; *Spine cells* solitary, rarely in pairs, variable, rudimentary and globose to well-developed (up to 1.3 mm. long) and spreading, ovoid and blunt; *Stipulodes* in 2 tiers, 2 sets per branchlets, typically contiguous but often separated, variable in size from obscure up to 1.6 mm. long, exceeding the branchlet segment but characteristically ovoid and regular, the upper tier frequently longer than the lower tier; *Branchlets* 6–10 per whorl, 0.8–5 cm. long, straight, incurved or rarely reflexed; the segments 4–8 of which 3–6 have two covering layers and 1–2 are naked; the end segment 2- to 3-celled, the basal 1 or 2 occasionally enlarged, the end cell sausage-shaped or conical, blunt to pointed, the nodes rarely swollen; *Bract cells* 2–6, one-sided, occasionally whorled, rarely forked; the anterior bract cells variable, 0.3–2.4 mm. long, one-half as long as the branchlet diameter to three times as long as the oögonium, tapering, blunt or pointed; the posterior bract cells usually rudimentary, globular or ovoid, but occasionally conical, rarely similar to the anterior bract cells; *Bracteoles* 2,

larger (rarely smaller) than the anterior bract cells, shorter to 4 times longer than the oögonium, 0.3–3 mm. long, tapering to obtuse, occasionally inflated, rarely forked; *Bractlet* rare, shorter than the oögonium; *Gametangia* (male and female sex organs) on different branches of the same plant, at the lowest 1–3 or all the branchlet nodes, solitary or paired, commonly encrusted; *Oögonia* (female sex organ) 0.5–0.8 mm. long (excluding the coronula), 0.315–0.5 mm. wide, the convolutions 12–16; *Coronula* 0.07–0.17 mm. high, 0.2–0.33 mm. wide, the cells spreading or rarely erect or meeting, blunt or with divergent tips, occasionally deciduous; *Oöspores* dark-red, brown (rarely golden) to black, 0.4–0.76 mm. long, 0.22–0.25 mm. wide, often encrusted; the ridges of 10–15 low to prominent, often prolonged into basal claws or cage; the fossa 0.041–0.053 mm. across; the membrane obscurely to clearly granulate, granular or papillate or diffusely spotted; *Antheridia* (male sex organ) peltate, 0.2–0.5 mm. in diameter, in 8 planes; *Bulbils* rare, spheroid. Summer.

Frequent to common in fresh water situations throughout the United States. Since this plant belongs to a group of plants with a reproductive system different from the other plants considered in this book, much of its terminology is unique to it. Most of the structures are identified on the plate (Fig. 1).

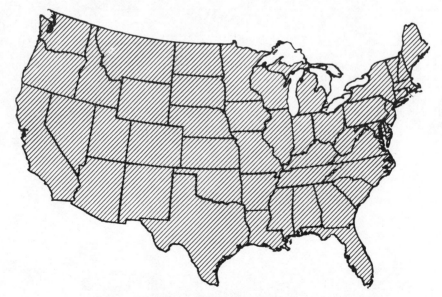

Distribution of *Chara vulgaris* L.

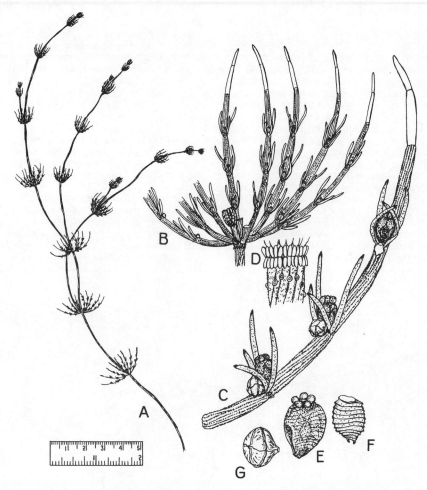

FIGURE 1.—*Chara vulgaris* L. Chara. *A*, Habit—× 0.5; *B*, whorl of branchlets—× 6; *C*, branchlet—× 12; *D*, stipulodes—× 24; *E*, oögonium—× 20; *F*, oöspore—× 20; *G*, antheridium—× 20.

EQUISETACEAE

Perennial fern ally, reproducing by spores and by rhizomes attached to small tubers (Fig. 2); *Rhizome* deep-seated and long-running; *Stems* erect or decumbent, 1.5–6 dm. tall or long, hollow, jointed; *Fertile stems* stout, producing a terminal cone, with large easily separated joints, up to 8 mm. thick, the sheaths 14–20 mm. long, the teeth large, partly united, 5–9 mm. long, unbranched, flesh-colored, yellowish or brownish; *Sterile* or *vegetative stems* tough, wiry, with much smaller joints, the lateral branches in whorls around the main stem, green, often rough with silicaceous crystals along it (hence the name scouring rush), solitary or in clusters, normally 10- to 12-ridged (dwarf plants only 4-ridged), internodes 1.5–6 cm. long, 1.5–5 mm. thick; *Branches* solid, numerous, regularly whorled, 3- or 4-angled, the sheaths with 3 or 4 teeth, the basal sheath pale-brown, the first internode longer than the subtending stem sheath; *Leaves* green, on the sterile stems only, forming cup-shaped sheaths at the joints, the sheaths 5–10 mm. long, gradually widening upward, the teeth dark-brown to light-tan, persistent, free or partly united, 1.5–2 mm. long, thin, dry, membranaceous, margined; *Fruiting heads*, or cones, terminal, containing masses of pale-greenish to yellow spores, usually on the fertile stems only, long-peduncled, not ending in an abrupt sharp-pointed tip; *Spores* globose, with a pair of elators for dissemination. Fertile shoots in early spring and soon disappearing; the sterile shoots coming up in late spring and persisting until frost.

Mostly on wet sandy or gravelly soils; railroad embankments, stream banks, woods, and roadsides. Poisonous to livestock, especially to horses and cattle, causing equisetosis. Cosmopolitan, but native. Throughout all the United States excepting the southeastern area; north into Canada, Alaska, and Greenland; Eurasia.

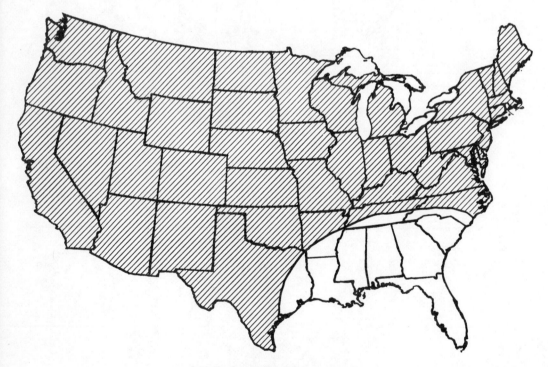

Distribution of *Equisetum arvense* L.

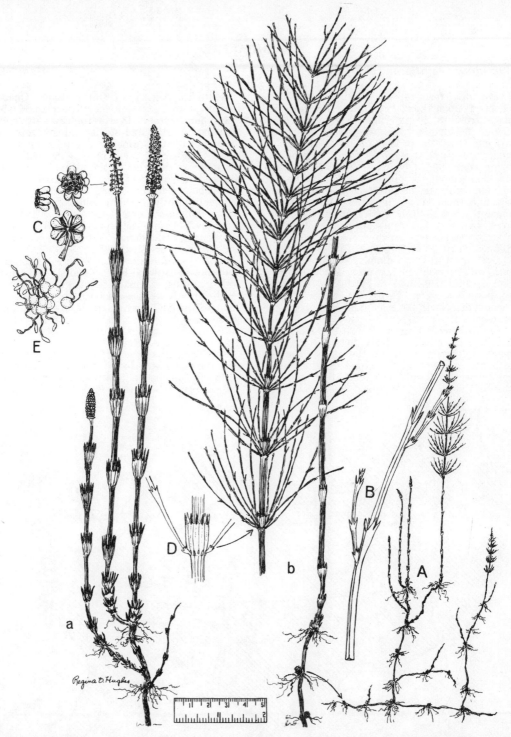

FIGURE 2.—*Equisetum arvense* L. Field horsetail. *A*, Habit— × 0.1: *a*, early, sporophyll-bearing plants— × 0.5: *b*, later, vegetative stems— × 0.5; *B*, enlarged branch, habit— × 0.5; *C*, sporangiophores— × 3; *D*, sheath— × 1.5; *E*, spores, showing elaters— × 50.

PTERIDACEAE

Pteridium aquilinum (L.) Kuhn

Perennial fern, reproducing by spores, or by shoots from a thick, black scaly rhizome that may grow to 20 ft. long (Fig. 3); *Fronds* coarse, deciduous, 3–15 dm. (up to 5 m.) tall, arising from the rhizome, broad, triangular, and divided into three main parts, each branch being compounded by numerous leaflets (pinnae and pinnules), which in turn may be segmented, glabrous or pubescent; *Sporangia* on the underside of the pinnules of the fronds, along the margin as a narrow brown band, covered by a thin membranaceous indusium; *Spores* tetrahedral, with a perispore, July–September.

Open pastures, woodlands, pinewoods, barrens, and hillsides, mainly on acid soils. Fronds and petioles poisonous to cattle and horses if consumed over a period of time. Native throughout North America; also in Europe and eastern Asia.

var. *pubescens* Underw.—WESTERN BRACKEN. Fertile and sterile indusia both ciliate, and more or less pubescent on the outer face; the ultimate segments of the frond usually pubescent beneath; pinnules nearly at right angles to the midribs.

Southern Alaska to Ontario and Quebec, southwest to Texas and northwestern Mexico.

var. *latiusculum* (Desv.) Underw.—EASTERN BRACKEN. Fertile and sterile indusia both glabrous; ultimate segments glabrous or rarely slightly pubescent beneath; pinnules oblique to the midribs; margins of the ultimate segments moderately pubescent; the longest entire segment about 4 times as long as broad; terminal segments mostly 5–8 mm. wide.

Newfoundland and Quebec to Minnesota, south to Virginia and upland North Carolina, Mississippi, Oklahoma, Wyoming, Colorado, and northeastern Mexico.

var. *pseudocaudatum* (Clute) Heller—SOUTHERN BRACKEN. Fertile and sterile indusia both glabrous; ultimate segments glabrous or rarely slightly pubsescent beneath; pinnules oblique to the midribs; margins of the ultimate segments glabrous; longest entire segment 6–15 times as long as broad; terminal segment mostly 2–4.5 mm. wide.

On or near the Coastal Plain from southeastern Massachusetts to Florida and inland to southern Illinois, Indiana, southern Missouri, and eastern Oklahoma.

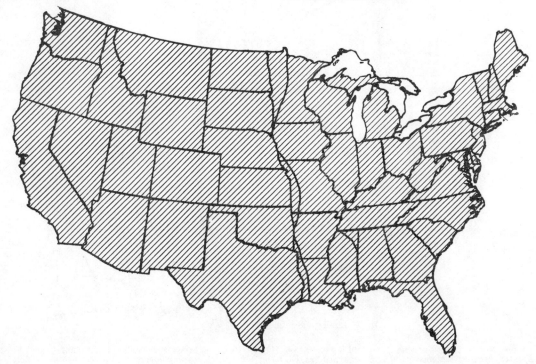

Distribution of *Pteridium aquilinum* (L.) Kuhn

FIGURE 3.—*Pteridium aquilinum* (L.) Kuhn. Bracken. *A*, Habit—× 0.4; *B*, pinnules showing marginal sori—× 2.5; *C*, nectary glands—× 1,5.

TYPHACEAE

Typha angustifolia L.

Perennial herb, from a creeping rhizome, up to 7–15 dm. tall (Fig. 4, *A*); *Leaves* usually less than 10, somewhat convex on the back, full green, herbaceous, 3–8 mm. wide; pistillate (below) and staminate (above) portions of the spike usually separated by a short interval; the pistillate portion reddish-brown, in fruit 6–15 mm. in diameter 0.3–1.5 dm. long, its surface minutely bristly with persistent linear stigmas; the staminate half of spike 0.7–2 dm. long, the pistillate flowers with a linear fleshy stigma and usually with a hairlike bractlet with dilated blunt tips among the bristles; denuded old axis covered with stout compound papillate pedicels 0.5-0.7 mm. long; *Fruit* 5–8 mm. long, subtended by copious white hairs arising distinctly above the middle. Late May–July.

Chiefly in basic or alkaline waters; waste wet areas, especially along the seaboard eastward. Throughout approximately all the eastern half of the United States excepting an area north of the gulf coast; along the Pacific coast from southern Washington through southern California and southwestern Arizona; Eurasia; Africa.

TYPHACEAE

Typha latifolia L.

Perennial herb, from a creeping rhizome, stout, 1–2.7 m. tall (Fig. 4, *B*); *Leaves* flat, sheathing, pale or grayish-green, 6–23 mm. wide; *Staminate* (7–13 cm. long) and dark-brown *pistillate* (2.5–20 cm. long) parts of the spike usually contiguous, in fruit 1.2–3.5 cm. thick, its surface appearing minutely pebbled with crowned persistent stigmas and scarcely bristly, pistillate flowers without branchlets among the bristles; stigmas lance-ovate, fleshy, persistent; denuded axis of old spike retaining slender pedicels 1–2 mm. long; *Fruit* about 1 cm. long, with copious white hairs arising near the base. Late May–July.

Marshes and shallow water, ditches, and wet wastes along rivers; the common inland species. Native. Throughout the United States; Eurasia; North Africa.

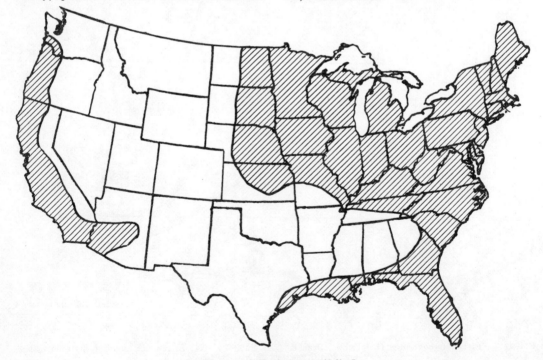

Distribution of *Typha angustifolia* L.

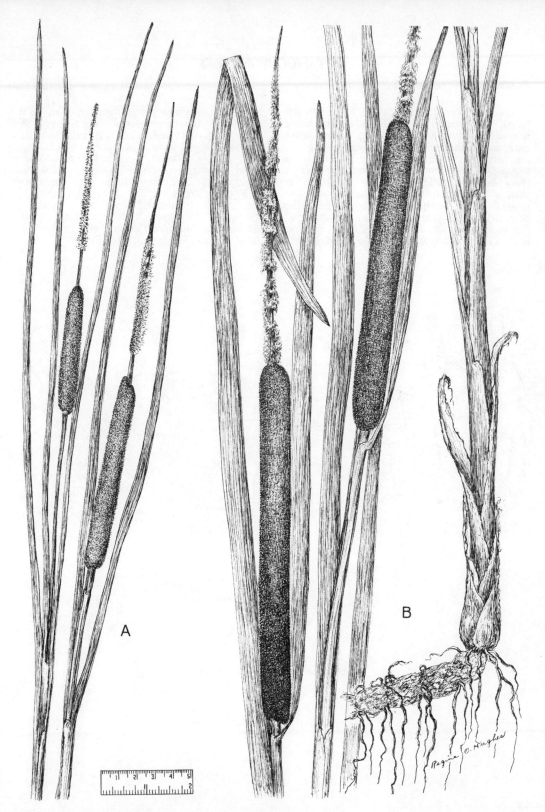

FIGURE 4.—*A, Typha angustifolia* L. Narrowleaf cattail. Habit—× 0.5. *B, Typha latifolia* L. Common cattail.
Habit—× 0.5.

POTAMOGETONACEAE

Potamogeton crispus L.

Aquatic perennial herb (Fig. 5); *Stem* flattened, the broader flattened sides channelled, branched above, 3–8 dm. long; *Leaves* alternate, all submersed, sessile, linear-oblong, 3–8 cm. long, 5–12 mm. wide, rounded, obtuse or minutely tipped with a sharp and firm point at the apex, often reddish, sharply and finely serrate, at maturity often crisped and wavy-margined 3- to 5-nerved; *Stipules* about 4 mm. long, thin, dry and membranaceous soon disintegrating and deciduous; *Peduncles* curved, 2–5 cm. long; *Spikes* loosely to densely flowered, slightly tipped with a sharp and firm point, up to 1.8 cm. long; *Achene* obliquely ovate to ovoid, 3–5 mm. long, flattened, shallowly pitted, with 3 rounded dorsal keels, the central one prolonged at the base, shaped somewhat like an arrow-head, into a projecting appendage, the beak erect, conic, 2–2.5 mm. long. May–September.

Fresh calcareous and brackish ponds and streams. Naturalized from Europe, locally introduced. Throughout Northeastern United States into southern Canada; also in three distinct areas in Western United States.

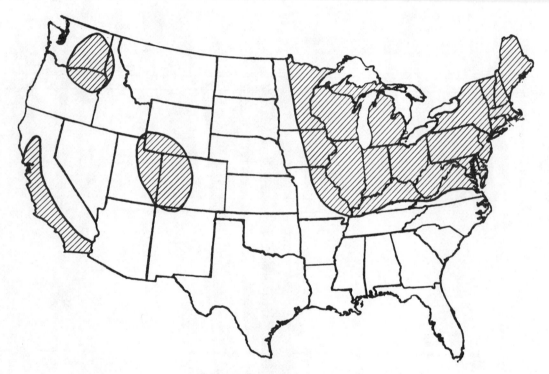

Distribution of *Potamogeton crispus* L.

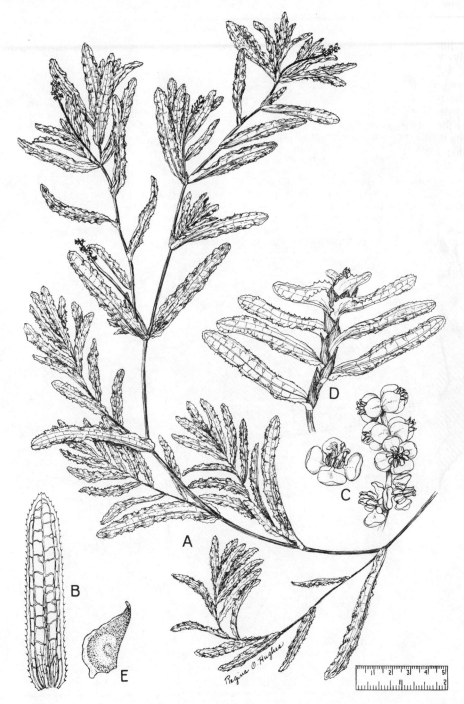

FIGURE 5.—*Potamogeton crispus* L.   Curlyleaf pondweed.   *A*, Habit—× 0.5; *B*, leaf venation—× 2.5; *C*, flowers— × 2.5; *D*, winter bud—× 1.5; *E*, achene—× 4.

POTAMOGETONACEAE

Potamogeton foliosus Raf.   LEAFY PONDWEED

Aquatic perennial herb (Fig. 6); _Rootstock_ long and slender, freely branching, rooting at the nodes; _Stems_ compressed-filiform, simple to loosely branched, up to 1 m. long; _Leaves_ alternate, all submersed, dark-green to bronze, narrowly linear, somewhat tapering at the base, usually without basal glands; the primary leaves 4–10 cm. long, 1.4–2.7 mm. wide, 3- to 5-nerved, the midrib prominent, compound below the middle, with 1–3 rows of air cells on each side at the base; _Stipules_ at first with united margins, forming tubular fibrous blunt sheaths 0.7–1.8 cm. long, soon splitting and deciduous; _Peduncles_ few, arising in the upper forks, slightly thickened upward, 3–10 mm. (rarely 30) long; _Spike_ nearly head-shaped or thick-cylindric, 2–5 mm. long, about 4 mm. thick, with 2 or 3 whorls of 2 flowers each; _Sepallike connectives_ 0.6–1 mm. long, brownish; _Achene_ brownish to olive-green, unequally circular, strongly compressed, 2–2.5 mm. long, the body circular to broadly inverted ovate, the dorsal keel thin and undulate or dentate, the beak 0.2–0.4 mm. long; _Winter buds_ sessile in the axils or terminating short branches, their hard bodies 1–1.6 cm. long, 1–2 mm. thick. July–October.

Streams and ponds. Throughout all the United States excepting southern Florida; north into southern Canada.

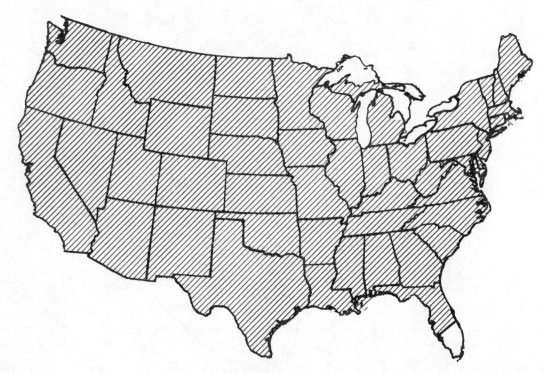

Distribution of _Potamogeton foliosus_ Raf.

FIGURE 6.—*Potamogeton foliosus* Raf. Leafy pondweed. *A*, Habit—× 0.5; *B*, enlarged habit—×2.5; *C*, flower diagram—× 5; *D*, achene—× 5; *E*, tip of leaf showing nerves—× 7.5.

POTAMOGETONACEAE

Potamogeton nodosus Poir.

(*P. americanus* Gray; *P. fluitans* Small; *P. rotundatus* Hagstr.)

Aquatic perennial herb (Fig. 7); *Stem* branched, up to 2 m. long; *Submersed leaves* alternate, linear- to elliptic-lanceolate, up to 3 dm. long, 1–3.5 cm. wide, tapering to petiole 2–13 cm. long, and to acutish tip, 7- to 15-nerved, with 2–5 rows of air cells each side of midrib, the young blades margined by temporary translucent minute teeth, submersed stipules early decaying, linear, 3–10 cm. long; *Floating leaves* long-petioled, lance-oblong to lance-elliptic, rounded to acutish at base and apex, 3–13 cm. long, 1.5–4.5 cm. broad, with petioles 5–20 cm. long, 9- to 21-nerved, emersed stipules similar to the submersed ones but broader; *Spike* dense, becoming loose, of 10–17 whorls, in fruit 3–7 cm. long, 0.8–1 cm. thick; *Achene* inverted oval to broadly nearly egg-shaped, 3.5–4.3 mm. long, 2.5–3 mm. wide, the dorsal keel sharp but narrow, often tuberculate, the lateral keels often rough with spines, in maturity brownish or reddish, the facial beak short. August–September.

Deep or shallow water; ponds and streams. Throughout all the United States excepting most of New England, northern New York, and southern Florida.

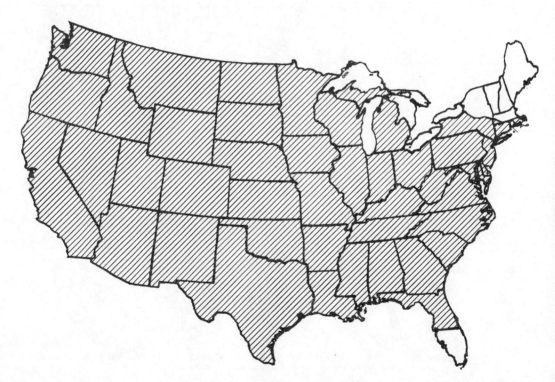

Distribution of *Potamogeton nodosus* Poir.

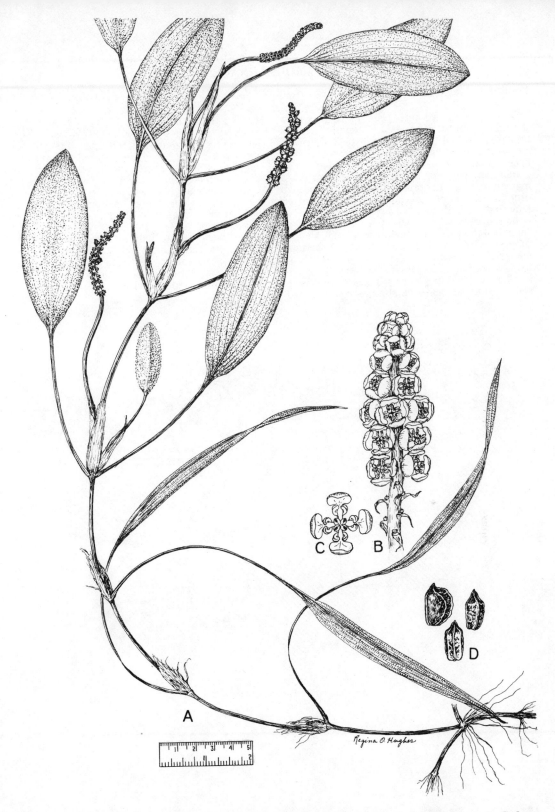

FIGURE 7.—*Potamogeton nodosus* Poir. American pondweed. *A*, Habit—× 0.5; *B*, flower spike—× 3; *C*, flower diagram, showing stamens—× 3; *D*, achenes—× 3.

POTAMOGETONACEAE

Potamogeton pusillus L.

Aquatic perennial herb (Fig. 8); *Stems* very slender, slighty flattened, usually much-branched toward the summit; *Leaves* alternate, all submersed, light-green, narrowly linear, firm, usually with 2 small translucent basal glands; the primary leaves 1–7 cm. long, 0.5–3 mm. wide, acute to obtuse, 3-nerved, the midrib prominent, the lateral veins delicate and often indistinct, usually not bordered by air cells, or with 1–4 rows of air cells at least in the lower half; *Stipules* thin, dry, membranaceous, slender tubular, with margins united to above the middle, finally rupturing and soon deciduous, 0.6–1.7 cm. long; *Peduncles* axillary, long and slender, 1.5–8 cm. long; *Spikes* elongate to short cylindric dense clusters, strongly interrupted, 6–15 mm. long, of 1 or 3–5 distant whorls; *Achene* olive-green, unevenly egg-shaped, often somewhat S-shaped, 1.9–2.8 mm. long, 1–1.8 mm. broad, smooth but often deeply impressed on the somewhat flattened sides, the back rounded, the ventral face arching to the prominent marginal beak; *Winter buds* axillary along the branches and terminal, their bodies 9–17 mm. long, 0.5–1.5 mm. broad. July–September.

In basic or alkaline lakes and ponds. Throughout all the United States excepting the southeastern area; north to Alaska, Canada, and Greenland and south to central Mexico; West Indies; Azores; Eurasia.

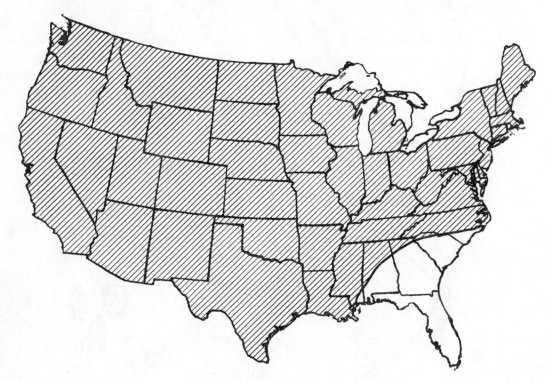

Distribution of *Potamogeton pusillus* L.

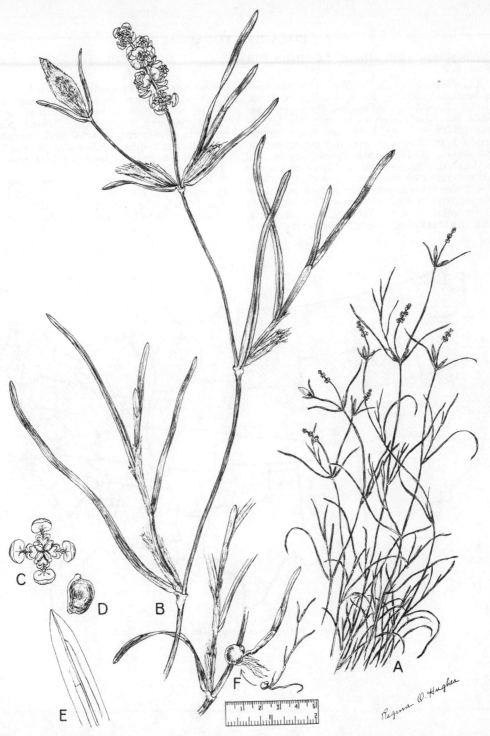

FIGURE 8.—*Potamogeton pusillus* L. Small pondweed. *A*, Habit—× 0.5; *B*, enlarged habit—× 2.5; *C*, flower diagram—× 4; *D*, achene—× 4; *E*, tip of leaf showing nerves—× 7.5; *F*, winter bud—× 2.5.

POTAMOGETONACEAE

Potamogeton richardsonii (A. Benn.) Rydb.

RICHARDSON PONDWEED

Aquatic perennial herb (Fig. 9); *Stems* freely branched, densely leafy, 1–2.5 mm. thick; *Leaves* alternate, all submersed, the lowest ones ovate to ovate-lanceolate, to narrowly lanceolate, 1.5–12 cm. long, 5–20 mm. broad, prominently 7- to 33-nerved, with 3–7 stronger than the others, cordate-based, closely sessile and cordate clasping one-half to three-fourths the circumference of the stem, somewhat acute to blunt, the margin minutely toohed on young leaves; *Stipules* whitish, coarsely nerved, ovate to lanceolate, obtuse, keelless, 1–2 cm. long, soon disintegrating into stringy white fibers;

Peduncles often upwardly thickened, about as thick as the stem, 0.15–2.5 dm. long; *Spikes* dense, with 6–12 whorls, cylindric, in fruit 1.5–4 cm. long, 1 cm. thick; *Achene* grayish-green to olive-green, inverted ovate, rounded on back and at the base, 2.5–4 mm. long, 2.3 mm. wide, the prominent beak up to 1 mm. long. July–September.

Ponds, lakes, rivers, and streams; frequently in brackish or alkaline waters. Throughout approximately the northern half of the United States; north to Labrador, Canada, and Alaska.

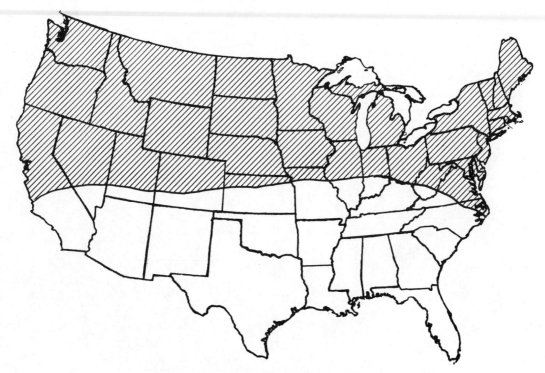

Distribution of *Potamogeton richardsonii* (A. Benn.) Rydb.

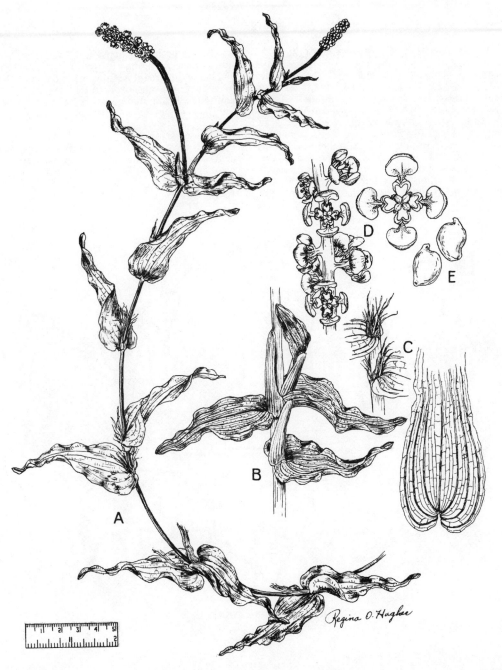

FIGURE 9.—*Potamogeton richardsonii* (A. Benn.) Rydb. Richardson pondweed. *A*, Habit—× 0.5; *B*, enlarged leaves with young stipules—× 1; *C*, enlarged bases of leaves—× 1.5; *D*, flowers—× 2.5; *E*, achenes—× 2.5.

NAJADACEAE

Najas flexilis (Willd.) Rostk. & Schmidt

Annual herb, aquatic, monoecious (Fig. 10); *Stems* fragile, bushy-branched, with crowded nodes or elongate and slender light-green to reddish or olive-green; *Leaves* linear or narrowly lanceolate, triangularly dilated at the base, unlobed, often with slightly inrolled margins and tapering to long, fine, recurving tips, 1–4 cm. long, 0.2–2 mm. wide, each margin with 20–40 minute 1-celled spinules; each edge of the gradually tapering to rounded herbaceous sheath with 6–13 teeth; *Flowers*: staminate 2.5–3.2 mm. long, borne near the tips of the fertile branches, the anthers 1-locular; pistillate 1.6–2.5 mm. long, borne in the middle and lower axils, the style and 2 commonly spinulose-based stigmas 0.8–2 mm. long; *Fruit* slenderly to broadly ellipsoid, 2–3.5 mm. long; *Seed* lustrous, obscurely reticulate with 30–40 rows of hexagonal areolae, closely covered by the yellowish to purplish pericarp. July–October.

Shallow fresh to brackish water; lakes and bays. Native. In the northeastern and north central areas of the United States; north into Canada; also along the Pacific Coast and in distinct areas in Missouri and Utah; northwestern Europe.

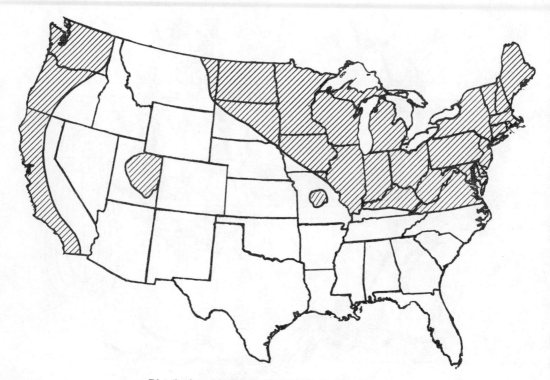

Distribution of *Najas flexilis* (Willd.) Rostk. & Schmidt

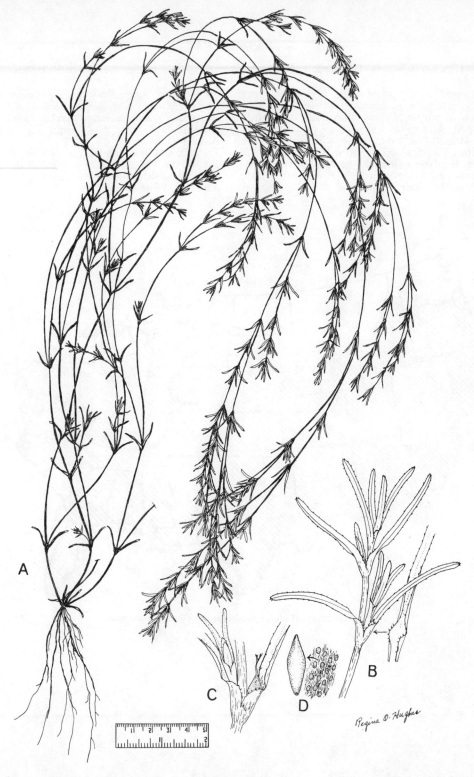

FIGURE 10.—*Najas flexilis* (Willd.) Rostk. & Schmidt. Slender naiad. *A*, Habit, as it grows in running water —× 0.5; *B*, leaf detail—× 2.4; *C*, flower detail, pistillate flower—× 2.5; *D*, seed—× 6, with enlargement showing rows of areolae.

NAJADACEAE

Najas guadelupensis (Spreng.) **Magnus**

Annual herb, aquatic (Fig. 11); *Stems* very leafy, often much elongate, rather firm, deep-green to purple; *Leaves* linear, flat or slightly crisped, dark-green, olive-green or tawny, 1–2 cm. long, 0.4–0. 8 mm. wide, with smaller ones clustered in the axils, obtuse or acute at the apex, the base ovate, the margins beset at intervals of 0.3–1 mm. with 3–10 minute spines; *Anther* 4-locular; *Style* and 2 or 3 stigmas 0.1–0.6 mm. long; *Fruit* purple-brown at maturity, 1.5–2.5 mm. long; *Seed* dull, straw-colored, 2.5–3 mm. long, marked with 15–20 longitudinal rows of squarish areolae. August–October.

Fresh and brackish waters. Native. Throughout all the United States excepting the northernmost areas; south into Central and South America; West Indies.

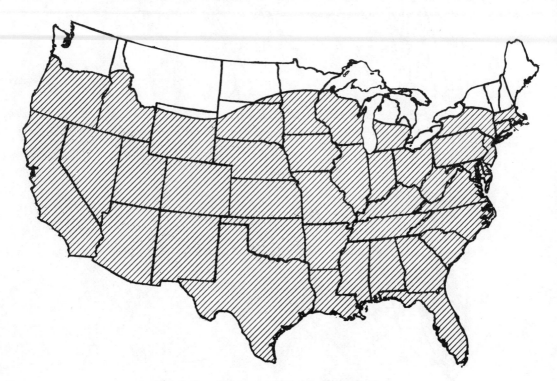

Distribution of *Najas guadelupensis* (Spreng.) Magnus

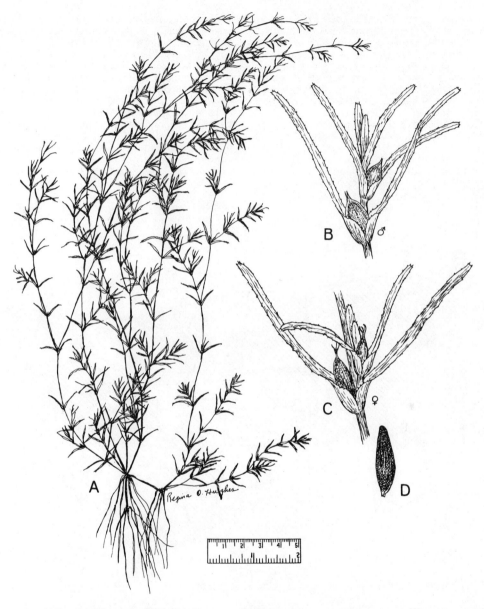

FIGURE 11.—*Najas guadelupensis* (Spreng.) Magnus. Southern naiad. *A*, Habit—× 0.5; *B*, staminate flowers, in spathe—× 5; *C*, pistillate flowers, lower one mature, upper one immature—× 5; *D*, seed, showing square areolae—× 7.5.

ALISMATACEAE

Sagittaria latifolia **Willd.**

SMALL COMMON ARROWHEAD

Perennial herb, aquatic or growing in marshes, erect, stoloniferous herb, with milky juice (Fig. 12); *Scape* erect, simple or branched, sheathed at base by the bases of the long petioles, 1–15 dm. high, angled, with one or more of the lower whorls pistillate, or all unisexual flowers; *Leaf blades* ovate to linear, rarely without lobes, mostly sagittate, the basal lobes triangular-ovate to linear, from one-half as long as the body of the leaf to longer than the body of the leaf, 5–40 cm. long, 2–25 cm. broad; *Bracts* distinctly united or slightly joined, thin, dry, membranaceous, obtuse to acute, 1 cm or less long; *Flowers* in whorls of 2–15, the upper staminate or perfect on short pedicels, the lower usually pistillate on longer, terete pedicels; *Sepals* ovate, obtuse, 5–7 mm. long; *Petals* showy, white, broadly ovate, 1–2 cm. long; *Achene* inverted ovate, 2.3–4 mm. long, 1.5–3 mm. broad, with broad marginal wings on both margins, the broad-based beak usually subhorizontal to slightly incurved or erect, 1–2.5 mm. long. July–September.

In water and wet places; along lakes, ponds, rivers, bays, and swamps; exceedingly variable, especially in leaf outline. Native. Throughout all the United States excepting along the Mexican border in California, Arizona, New Mexico, and central Texas; southern Canada; Mexico.

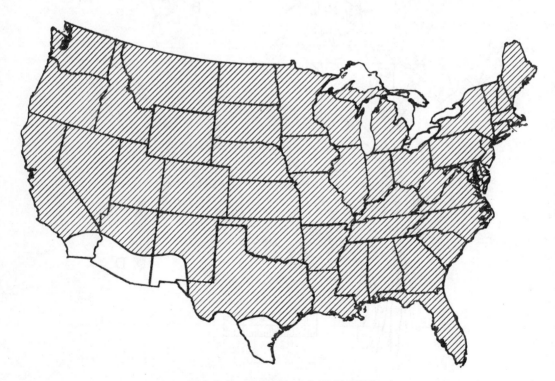

Distribution of *Sagittaria latifolia* Willd.

26

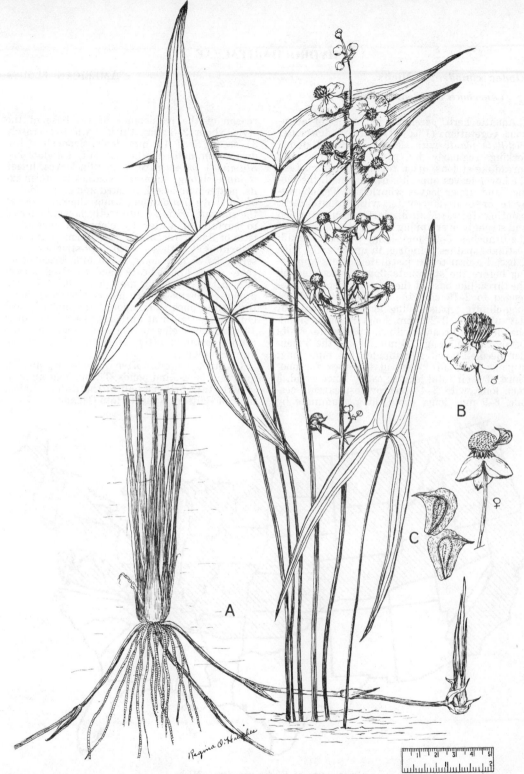

FIGURE 12.—*Sagittaria latifolia* Willd. Common arrowhead. *A*, Habit—× 0.5; *B*, flowers—× 0.5; *C*, achenes— × 5.

Elodea canadensis Michx.

AMERICAN ELODEA

(Anacharis canadensis Planch.)

Aquatic herb, *perennial* by means of abundant vegetation (Fig. 13); plants dioecious: *Pistillate plants* with slender branched stems, forking regularly by pairs, from creeping threadlike stolons, often forming large masses; the lower leaves opposite, ovate, small, the median and upper leaves whorled in 3's, oblong-ovate or ovate-lanceolate, with minute teeth pointing forward, firm, dark-green, crowded and strongly overlapping toward the summit of the branches, 6–13 mm. long, 1–5 mm. broad; pistillate spathes cylindric, in upper axils, with 2 broad apical teeth; pistillate flowers appearing before the staminate flowers, exserted by the threadlike base of the flower receptacle prolonged to 2–15 cm., the dark-striate and oblong-elliptic sepals falling at anthesis without flattening out, 2–2.2 mm. long, 1.1 mm. broad, the delicate broadly elliptic-spathulate white petals 2.6 mm. long, 1.3 mm. broad, the 3 slender needle-shaped staminoides 0.7 mm. long; stigmas 3, broad, 2-cleft at the apex for one-third of their total length; ovary lance-ovoid, 3 mm. long, with 3–4 erect ovules; capsule sessile, 6–9 mm. long, ovoid, long acuminate by

reason of the persistence of the base of the style, about 2–3 mm. thick, with 1–2 (rarely 3) seeds; *Seed* 4.5 mm. long, slenderly cylindric, acuminate at the summit, subglabrous. *Staminate plants* rare, with thin leaves, linear to lance-oblong; staminate spathes in upper axils, peduncular-based, inflated and ellipsoidal or ovoid above, 7 mm. long, 4 mm. thick, gaping at the summit, with 2 acute teeth; flowers carried to surface of water by elongated threadlike base of flower receptacle (10–20 cm. long), not detaching at anthesis, with dark-striate elliptic sepals 3.5–5 mm. long, 2–2.5 mm. broad, concave-convex and delicate slender-clawed lanceolate petals about 5 mm. long, 0.3–0.7 mm. broad; *Stamens* 9, with almost sessile anthers, the 6 outer ones (3 mm. long) falling backward onto the perianth at anthesis, the 3 inner ones (4 mm. long) elevated on a common stalk, becoming petaloid after emission of the pollen. July–September.

In quiet waters, often calcareous, and in quarries, lakes, and ponds. Throughout approximately the northern half of the United States; most of California; north into Canada.

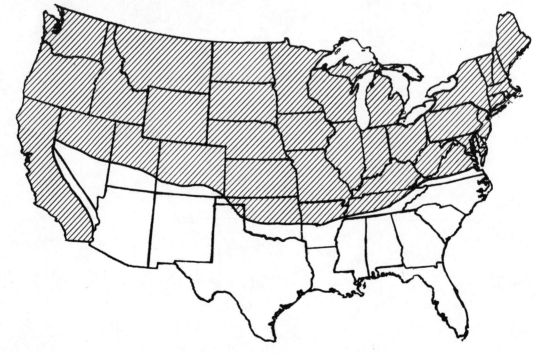

Distribution of *Elodea canadensis* Michx.

FIGURE 13.—*Elodea canadensis* Michx. American elodea. *A*, Habit, pistillate plant—× 0.5; *B*, flower and leaf detail, pistillate plant—× 2.5; *C*, flower and leaf detail, staminate plant, flower fully expanded, sepals and outside anthers fallen—× 1.5; *D*, flowers, female—× 4: male, before full expansion, with all anthers upright—× 2.5; *E*, capsules—× 4; *F*, seeds—× 4.

HYDROCHARITACEAE

Elodea densa (Planch.) Caspary   <small>DENSELEAVED ELODEA, EGERIA</small>

(Anacharis densa (Planch.) Vict.; *Egeria densa* Planch.)

Aquatic herb (Fig. 14); *Leaves* in whorls of 4–6, the principal leaves 2–3.3 cm. long, linear-lanceolate, tapering gradually to a point, the lower leaves remote, the upper ones crowded; *Flowers* at anthesis 15–20 mm. wide; the staminate spathes with 2 or more exserted flowers with relatively showy petals 9–11 mm. long and 6–9 mm. broad; the pistillate flowers not known in United States. June–October.

Commonly cultivated in aquaria; occasionally established in ponds, pools, and quiet streams. Native of Argentina. Throughout the area in the United States with Massachusetts, Florida, eastern Texas, and eastern Utah at its extreme boundaries; along most of the Pacific coast.

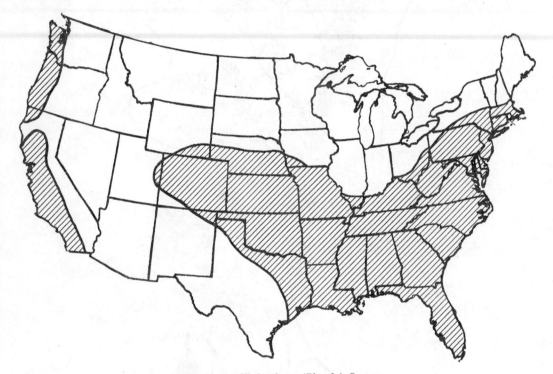

Distribution of *Elodea densa* (Planch.) Caspary

FIGURE 14.—*Elodea densa* (Planch.) Caspary. Denseleaved elodea. *A*, Habit—× 0.5; *B*, spathe detail—× 2; *C*, flower detail—× 1.

Aegilops cylindrica Host

Annual (Fig. 15); *Culms* erect, branching at the base, 2–6 dm. tall; *Root system* fibrous; *Leaves* alternate, simple, with auricles at the base of the blade, smooth or hairy; *Spike* 5–8 cm. long; *Spikelets* few, 2–5 flowers placed with the side against the articulated rachis and closely appressed to it, the rachis joints upwardly enlarged; *Glumes* with lateral keel prolonged into an awn; *Lemmas* of upper spikelets with harsh awns 4–5 cm. long, those of the lower spikelets shorter; *Seed* ripening before wheat, shattering easily. June–August.

Waste places, railroads, and fields, mainly in wheatfields, spreading to roadsides and wastes. Naturalized from Europe. Throughout approximately the south central and southwestern areas of the United States, east into Illinois and Indiana; distinct areas in Nevada, Washington, Oregon, and New York.

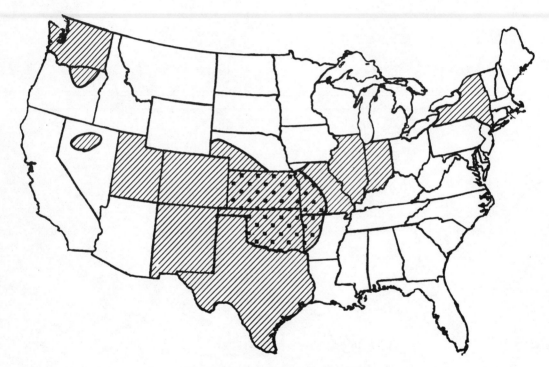

Distribution of *Aegilops cylindrica* Host

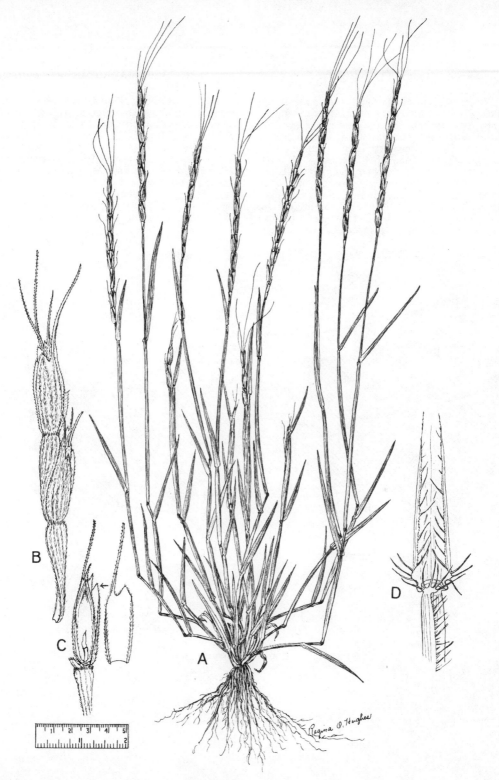

FIGURE 15.—*Aegilops cylindrica* Host. Jointed goatgrass. *A*, Habit—× 0.5; *B*, spike detail—× 2.5; *C*, floret— × 2.5; *D*, ligule—× 3.

GRAMINEAE

Agropyron repens (L.) Beauv.

Perennial, reproducing by seeds and extensively creeping underground slender rhizomes, roots arising only at the nodes (Fig. 16); *Culms* 3–12 dm. tall, smooth, with 3–6 joints, hollow at the tip; the cartilaginous bands of upper nodes longer than thick; *Leaves* with auricles, soft, flat, with crowded fine ribs, scabrous or sparsely pilose above; *Ligules* 0.5 mm. long; *Sheaths* the lower ones hairy, the upper ones glabrous or slightly pilose; *Spike* dense or lax, 0.5–2.5 dm. long, 2–9 short-awned florets in the compressed spikelet (0.6–2.2 cm. long);

Glume herbaceous, oblong to lanceolate, narrowed from above the middle, strongly 5- to 7-nerved; *Lemmas* obtuse, acute or awned. A highly variable species. Late May–September.

Open waste places, in most cropped areas and in pastures; on gravelly and sandy shores. Often used for pasture and as a grass hay plant; rhizomes used in treating urinary disorders; considered a primary noxious weed. European origin. Throughout all the United States excepting the southern area; all of California.

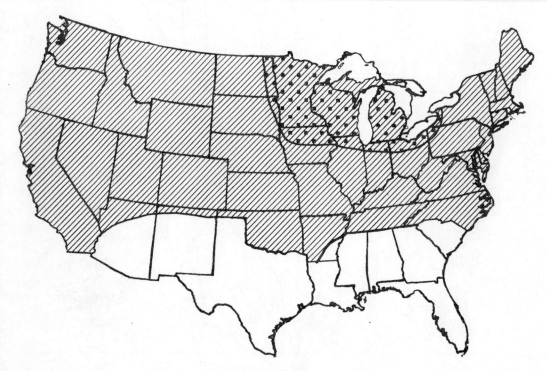

Distribution of *Agropyron repens* (L.) Beauv.

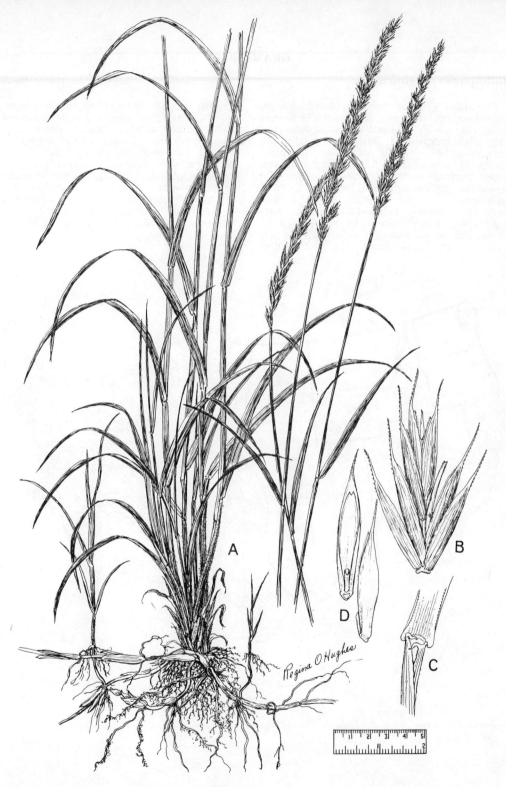

FIGURE 16.—*Agropyron repens* (L.) Beauv. Quackgrass. *A*, Habit—× 0.5; *B*, spikelet—× 3; *C*, ligule—× 2.5; *D*, florets—× 3.25.

Andropogon virginicus L.

Perennial, growing erect in small clumps, reddish-brown when dry; *Roots* densely fibrous (Fig. 17); *Culms* slender to stout, several in a tuft, slightly flattened, 30–90 cm. tall, upper part branched; *Leaves* green or glaucous, 15–30 cm. long, flat or folded, very hairy on upper surface where attached to stem, the sheaths strongly compressed, keeled, and enfold each other; *Racemes* mostly paired of 2–4 finger-like clusters, each 1–4.5 cm. long, bearing tufts of conspicuous white hairs, enclosed by reddish-brown leaves; *Sessile spikelets* 3–4 mm. long, the rachis joints long and slender, the awn straight or spiraling only at the base, 1–2 cm. long; *Pedicelled spikelets* represented by an awllike scale or absent, the divergent beard longer than the axis of the pedicel; *Seed* about 3 mm. long, brown, bearded. A highly variable species. September–January.

Wastes, plains, old fields, and sterile areas. A serious pasture weed on marginal lands. Throughout approximately all the eastern half of the United States excepting the area in northern New England; California; West Indies; South America.

Distribution of *Andropogon virginicus* L.

FIGURE 17.—*Andropogon virginicus* L. Broomsedge. *A*, Habit—× 0.5; *B*, ligule (left, opened; right, compressed as in nature)—× 2.5; *C*, inflorescence—× 2.5; *D*, florets—× 7.5.

Avena fatua L.   WILD OAT

Annual, reproducing by seeds (Fig. 18); *Root system* extensive and fibrous; *Culms* smooth, erect, stout, 4–12 dm. tall, in small tufts; *Leaf blades* 7–20 cm. long, 5–8 mm. wide, resembling those of tame oats; *Panicle* loose and open, the slender branches ascending; *Spikelets* pendulous, 2.2–2.5 cm. long; *Glumes* smooth, striate, acuminate; *Lemmas* with long, dark awns, 3 cm. long or more, the lower parts twisted, the upper parts bent sharply at right angles to the twisted parts, and with a ring of hairs at the base and more or less appressed-pubescent with long stiff brownish hairs, or glabrous; *Caryopsis* varying from white to yel-low, brown, gray or black, usually hairy, especially near the base. June–October.

In fields under continuous cultivation to small grains and flax; probably the most serious annual weed in the hard red spring wheat area; seeds usually ripen earlier than most cereals and many drop to ground before time to harvest cultivated cereals. Naturalized from Europe. Throughout all the United States excepting an area along the Atlantic Coast, the Gulf States, and the southern Great Plains into Texas; north into southern Canada and south into Mexico.

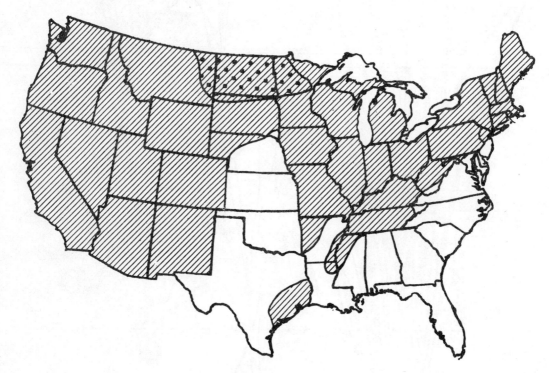

Distribution of *Avena fatua* L.

FIGURE 18.—*Avena fatua* L. Wild oat. *A*, Habit—× 0.5; *B*, spikelet—× 2; *C*, florets, 3 views—× 3.5.

Bromus commutatus Schrad.

HAIRY CHESS

Winter annual plants, mostly 3–10 dm. tall, erect or decumbent at the base (Fig. 19); *Leaf blades* sparsely to densely pubescent, 2–7 mm. wide; *Sheaths* sparsely to densely pubescent or short-pilose, the hairs usually retrorse; *Ligules* 1–2 mm. long; *Panicle* 10–12 cm. long, open, with 2–6 rather stiffly ascending or drooping branches; *Spikelets* 1–2.5 cm. long, 6- to 10-flowered, somewhat flattened with rather closely imbricated florets; *First glume* 4.5–6 mm. long, 3- to 5-nerved; *Second glume* 6–8 mm. long, 7- to 9-nerved, both glumes glabrous to scaberulous; *Lemmas* 7–11 mm. long, 7- to 9-nerved, minutely scabrous, thin, and acute, awns 7–9 mm. long. This species intergrades with *B. secalinus* L., *B. japonicus* Thunb., and *B. racemosus* L., being most similar to and probably not separable from *B. racemosus* L. June–early August.

Dry roadsides, waste places, pastures, and fields. Introduced from Europe. Throughout the United States, but less common in the Southeast, the Southwest, and an area between Lake Superior and the Rockies.

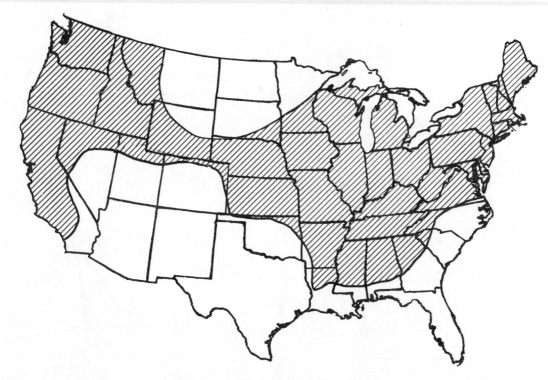

Distribution of *Bromus commutatus* Schrad.

FIGURE 19.—*Bromus commutatus* Schrad. Hairy chess. *A*, Habit—× 0.5; *B*, spikelet—× 5; *C*, floret, 3 views —× 4; *D*, seed—× 4; *E*, ligule—× 2.5.

GRAMINEAE

Bromus japonicus Thunb.

Winter annual, reproducing by seeds (Fig. 20); *Culms* erect, 0.2–1 m. tall; *Leaves*, both blades and sheaths, covered with soft hairs; *Panicle* open, the divergent branches with drooping tips, 2–2.5 cm. long, somewhat hairy, borne on long, slender pedicels; *First glume* 3-nerved, acute; *Second glume* 5-nerved, obtuse; *Lemmas* glabrous, 7–9 mm. long, obtuse, firm, obscurely 9-nerved, the margins somewhat in-rolled at maturity, with a twisted or divaricate awn, 8–12 mm. long, with stiff beards, 0.7–1.3 cm. long, bent conspicuously outward at maturity; *Palea* distinctly shorter than its glume. Maturing in May–August.

Grainfields, meadows, wasteland, and roadsides. Naturalized from Eurasia. Throughout all the United States excepting northern Maine and Southern Florida.

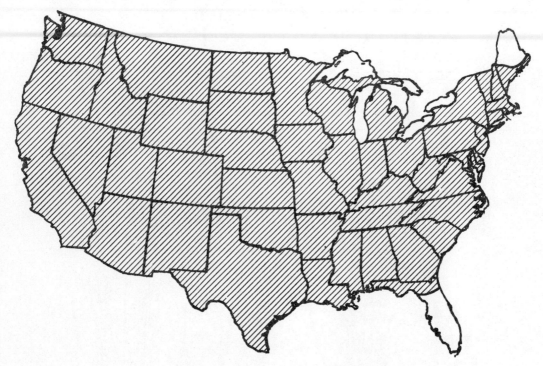

Distribution of *Bromus japonicus* Thunb.

FIGURE 20.—*Bromus japonicus* Thunb. Japanese brome. *A*, Habit—× 0.5; *B*, spikelet—× 3; *C*, ligule—× 2; *D*, floret—× 5; *E*, caryopsis—× 5.

Bromus secalinus L.

Winter annual, reproducing by seeds (Fig. 21); *Culms* erect, 0.1–1.3 m. tall; *Leaves*, upper sheaths smooth and strongly nerved, blades with moderately stiff hairs above and harsh; *Panicle* 0.3–2 dm. long, branches ascending or the lowest becoming divergent; *Spikelets* borne on elongate pedicels, 5- to 15-flowered, glabrous or scabrous, in maturity lax; *Lemmas* spreading-ascending at maturity, strongly inrolling, firm, subequal, obscurely 7-nerved, mostly 5–8 mm. long; awn straight or flexuous, 1–6 mm. long, deciduous, sometimes slightly projecting in maturity; *Caryopsis* plumper and heavier than those of other brome species. June–September.

Grainfields, meadows, and waste places. Naturalized from Europe. Throughout all the United States excepting an area between Lake Superior and the Rockies.

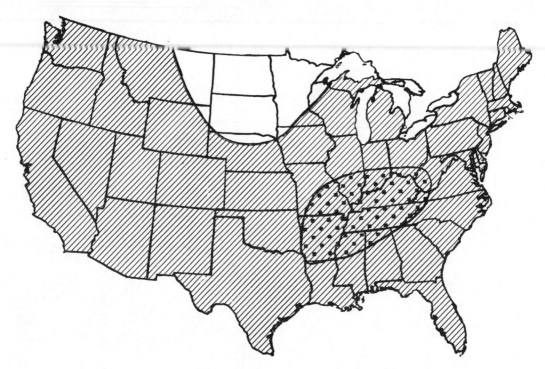

Distribution of *Bromus secalinus* L.

FIGURE 21.—*Bromus secalinus* L. Cheat. *A*, Habit—× 0.5; *B*, spikelet—× 2.5; *C*, ligule—× 1.5; *D*, floret, 3 views—× 3; *E*, caryopsis—× 3.

GRAMINEAE

Bromus tectorum L.

DOWNY BROME, DOWNY CHESS, CHEATGRASS

Winter annual, reproducing by seeds (Fig. 22); *Culms* erect or spreading, slender, 0.2–1 m. tall; *Leaves,* both blades and sheaths, light-green, covered with long soft hairs; *Panicle* rather dense, soft, very drooping, often purplish, flowering in April–May, 0.5–2 dm. long with spreading or recurving flexuous branches, the branches often with several spikelets; *Spikelets* 2–3.5 cm. long, including awns (1–1.7 cm. long); *Glumes* sparsely pilose; *Lemmas* slenderly 5- to 7-nerved, hispid, bearing long beards, 1–1.5 cm. long; *Caryopsis* long and narrow. Maturing in May–June.

Meadows, pastures, ranges, small grainfields, wastelands, and roadsides; often too abundant. Throughout all the United States excepting the extreme southeastern area.

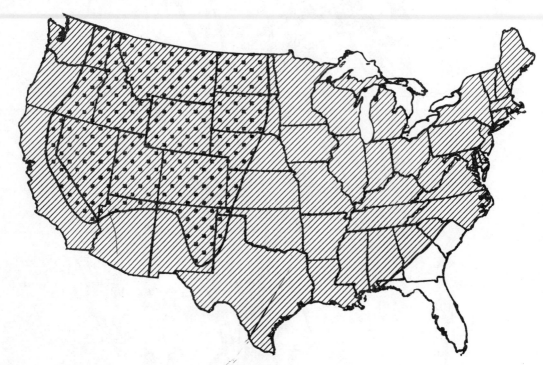

Distribution of *Bromus tectorum* L.

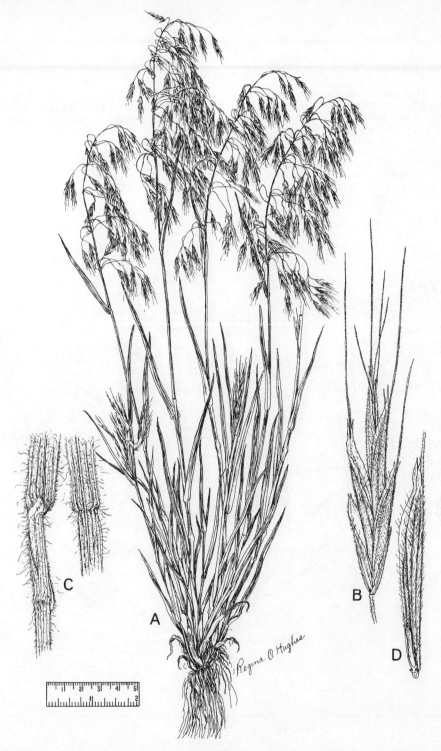

FIGURE 22.—*Bromus tectorum* L. Downy brome. *A*, Habit—× 0.5; *B*, spikelet—× 4; *C*, ligules—× 2.5; *D*, floret—× 5.

Cenchrus echinatus L.

Annual (Fig. 23); *Culms* round in cross section, ascending from an abruptly bent base, 15–85 cm. long; pubescence variable; *Leaves* glabrous to pubescent, 4–26 cm. long, 3.5–11 mm. wide; *Sheaths* flattened, with moderately stiff hairs on the margins near the summit; *Ligule* with marginal hairs, 0.7–1.7 mm. long; *Inflorescence* open, 2–10 cm. long, 0.8–1.8 cm. wide; *Rachis* strongly flexuous, scabrous, the internodes 2–3.0 mm. long; *Spikelets* 2 or 3 per bur, sessile, 5–7 mm. long; *Burs* truncate at the base, globose, 5–10 mm. long, 3.5–6 mm. wide, the spine tips usually turning purple with age; *Seed* ovoid, 1.6–3.2 mm. long, 1.3–2.2 mm. wide. June–September.

Open ground and waste places; a common weed in tropical areas. Along the South Atlantic coast and the southern border area of the United States.

Distribution of *Cenchrus echinatus* L.

FIGURE 23.—*Cenchrus echinatus* L. Southern sandbur. *A*, Habit—× 0.5; *B*, ligule—× 2; *C*, inflorescence—× 0.5; *D*, bur—× 4; *E*, spikelet—× 4; *F*, seed, 3 views—× 5.

GRAMINEAE

Cenchrus incertus M. A. Curtis (1837)
(*C. pauciflorus* Benth. 1844)

FIELD SANDBUR, BURGRASS

Annual, often biennial and overwintering, reproducing by seeds (Fig. 24); *Roots* fibrous, rooting sometimes at the nodes of the stems when they contact the soil; *Culms* decumbent or erect, sometimes with many spreading branches from the base, 5–80 cm. tall, smooth; *Leaves* glabrous, the margins scabrous, 2–18 cm. long, 2–6 mm. wide; *Ligule* with marginal hairs, 0.5–1.5 mm. long; *Spike* short, composed of 2–4 sessile, glabrous spikelets, enclosed in sharp spiny burs (8–40 spines); *Burs* each containing 1–3 seeds, usually 2, straw-colored to mauve or purple. June–September.

Mostly on sandy soil, fields, wastes, and roadsides; a troublesome weed in garden crops, lawns, and fields, mainly because of the spiny burs. Along the South Atlantic Coastal Plain from Virginia to Texas, west to southern California.

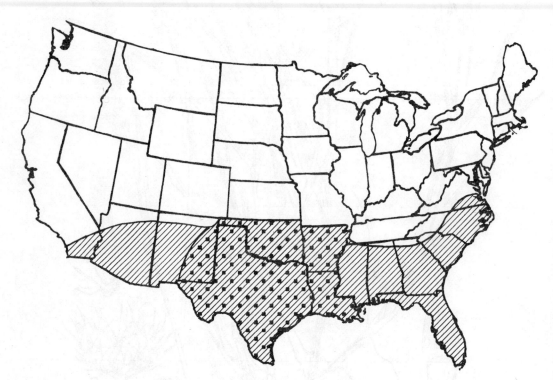

Distribution of *Cenchrus incertus* M. A. Curtis (1837)

50

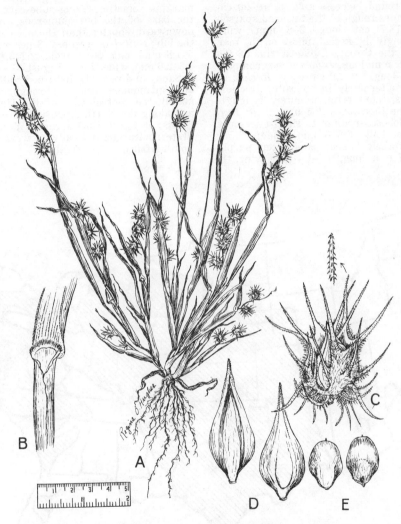

FIGURE 24.—*Cenchrus incertus* M. A. Curtis. Field sandbur. *A*, Habit—× 0.5; *B*, ligule—× 2; *C*, bur—× 4; *D*, florets—× 6; *E*, seeds—× 6.

Cenchrus longispinus (Hack.) Fern.

Annual, often forming large clumps (Fig. 25); *Culms* round in cross section, 10–90 cm. tall; *Leaf blades* rough to the touch to sparsely pilose, 6.3–18.7 cm. long. 3–8 mm. wide; *Sheaths* strongly flat-keeled, pilose on the margins and at the throat; *Ligule* a rim of fine hairs, 0.7–1.7 mm. long; *Inflorescence* compact, 4.1–10.2 cm. long, 1.2–2.2 cm wide; *Rachis* angled, curved alternately in opposite directions and glabrous, more often minutely rough to the touch, the internodes 2–5 mm. long; *Burs* somewhat globose, medium to short-pubescent, 8.3–11.9 mm. long, 3.5–6 mm. wide; *Spines* slender, retrorsely barbed, and often purple-tinged, 3.5–7 mm. long, 0.7–1.4 mm. wide, the margins often narrowly grooved, the lower margins sometimes long-pubescent; *Spines* at the base of the bur numerous and pointing downward, shorter than those on the body of the bur; *Spikelets* sessile, 2–3 per bur, rarely 4, 6–7.8 mm. long; *Seed* ovoid, 2.2–3.8 mm. long, 1.5–2.6 mm. wide. June–August.

Sandy and recently disturbed soils; roadsides and abandoned fields. Throughout approximately the central part of the United States and along the North Atlantic and mid-Atlantic coasts; also in distinct areas in Western United States; naturalized locally in western Europe, South Africa, and Australia.

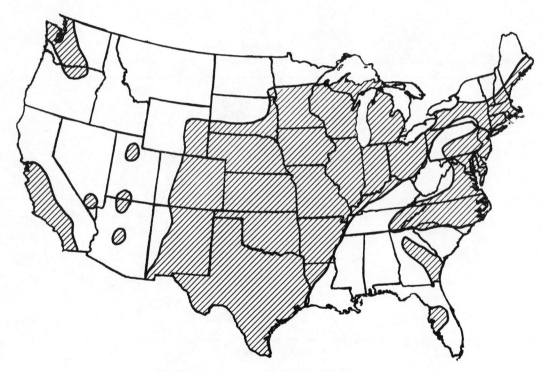

Distribution of *Cenchrus longispinus* (Hack.) Fern.

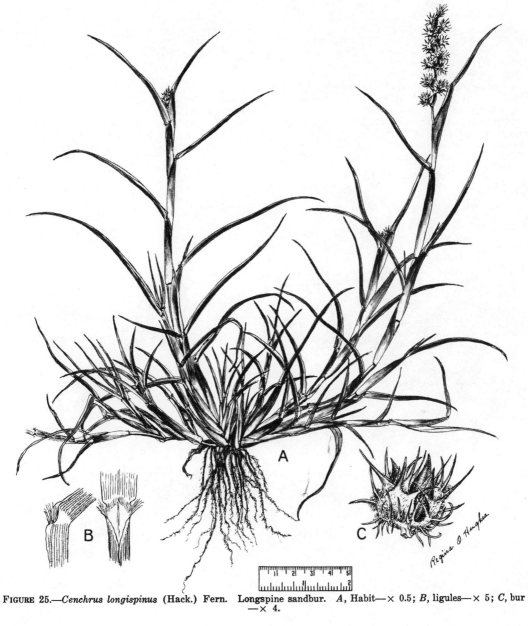

FIGURE 25.—*Cenchrus longispinus* (Hack.) Fern. Longspine sandbur. *A*, Habit—× 0.5; *B*, ligules—× 5; *C*, bur —× 4.

Cynodon dactylon (L.) Pers.

BERMUDAGRASS, DEVILGRASS

Perennial, reproducing by seed (rarely), rootstocks, and stolons (Fig. 26); *Rootstock* hard, scaly, sharp-pointed, forming dense heavy sod; *Stolons* (stems) flat, glabrous, extensively creeping, bearing at each joint the dead bladeless sheath; *Flowering culms* erect or ascending, 15–45 cm. tall; *Leaf blades* 3 mm. wide, gray-green, slightly hairy or glabrous, except for a fringe of long hair at the edge just above the collar; *Sheath*, often two opposite per node, sparsely hairy or hairless, strongly flattened; *Ligule* a conspicuous ring of white hairs; *Inflorescence* fingerlike, 3–7 parted, 2–7 cm. long; *Spikelets* in two rows tightly appressed to one side of the rachis, 2 mm. long; *Lemma* boat-shaped, acute, longer than the glume; *Caryopsis* free within the lemma and palea. Summer.

Open places, pastures, and most cultivated areas; a serious weed when established; sometimes used for lawns; an important pasture grass in Southern States. Introduced from Africa. Throughout approximately the southern two-thirds of the United States, but occurring as far north as central Washington and central New York, New Hampshire, and Vermont.

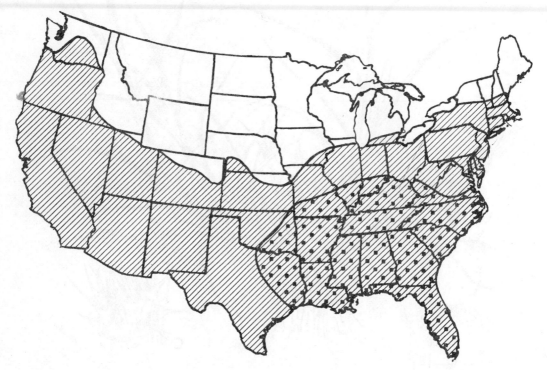

Distribution of *Cynodon dactylon* (L.) Pers.

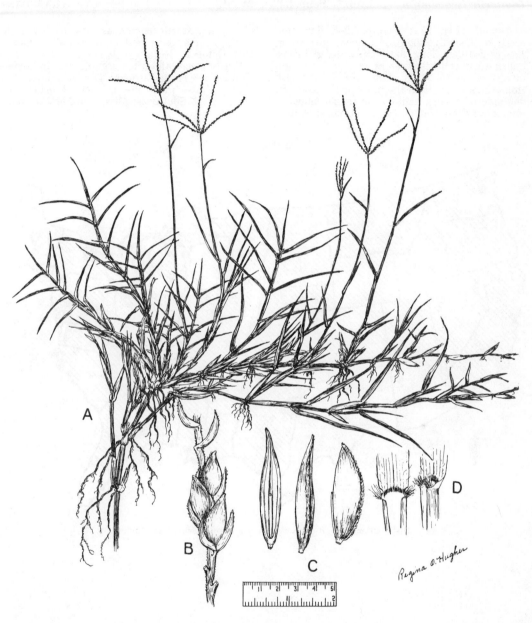

FIGURE 26.—*Cynodon dactylon* (L.) Pers. Bermudagrass. *A*, Habit—× 0.5; *B*, spike—× 7.5; *C*, florets—× 15; *D*, ligules—× 5.

GRAMINEAE

Digitaria ischaemum (Schreb.) Schreb. ex Muhl.   SMOOTH CRABGRASS

Annual (Fig. 27); *Culms* 0.2–4 dm. tall, erect or usually soon decumbent-spreading; *Leaves* 2–10 cm. long, 3–6 mm. wide, glabrous, bluish to purplish; *Racemes* mostly 2–6, commonly purple, 4–10 cm. long, the rachis with thin wings wider than the midrib; *Spikelets* on one side of rachis, solitary or in 2's, about 2 mm. long; *First glume* hyaline, obscure; *Second glume* and sterile lemma as long as the dark fertile lemma, pubescent with capitellate hairs. July–October.

Waste places and often troublesome in lawns. Naturalized from Eurasia. Throughout all the United States excepting southern Florida and parts of the Southwest along the Mexican border.

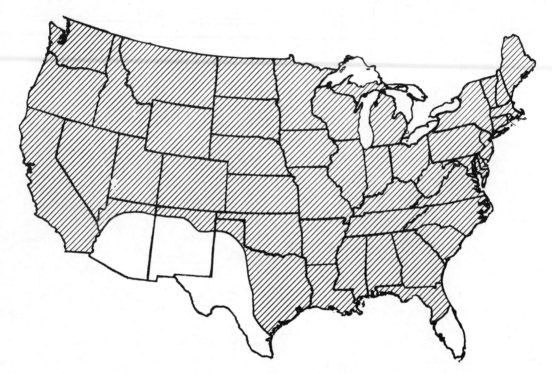

Distribution of *Digitaria ischaemum* (Schreb.) Schreb. ex Muhl.

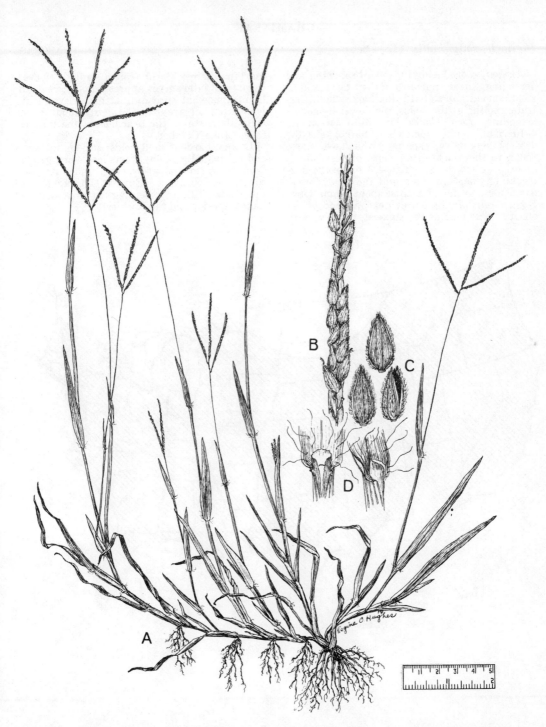

FIGURE 27.—*Digitaria ischaemum* (Schreb.) Schreb. ex Muhl. Smooth crabgrass. *A*, Habit—× 0.5; *B*, spike detail, showing arrangement of florets on rachis—× 5; *C*, florets—× 7.5; *D*, ligules—× 5.

Digitaria sanguinalis (L.) Scop.   LARGE CRABGRASS

Annual, reproducing by seed, branching and spreading, often purplish (Fig. 28); *Culms* stout, smooth, up to 3–12 dm. long, when prostrate, rooting at the nodes, the flowering shoots ascending; *Leaf blades* lax, 5–15 cm. long, 4–10 mm. wide, somewhat hairy, sheaths densely long-hairy, especially the lower ones, rough to the touch, often more or less pilose; *Spike* 5–15 cm. long, with 3–13 fingerlike segments, in whorls at the top of the stem; *Spikelets* along one side of rachis, about 3 mm. long; *First glume* minute, but evident; *Second glume* about half as long as the spikelet, narrow, with marginal hairs; *Sterile lemma* strongly nerved, the lateral internerves appressed-pubescent, the hairs somewhat spreading at maturity; *Fertile lemma* pale or grayish; *Caryopsis* about 2 mm. long, alternate on the branches of the inflorescence. June–October.

Lawns, gardens, and fields; serious in lawns and cultivated ground. Starts late when ground is quite warm and grows well under dry, hot conditions. Native of Europe. Throughout all the United States excepting an area between Lake Superior and the Rockies.

Distribution of *Digitaria sanguinalis* (L.) Scop.

FIGURE 28.—*Digitaria sanguinalis* (L.) Scop. Large crabgrass. *A*, Habit—× 0.5; *B*, florets, front and back views—× 5; *C*, caryopsis—× 6.

Echinochloa crus-galli (L.) Beauv.   BARNYARDGRASS

Annual, with fibrous, rather shallow roots (Fig. 29); *Culms* stout, erect to decumbent, often branching from the base, usually less than 1 m. (but occasionally up to 1.5 m.) tall; *Sheaths* glabrous; *Ligule* absent; *Leaf blades* glabrous, elongate, 5–15 mm. wide, light-green; *Panicle* erect or nodding, green or purple-tinged, 10–20 cm. long; *Racemes* numerous, 2–4 cm. (but occasionally up to 10 cm.) long, spreading, ascending, sometimes branched; *Spikelets* crowded, about 3 mm. long, excluding the awns; *First glume* nearly half as long as the spikelet; *Second glume* and sterile lemma with short bristly hairs on the nerves, typically awnless; *Awns* variable, mostly 5–10 mm. (but occasionally up to 3 cm). long. (A form with conspicuous awns is known as **forma *longiseta* (Trin.) Farw.**); *Caryopsis* ovate, obtuse, usually 2.5–3.5 mm. long, the short beak withering, somewhat inflexed and sharply differentiated from the obtuse body: *Seed* tan to brown, and with longitudinal ridges on the convex surface. June–October.

Cultivated areas, waste ground, ditches, and fields, especially soybeans, clover, and alfalfa fields, in late summer and fall. Native of Europe. Throughout all the United States excepting the extreme southeastern area.

A very variable species with several varieties that intergrade:

var. *mitis* (Pursh) Peterm.—Racemes dense, mostly spreading-flexuous, with spikelets awnless or nearly so (awns less than 3 mm. long) and the sheaths occasionally pubescent with stiff hairs. Over much of the same range as the species and nearly as common.

var. *zelayensis* (H.B.K.) Hitchc.—Racemes more or less appressed, the spikelets less strongly hispid but papillose, usually green, the culms less succulent. Most often in alkaline places; Oklahoma to Oregon, south to Texas and California; Mexico; Argentina.

var. *frumentacea* (Roxb.) W. F. Wight—JAPANESE MILLET, BILLION-DOLLAR GRASS. Racemes thick, appressed, incurved, with turgid, awnless, mostly purple spikelets, the nerves hispid but not tuberculate. Occasionally cultivated as a forage plant and escaped.

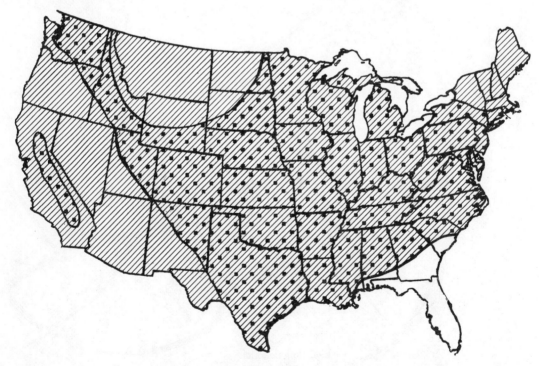

Distribution of *Echinochloa crus-galli* (L.) Beauv.

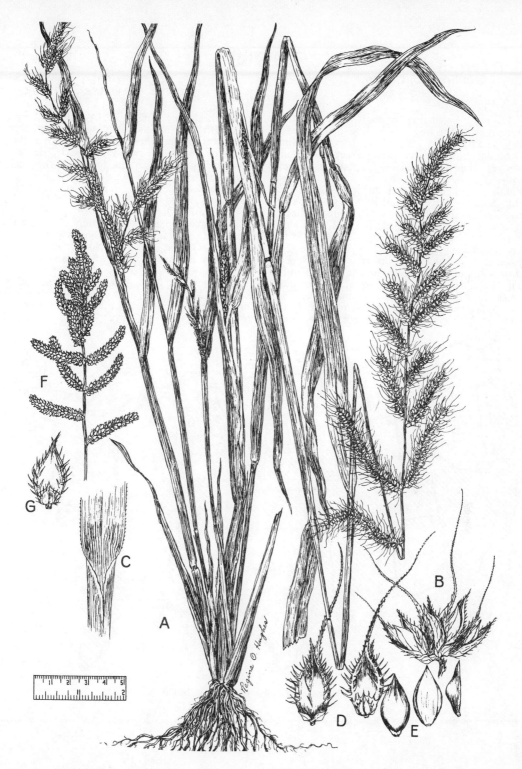

FIGURE 29.—*Echinochloa crus-galli* (L.) Beauv. Barnyardgrass. *A*, Habit, forma *longiseta* (Trin.) Farw.—×
0.5; *B*, spikelet—× 2.5; *C*, ligule—× 2.5; *D*, florets—× 4; *E*, caryopses—× 4; *F*, spike, var. *mitis* (Pursh) Peterm.—× 0.5; *G*, floret of awnless variety—× 4.

GRAMINEAE

Eleusine indica (L.) Gaertn.

GOOSEGRASS, YARDGRASS,
SILVER CRABGRASS, WIREGRASS

Annual, reproducing by seeds, coarse tufted, branching at the base, ascending to prostrate, very smooth (Fig. 30); *Roots* fibrous; *Culms* 15–60 cm. (up to 1 m.) long, erect or decumbent at the base, flattened, glabrous; *Leaf blades* flat or folded, smooth but sometimes slightly roughened, 3–8 mm. wide, 5–25 cm. long; *Sheaths* flattened and keeled, glabrous or somewhat scabrous, margin sometimes pilose; *Ligules* with short marginal hairs, 1 mm. long or less; *Spikes* 4–15 cm. long, fingerlike with 2–6 fingerlike segments (2.5–7.5 cm. long), crowded and whorled or 1 inserted lower; *Spikelets* sessile on one side of the rachis, 3–5 mm. long, 3–6 florets along the edges of the rachilla, crowded; *First glume* 2–2.5 mm. long, 1-nerved; *Second glume* about 3 mm. long, 3- to 9-nerved, both glumes acute, rough to the touch

on the keel, dry and thin; *Lemmas* 3–4 mm. long, with 3 strong nerves close together forming a keel and another pair near the margins, obtuse or nearly so, rarely abrupt tipped. glabrous except rough to the touch on the keel; *Paleas* shorter than the lemmas; *Caryopsis* very small, 1–1.5 mm. long, reddish-brown, granular, ridged, loosely inclosed within the pericarp. July–October.

Waste places, fields, open ground, lawns, gardens, and roadsides; a common weed in the warmer regions; often confused with crabgrass, but is darker green and grows only in tufts. Naturalized from the Old World. Throughout all the United States excepting northern Maine and parts of the north-central and northwestern areas of the United States.

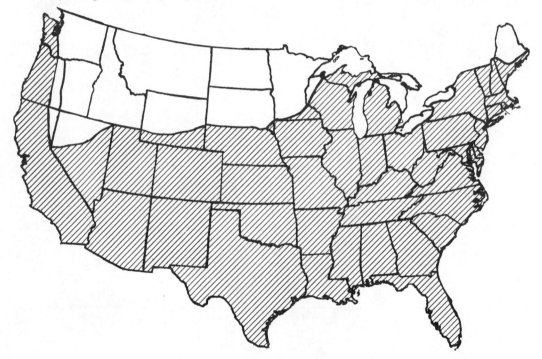

Distribution of *Eleusine indica* (L.) Gaertn.

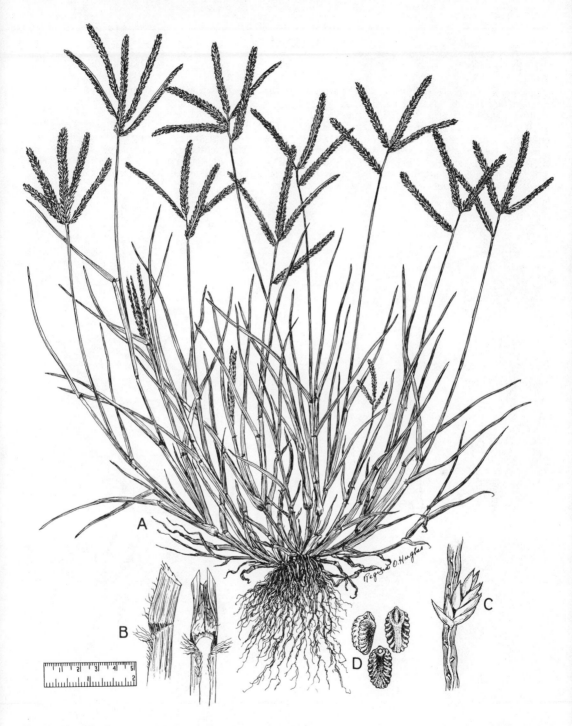

FIGURE 30.—*Eleusine indica* (L.) Gaertn. Goosegrass. *A*, Habit—× 0.5; *B*, ligules—× 2.5; *C*, spikelet—× 3; *D*, caryopses—× 12.5.

GRAMINEAE

Holcus mollis L.

Perennial (Fig. 31); *Rhizomes* slender, vigorous; *Culms* glabrous, 5–10 dm. tall; *Leaves* with the blades with long soft hairs or velvety, 4–10 mm. wide and the sheaths except the lower ones glabrous; *Panicle* ovate or oblong, rather loose, 6–10 cm. long; *Spikelets* 2-flowered, the pedicel disarticulating below the glumes, 4–5 mm. long; *Glumes* about equal, longer than the 2 florets, glabrous; the *first floret* perfect, the *lemma* awnless; the *second floret* staminate, the *lemma* bearing a short awn (about 3 mm. long) on the back. Summer.

Damp places. Recently introduced from Europe and spreading. Along the Atlantic coast from Massachusetts through Pennsylvania and New Jersey; along the Pacific coast from Washington through northern California.

Distribution of *Holcus mollis* L.

FIGURE 31.—*Holcus mollis* L. German velvetgrass. *A*, Habit—× 0.5; *B*, inflorescence—× 2.5; *C*, spikelet (lower floret perfect, awnless: upper floret staminate, awned)—× 5; *D*, glumes—× 5; *E*, ligule—× 2.5; *F*, leaf sheath (retrorse hairs of sheath at joint)—× 2.5.

Hordeum jubatum L.   FOXTAIL BARLEY

Perennial, in clumps or tufted (Fig. 32); *Roots* densely fibrous; *Culms* usually erect, 30–60 cm. tall, or decumbent at the base; *Leaves* alternate, sheaths smooth, the blades 3–6 mm. wide, rough on the upper surface; *Spike* 5–12.6 cm. long, about as wide, nodding with rather soft, yellowish-green or purplish bristles about 5 cm. long; *Lateral spikelets* reduced to 1–3 spreading awns; *Glumes* of central perfect spikclet awnlike, 2.5–6 cm. long, spreading; *Lemma* 6–8 mm. long, with an awn as long as the glumes; *Caryopsis* about 3 mm. long, yellow, hairy. June–September.

Open wastes, meadows, and pastures, where it may be troublesome as the bristles may injure the mouths of livestock; other uncultivated areas and wastes. Throughout all the United States excepting the South Atlantic and Gulf Coast States, north into Canada to Newfoundland and Alaska.

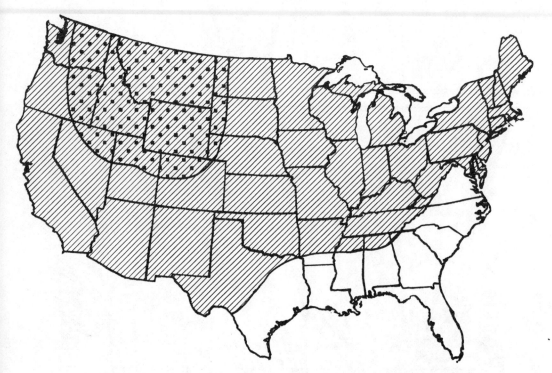

Distribution of *Hordeum jubatum* L.

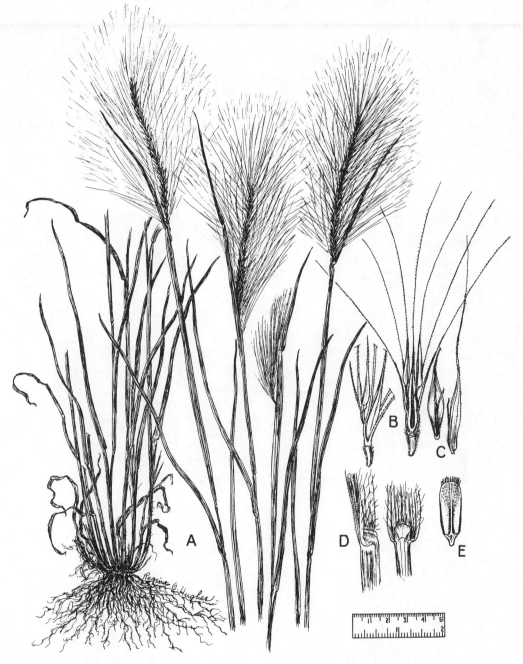

FIGURE 32.—*Hordeum jubatum* L. Foxtail barley. *A*, Habit—× 0.5; *B*, spikelets, side and face views—× 2.5; *C*, florets—× 2.5; *D*, ligules—× 2.5; *E*, caryopsis—× 5.

Hordeum pusillum Nutt.

Annual or *winter annual* (Fig. 33); *Roots* shallow, fibrous; *Culms* smooth, 1–4 dm. tall, bent slightly at each node; *Leaves* erect, 2–7 cm. long, 10–14 mm. wide, rough on the upper surfaces; *Spike* resembling small dense head of rye, erect, 3.3–8.3 cm. long, 1–1.5 cm. wide, with short (1.2–1.5 cm.) stiff bristles; *First glume* of the lateral spikelet and both glumes of the fertile spikelet dilated at the base, atten-uate into a slender awn, 8–15 mm. long, the glumes very rough to the touch; *Lemma* of central spikelet awned, of the lateral spikelets awn-pointed; *Caryopsis* 3–8 mm. long, hairy at the apex, yellow, May–June.

Plains, pastures, other uncultivated areas, and open places; especially in alkaline ground. Native. Throughout most of the United States; South America.

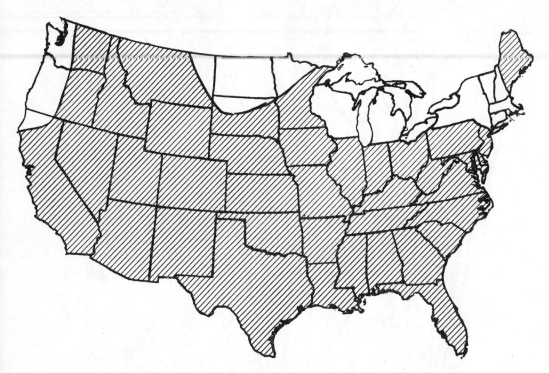

Distribution of *Hordeum pusillum* Nutt.

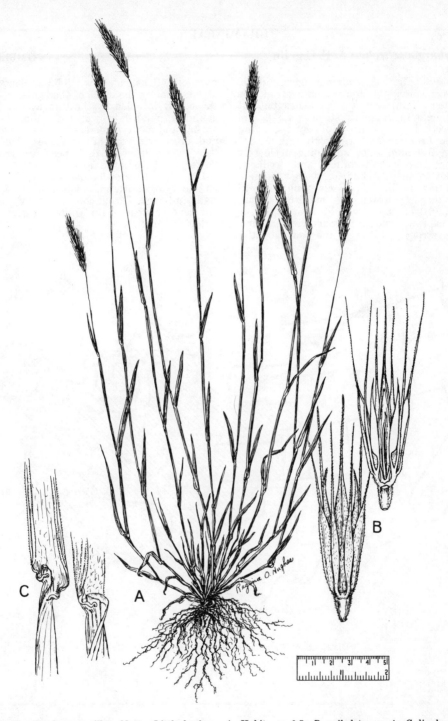

FIGURE 33.—*Hordeum pusillum* Nutt. Little barley. *A*, Habit—× 0.5; *B*, spikelets—× 4; *C*, ligules—×5.

Muhlenbergia schreberi J. F. Gmelin

NIMBLEWILL

Perennial (Fig. 34); *Culms* slender, diffuse, branching, spreading and decumbent at the base, often rooting at the lower nodes, but not forming definite creeping stolons, 1.5–6 dm. long, freely forking into capillary ascending branches; *Leaf blades* flat, mostly less than 5 cm. long, 2–4 mm. wide, spreading or loosely ascending; *Panicles* terminal and axillary, threadlike to linear-cylindric, slender, loosely flowered, lax, nodding, 6–18 cm. long; *Glumes* minute, the first often obsolete, the second rounded, 0.1–0.2 mm. long; *Lemma* green or purple, narrow, somewhat pubescent around the base, strongly 3-nerved, the body about 2 mm. long, the slender awn 2–5 mm. long; *Palea* about equaling the blade of the lemma; *Caryopsis* loosely infolded by the thin lemma, linear-cylindric, reddish-brown, 1–1.4 mm. long. In spring and early summer the culms are short and erect with spreading blades, the plants being very different in appearance from the flowering phase in the fall.

Damp places, woodlands, thickets, roadsides, and dooryards; often a troublesome weed, especially in lawns. Throughout most of the eastern and central areas of the United States; central Colorado; Mexico.

Distribution of *Muhlenbergia schreberi* J. F. Gmelin

FIGURE 34.—*Muhlenbergia schreberi* J. F. Gmelin. Nimblewill. *A*, Habit—× 0.5; *B*, ligules—× 2.5; *C*, part of spikelet to show glumes—× 17.5; *D*, florets—× 17.5.

Panicum dichotomiflorum Michx.

Annual, simple or commonly divergently branching from the base and the nodes (Fig. 35); *Culms* ascending or spreading, bent abruptly at the joints at the base, 5–10 dm. (but occasionally up to 20 dm.) long, flattened, succulent, lower nodes enlarged; *Ligule* a dense ring of white hairs, 1–2 mm. long; *Leaf blades* narrowly lanceolate, rough to the touch and sometimes sparsely pilose on the upper surface, 10–50 cm. long, 3–25 mm. wide, the white midrib usually prominent; *Panicles* terminal and axillary, mostly included in the sheath at the base, 10–40 cm. long or more, the main branches ascending; *Spikelets* narrowly oblong-ovate, 1.8–3.6 mm. (usually 2.5 mm.) long, acute, mostly longer than their rough-angled pedicels and on one side only toward the tips of the branchlets; *First glume* rounded-triangular, one-fifth to one-fourth as long as the second and the sterile lemma. A variable species. June–October.

Moist ground and along streams; a weed in waste places and in cultivated soil. Throughout all the United States excepting parts of the North Central and Northwestern States and Texas.

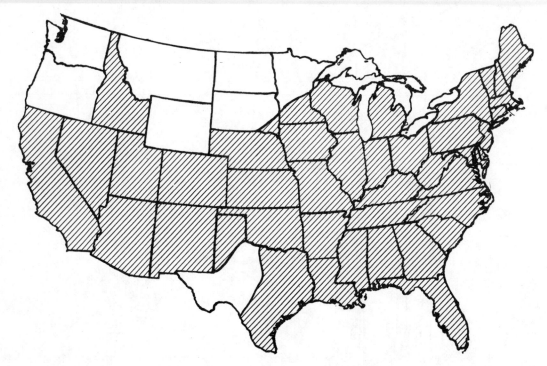

Distribution of *Panicum dichotomiflorum* Michx.

FIGURE 35.—*Panicum dichotomiflorum* Michx. Fall panicum. *A*, Habit—× 0.5; *B*, spikelet, showing the dichotomous florets—× 7.5; *C*, ligule—× 4; *D*, caryopses—× 7.5.

Paspalum dilatatum Poir.   DALLISGRASS

Perennial, from a short rhizome (Fig. 36); *Culms* tufted, stoutish, 4.5–17 dm. tall, glabrous except the ligules and crowded spikelets; *Leaves* elongated, 10–25 cm. long, 4–12 mm. wide; *Racemes* 3–5 (occasionally 2–10), 5–19 cm. long, loosely ascending and spreading; *Spikelets* egg-shaped, tapering to a point, 2.8–4 mm. long, 2–2.5 mm. broad; *Glume* and *sterile lemma* silky, long soft hairs, overtopping the caryopsis. May–October.

Low ground, from rather dry prairie to marshy meadows, roadsides, and borders of ditches; occasionally on ballast northward; a valuable pasture grass. Introduced and naturalized from Uruguay and Argentina. Atlantic Coast States south from New Jersey and across the southern border area of the United States, inland as far north as Missouri; distinct areas in other parts of the United States.

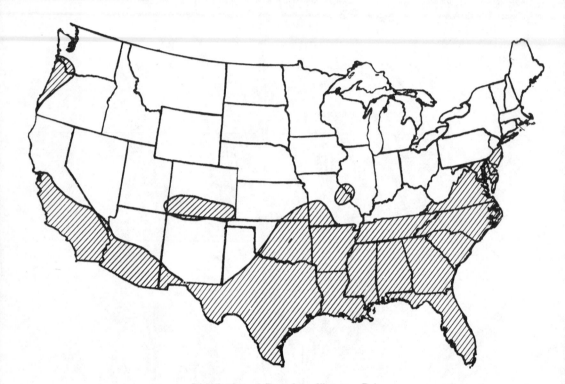

Distribution of *Paspalum dilatatum* Poir.

FIGURE 36.—*Paspalum dilatatum* Poir. *Dallisgrass. A,* Habit—× 0.5; *B,* ligule—× 1.5; *C,* spikelet—× 3; *D,* florets—× 5; *E,* caryopses—× 5.

Paspalum distichum L.   KNOTGRASS

Perennial, stoloniferous (Fig. 37); *Culms* creeping, rooting at the pubescent nodes, with ascending culms 1–6 dm. long; *Leaves* short, 2–8 cm. long, 2–5 mm. wide, usually crowded, sometimes sparsely hairy on the margins, ciliate at the base; *Racemes* 2 (rarely 3 or 4), strictly terminal, 1.5–7 cm. long, ascending and often incurved; *Spikelets* solitary, 2.5–4 mm. long, 1.3–1.5 mm. wide, ovate, abruptly acute, sparsely pubescent, pale-green; *First glume* occasionally present, triangular, to 1 mm. long; *Second glume* appressed-pubescent, 5-nerved; *Sterile lemma* 5-nerved, glabrous. July–October.

Swamps, ditches, muddy and sandy shores, and, rarely, in brackish areas. Native. Throughout most of the Mideastern, Southern, and Western States of the United State Mexico; West Indies; South America.

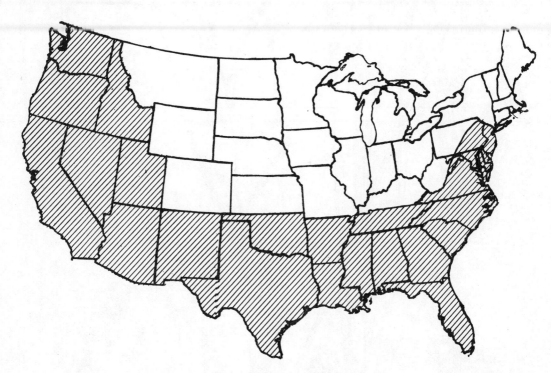

Distribution of *Paspalum distichum* L.

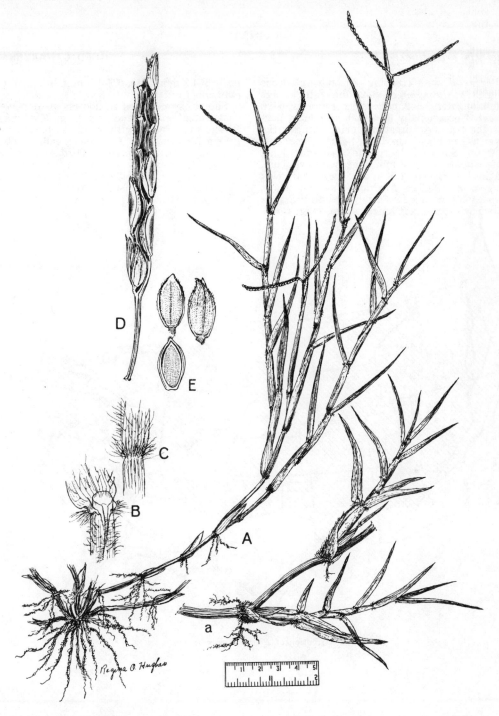

FIGURE 37.—*Paspalum distichum* L. Knotgrass. *A*, Habit—× 0.5, with *a*, young shoot—× 1; *B*, ligule—× 2; *C*, back of leaf, showing fringe of long hairs at base of blade—× 2; *D*, spike—× 4; *E*, florets—× 5.

GRAMINEAE

Phalaris arundinacea L.   REED CANARYGRASS

Perennial, with creeping rhizomes, glaucous (Fig. 38); *Culms* erect, 6–20 dm. tall; *Leaves* flat, elongate, 0.6–2 cm. wide; *Panicles* 5–20 cm. (but occasionally up to 30 cm.) long, narrow, the branches spreading during anthesis, the lower as much as 5 cm. long, tightly contracted in fruit; *Spikelets* lanceolate, 4–6 mm. long, pale; *Glumes* about 5 mm. long, narrow, acute, the keel rough to the touch, very narrowly winged, or wingless; *Fertile lemma* lanceolate, 4 mm. long, with a few flat-lying hairs; *Sterile lemma* with long soft hairs, 1 mm. long; *Cary-*

opsis 3–4.2 mm. long, 0.7–1.5 mm. broad. June–September.

Shores, swales, and meadows; an important constitutent of lowland hay from Montana to Wisconsin. Form with white-striped leaves grown for ornament in gardens, called ribbon-grass or gardener's garters. Throughout all the United Sates excepting areas in the South Atlantic Coast and Gulf Coast States, eastern California, and southeastern Arizona; southern Canada to Alaska.

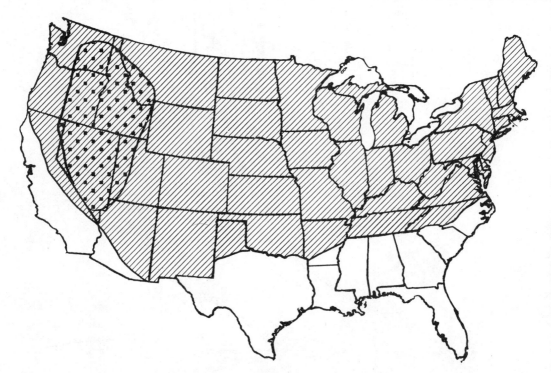

Distribution of *Phalaris arundinacea* L.

FIGURE 38.—*Phalaris arundinacea* L. Reed canarygrass. *A*, Habit—× 0.5; *B*, ligule—× 1.5; *C*, spikelet—× 5; *D*, florets—× 5; *E*, caryopsis—× 5.

GRAMINEAE

Phragmites australis (Cav.) Trin. ex Steud.

(**P. communis** Trin.)

COMMON REED, GIANT REED

Perennial reedgrass, with broad flat, linear blades and large terminal panicles (Fig. 39); *Culms* erect, 2–4 m. (but occasionally up to 6 m.) tall, with stout creeping rhizomes, often also with stolons; *Leaf blades* flat, 1.5–6 dm. long, 1–6 cm. wide, glabrous, the sheaths overlapping; *Panicle* tawny or purplish, 15–40 cm. long, the branches ascending, rather densely flowered; *Spikelets* 10–17 mm. long, the florets exceeded by the hairs of the rachilla; *First glume* 2.5–5 mm. long; *Second glume* 5.7 mm. long. Late July–September.

Marshes, banks of lakes and streams, and most wet wastelands. In the Southwest, used for lattices in the construction of adobe huts; stems used by Indians for shafts or arrows; in Arizona and Mexico, used for mats, screens, thatching, cordage, and for carrying nets. Throughout all the United States excepting the inland areas of the South Atlantic and the South Central States; distinct area in North Carolina; Mexico; Eurasia.

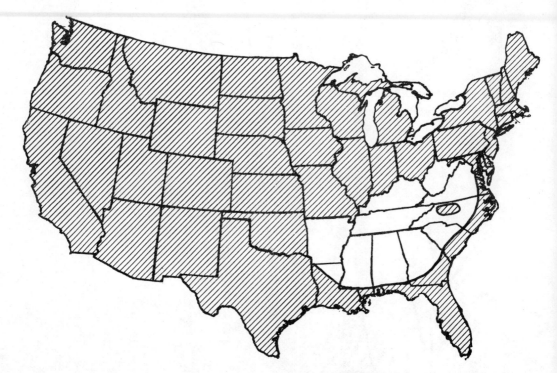

Distribution of *Phragmites australis* (Cav.) Trin. ex Steud.

FIGURE 39.—*Phragmites australis* (Cav.) Trin. ex Steud. Common reed. *A,* Habit—× 0.25; *B,* ligule—× 0.5; *C,* spikelet—× 5.

Setaria faberi Herrm.

Annual, branching at the base, reproducing by seed (Fig. 40, *A*); *Culms* 8–18 dm. tall, plants often so weak as to fall over unless supported by each other or by other vegetation; *Leaf blades* usually softly pubescent beneath to becoming glabrous, and with flattened straight stiff hairs on the upper surface, 8–17 mm. broad; *Panicle* dense, 7.5–20 cm. long, flexuous to conspicuously nodding, 1–1.7 dm. long, 2.3 cm. thick; *Spikelets* about 3 mm. long, with 3–6 bristles extending from the base of each spike-let, the second glume shorter than the wrinkled seed; *Caryopsis* usually greenish, about 1.5 mm. long, transversely and abundantly cross-wrinkled. June–September.

Fields, waste places, disturbed soils, roadsides, and cultivated ground; a serious weed in Illinois and Missouri. Introduced from China, probably in seed of Chinese millet (1931). Throughout all but the northernmost and southernmost States or parts of the States in the eastern half of the United States.

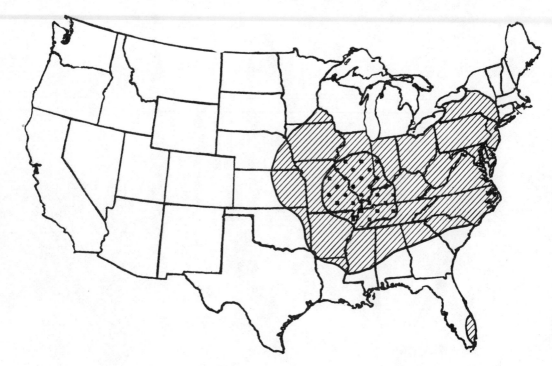

Distribution of *Setaria faberi* Herrm.

Figure 40.—*A*, *Setaria faberi* Herrm. Giant foxtail. *a*, Habit—× 0.5; *b*, spikelet, showing subtending bristles —× 5; *c*, ligule—× 1.5; *d*, caryopses—× 5. *B*, *Setaria viridis* (L.) Beauv. Green foxtail. *a*, Habit—× 0.5; *b*, spikelet—× 5; *c*, ligule—× 1.5; *d*, caryopses—× 5. *C*, *Setari glauca* (L.) Beauv. Yellow foxtail. *a*. Habit— × 1; *b*, spikelet—× 5; *c*, ligule—× 1.5; *d*, caryopses—× 5.

GRAMINEAE

Setaria glauca (L.) Beauv.

   (*S. lutescens* (Weigel) Hubb.)

Yellow Foxtail, Yellow Bristlegrass

Annual, branching at the base (Fig. 40, *C*); *Culms* flattened, often tufted, erect to prostrate, mostly 5–12 dm. tall; *Leaves* with keeled sheaths; *Blades* as much as 25 cm. long and 3–10 mm. wide, flat, twisted in a loose spiral, with hairs long and soft toward the base above; *Panicle* dense, evenly cylindric, spikelike, yellow at maturity, mostly 1.5–12 cm. long, 0.9–1.4 cm. thick, the axis densely pubescent;

Bristles 5–20 in a cluster, 3–8 mm. long, the longer ones 2 to 3 times as long as the spikelet; *Spikelets* 3 mm. long, with undulate-wrinkled fertile lemma; *Caryopsis* strongly wrinkled. June–September.

Cultivated soils, waste areas, and other disturbed soil. Introduced from Europe. Throughout all the United States; north into British Columbia and New Brunswick.

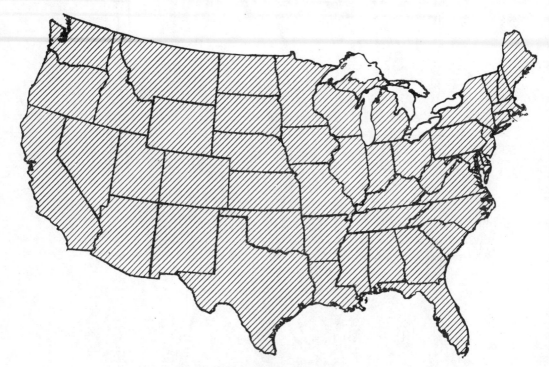

Distribution of *Setaria glauca* (L.) Beauv.

GRAMINEAE

Setaria viridis (L.) Beauv.   GREEN FOXTAIL, GREEN BRISTLEGRASS, BOTTLEGRASS

Annual, simple or tufted, branching at the base, sometimes spreading (Fig. 40, *B*); *Culms* 20–40 cm. (but occasionally up to 1 m.) tall; *Leaf blades* flat, usually less than 15 cm. long, 5–15 mm. wide, glabrous; *Panicle* erect or somewhat nodding, densely flowered, green or purple, cylindric but tapering a little at the summit, usually 1.5–15 cm. long, 1–2.3 cm. wide; *Bristles* 1–3 below each spikelet, mostly 3–4 times their length; *Spikelets* 1.8–2.5 mm.

long, green, the green to purplish bristles upwardly rough to the touch, spreading-ascending and 3–4 times as long; *Caryopsis* very finely rugose. June–September.

One of the most serious and widespread grass weeds of cultivated soils and waste places. Introduced from Europe. Common throughout all the cooler parts of the United States.

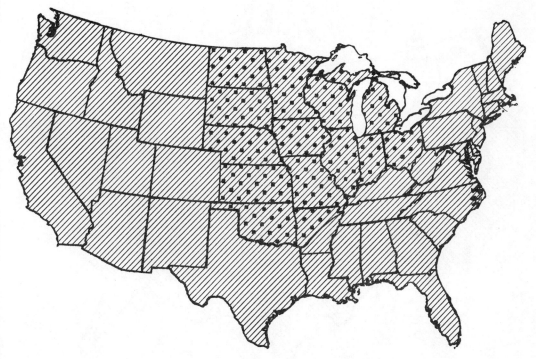

Distribution of *Setaria viridis* (L.) Beauv.

Sorghum halepense (L.) Pers. JOHNSONGRASS

Perennial, reproducing by large rhizomes and by seeds (Fig. 41); *Root* system freely branching, fibrous, the rhizomes stout, creeping, with purple spots, usually with scales at the nodes; *Stems* erect, stout, 5–15 dm. tall; *Leaves* alternate, simple, smooth, 20-50 cm. long, less than 2 cm. wide; *Panicles* large, purplish, hairy, 15–50 cm. long; *Sessile spikelet* 4.5–5.5 mm. long, ovate, with flat-lying straight hairs, the readily deciduous awn 1–1.5 cm. long, bent abruptly, twisted below; *Pedicillate spikelet* 5–7 mm. long, lanceolate; *Caryopsis* nearly 3 mm. long, oval, reddish-brown, marked with fine lines on the surface. June–October.

Open ground, fields, and waste places; cultivated for forage, but becomes a troublesome weed. Native of the Mediterranean region. Throughout approximately the southern half of the United States, extending as far north as central New York, New Hampshire, and Vermont in the East and southern Oregon in the West; a distinct area in central Washington and Oregon.

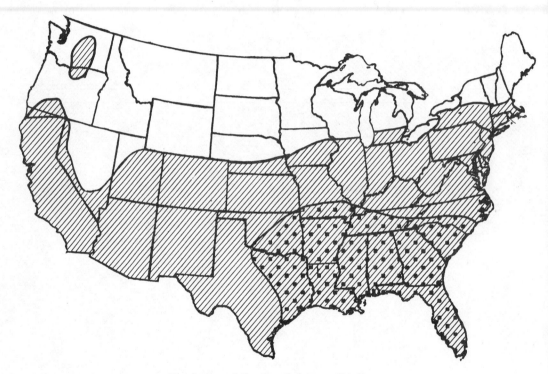

Distribution of *Sorghum halepense* (L.) Pers.

FIGURE 41.—*Sorghum halepense* (L.) Pers. Johnsongrass. *A*, Habit—× 0.5; *B*, spikelet—×4; *C*, ligule—× 1.5; *D*, florets—× 5; *E*, caryopses—× 5.

Sporobolus poiretii (Roem. & Schult.) Hitchc.   SMUTGRASS

Perennial (Fig. 42) ; Culms solitary or tufted, 3–10 dm. tall, erect, wiry; with 2 or 3 leaves; *Leaves* flat to slightly rolled inward, rather firm, 10–30 cm. long, 2–5 mm. wide at base, slenderly tapering; *Panicle* linear-cylindric, stiff, one-fourth to one-half the entire length of the plant, 10–40 cm. long. the branches close to the central axis or ascending; *Spikelets* 1.5–2 mm. long, shining, crowded on the slender erect branches; *Glumes* obtuse, unequal, the second half as long as the tapering pointed lemma, which is slightly longer than the blunt palea. May–October.

Dry sandy soils, open ground, and waste places; on ballast in New Jersey and Oregon. Naturalized from tropical America. Throughout approximately the southeastern fourth of the United States; a distinct area along the coast of Oregon.

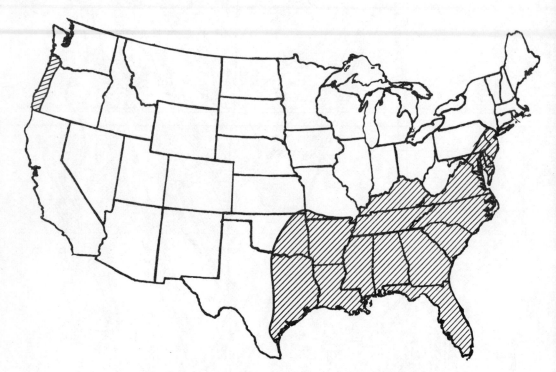

Distribution of *Sporobolus poiretii* (Roem. & Schult.) Hitchc.

FIGURE 42.—*Sporobolus poiretii* (Roem. & Schult.) Hitchc. Smutgrass. *A*, Habit—× 0.5; *B*, ligules—× 2.5 (*left*, as in nature: *right*, spread open); *C*, spikelet—× 5; *D*, floret—× 7.5; *E*, caryopses—× 10.

GRAMINEAE

Taeniatherum asperum (Simonkai) Nevski

MEDUSAHEAD

("*Elymus caput-medusae*")

Annual (Fig. 43); *Culms* ascending from a decumbent, branching base, slender, 2.6 dm. tall; *Leaf blades* narrow, short; *Spike* very bristly, 2–5 cm. long, excluding the long spreading awns; *Spikelets* 2 (occasionally 3), each containing 1 seed located on each node of the rachis; *Glumes* awl-shaped, smooth, hardened below, tapering into a slender awn, 1–2.5 cm. long; *Lemmas* lanceolate, 3-nerved, 6 mm. long, very rough to the touch, tapering into a flat awn 5–10 cm. long, containing upward pointing barbs. Summer.

Open ground; a bad weed, spreading on the ranges in northern California, Oregon, Washington, and Idaho. Introduced from Europe. Throughout part of the northwestern area of the United States, south into central California; north into British Columbia.

Distribution of *Taeniatherum asperum* (Simonkai) Nevski

FIGURE 43.—*Taeniatherum asperum* (Simonkai) Nevski. Medusahead. *A*, Habit—× 0.5; *B*, spikelet, showing arrangement of florets in pairs—× 3; *C*, florets, front and back—× 5; *D*, ligule—× 2.5.

CYPERACEAE

Carex lasiocarpa Ehrh. var. *latifolia* (Boeckl.) Gilly

BULL SEDGE

(*C. lanuginosa* Michx.)

Perennial rhizomatous sedge, forming large colonies (Fig. 44); *Culms* 5–10 dm. tall, 3-sided, acutely angled and rough to the touch in the upper regions; *Leaves* very long and slenderly tapering, the leaf blades rough to the touch, 2–5 mm. wide, flat, the margins rolled backward; *Staminate spikes* usually 2, 2–6 cm. long; *Pistillate spikes* 1–3, widely spaced, cylindric, 1–3 cm. long, rarely longer, sessile or nearly so; *Lowest bract* overtopping the culm; *Pistillate scales* ovate-lanceolate, from shorter than to longer than the perigynia, purplish-brown, acute to abruptly tipped or gradually tapering to the end; *Perigynia* oblong egg-shaped, 2.5–5 mm. long, 1.2–3 mm. thick, densely pubescent, the teeth 0.3–0.8 long; *Achene* angled, egg-shaped. Variable in the leaf characters. May–August.

Marshes, swamps, swales, rich meadows, and shores. Native. Throughout all the United States excepting the extreme southeastern area; north into southern Canada.

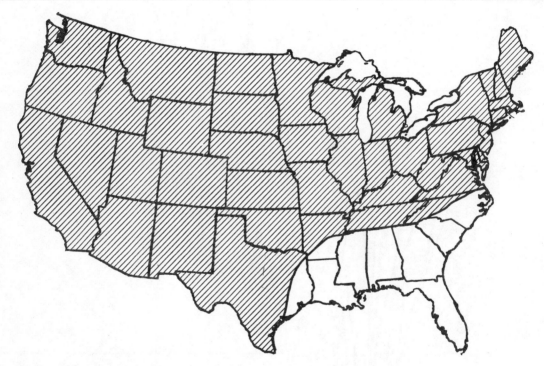

Distribution of *Carex lasiocarpa* Ehrh. var. *latifolia* (Boeckl.) Gilly

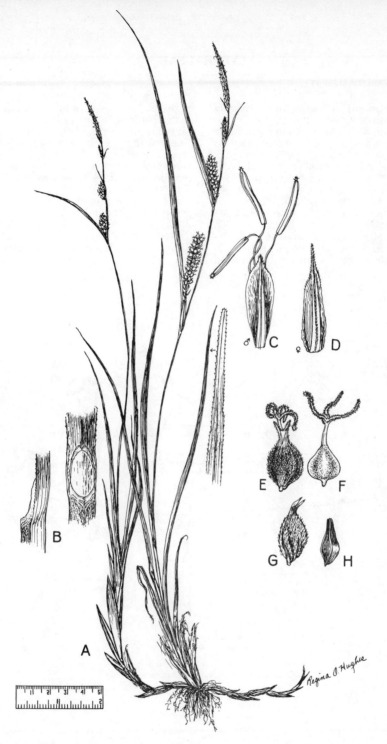

FIGURE 44.—*Carex lasiocarpa* Ehrh. var. *latifolia* (Boeckl.) Gilly. Bull sedge. *A*, Habit—× 0.5; *B*, ligules—×
2.5; *C*, staminate flower (scale subtending 3 stamens)—× 5; *D*, pistillate scale—× 5; *E*, pistillate flower with
perigynium—× 5; *F*, pistillate flower without perigynium—× 5; *G*, perigynium enclosing the achene—× 5; *H*,
achene—× 10.

CYPERACEAE

Carex nebraskensis Dewey

Perennial (Fig. 45); Rhizome long-creeping and stoloniferous; *Culms* 2.5–12 dm. tall; *Leaves* 3–12 mm. wide, flat or channeled, more or less divided into partitions and swollen at the nodes; *Sheaths* smooth; *Stȧminate spike* usually solitary or with smaller ones at base, terminal; *Pistillate spike* 1.5–6 cm. long, 5–9 mm. wide, oblong to cylindrical, erect, upper nearly sessile, the leaves short- to long-peduncled, rather ccntiguous, 2–5, with many ascending perigynia; *Lowest bract* leaflike, sheathless, usually longer than the inflorescence; *Sales* narrower and from longer to shorter than the perigynia, lanceolate, rounded at the end to tapering to a gradual point, purplish, brown or brownish-black, often with narrow hyaline margins, lighter centers, 1- to 3-nerved; *Perigynia* ascending, 3–3.5 mm. long, about 2 mm. wide, oblong-ovate, flat-convex or unequally double convex, flattened, straw-colored, leathery in texture, strongly many-ribbed, abruptly contracted to a 2-toothed beak 0.4–1 mm. long; *Styles* jointed; *Stigmas* 3. May–July.

Wet meadows and swamps. Native. Throughout approximately all the western half of the United States excepting that area along the Pacific coast; north into British Columbia.

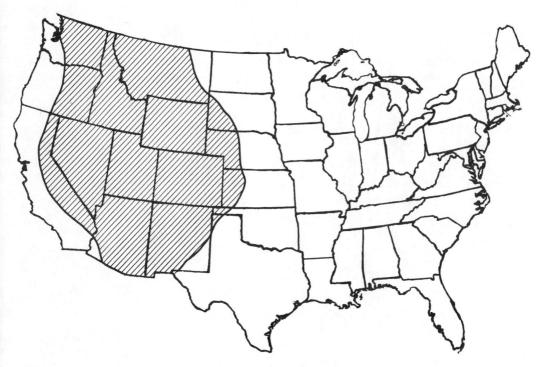

Distribution of *Carex nebraskensis* Dewey

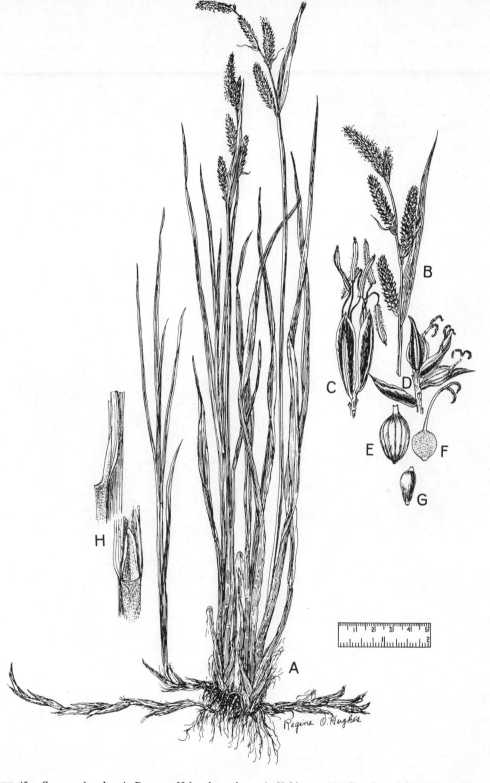

FIGURE 45.—*Carex nebraskensis* Dewey. Nebraska sedge. *A*, Habit—× 0.5; *B*, enlarged flowering spike—× 1; *C*, staminate flower—× 4; *D*, pistillate flowers, showing scales—× 4; *E*, perigynium—× 4; *F*, pistillate flower without perigynium—× 4; *G*, achene—× 7.5; *H*, ligule—× 3.

Cyperus esculentus L.   YELLOW NUTSEDGE

Perennial herb, reproducing by seeds and weak thread like stolons, terminated by hard tubers (Fig. 46); *Tubers* 1–2 cm. long; *Roots* fibrous; *Stems* (culms) erect, 2–9 dm. tall, simple, triangular; *Leaves* 3-ranked, pale-green, 4–9 mm. wide, about as long as the stem, with closed sheaths mostly basal; *Umbel* terminal, simple to compound, the longest involucral leaf much exceeding the umbel; *Spikelets* 0.5–3 cm. long, 1.5–3 mm. broad, yellowish to golden-brown, strongly flattened, mostly 4-ranked (occasionally 2-ranked) along the wing-angled rachis, blunt, the tip acute to round; *Scales* thin, oblong, obtuse, distinctly nerved, thin and dry at the tip, 2.3–3 mm. long; *Achene* yellowish-brown, 3-angled, lustrous, ellipsoid or linear to oblong-cylindric, rounded at the summit, 1.2–1.5 mm. long, granular-streaked. July–September.

Cultivated fields, gardens, and grainfields; rich or sandy soils; often limited to low, poorly drained areas in fields; a serious weed. Native of North America. Throughout most of the United States; north to Nova Scotia, southern Quebec, southern Ontario, and southern Manitoba; Mexico; tropical America; Eurasia.

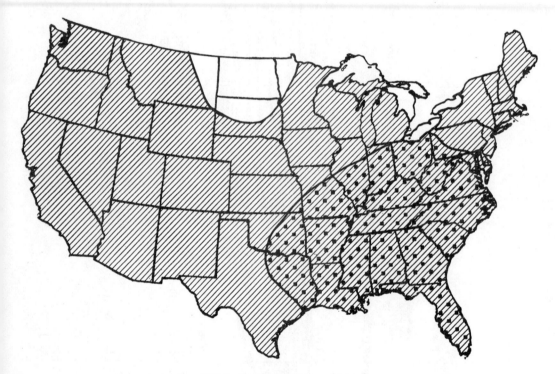

Distribution of *Cyperus esculentus* L.

FIGURE 46.—*Cyperus esculentus* L. Yellow nutsedge. *A*, Habit—× 0.5; *B*, spikelet—× 5; *C*, achene—× 10.

CYPERACEAE

Cyperus rotundus L.

Perennial herb, reproducing by seeds and tuber-bearing rhizomes (Fig. 47); *Stems* (culms) erect, 1–6 dm. tall, simple, triangular, longer than the leaves; *Leaves* 3–6 mm. wide; *Umbel* simple or slightly compound, about equaling the involucre; *Spikelets* 0.8–2.5 cm. long, chestnut-brown to chestnut-purple, acute, 12- to 40-flowered; *Scales* ovate, closely appressed, nerveless except on the keel, 2–3.5 mm. long, bluntish; *Achene* linear-oblong, 1.5 mm. long, 3-angled, the base and apex obtuse, granular, dull, olive-gray to brown, covered with a network of gray lines. July–October.

Cultivated sandy fields and gardens, especially in the Cotton Belt; often a troublesome weed. Introduced and naturalized from Eurasia. Throughout most of the South Atlantic and Gulf Coast States, west to Texas and Mexico; occasionally north to New England; along most of the coast of California, east to southwestern Arizona.

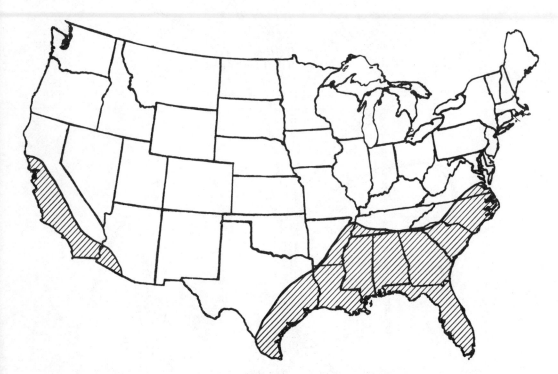

Distribution of *Cyperus rotundus* L.

FIGURE 47.—*Cyperus rotundus* L. Purple nutsedge. *A*, Habit—× 0.5; *B*, flowering spikelet—× 5; *C*, achenes, showing type of reticulation and cross section in detail—× 10.

Scirpus acutus Muhl.

Perennial herb (Fig. 48); *Rhizome* stout, often drab and brown; *Culms* circular in cross section, erect, up to 3 m. tall, olive-green; *Inflorescence* of a few nearly sessile spikelets and of several flattened peduncles 1–8 cm. long, each having 1–5 spikelets; *Bract* erect, usually 1–4 cm. (occasionally up to 10 cm.); *Spikelets* mostly in compact clusters, several, ovate to cylindric, acute, 7–20 mm. long, reddish to grayish-brown; *Scales* red-spotted, sticky, broadly ovate, about 4 mm. long, conspicuously exceeding the achene, usually short-pubescent, the margin thin and hyaline and often fringed, the apex notched and abrupt tipped; *Achene* becoming black and lustrous, thickly flat-convex, 2–2.5 mm. long, abrupt short-pointed, bristles variable in length. July–August.

Swamps, shores, and shallow water. Native. Throughout all the United States excepting some of the South Atlantic and Gulf Coast States; north into southern Canada from Newfoundland to British Columbia.

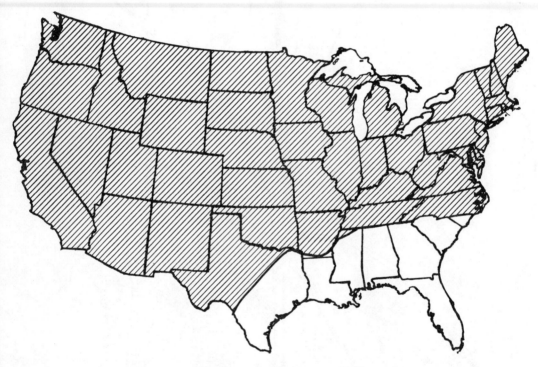

Distribution of *Scirpus acutus* Muhl.

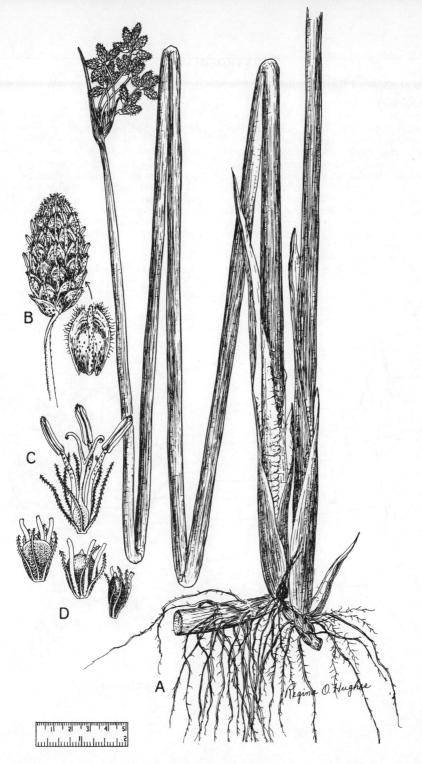

FIGURE 48.—*Scirpus acutus* Muhl. Hardstem bulrush. *A*, Habit—× 0.5; *B*, spikelet—× 2.5; *C*, flower—× 7.5; *D*, achenes—× 5.

Eichornia crassipes (Mart.) Solms   WATERHYACINTH

(*Eichhornia*)

Perennial aquatic herbs (Fig. 49); *Rhizome* and *stems* normally floating, rooting at the nodes, with long black pendent roots; *Leaves* usually with greatly inflated spongy petioles, the leaf blades circular to kidney-shaped, 4–12 cm. wide; *Inflorescence* a contracted panicle, 4–15 cm. long, with several flowers; *Perianth* lilac, bluish-purple, or white, the upper lobe bearing a violet blotch with a yellow center; *Stamens* 6; *Stalk* of the inflorescence soon becoming goose-necked, forcing the dead flowers under the water; *Capsule* dehiscent, surrounded by the perianth, membraneous, many-seeded.

July–October; longer in the warmer regions.

Ditches, quiet streams, rivers and waterways, lakes, and ponds; usually very prolific and troublesome, often clogging and obstructing waterways. Widely naturalized in all tropical regions; sometimes cultivated in the northern regions of the range as the water orchid. Introduced and naturalized from South America. Throughout approximately all the southeastern fourth of the United States, from the Potomac River south; along the coast of central California; south into Mexico and Central America; introduced in Europe and Asia.

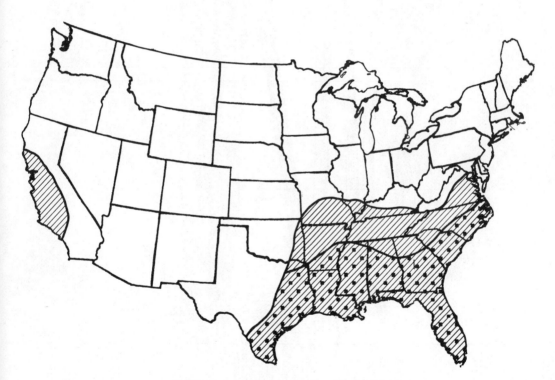

Distribution of *Eichornia crassipes* (Mart.) Solms

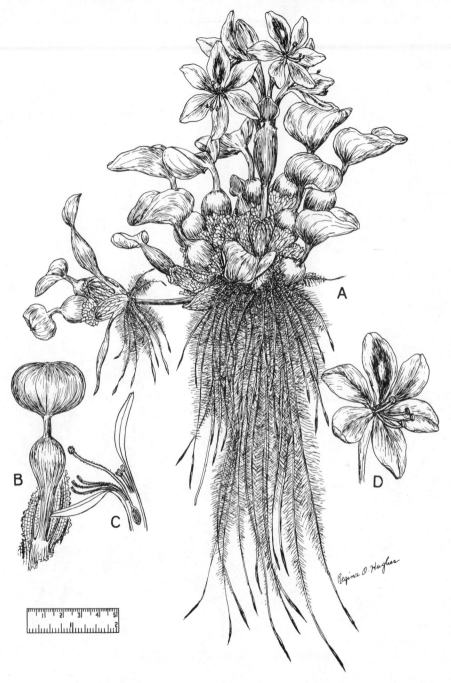

FIGURE 49.—*Eichornia crassipes* (Mart.) Solms. Waterhyacinth. *A*, Habit—× 0.25; *B*, leaf—× 0.25; *C*, diagram of flower—× 0.5; *D*, flower—× 0.5.

PONTEDERIACEAE

Heteranthera dubia (Jacq.) MacM.

(*Zosterella dubia* (Jacq.) Small)

Aquatic herb submersed, floating, or sometimes stranded (Fig. 50); *Stems* elongate, branched, slender, submersed; *Leaves* linear, grasslike, sessile, translucent, 2–6 mm. wide, up to 15 cm. long; *Inflorescence* 1-flowered, nearly sessile, completely enclosed by the 1-leaved spathe; *Spathe* 2–5 cm. long, slender, sessile in the axils, the small flowers expanded on the water surface, the spathe abruptly short-caudate at the spreading tip; *Flowers* often fertilized in unopened buds, or perianth tube 2–7 cm. long, the limb spreading, pale-yellow, the outer segments linear, the inner linear-lanceolate; *Stamens* 3, all alike, with filaments dilated near the middle, tapering at both ends; *Fruit* an indehiscent 1-locular, few-seeded capsule, narrowly egg-shaped, about 1 cm. long. June–September.

Quiet water, streams, meadows, and shores of quiet water areas, as lakes and ponds. Tropical America. Throughout all the United States excepting an area in the Southwest; distinct area in southwestern Arizona; north into southern Canada; Mexico; Cuba.

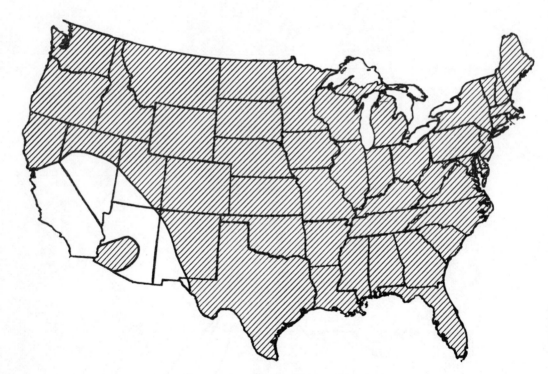

Distribution of *Heteranthera dubia* (Jacq.) MacM.

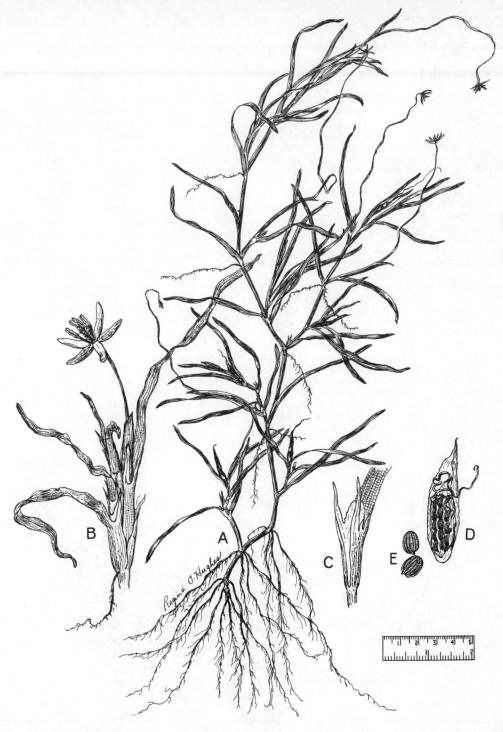

FIGURE 50.—*Heteranthera dubia* (Jacq.) MacM. Waterstargrass. *A*, Habit—× 0.5; *B*, enlarged habit, showing flower—× 1.5; *C*, sheath at base of leaf, showing the stipulelike appendages—× 2; *D*, capsule—× 5; *E*, seeds— × 10.

LILIACEAE

Allium vineale L.   Wild garlic

Perennial bulbous herb, the outer layers of the bulb formed from the sheathing leaves of the foliage leaves (Fig. 51): *Stem* becoming stiff, erect, leafy to near the middle, 0.3–1.3 m. tall; *Leaves* 2-ranked, with sheathing bases, the leaf blades circular, hollow in cross section, striped, the younger ones easily flattened, slenderly tapering; *Spathe* usually 1, dry and thin, short, beaked, its edges united above; *Umbel* projecting through the base of the deciduous spathe, nearly head-shaped, 2–5 cm. in diameter; *Two plant types*: the larger, *scapigerous plants* bearing scapes that produce aerial bulblets and sometimes flower; the flowers having greenish to purplish perianths with lanceolate to elliptic segments, the segments obtuse to acutish and about as long as the stamens; seeds black, flat on one side, about 3 mm. long; the smaller, *nonscapigerous* plants bearing slender foliage and fewer leaves, and not producing a scape at the end of the growing season; *Four types of bulbs* found at the end of season in late spring: *Aerial bulblets* (as many as 300 in one scape of the scapigerous plant); *Hard-shell bulbs*, having a single bladeless storage leaf that contains a growing point at its base, formed underground, in the axils of the outer leaves of scapigerous and nonscapigerous plants; *Central bulbs*, formed underground by nonscapigerous plants, conspicuous at the end of the season's growth, formed around the main axis of the plant, circular in cross section, varying from the size of an aerial bulblet to that of a soft offset bulb; *Soft offset bulb* formed underground in the axil of the innermost leaves of scapigerous plants, largest of the four types of bulbs, ovate in longitudinal section, with a convex abaxial face and a flat adaxial face that form two distinct ridges where the faces meet, these ridges clasping the sides of the flattened scape to which they are attached; *Seed* produced in the spring, germinate the following fall; usually spreading by bulbs rather than by seed; and most usually by the numerous aerial bulbs. May–July.

A ubiquitous weed, drought-hardy, cold-hardy, tolerant to wet soils, liking heavy soils best; poorly drained land along rivers and streams, hillsides; a pest and troublesome weed in fields of small grain, pastures, hayfields used for milk cows (the allyl sulfide imparting the garlicky flavor to agricultural products, as milk, along with a disagreeable odor), gardens, roadsides, lawns, and noncrop areas. Difficult to eradicate. Native of Eurasia. Throughout most of the Eastern and Central States excepting those in the northern part of the United States; along the Pacific Coast from Washington through northern California; distinct area in Wyoming.

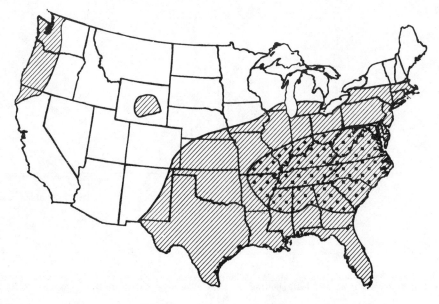

Distribution of *Allium vineale* L.

106

FIGURE 51.—*Allium vineale* L. Wild garlic. *A,* Habit—× 0.5; *B,* flower cluster—× 0.5; *C,* bulblets—× 2.5; *D,* flower—× 3.5; *E,* bulbs, hard-shell—× 0.5; *F,* bulbs, soft-shell—× 0.5.

CANNABINACEAE

Cannabis sativa L.

Annual, reproducing by seed (Fig. 52); *Taproot* much-branched; *Plant* bushy unless crowded; *Stems* simple or sparingly branched, 6–30 dm. tall, coarse, somewhat grooved, rough and hairy, the hairs on the upper parts exuding a sticky resin with a characteristic odor, the inner bark of very tough fibers; *Leaves* opposite, but alternate above, palmately divided, with 5 to 9 hairy leaflets with notched edges; *Flowers* dioecious, small and green, the male and female flowers borne on separate plants: *male plants* turning yellow and dying after shedding pollen, male flowers in axillary compound racemes or panicles in the axils of the upper leaves, 5 perianth segments and 5 stamens; *female plants* vigorous and dark-green until frost, female flowers in spikelike clusters, without petals, in the axils of the leaves; *Fruit* (achene) about 4 mm. long, ovoid to nearly round with obtuse edges, yellow to olive-brown; *Seed* oval, mottled-brown, about 3 mm. long. June–October.

Neglected fields, farmyards, ditches, roadsides, moist fertile soil, on wastelands, and fence rows; cultivated varieties grown as fiber crop; chiefly sporadic and derived from foreign packing, ballast lots. Prolific seed and pollen producers; source of marijuana and of hemp fibers. Adventive from Asia. Throughout all the United States excepting the extreme southeastern and southwestern areas, western Texas, and on an area between central Montana and southern Michigan

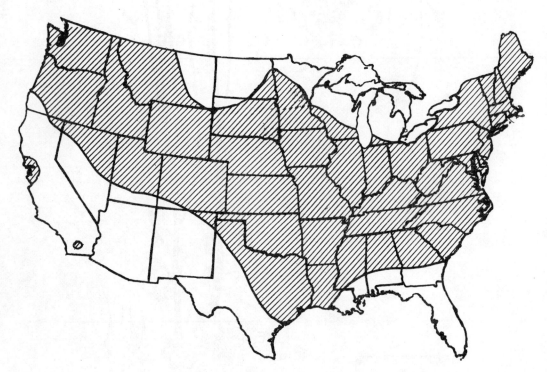

Distribution of *Cannabis sativa* L.

FIGURE 52.—*Cannabis sativa* L.   Hemp.   *A*, Male plant: *a*, habit—× 0.5; *b*, enlarged staminate flower panicle—× 3; *c*, flower—× 6. *B*, female plant: *a*, habit—× 0.5; *b*, enlarged pistillate flower cluster—× 3; *c*, flower—× 6; *d*, achene—× 3; *e*, seeds—× 3.

Urtica dioica L.

Perennial, reproducing by seeds and creeping rootstocks (Fig. 53); *Stems* erect, 1–2 m. tall, ridged, bristly-hairy with stinging bristles (0.75–2 mm. long); *Leaves* opposite, simple, egg-shaped to heart-shaped, coarsely serrate, hairy or glabrous, with or without stinging bristles, usually twice as wide as the length of the petiole, the stipules linear-lanceolate, 5–15 mm. long, green to pale-brown, minutely pubescent; *Inflorescence* branched, many-flowered, loose to dense, panicled spikes; *Flowers* mostly dioecious, small, greenish; *Staminate flowers* with 4 perianth segments and 4 stamens; *Pistil-late flowers* with 4 perianth parts and a 1-celled ovary; *Fruit* (achene) 1–1.5 mm. long, flattened, egg-shaped, minutely glandular, yellow to grayish-tan, the calyx and remnant of the style often persistent. Most frequently represented by **var. procera (Muhl.) Wedd.** June–September.

Waste places, roadsides, vacant lots, rich soil, and edge of damp woods. Naturalized from Eurasia. Throughout all the United States excepting southern Georgia, most of Florida, and that part of the United States from northwestern Washington through most of Texas.

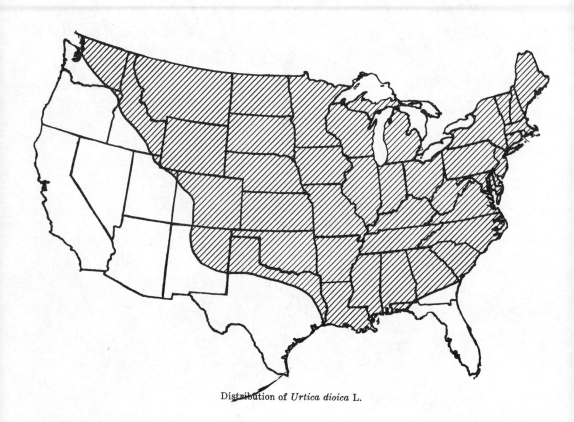

Distribution of *Urtica dioica* L.

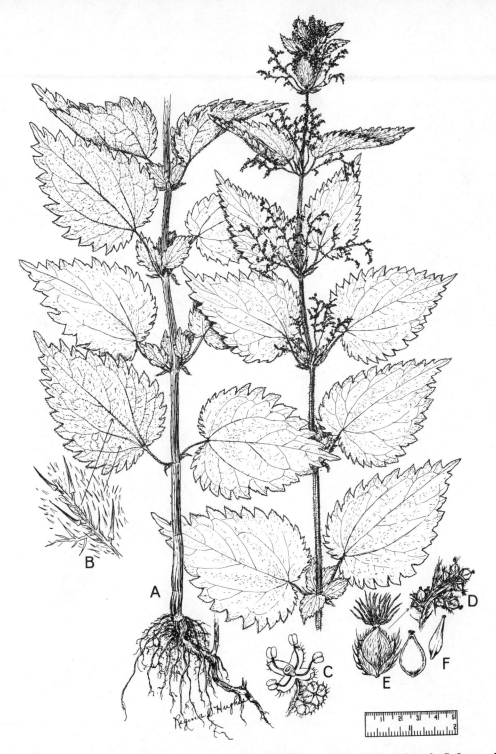

FIGURE 53.—*Urtica dioica* L. Stinging nettle. *A*, Habit—× 0.5; *B*, stinging hairs, enlarged; *C*, flower, closed and open—× 7.5; *D*, fruiting spike—× 1.5; *E*, fruit—× 6.5; *F*, achenes, face and edge views—× 7.5.

Brunnichia cirrhosa Gaertn.

Perennial woody tendril-bearing vine (Fig. 54); *Stems* high-climbing, much-branched, sometimes 2 cm. thick; *Leaves* alternate, deciduous, the ocreae (tubular stipules) obsolete, the blades ovate to ovate-lanceolate, 3–15 cm. long; *Flowers* in branching panicles; *Perianth* becoming 3–3.5 cm. long; *Sepals* 5, oblong, about 5 mm. long, surmounting the hypanthium; *Hypanthium* developing into an indehiscent winged fruit, 2.5–3.5 mm. wide, extending the length of the elongate pedicellike base; *Stamens* 8; *Stigmas* 3, each 2-cleft; *Achene* 7–10 mm. long, 3-angled, included in the dry hypanthium. May–September.

Mostly on river banks. In the extreme southeastern coastal area of the United States, along the Gulf coast, north paralleling each side of the Mississippi River to Illinois.

Distribution of *Brunnichia cirrhosa* Gaertn.

Figure 54.—*Brunnichia cirrhosa* Gaertn. Redvine. *A*, Habit—× 0.5; *B*, branch showing fruiting calyces—× 0.5; *C*, flowers—× 2.5; *D*, achenes—× 2.

POLYGONACEAE

Polygonum amphibium L. (incl. var. *stipulaceum* (Coleman) Fern.) WATER SMARTWEED

(*P. natans* Eat.)

Perennial herb, with aquatic and terrestrial forms, reproducing by seeds and by slender and tough forking rhizomes; stolons, and rooting stems (Fig. 55); *Branches* elongate, simple, leafy to the summit, the young stems, ocreae (tubular stipules) and leaves glabrous to pubescent; *Leaves* alternate, floating or spreading to ascending, elliptic-oval to lanceolate, petioled, gradually tapering or rounded at the base, rarely subcordate; *Ocreae* cylindric, with or without spreading and hairy summit margins; *Spikes* 1–4, dense, straight, erect on erect or terminal glabrous peduncles, cylindric, oval or egg-shaped, the leading spike 1–4 cm. long, at maturity 1–2 cm. thick; *Calyx* pink or rose-col-ored, the sepals spreading and blunt in anthesis, closed in fruit; *Achene* lens-shaped, broadly egg-shaped to circular, 2.5–3 mm. long. Highly variable in appearance as to habitat. July–October.

Gravelly shores, slopes, prairies, open and wooded swamps, and meadows; also in aquatic situations as margins of lakes and ponds, in quiet waters, and in floating and stranded situations. Throughout the northern areas of the world and in south Africa. Adventive from Europe. Throughout all the northern half of the United States excepting parts of States in the West; north into Canada to Labrador and Alaska.

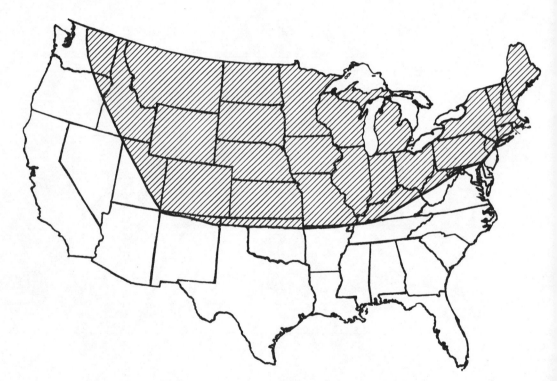

Distribution of *Polygonum amphibium* L. (incl. var. *stipulaceum* (Coleman) Fern.)

FIGURE 55.—*Polygonum amphibium* L. Water smartweed. *A*, Habit—× 0.5; *B*, ocrea—× 2.5; *C*, flower cluster, showing sheath and bilobed sheathing bracts—× 3; *D*, flowers—× 3; *E*, achene—× 3.

POLYGONACEAE

Polygonum aviculare L.

Annual herb, reproducing by seeds (Fig. 56); *Stems* 10–100 cm. long, prostrate or loosely ascending to erect, the main stem corrugated, much-branched, mostly forming mats from thin taproots; *Leaves* alternate, entire, sharp-pointed to rounded at the end, narrowed at the base, blue-green, lanceolate, linear to oblong or elliptic, 5–30 mm. long, 1–8 mm. wide, scattered to close together on the stem, petioles very short, united to the short sheath formed by the stipules, veinless or inconspicuously veined; *Flowers* in axillary clusters, perfect, small; *Pedicels* soon exserted beyond the hyaline and flaccid soon torn ocreae (tubular sheaths); *Perianth* (fruiting calyx) 2–3 mm. long, with 5–6 lobes, green with pinkish or whitish margins, appressed at maturity; *Stamens* mostly 8; *Pistil* solitary, ovary 1-celled, styles 3; *Achene* egg-shaped, 2–2.5 mm. long, 3-angled, dark reddish-brown to black, dull to nearly lustrous, granular-striate to minutely punctuate, the remains of the perianth usually attached. Variable species with many forms and varieties. July–November.

Disturbed soils, lawns, along streets, gardens, roadsides, and wastes; a ubiquitous weed. Native to North America but also naturalized from Europe. Throughout all the United States and southern Canada; north to Alaska and Newfoundland.

var. *littorale* (Link) W. D. J. Koch—Seashores, salt marshes, alkaline habitats inland, and rich nonsaline soils.

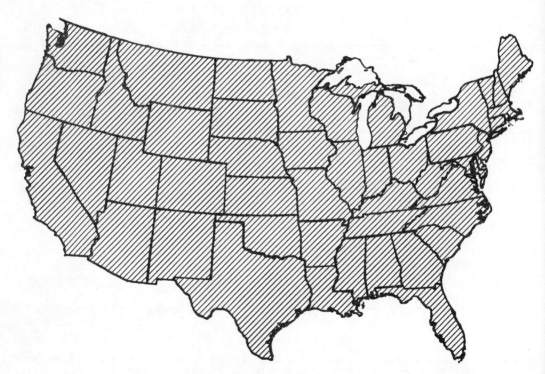

Distribution of *Polygonum aviculare* L.

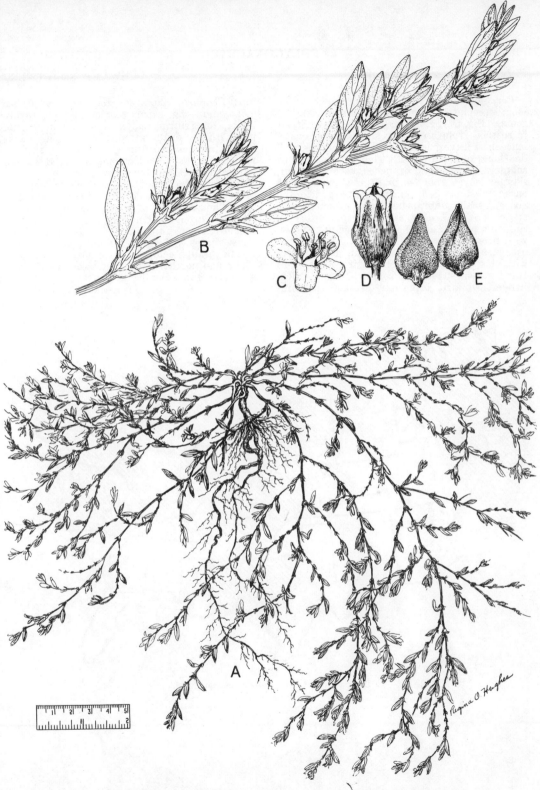

FIGURE 56.—*Polygonum aviculare* L. Prostrate knotweed. *A*, habit—× 0.5; *B*, flowering branch, enlarged—× 2.5; *C*, flower—× 7.5; *D*, fruiting calyx—× 7.5; *E*, achenes—× 7.5.

Polygonum coccineum Muhl.

Perennial herb, reproducing by seeds and by long, creeping, tough, woody, horizontal rhizomes (Fig. 57); *Root system* extensive; *Stems* terrestrial from ascending stolons with ovate-lanceolate leaves, long slenderly tapering, 1–2 dm. long, or aquatic with glabrous floating or submersed leaves and branches, with smoother, thinner leaves, rounded or heart-shaped at the base, the stems 3–9 dm. long, enlarged at the nodes, usually unbranched, may produce roots at the nodes; *Leaves* alternate, oblong, 7–18 cm. long, pointed at the tip, rounded at the base with prominent veins, a sheath (ocrea) at the base of leaf surrounding the stem, close, mostly with close-lying straight stiff hairs; *Flowers* in 1 or 2 racemes, 4–18 cm. long, 7–15 mm. thick, slender, cylindric, often narrowest at the summit; *Peduncle* pubescent to glabrous; *Calyx* 4.5–5 mm. long, sepals scarlet to pink, rarely white, the fruiting calyx veiny, about 7 mm. long; *Achene* oval, flattened on one side, dark-brown to black, 2.5–3 mm. long, shiny, slightly rough, but usually does not set seed in the northern areas. July–October.

Low wet places in fields, shallow or deep water, ditches, gardens, roadsides, meadows, shores and margins of ponds, and wet prairies. Native. Throughout most of the United States excepting areas in the South Atlantic and Gulf Coast States and an area from southern California through central Texas, north to western Idaho and northern Wyoming; eastern Canada in Quebec and Nova Scotia.

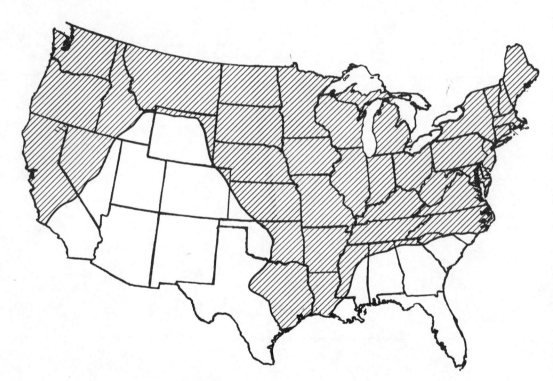

Distribution of *Polygonum coccineum* Muhl.

FIGURE 57.—*Polygonum coccineum* Muhl. Swamp smartweed. *A*, Habit—× 1; *B*, rootstock—× 0.25; *C*, spike— × 3; *D*, achenes, 2 views—× 5.

POLYGONACEAE

Polygonum convolvulus L.

Annual herb, reproducing by seeds (Fig. 58); *Stems* glabrous to slightly roughish, scurfy, branched at the base, twining or procumbent, 20–100 cm. long, the internodes long; *Leaves* alternate, 2–6 cm. long, heart-shaped with basal lobes directed backward, pointed with smooth margins, dull-green, long-petioled; the upper leaves lanceolate, with basal lobes directed backward, tapering to a gradual point; *Stipule sheaths* (ocreae) with entire margins; *Flowers* small, greenish-white, borne in short axillary clusters, or axillary and terminal interrupted or spikelike racemes; *Pedicels* mostly shorter than the minutely pubescent green or purple-tipped calyx; *Fruiting calyx* nearly oblique-angled to egg-shaped, 4–5 mm. long, 3-angled, with scarcely developed keels; *Achene* 3-angled, black, often covered with a dull-brown minutely roughened hull. May–November.

Most cultivated areas, waste grounds, gardens, grainfields, and thickets, und along fences; a serious weed. Naturalized from Eurasia. Widely distributed in North America and throughout United States.

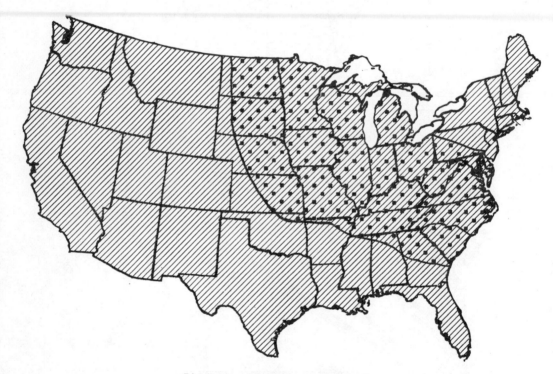

Distribution of *Polygonum convolvulus* L.

FIGURE 58.—*Polygonum convolvulus* L. Wild buckwheat. *A*, Habit—× 0.5; *B*, branchlet with fruiting calyx—× 4; *C*, flower—× 5; *D*, achenes—× 5.

Polygonum hydropiper L.

Annual herb, reproducing by seeds (Fig. 59); *Stems* jointed, somewhat flattened, ascending or erect, 3–6 dm. tall, glabrous, green or more or less reddened, intensely acrid or peppery; *Leaves* alternate, simple, narrowly lanceolate to oblanceolate, acute or tapering to a gradual point, entire, 9 cm. long, sessile or extending downward into short petioles, glabrous, with wavy margins; *Ocreae* (tubular stipules) thin, dry, membranaceous, brown, truncate, bristly, hairy-margined, the hairs 1–2 mm. long; *Spikes* slender and lax, arching at the tips of the branches, with distant cleistogamous fascicles extending down to and often inclosed in the upper sheaths; *Ocreolae* (small secondary sheaths) inversely top shaped, greenish, some-

times with red tips, without hairs or with short hairs; *Pedicels* included or exserted; *Calyx* greenish or red-tipped, 2–4.5 mm. long in fruit, covered with dark sessile glands; *Stamens* 6; *Pistil* with 1-celled ovary, the style 2- to 3-parted; *Achene* lens-shaped to 3-angled, dull, minutely dotted with depressions in lines, 2–3.5 mm. long, dark-brown to black, the tip often slightly exserted, with the remains of the perianth usually attached. June–November.

Damp soils, low meadows, pastures, cultivated ground, and waste places. Native to North America and Europe, widespread. Throughout all the United States excepting southern Georgia and Florida.

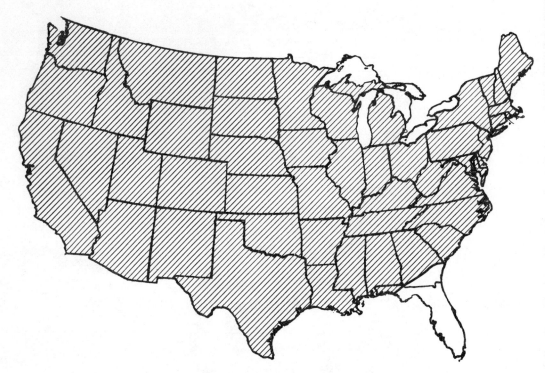

Distribution of *Polygonum hydropiper* L.

FIGURE 59.—*Polygonum hydropiper* L. Marshpepper smartweed. *A,* Habit—× 0.5; *B,* node showing ocrea—× 2.5; *C,* spike—× 5; *D,* flower—× 5; *E,* achenes—× 5.

POLYGONACEAE

Polygonum pensylvanicum L. PENNSYLVANIA SMARTWEED

Annual herb, reproducing by seeds (Fig. 60); *Stems* ascending to erect, up to 1.2 m. tall, swollen at the nodes, branching, glandular to nearly glabrous, often strigose-hispid; *Leaves* alternate, glabrous, often with close-lying stiff hairs, pointed, lanceolate to elliptic or oval, 5–15 cm. long; *Sheath* (ocrea) at the base extending around the stem, thin, membranaceous, cylindric, soon falling away, without hairs, the upper sheaths often glandular or strigose; *Flowers* in dense erect spikes, bright-pink or rose, nearly round to thick-cylindric, 1–6 cm. long, 1–1.5 cm. thick, the larger ones pedun-cled; the flowers all alike or if occasionally of two types (sexes) borne in the same inflorescense; *Achene* shiny, black, smooth, lens-shaped, round-ovoid to circular, flattened on one face, concave on the other, 2.2–3.5 mm. broad. Several varieties may be distinguished. Late May–October.

Cultivated ground and waste places and along ditches, damp shores, and thickets. Native. Throughout approximately the eastern and central parts of the United Steas, west as far as southeastern Wyoming.

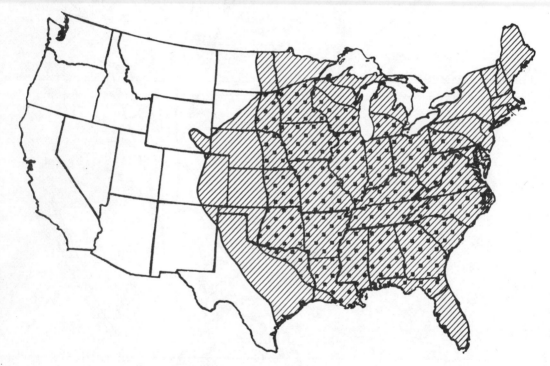

Distribution of *Polygonum pensylvanicum* L.

FIGURE 60.—*Polygonum pensylvanicum* L. Pennsylvania smartweed. *A*, Habit—× 0.5; *B*, spike—× 2.5; *C*, achenes—× 4.

POLYGONACEAE

Polygonum persicaria L.

Annual herb, reproducing by seeds (Fig. 61); *Stems* smooth, sometimes hairy, simple to much-branched, ascending or decumbent, 0.2–1 m. tall; *Leaves* alternate, narrowly to broadly lanceolate, pointed at both ends, 2.5–15 cm. long, 0.5–3 cm. broad, with smooth edges and usually with a purplish blotch in the middle; *Sheath* (ocreae) at base of the leaf fringed with short bristles; *Flowering spikes* 1 to several in a panicle, glabrous-peduncled or the secondary spikes short-peduncled to nearly sessile, oblong to thick-cylindric, dense, 7–11 mm. thick, the leading spikes 1.5–4.5 cm. long; *Ocreolae* (secondary sheaths) usually with hairy margins; *Calyx* pink, purplish, or green and pink, rarely white, 2.3 mm. long (4 mm. in fruit), the mature sepals with prominently netted-veined bases; *Achene* almost circular, flattened or 3-angled, smooth, black, shiny, 2.5–3 mm. long. June–October.

Cultivated ground, waste places, and roadsides and along ditches, damp clearings, and shores. Naturalized from Europe. Throughout all the United States excepting the southwestern area and Texas; north to Quebec and Nova Scotia.

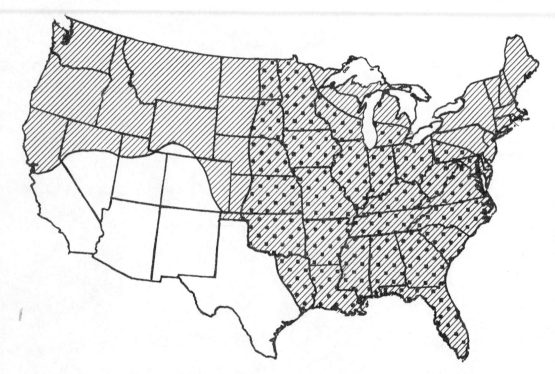

Distribution of *Polygonum persicaria* L.

FIGURE 61.—*Polygonum persicaria* L. Ladysthumb. *A*, Habit—× 0.5; *B*, spike—× 3; *C*, ocrea—× 1.5; *D*, achenes—× 5.

POLYGONACEAE

Rumex acetosella L. Red sorrel

Perennial, reproducing by seeds and creeping rhizomes (Fig. 62); *Roots* and *rhizomes* extensive but rather shallow; *Stems* slender, erect, 1.5–4.5 dm. tall, branched at the top, several stems from one crown or from the rhizomes; *Leaves* alternate, simple and entire, a rosette of basal leaves in early growth, the stem leaves arrow-shaped with the 2 basal lobes somewhat divergent, thick, glabrous, narrowly lanceolate to almost linear upward, 2.5–7 cm. long, acid to the taste; *Inflorescence* of slender racemes near the top of the plant, erect in panicles; *Flowers* yellow to red, male and female flowers on different plants, nodding on short-jointed pedicels, the outer sepals lanceolate, the inner sepals in staminate flower 1.5–2 mm. long, obovate, in pistillate flower broadly ovate; *Hull* reddish-brown, rough, often adhering to the seed; *Achene* 3-sided, about 1.5 mm. long, reddish-brown to golden-brown, shiny, exserted from and divested of the calyx. A highly variable species in color and size of plant. June–October.

A ubiquitous weed in gardens, pastures, meadows, and lawns; persists in areas of poor drainage and low soil fertility; in gravelly sterile fields; very difficult to eradicate. Naturalized from Eurasia. Throughout the United States.

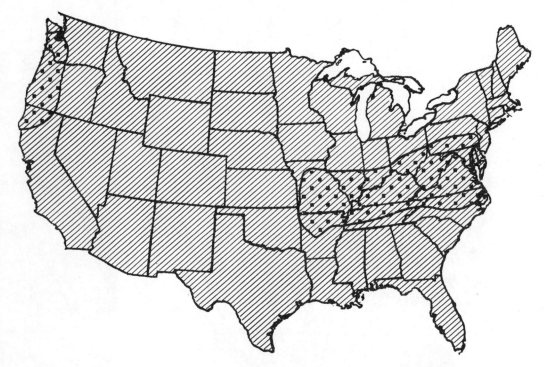

Distribution of *Rumex acetosella* L.

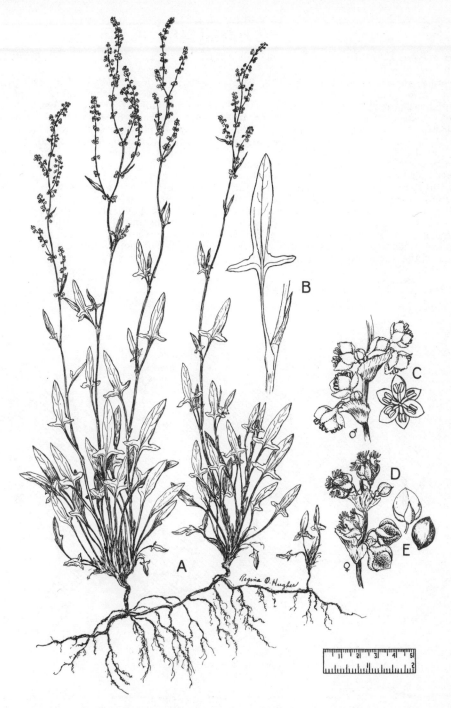

FIGURE 62.—*Rumex acetosella* L. Red sorrel. *A*, Habit—× 0.5; *B*, leaf detail—× 1.5; *C*, staminate flowers—× 7.5; *D*, pistillate flowers—× 7.5; *E*, achenes, in and out of calyx—× 10.

Rumex crispus L.   CURLY DOCK

Perennial, reproducing by seeds (Fig. 63); *Taproot* large, yellow somewhat branched; *Stems* glabrous, erect, single or in groups from the root crown, simple to the inflorescence, up to 1 m. tall; *Leaves* simple, mostly basal, glabrous, 15–30 cm. long, lanceolate, the larger leaves rounded to nearly heart-shaped at the base, with wavy-curled or crisped margins; upper leaves alternate, the base of the short petiole with a papery sheath surrounding the stem. *Inflorescence* large with many erect or ascending branches, with few to many linear leaves intermingled; *Flowers* small, greenish, becoming reddish-brown at maturity, in dense clusters of ascending racemes in branches at the ends of the stems, on long-slender pedicels 5–10 mm. long; *Calyx* of 6 greenish sepals more or less persistent, the 3 inner enlarged (in fruit called the valves), heart-shaped, and nearly entire, 4–6 mm. wide, and each bearing a rounded plump grain (tubercule); *Grains* 3, often unequal, the larger ovoid, very turgid, rounded at both ends, about half as long as the valves; *Achene* brown, shiny, triangular, and sharp-edged, about 2 mm. long, surrounded with 3 heart-shaped valves with smooth edges. June–September.

Pastures, hayfields, meadows, waste areas, and gardens and along roadsides; often a pernicious weed. Introduced and naturalized from Eurasia. Throughout the United States.

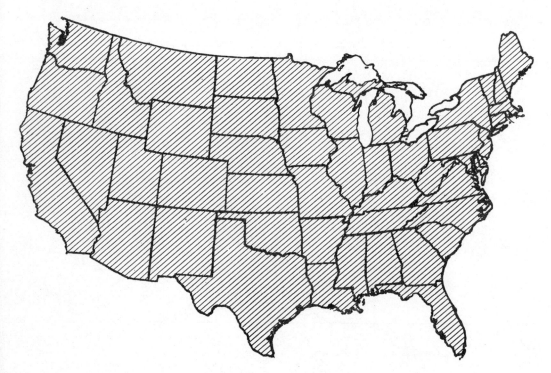

Distribution of *Rumex crispus* L.

FIGURE 63.—*Rumex crispus* L. Curly dock. *A*, Habit—× 0.5; *B*, Fruit, *a*, surrounded by persistent calyx, *b*, showing 3 valves—× 3.5; *C*, achene—× 5.

Chenopodium album L.

Annual herb, reproducing by seeds (Fig. 64); *Taproot* short and much-branched; *Stems* erect, much-branched above, 0.2–2 m. tall, glabrous, grooved, often with red or light-green streaks, branching varying from slight to much; *Leaves* alternate, simple, ovate to lanceolate, without stipules, the upper leaves sometimes linear and sessile, glabrous, usually white mealy-coated, especially on the underside and in the early stages, the edges with a few low broad teeth; *Inflorescence* in irregular spikes clustered in panicles at the ends of the branches and in the keeled and nearly covering the mature fruit;

axils of leaves; *Flowers* perfect, small, sessile, green; *Calyx* of 5 sepals that are more or less keeled and nearly covering the mature fruit; *Petals* none; *Stamens* 6; *Pistil* 1, with 2 or 3 styles, ovary 1-celled, attached at right angles to the flower axis; *Fruit* a utricle (a seed covered by the thin papery pericarp); *Seed* shining, black, lens- to disk-shaped, 1.3–1.5 mm. in diameter, with a marginal notch. June–October.

Cultivated crops, gardens, grain fields, and waste ground. Introduced and naturalized from Eurasia. Throughout the United States.

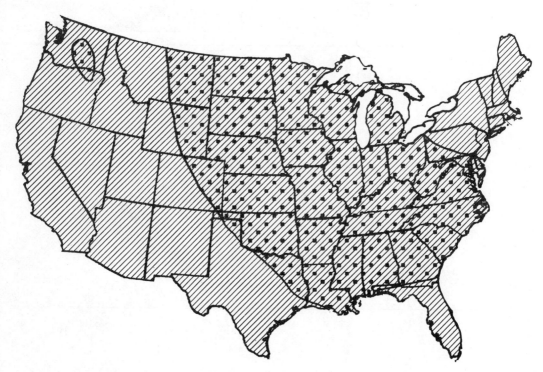

Distribution of *Chenopodium album* L.

FIGURE 64.—*Chenopodium album* L. Common lambsquarters. *A*, Habit, small plant; *B*, floral spike—× 2.5; *C*, flowers—× 7.5; *D*, utricle—× 4; *E*, seed—× 4.

CHENOPODIACEAE

Halogeton glomeratus (M. Bieb.) C. A. Mey.   HALOGETON, BARILLA

Annual herb, branching from the base, the stems at first spreading, then usually becoming erect, 0.5–5 dm. tall, often with numerous short lateral branches (Fig. 65); *Plant* glabrous or pubescent, fleshy, bluish-green in early spring becoming yellow or red in late summer; *Leaves* alternate but in bunches along the stems, fleshy, round, abruptly ending in a slender needlelike hair, sessile, 6–20 mm. long, with tufts of cottony hairs in the angles between the leaves and the stems; *Flowers* in compact clusters in the leaf axils, 2-bracted, greenish-yellow, inconspicuous, numerous, of 2 kinds: the larger flowers with wing-tipped sepals surrounding the seed cases, the smaller flowers with toothlike sepals at the apex; *Seed cases* 5, wide-winged bracts (sepals) on black seed produced during short days of late summer densely crowded on the stems and short branches at maturity giving an appearance of being in flower in autumn, the brown seeds produced during the long days of early summer encased in short adherent thickened bases of bracts (sepals); *Seed* numerous and of two types: black seed (very dark chocolate brown) and brown seed (light-tan), more or less flattened, about 1 mm. long, the spiral form of the embryo clearly evident; *Black seed* all germinating during first growing season after production; *Brown seed* dormant but remaining viable in soil for many years; *Winged bracts* on black seed facilitating spread by wind. Plants also become tumbleweeds, distributing the seeds. Fruiting July–October.

Dry deserts and dry lakebeds; barren eroded burned-over areas, overgrazed ranges, roadsides, alkaline and disturbed soils, and abandoned farmlands; and along railroad beds and sheep trails. Introduced from Siberia about 1930. Poisonous to livestock, especially sheep and cattle, because of high oxalate content. In distinct areas in the West Central States.

Distribution of *Halogeton glomeratus* (M. Bieb.) C. A. Mey.

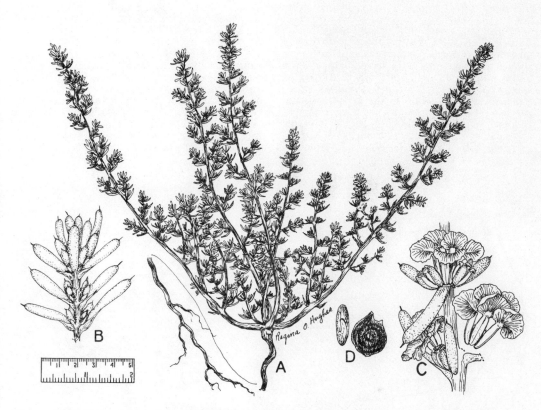

FIGURE 65.—*Halogeton glomeratus* (M. Bieb.) C. A. Mey.   Halogeton.   *A*, Habit—× 0.5; *B*, enlarged leaves—× 2.5; *C*, flower—× 5; *D*, seed, 2 views—× 6.

CHENOPODIACEAE

Kochia scoparia (L.) Roth

KOCHIA

Annual, with taproot, reproducing from seeds (Fig. 66); *Stems* erect, much-branched, 3–10 dm. tall, smooth but usually hairy above; *Leaves* alternate, simple, pubescent to nearly glabrous, 2.5–5 cm. long, lanceolate to linear, with hairy margins, without petioles; *Spikes* 5–100 mm. long, hairy, left bracts 3–10 mm. long; *Flowers* perfect, solitary or paired, small, greenish, without petals, in the axils of the upper leaves and in terminal panicles; *Calyx* 5-10-lobed, each lobe developing into a winglike appendage; *Seed* about 1.8 mm. long, ovate, flattened with a groove on each side from the narrow end, finely granular, surface dull, brown with yellow markings, a fragile shell-like hull (calyx) may enclose seed. July–September.

Waste places, ballast grounds, dry pastures, rangeland, and cropland; a drought-resistant weed serious in the Plains States; introduced as an ornamental for its bright-red autumnal color (burning bush, summer cypress) ; often escaped from cultivation. Naturalized from Eurasia. Throughout most of the northern half of the United States excepting Washington, most of Oregon, and parts of Idaho and Montana.

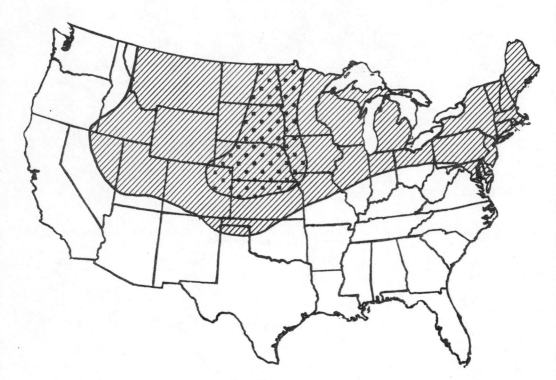

Distribution of *Kochia scoparia* (L.) Roth

FIGURE 66.—*Kochia scoparia* (L.) Roth.   Kochia.   *A*, Branch of plant—× 0.5; *B*, magnified branchlet, showing flowers at different stages—× 2.5; *C*, rootstock—× 0.5; *D*, flower—× 5; *E*, fruits—× 5; *F*, seeds—× 6.

CHENOPODIACEAE

Salsola kali L. var. *tenuifolia* Tausch   RUSSIAN THISTLE

(*S. pestifer* A. Nels.)

Annual herb, reproducing by seeds (Fig. 67); *Taproot* spreading; *Stems* bushy, much-branched, 1.5–12 dm. tall, 3–15 dm. in diameter, rigid, spiny, spherical, often reddish in age, young stems and leaves green and succulent; *Leaves* alternate, the first-formed leaves (in seedlings and young plants) fleshy, cylindrical or awl-shaped, 0.5 mm. broad, 1.2–6.5 cm. long, pointed at the tips, usually bearing a short shoot in the axil; the later-formed leaves shorter, stiff, dilated and thickened at the base, ending in a hard sharp spine; *Flowers* small, greenish, mostly solitary from the lowest to the uppermost leaf axils; *Petals* none; *Sepals* 5, papery and persistent; *Stamens* 5; *Pistil* 1, with a style; *Bracts* at the base of each flower 2, rigid, spine-tipped, resembling the leaf;

Fruit surrounded by the 5 enlarged sepals, each developing a fan-shaped, strongly veined wing on its back, 3–9 mm. broad, thus forming a beaked or conical cover over the 1-seeded fruit; *Seed* numerous (thousands per plant), top-shaped, about 2 mm. broad, with a yellowish coiled embryo, visible through the thin gray wall of the fruit. Flowering July until frost; fruiting from August into winter.

Disturbed areas, roadsides, ditchbanks, fallow abandoned grainfields, overgrazed ranges, and pastures. Old plants break loose to form "tumbleweeds." Common to abundant in Western and parts of the Central States, occasional to frequent in the States along the eastern and southern coasts, where it is spreading rapidly.

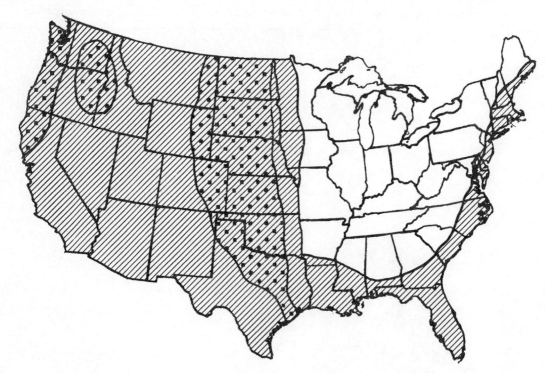

Distribution of *Salsola kali* L. var. *tenuifolia* Tausch

FIGURE 67.—*Salsola kali* L. var. *tenuifolia* Tausch. Russian thistle. *A*, Habit—× 0.5; *B*, flowering branch—
× 5; *C*, fruiting calyces—× 5; *D*, seeds—× 5.

Alternanthera philoxeroides (Mart.) Griseb.   ALLIGATORWEED

Perennial aquatic herb, nearly glabrous, reproducing by seeds (Fig. 68); *Stems* or their branches prostrate or decumbent, freely creeping, the ascending portion often 1–5 dm. long, the upper internodes often slightly pubescent; *Leaves* opposite, 3–11 cm. long, the leaf blades somewhat fleshy, linear to linear-oblanceolate, 2–10 cm. long, usually acute or small short abrupt tip, entire, narrowed to the sessile base; *Flower heads* in spikes, nearly globose or cylindric, long-peduncled, silvery-white, the peduncles 2–7 cm. long, glabrous or pubescent in lines; *Flowers* perfect; *Sepals* 5, glabrous, 5–6 mm. long, unequal, 4-nerved, lanceolate, acute, firm; *Sterile stamens* narrow, usually entire; *Utricle* flattened, indehiscent; *Seed* lens-shaped, smooth. June–October.

Wet waste places, often choking watercourses. Introduced from South America. Southeastern United States, from south.. .stern Virginia to Florida, west to eastern Texas; also in southern California.

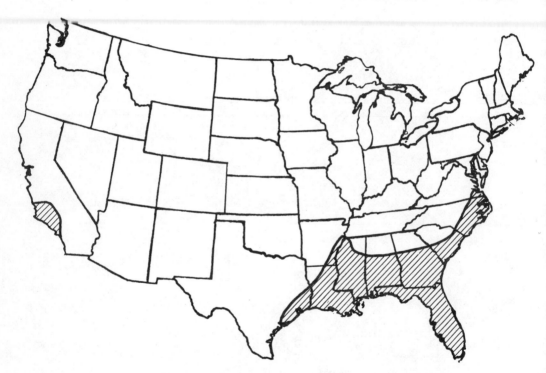

Distribution of *Alternanthera philoxeroides* (Mart.) Griseb.

FIGURE 68.—*Alternanthera philoxeroides* (Mart.) Griseb. Alligatorweed. *A*, Habit—× 0.5; *B*, roots and young plant—× 0.5; *C*, part of aquatic growth, new shoot from rooting node—× 0.5; *D*, flower—× 2.5; *E*, persistent chaffy flower with the single mature achene—× 2.5; *F*, achenes—× 2.5; *G*, seeds—× 5.

AMARANTHACEAE

Amaranthus albus L.

Annual herb, reproducing by seed (Fig. 69); *Stem* pale-green, slender, with whitish erect or ascending slender stems, diffusely branched, 0.1–1 m. tall, plants breaking off at ground at maturity and rolling over open ground, often piled up along fence rows; *Leaves* egg-shaped to spatulate-oblong, blunt or notched at the rounded apex, with veiny blades, 1–7 cm. long, short-petioled; *Flowers* monoecious in small axillary clusters, greenish; *Bracts* rigid, awl-shaped, pungent, about twice as long as the calyx; *Sepals* of pistillate flowers commonly 3, uneven, the longest about equaling the utricle, oblong; *Stamens* 3; *Utricle* lens-shaped, wrinkled when dry, 1.3–1.7 mm. long, dehiscing by a transverse line at the middle; *Seed* about 0.7–1 mm. broad, round, shiny, black, each contained in a bladderlike hull. July–October.

Waste ground, fallow ground. Originally probably native of only the Great Plains; now throughout United Sates.

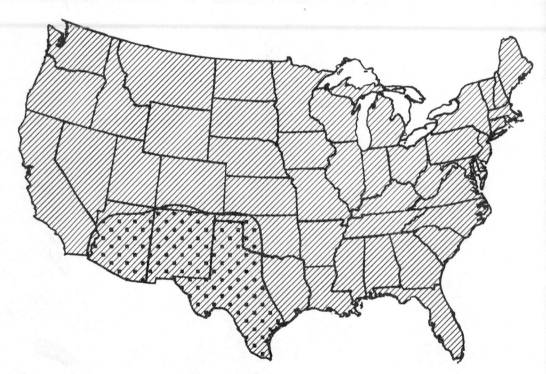

Distribution of *Amaranthus albus* L.

FIGURE 69.—*Amaranthus albus* L. Tumble pigweed. *A*, Habit—× 0.5; *B*, enlarged node showing flowers and leaf—× 5; *C*, flower spike—× 5; *D*, utricles—× 5; *E*, seeds—× 6.

Amaranthus blitoides S. Wats.   PROSTRATE PIGWEED

Annual, reproducing by seeds (Fig. 70); *Stems* prostrate, smooth, much-branched, 2–6 dm. long, reddish, spreading flat over the ground, mostly erect at the tips; *Leaves* numerous, small, slenderly tapering, simple, oblong to obovate, 1–4 cm. long, blunt or rounded, slenderly tapering into a long petiole; *Flowers* inconspicuous in short dense axillary clusters, without petals; *Bracts* about equaling the sepals, tapering to a protracted point, nearly bristlelike; *Sepals* of the pistillate flowers normally 5 (occasionally 4), egg-shaped to oblong, unequal in length; *Utricle* thick, lens-shaped, 22.5 mm. long, about equaling the longest sepal, smooth or nearly so, dehiscing by a transverse line at the middle; *Seed* flattened, shiny-black, nearly circular, 1.4–1.7 mm. wide. July–October.

Fields, wastes, gardens, and vacant lots. Native of Western United States. Common as a weed toward the East, excepting the extreme Northeast. Throughout all the United Sates excepting the extreme southern coastal areas and the extreme Southwest.

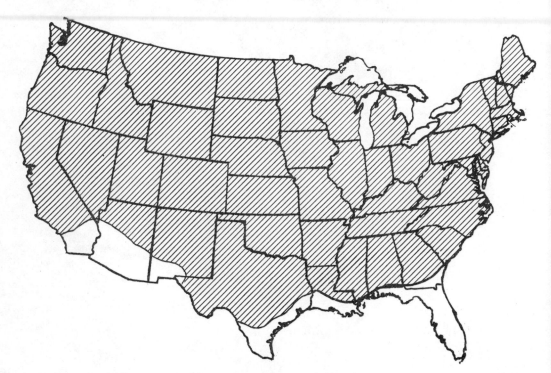

Distribution of *Amaranthus blitoides* S. Wats.

FIGURE 70.—*Amaranthus blitoides* S. Wats. Prostrate pigweed. *A*, Habit, as seen from above—× 0.5; *B*, flowering branchlet—× 5; *C*, rootstock—× 0.5; *D*, utricles—× 2.5; *E*, seeds—× 5.

Amaranthus retroflexus L.   Redroot Pigweed

Annual, reproducing by seeds (Fig. 71); *Taproot* shallow, red; *Stems* erect, branching freely if not crowded, up to 2 m. high, finely hairy; *Leaves* dull-green, long-petioled, egg-shaped or rhombic-ovate, up to 1 dm. long; *Flowers* green, small, the terminal panicle of several to many, short, densely crowded, ovoid, blunt spikes (1–5 cm. long), the whole 5–20 cm. long; smaller panicles produced in the upper axils; each flower surrounded by 3 spiny bracts, the bracts rigid, awl-shaped, much exceeding the calyx, 4–8 mm. long; *Utricle* flattened, 1.5–2 mm. long, dehiscing by a transverse line at the middle, the upper part wrinkled; *Seed* oval to egg-shaped, lens-shaped, notched at the narrow end, 1–1.2 mm. long, shiny-black to dark red-brown. August–October.

Cultivated fields, yards, fence rows, and waste ground. A troublesome semicosmopolitan weed. Sometimes accumulates excess nitrites and thus is poisonous to cattle, causing them to bloat. Native of tropical America. Throughout the United States.

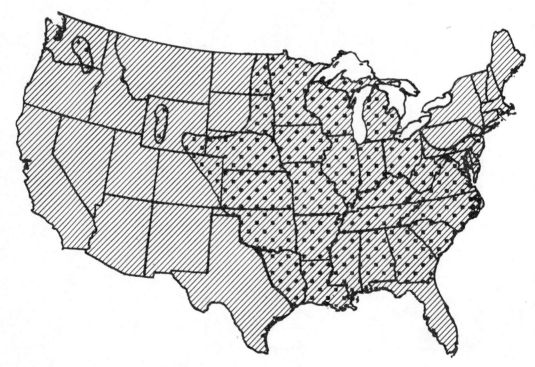

Distribution of *Amaranthus retroflexus* L.

FIGURE 71.—*Amaranthus retroflexus* L. Redroot pigweed. *A*, Habit—× 0.5; *B*, pistillate spikelet—× 5;j *C*, utricle—× 5; *D*, seeds—× 3.

PHYTOLACCACEAE

Phytolacca americana L.

(Ph. decandra L.)

Perennial herb, reproducing by seeds or from a very large (up to 15 cm. across) poisonous taproot (Fig. 72); *Stems* erect, stout, glabrous, 2–3 m. tall, branches above, often reddish, single or several from the large fleshy, white root; *Leaves* alternate, simple, entire, oblong-lanceolate to egg-shaped, 1–3 dm. long, with long petioles 1–5 cm. long, glabrous; *Inflorescences* long, narrow, in terminal peduncled racemes, 1–2 dm. long, becoming lateral and opposite to the leaves; *Flowers* small, about 6 mm. wide; *Sepals* 5, greenish-white to white, or suffused with pink, petallike and rounded; *Stamens* 10; *Pistil* 1, of about 10 united carpels, each with 1 vertical seed; *Fruit* a nearly globose berry, dark-purple, with a crimson juice, depressed 10-seeded, about 1 cm. in diameter; *Seed* lens-shaped, about 3 mm. in diameter, glossy, black. July–September.

Rich pastures, fields, waste places, gardens, and open places in woodlands, and along fence rows; mostly on deep, rich, gravelly soils. Young shoots used for greens or potherbs when thoroughly cooked; roots, leaves, and berries poisonous, used in preparation of medicines. Native. Throughout all the eastern half of the United States excepting the northwestern parts of that area; north to Quebec and Ontario; south into Mexico; introduced into Europe.

Distribution of *Phytolacca americana* L.

FIGURE 72.—*Phytolacca americana* L. Pokeweed. *A*, Habit, in flower—× 0.5; *B*, fruiting raceme—× 0.5; *C*, flower—× 5; *D*, berry—× 2; *E*, seeds—× 2.5.

Mollugo verticillata L. CARPETWEED

Annual herb, reproducing by seeds (Fig. 73); *Taproot* little-branched; *Stems* 5–30 cm. long, green, smooth, branched at the base, prostrate along the ground in all directions from the root, making large flat mats on the soil surface; *Leaves* whorled, 5 or 6 (occasionally 3–8) at each joint of the stem, smooth, 1–2.5 cm. long, spathulate to linear-oblanceolate, obtuse to acute at apex, narrowly triangular below to a short petiole; *Stipules* obsolete; *Flowers* small, 2–5 from each node, on slender pedicels, 3–14 mm. long; *Sepals* 5, 1.5–2.5 mm. long, white inside, oblong; *Capsule* 3-locular, 3-valved, the partitions breaking away from the many-seeded axis; *Seed* small, orange-red, somewhat kidney-shiped, ridged on the back and sides. June–November.

A late-starting but quick-growing summer annual weed, quickly covering any fertile bare soil; gardens, tilled crops, lawns, waste places, and sandy riverbanks. Native of tropical America. Throughout all the United States excepting an area between central Montana and central Minnesota; north into southern Canada; also in the Eastern Hemisphere.

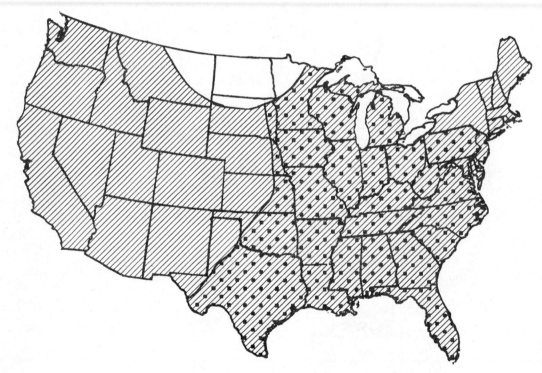

Distribution of *Mollugo verticillata* L.

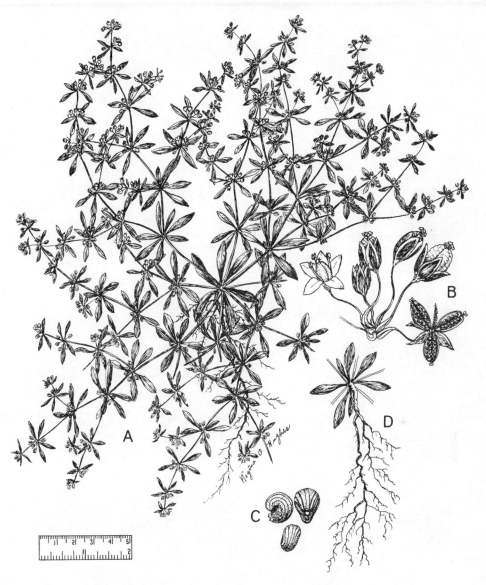

FIGURE 73.—*Mollugo verticillata* L. Carpetweed. *A*, Habit—× 0.5, as seen from above; *B;* flowers and fruits—× 5; *C*, seeds—× 6; *D*, taproot—× 0.5.

PORTULACACEAE

Portulaca oleracea L.

Annual herb, reproducing by seeds and stem fragments on moist soil (Fig. 74); *Stems* succulent, smooth, fleshy, commonly prostrate, arising from a taproot, usually purplish-red and often forming mats, freely branched, 10–56 cm. long, glabrous; *Leaves* alternate or nearly opposite, often in clusters at the ends of the branches, thickened, sessile, margins smooth and broad rounded tips, 0.4–2.8 cm. long; *Flowers* yellow, sessile, solitary in the leaf axils or several together in the leaf clusters at the ends of the branches, 3–10 mm. broad, including the 5 pale-yellow petals (which open only on sunny mornings); *Styles* 4–6; *Calyx* with the lower portion fused with the ovary, the upper part with 2 free sepals, pointed at the tip and 3–4 mm. long; *Petals* and the 6–12 stamens appearing to be inserted on the calyx; *Fruit* a globular, many-seeded capsule, 4–8 mm. long, splitting open around the middle, the upper half (with the 2 sepals on top) falling away like a lid; *Seed* nearly oval, tiny, only about 0.5 mm. in diameter and length, the surface covered with curved rows of minute wrinkles, black with a whitish scar at one end. Flowering and fruiting from June or July until frost; in hot regions from April to June, disappearing in the hottest period, reappearing in late summer, and continuing until frost.

Common locally in cultivated lands; a serious pest in vegetable crops, ornamental crops, citrus and other fruit and nut orchards, small fruits and berries, cotton, lawns, and peanuts in some Southern States; also waste places, barren driveways, eroded slopes, and bluffs, from sea level to 8,500 feet. Native of western Asia, introduced into the United States from southern Europe. Throughout most of the United States, most abundant in the Northeastern States, least common in the Pacific Northwest.

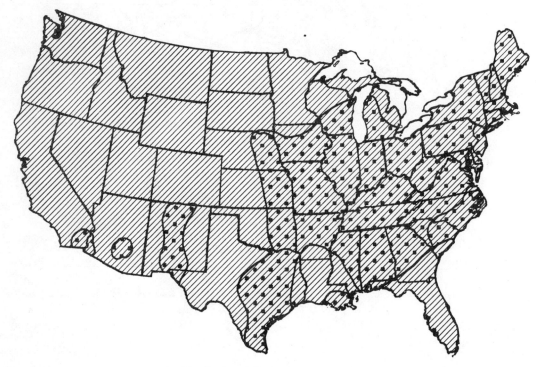

Distribution of *Portulaca oleracea* L.

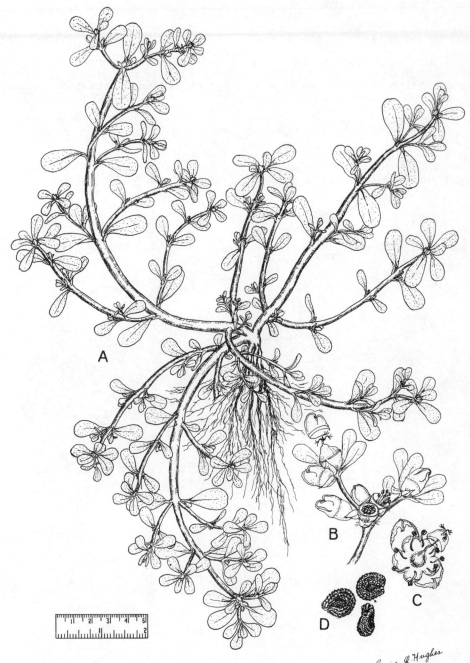

A

B

C

D

Regina O. Hughes

FIGURE 74.—*Portulaca oleracea* L. Common purslane. *A*, Habit—× 0.5; *B*, flowers and capsules—× 1.5; *C*, flower open—× 4; *D*, seeds—× 18.

CARYOPHYLLACEAE

Agrostemma githago L.

Winter annual, reproducing by seeds (Fig. 75); *Taproot* shallow; *Stems* rough, silky, hairy, erect, linear 6–10 dm. tall, swollen at the nodes, simple or branching slightly above; *Leaves* linear or lanceolate, acute, hairy, 8–12 cm. long, 5–10 mm. wide, opposite and jointed at the base; *Flowers* in cymes or solitary, on long peduncles up to 2 dm. long, large, 2.5–4 cm. in diameter, purplish-red, with narrow green sepals longer than the colored petals; *Capsule* 1-locular, 14–18, mm. long ovoid-ob-

long, enclosed in a 10-ribbed urnlike calyx tube (12–18 mm. long); *Seed* black, 2–3 mm. in diameter, triangular, rounded on the back, covered with rows of sharp tubercles. May–September.

Cultivated land, in association with fall-sown grain crops, especially winter wheat and rye. Seeds poisonous, highly objectionable in grains used for milling or feed, dangerous to stock and poultry. Naturalized from Eurasia. Widely distributed throughout the United States.

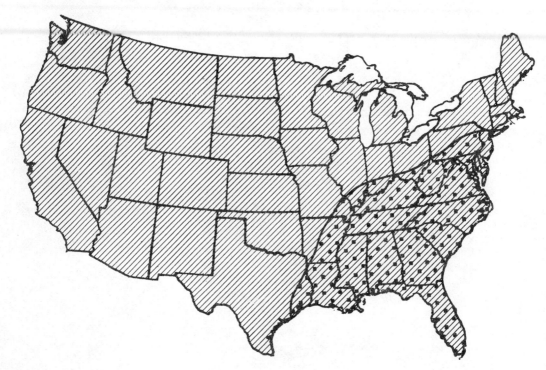

Distribution of *Agrostemma githago* L.

FIGURE 75.—*Agrostemma githago* L. Corn cockle. *A*, Habit—× 0.5; *B*, flower—× 1; *C*, calyx—× 1; *D*, capsule—× 1.25; *E*, seed—× 4.

CARYOPHYLLACEAE

Cerastium arvense L.

Perennial herb, forming mats or tufts, reproducing by seeds and creeping stems, rooting at the lower nodes (Fig. 76); *Stems* slender, erect or ascending, glabrous to densely villous, glandular or nonglandular, 1.5–6 dm. tall; *Leaves* opposite, simple, linear to lanceolate or narrowly ovate, acute to obtuse, 2–7 cm. long, 1–15 mm. wide, glabrous to pubescent, glandular or nonglandular; axillary fascicles or short sterile shoots often subtended by the primary leaves; *Inflorescences* with few to many flowers, the pedicles subcapillary; *Sepals* 5 (rarely 4), lanceolate acute, mostly 5–8 mm. long, 2–3 times exceeded by the conspicuous white petals; *Petals* 5 (rarely 4), about 1 cm. long; *Capsule* 1-celled, about 1 cm. long, many-seed-ed, cylindric, equaling or much exceding the sepals; *Seed* 0.6–1 mm. long, obovoid, flat on the sides, strongly papillate-tuberculate, especially dorsally, reddish-brown to chestnut-brown. Has many different forms. April–August.

Lawns, wastes, barrens, grasslands, abandoned fields, and meadows; rocky, gravelly, and sandy areas, chiefly on calcareous and magnesian soils; most introduced where it appears in lawns; does not persist under cultivation. Native of North America and Eurasia. Throughout all the United States excepting the Mid-Atlantic Coast States and States or parts of States along the southern boundary; north through Canada to Alaska, Newfoundland, and Labrador.

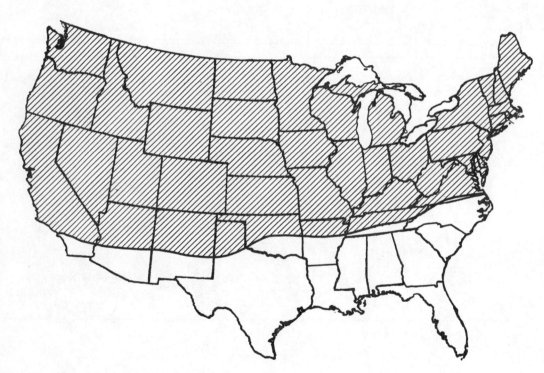

Distribution of *Cerastium arvense* L.

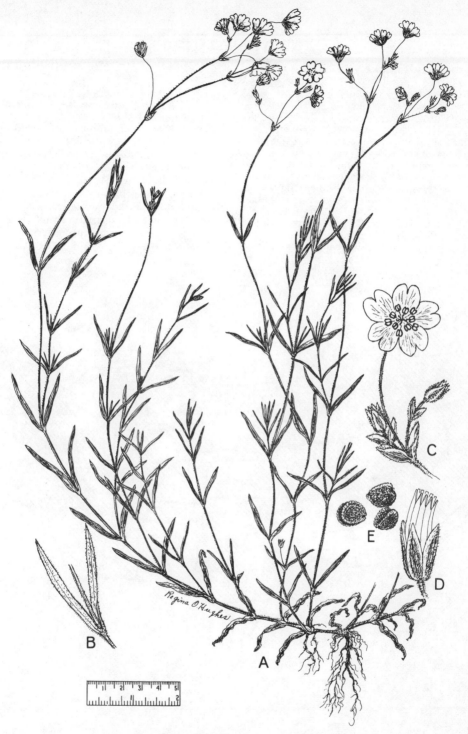

FIGURE 76.—*Cerastium arvense* L. Field chickweed. *A*, Habit—× 0.5; *B*, enlarged leaves—× 1; *C*, flower—× 1.5; *D*, capsule—× 3; *E*, seeds—× 10.

CARYOPHYLLACEAE

Cerastium vulgatum L.   MOUSEEAR CHICKWEED

Perennial herb, reproducing by seeds, occasionally by root development on the creeping stems (Fig. 77): *Roots* shallow, branched, fibrous; *Stems* sticky-pubescent, slender, 1.5–5 dm. long, partly spreading to erect, often rooting at the lower nodes, forming mats; *Leaves* opposite, small, 1–2 cm. long, 3–12 mm. wide, 1-nerved, very hairy, attached directly at the stem, mostly oblong to ovate-lanceolate, or oblanceolate, or spathulate; *Inflorescence* rather open, the mature pedicels 5–12 mm. long; *Sepals* 4–6 mm. long, oblong-lanceolate, acute or obtuse, pubescent, 1-nerved toward the base, scarious-margined; *Petals* (sometimes absent) about the same length as the sepals, white, notched at the tips; *Capsules* very small, 8–10 mm. long, 2–3 mm. wide, cylindrical, sometimes curved, containing many seeds; *Seed* chestnut-brown, very small, 0.75 mm. long, circular to angular-obovate, flattened with a rounded back bearing irregular knobs; seed long-lived in the soil. April–October.

Woods, lawns, pastures, abandoned cultivated land, and meadows; often a troublesome weed. Introduced and naturalized from Eurasia. Widespread throughout most of the United States.

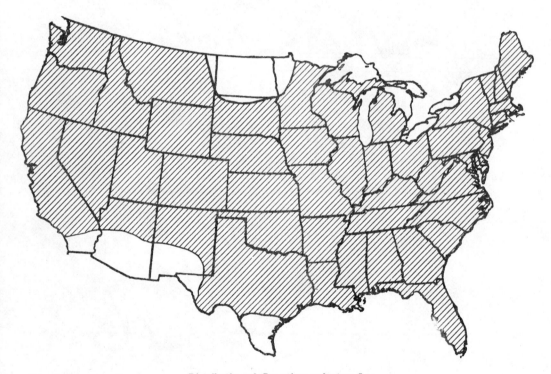

Distribution of *Cerastium vulgatum* L.

FIGURE 77.—*Cerastium vulgatum* L. Mouseear chickweed. *A*, Habit—× 0.5; *B*, mature dichotomous cymes—
× 0.5; *C*, enlarged leaves—× 1.25; *D*, flowers—× 3.5; *E*, capsules—× 3.5; *F*, seeds—× 15.

Lychnis alba Mill.

WHITE COCKLE

(Melandrium album Garcke)

Biennial herb or short-lived perennial, reproducing by seeds, plants green, glandular, minutely pubescent above (Fig. 78); *Lateral roots* thick, sending up a few short barren shoots and long, branching flowering stems; *Stems* erect, loosely branching, leafy, quite hairy and sticky, 3–7.5 dm. tall; *Leaves* opposite, long and narrow, sessile, covered with short hair, pointed at the tip and rather light-green; *Flowers* white to pink, several to many, with 5-notched petals, up to 2 cm. in diameter, opening in the evening, fragrant, borne on erect stems in the leaf axils or in loose panicles, the flowers at the forks longer pedicelled; Male and female flowers on separate plants; *Calyces*

of staminate flowers ellipsoid, those of the pistillate flowers ovoid and inflated at maturity, the teeth elongate, lance-linear, gradually tapering; *Capsule* conic-ovoid, with a narrow opening, with 10 teeth at the top, erect or only slightly spreading. *Seed* numerous, flat, nearly round, pale-gray, covered with small knobs, about 1 mm. in diameter. Late May–September.

Borders of fields, waste places, and roadsides; a troublesome weed in fields of grains and legumes. Naturalized from Eurasia. Throughout approximately the northern half of the United States; north into southern Canada from British Columbia to Nova Scotia.

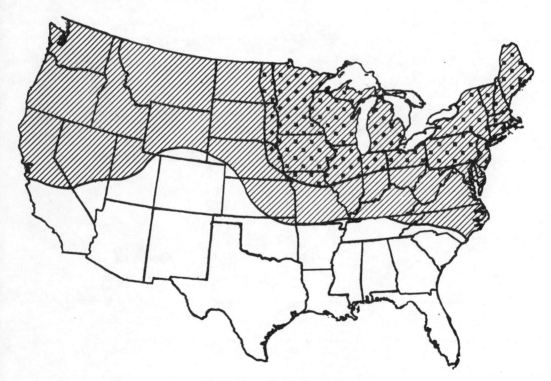

Distribution of *Lychnis alba* Mill.

FIGURE 78.—*Lychnis alba* Mill. White cockle. *A*, Habit, branchlet of staminate plant—× 0.5; *a*, staminate flower—× 1.5; *B*, habit, branchlet of pistillate plant—× 0.5; *a*, pistillate flower—× 1.5; *b*, capsule—× 1.5; *c*, seeds—× 6.

CARYOPHYLLACEAE

Scleranthus annuus L.

Annual or winter annual herb, reproducing by seeds (Fig. 79); *Stems* much-branched, low, spreading, 5–15 cm. high, glabrous or puberulent; *Leaves* opposite, simple, awl-shaped, without stipules; *Flowers* small, green, sessile to nearly sessile, in axillary clusters; *Sepals* 5, fused below into a cup that surrounds the 1-seeded fruit, the clayx lobes scarcely margined; *Fruit* a utricle, enclosed in the 5-toothed, 10-an-gled, straw-colored calyx, about 3–4 mm. long; *Seed* ovoid, beaked at the micropylar end, straw-colored, 1–1.3 mm. long. May–October.

A common weed in gardens, fields, waste places, and lawns; on dry, sandy, or gravelly soils. Introduced from Europe. Throughout approximately the eastern half of the United States and along the Pacific coast; north into eastern Canada to Quebec and Ontario.

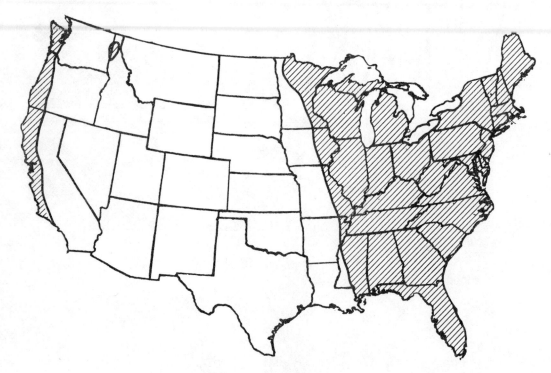

Distribution of *Scleranthus annuus* L.

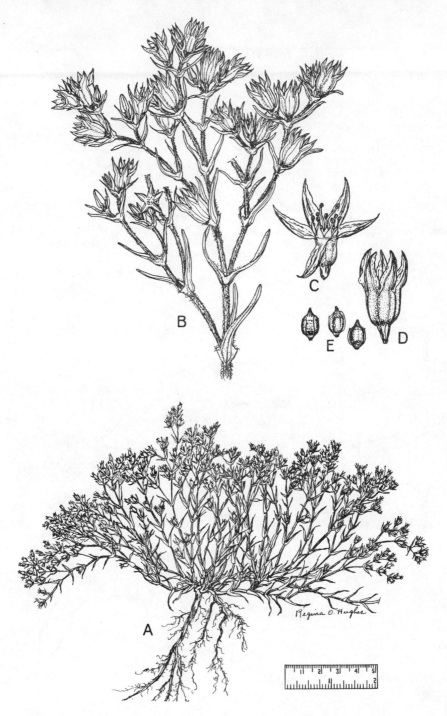

FIGURE 79.—*Scleranthus annuus* L. Knawel. *A,* Habit—× 0.5; *B,* enlarged branch—× 2.5; *C,* flower—× 5; *D,*
fruit (utricle, 1-seeded)—× 5; *E,* seeds—× 5.

CARYOPHYLLACEAE

Silene noctiflora L.

Annual herb, reproducing by seeds (Fig. 80); *Stems* erect, stout, up to 1 m. tall, simple or branched, covered with sticky hairs, at least above; *Leaves* lanceolate or ovate-lanceolate, 5–12 cm. long, 2–4 cm. wide, the lower leaves obovate to oblanceolate, blunt, narrowed to a broad petiole, the upper leaves ovate-lanceolate, acute or tapering to a protracted point and sessile; *Inflorescence* an open, loosely branched cyme or panicle; *Flowers* fragrant, opening at night, erect, rather few, often unisexual; Calyx 1.5–2.3 cm. long, with 10 prominent green ribs, glandular and freely cross-veined, the 5 awl-shaped teeth enclosing the capsule, the lobes linear-lanceolate, cylindrical at first, in fruit becoming inflated-ovoid; *Petals* 5, white, shading into pink, usually pinkish at base, the deeply cleft limb creamy-white, 7–10 mm. long; *Styles* normally 3, sometimes 4, rarely 5; *Capsule* 3-celled, sessile, ellipsoid; *Seed* rounded, 0.8–1 mm. in diameter, gray, uniformly wrinkled with minute projections. Late May–September.

Cultivated ground and waste places; often a troublesome weed. Throughout approximately the northern half of the United States and some South Central States; north into southern Canada.

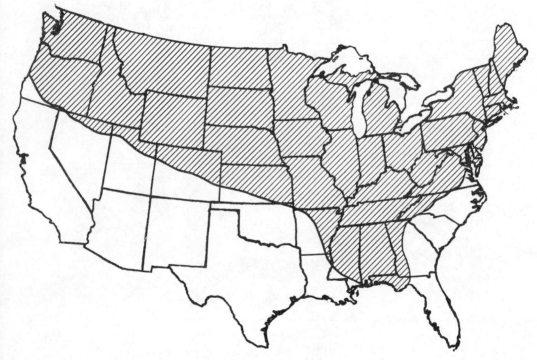

Distribution of *Silene noctiflora* L.

FIGURE 80.—*Silene noctiflora* L. Nightflowering catchfly. *A*, Habit of young plant—× 0.5; *B*, upper part of mature plant—× 1; *C*, capsule—× 1.5; *D*, seeds—× 7.5.

CARYOPHYLLACEAE

Spergula arvensis L.

Annual herb, reproducing by seeds (Fig. 81); *Stems* erect or spreading, much-branched, very slender, jointed, 15–45 cm. high, glabrous or only slightly hairy or sticky; *Leaves* bright-green, narrowly linear or awl-shaped, 2–5 cm. long, in whorls of 6–8 at each node, appearing disposed in a whorl, channel at base of leaf, stipules minute; *Flowers* small, perfect, in terminal clusters, or spreading open cymes; *Sepals* nearly separate; *Petals* 5, white; *Stamens* 10 (occasionally 5); *Pistil* with 5 styles, 5-valved; *Capsule* 1-celled, many-seeded, broadly ovoid, splitting into 5 sections; *Seed* lens-shaped, 1–1.5 mm. wide, dull-black with minute whitish projections, with a very narrow whitish wing margin. March–October.

Cultivated ground and waste places, especially on sandy and gravelly soils; locally in small grains and other annual crops in the Midwest; abundant on the Piedmont and Coastal Plain. Naturalized from Europe. throughout approximately all the eastern half of the United States excepting a distinct area in the center; along the Pacific coast; distinct area in Colorado and southern Wyoming.

var. *sativa* (Boenn.) Reichenb.—Dull-green and very sticky to essentially glabrous; *Seed* obscurely net-veined, without projections. Fields and wastes. Infrequent from western New England to Ohio and Virginia. Naturalized from Europe (sown formerly in Europe as forage for cattle and sheep).

Distribution of *Spergula arvensis* L.

FIGURE 81.—*Spergula arvensis* L. Corn spurry. *A*, Habit—× 0.5; *B*, enlarged branch—× 2; *C*, flowers—
× 2.5; *D*, seeds—× 10.

CARYOPHYLLACEAE

Stellaria media (L.) Cyrillo

Annual or winter annual, weakly tufted, reproducing by seeds and creeping stems, rooting at the nodes (Fig. 82); *Root system* fibrous, shallow; *Stems* much-branched, often trailing, matted or loosely ascending, up to 8 dm. long, minutely pubescent in lines; *Leaves* opposite, simple, usually 1–3 cm. long, ovate, elliptic, oblong-ovate or obovate, pointed at the tip, glabrous, the upper ones sessile, the lower ones petiolate, ovate, often hairy toward the base or on the petioles, 0.5–4 cm. long; *Flowers* solitary or in few-flowered terminal, leafy cymes; pedicels nearly capillary, ascending, reflexed or recurved, frequently pubescent; *Sepals* lanceolate-oblong, 3.5–6 mm. long, blunt to acute, usually with long soft hairs; *Petals* 5, white, small, shorter than the sepals, 2-parted or absent; *Stamens* 3–10; *Capsule* ovoid, usually a little longer than the sepals, reaking into 5 segments at maturity, many-seeded; *Seed* 1–1.2 mm. long, nearly circular, dull reddish-brown, conspicuous projections, the marginal projections more prominent. Has many different forms. February–December, but may flower throughout the year.

Dooryards, lawns, waste places, cultivated areas, woodlands, thickets, and meadows; especially bad in gardens, alfalfa, strawberry beds, and nurseries; a cosmopolitan weed. Putatively introduced from the Old World, but often appears to be native. Throughout the United States; also naturalized in Central and South America.

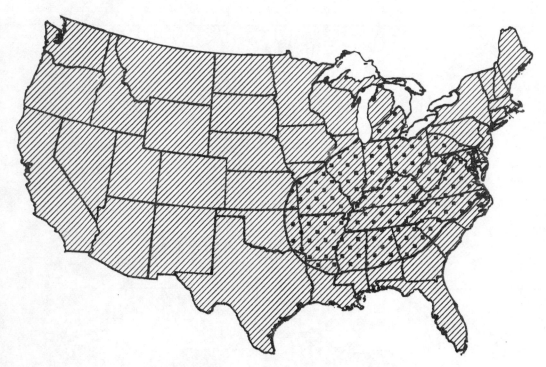

Distribution of *Stellaria media* (L.) Cyrillo

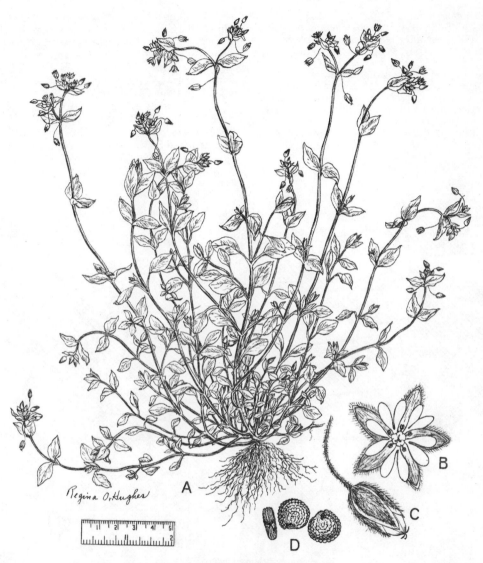

Figure 82.—*Stellaria media* (L.) Cyrillo. Common chickweed. *A*, Habit—× 0.5; *B*, flower—× 3; *C*, capsule—× 3.5; *D*, seeds—× 7.5.

CERATOPHYLLACEAE

Ceratophyllum demersum L.

Submersed aquatic plants, usually without roots (Fig. 83); *Stems* elongate, freely branched, forming large masses, varying from brittle and stiffly branched to more cordlike and flexuous; *Leaves* in whorls of 5–12, 2 or 3 times palmately divided, 1–3 cm. long, the ultimate divisions linear, flat, about 0.5 mm. wide, conspicuously serrate on one side, often more crowded toward the end of the branches; *Flowers* unisexual, minute, solitary and sessile in the axils, each subtended by a calyxlike involucre of 8–14 bracts; *Perianth* none; *Stamens* 12–16, filaments very short, anthers sessile, oblong, terminating in two short sharp points; *Pistil* 1, simple, 1-celled, narrowed above into a filiform style (4.5–6 mm. long), with 1 suspended ovule; *Achene* ellipsoid, wingless, smoothish, 4–6 mm. long, with 2 basal spines 2–5 mm. long. July–October.

Quiet waters and ponds. Achenes important food for aquatic birds. Throughout temperate North America, south to Mexico; West Indies; Central and South America; Asia; Europe.

Distribution of *Ceratophyllum demersum* L.

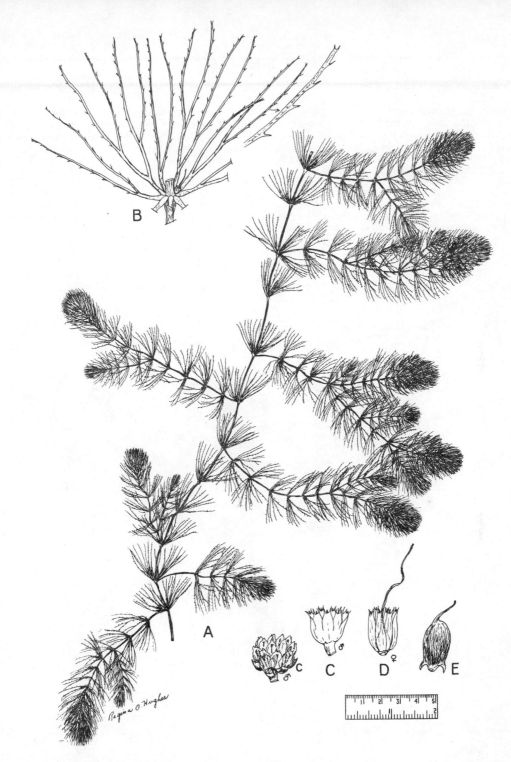

FIGURE 83.—*Ceratophyllum demersum* L. Common coontail. *A*, Habit—× 0.5; *B*, leaf detail, showing a pistillate flower—× 3; *C*, staminate flower—× 10; *c*, staminate flower showing developed stamens—× 10; *D*, pistillate flower—× 10; *E*, achene—× 2.5.

NYMPHAEACEAE

Nelumbo lutea (Willd.) Pers.

AMERICAN LOTUS

Perennial, aquatic herb, with thick rhizomes, or tubers that are starchlike and edible (Fig. 84); *Rhizome* underwater in the mud; *Leaves* circular, centrally shield-shaped, 3–7 dm. broad, with the center depressed or cupped, normally raised above the water surface; *Flowers* pale-yellow, solitary, 15–15 cm. wide; *Sepals* and *petals* numerous, usually 20 or more, grading into each other, the outermost in the bud green and sepallike; *Stamens* numerous, closely surrounding the pistils, the anthers tipped with a slender hooked appendage; *Fruiting receptacle* about 1 dm. broad, prolonged, in-versely conical, the numerous 1-celled ovaries sunk in small pits on its abrupt-ending summit; *Fruit* large, indehiscent, nutlike, each separately embedded in the receptacle, about 1 cm. in diameter. July–September.

Quiet water along ponds, lakes, estuaries, and sluggish rivers; usually local in distribution; along Illinois River most abundant, forming colonies many acres in extent. Tubers and seed edible. Native. Throughout approximately all the eastern half of the United States excepting northern New England and southern Florida; north into Ontario; West Indies.

Distribution of *Nelumbo lutea* (Willd.) Pers.

172

FIGURE 84.—*Nelumbo lutea* (Willd.) Pers. American lotus. *A*, Habit—× 0.3; *B*, pod, vertical section—× 0.25; *C*, seed—× 1; *D*, stamens—× 2.

NYMPHAEACEAE

Nuphar luteum (L.) Sibth. & Sm. SPATTERDOCK

(N. advena (Ait.) Ait. f.; *Nymphozanthus advena* (Ait.) Fern.)

Perennial from rhizomes, aquatic herb (Fig. 85); *Rhizome* creeping in the mud, cylindrical; *Leaves* erect (floating or submersed leaves rare and only in very deep water), the stout petiole nearly circular in cross section, rising above the water level, blades erect, ovate to rounded-oblong, 1–4 dm. long, with broad V- or U-shaped cleft between the two lobes 4–15 cm. wide between the nearly triangular basal lobes; *Flowers* usually on erect peduncles, raised above the water, 3–4 cm. high, when spread open 6–10 cm. broad, outer sepals green out-side, inner sepals yellow with yellowish tips, only rarely tinged with red; *Stamens* in 5–8 circles; *Disk* pale-green to yellowish, with 9–23 stigmatic rays; *Fruit* erect or lopping into the mud, furrowed, green, 2–5 cm. high, with very stout and thick neck, the mature disk 1.3–2.5 cm. across. May–October.

Tidal waters, pond margins, and swamps. Native. Throughout approximately most of the eastern half of the United States; not into Ontario; south into northeastern Mexico; West Indies.

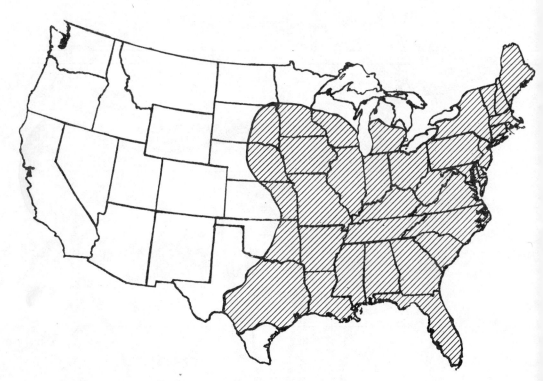

Distribution of *Nuphar luteum* (L.) Sibth. & Sm.

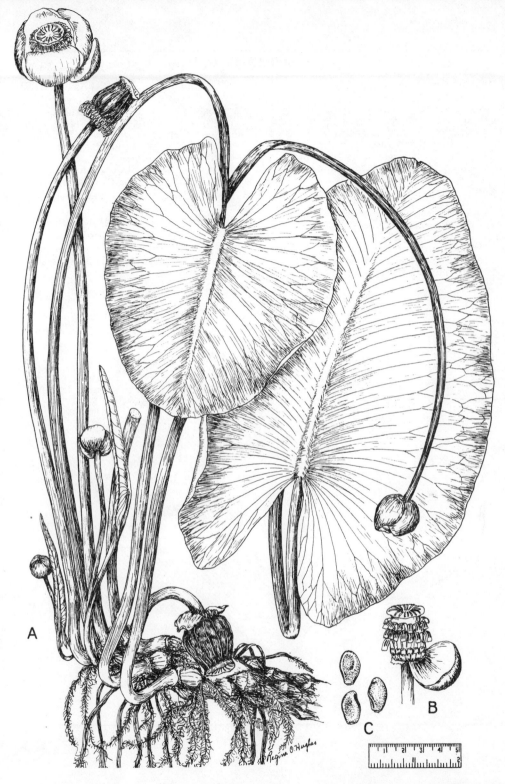

FIGURE 85.—*Nuphar luteum* (L.) Sibth. & Sm. Spatterdock. *A,* Habit—× 0.5; *B,* petal and stamen detail—
× 0.5; *C,* seeds—× 2.

NYMPHAEACEAE

Nymphaea odorata Ait.

FRAGRANT WATERLILY

Perennial, aquatic, with horizontal, elongate, rhizome without tubers (Fig. 86); *Rhizome* forking, the branches not strongly constricted at the base nor readily detached; *Leaves* arising along the rhizome, the nonstriped petioles purplish-green to red, the blades nearly circular, floating, depressed in the mud or ascending, flat, green above, usually purple to purplish-red beneath, 0.5–2.5 dm. in diameter, with a narrow cleft between the two lobes; *Flowers* very fragrant, expanded on 3 or 4 days from early morning until about noon, 5–15 cm. broad; *Sepals* often purplish on the back, ovate to ovate-lanceolate, 2.8–8 cm. long, 1–2.5 cm. broad, with rounded tips; *Petals* 17–32, 1–2.2 cm. broad, white to roseate, gradually tapering above to ovate rounded tips; *Stamens* 36–100, the inner filaments narrower than their anthers; *Fruit* depressed-globular, usually covered by the bases of the decayed petals, maturing under water; *Seed* enveloped in a saclike aril, ellipsoid, 1.5–2.3 mm. long, exceeded by the aril. A variable species with some named varieties and forms. June–September.

Quiet waters, ponds, dead waters, bogs, and edge of lakes. Native. Throughout approximately all the eastern half of the United States; north into southern Canada from Newfoundland to Manitoba.

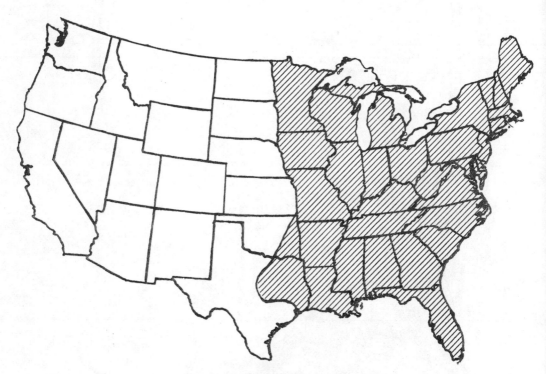

Distribution of *Nymphaea odorata* Ait.

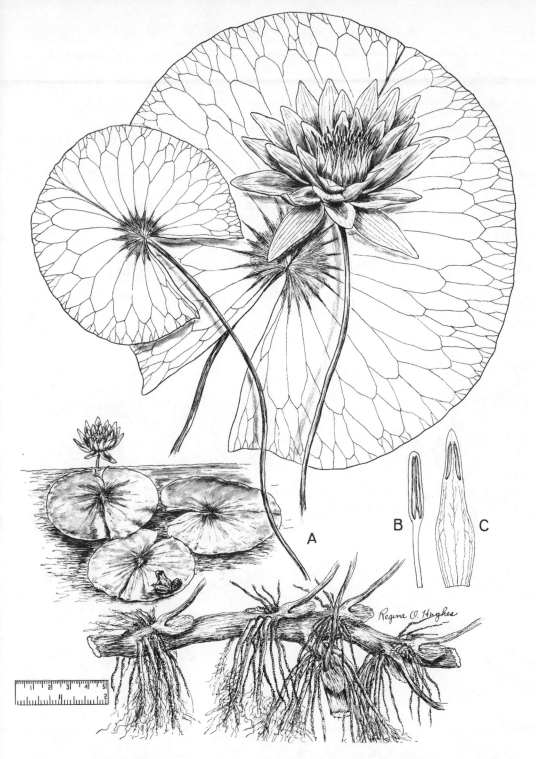

FIGURE 86.—*Nymphaea odorata* Ait. Fragrant waterlily. *A*, Habit—× 0.5; *B*, inner stamen—× 3.5; *C*, outer stamen—× 2.

Delphinium barbeyi Huth

TALL LARKSPUR

(D. subalpinum (Gray) A. Nels.; D. cockerellii A. Nels.)

Perennial herb, reproducing by seeds (Fig. 87); *Rootstocks* stout, woody; *Stems* 5–20 dm. tall, hollow, more or less glandular stiff-haired, densely so in the inflorescence, often nearly glabrous near the base; *Leaves* 5–15 cm. broad, pubescent, a little reduced above, broader than long, divided or cleft into 3 primary segments, segments entire in the lower half and cleft or coarsely toothed in the upper half; *Racemes* rather compact, short-oblong; *Flowers* scented and showy with conspicuous bracts below; *Sepals* 14–16 mm. long, narrowly ovate, slenderly tapering or acute, rich dark-purple, the spur about 10 mm. long, curved near the tip; *Petals*, the lower ones dark-purple, the clefts between lobes about 3 mm. deep, the upper petals little exserted, edged with white; *Follicle* 14–17 mm. long, oblong-ovate, with purplish veins, nearly glabrous; *Seed* smoky-brown, wing-angled. July–August.

Meadows and open woods. Native. Poisonous to cattle. In two distinct areas in the Western States.

Distribution of *Delphinium barbeyi* Huth

FIGURE 87.—*Delphinium barbeyi* Huth.   Tall larkspur.   *A*, Habit—× 0.5; *B*, flower diagram—× 1; *C*, capsules—× 0.5; *D*, seeds—× 4.

Delphinium geyeri Greene

GEYER LARKSPUR, PLAINS LARKSPUR

Perennial herb, reproducing by seeds (Fig. 88); *Rootstocks* tough, woody, fibrous, usually vertical; *Stems* 2–7 dm. tall, usually several strict, ashy-puberulent especially below; *Leaves* several, usually toward the base, 5–8 cm. broad, divided, the divisions repeatedly dissected, the ultimate divisions straight and linear to linear-filiform; *Racemes* narrow, strict and rather dense, flowers showy; *Sepals* 10–15 mm. long, oblong-ovate, acute to obtuse, the spur up to 1½ times as long as the sepal, straight or nearly so, deep-blue; *Petals*, the lower ones hairy near the middle, the lower sinuses obsolete or short, closed, the upper petals whitish; *Follicle* 12–15 mm. long, finely hirsutulose; *Seed* 2–3.5 mm. long, flat, the body roughened. July–August.

Open plains, slopes, dry mesas, and rocky hills; often among bushes. Native. In one distinct area in the Western States.

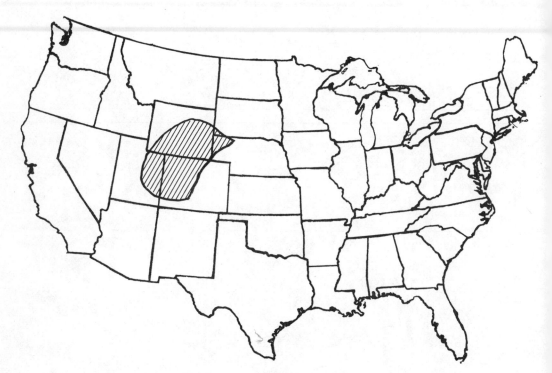

Distribution of *Delphinium geyeri* Greene

FIGURE 88.—*Delphinium geyeri* Greene. Geyer larkspur. *A*, Habit—× 0.5; *B*, enlarged leaf—× 1.5; *C*, flower—
× 1.5; *D*, capsule—× 1.5; *E*, seeds—× 2.5.

RANUNCULACEAE

Delphinium menziesii DC.

Perennial herb, reproducing by seeds, with tubers in small shallow globose clusters (Fig. 89); *Stems* 2–7 dm. high, soft-pubescent, with spreading white hairs; *Leaves* both on stems and basal, reduced upward to leafy bracts, the blades round 5-sided, 3–6 cm. wide, pubescent, palmately arranged into broad approximate wedge-shaped divisions, these shallowly to deeply lobed, the ultimate segments blunt to short-acute, the lower petioles 5–10 cm. long; *Racemes* 3- to 10-flowered, short, hairy; *Pedicels* spreading; *Sepals* deep rich blue, oblong-ovate, 10–15 mm. long, 9–11 mm. wide, ending in an abrupt short-pointed tip, hairy; *Upper petals* pale, rhombic, lower petals rounded, dark-blue, sometimes white-lined, 7–9 mm. wide, shallowly notched at rounded apex to 2-lobed; *Follicle* somewhat spreading, 10–14 mm. long, white-hairy; *Seed* few, oblong-prismatic, brownish, 1.5 mm. long, narrowly wing-margined. March–May.

Open places above the Pacific Ocean. Along the north Pacific coast; in a distinct area in eastern Washington and western Idaho.

Distribution of *Delphinium menziesii* DC.

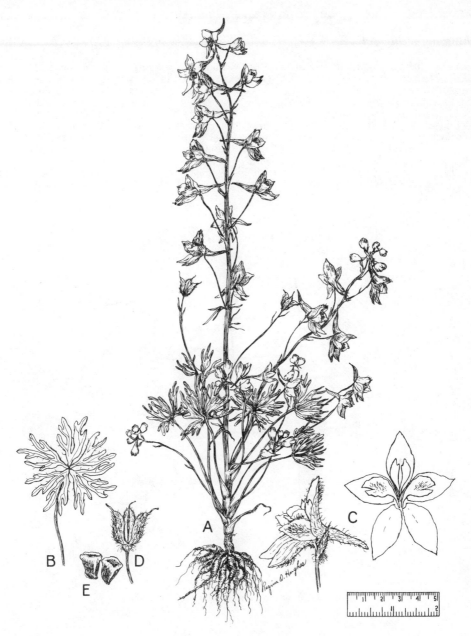

FIGURE 89.—*Delphinium menziesii* DC. Menzies larkspur. *A*, Habit—× 0.5; *B*, leaf—× 1; *C*, flowers—× 2; *D*, capsule—× 1; *E*, seeds—× 5.

RANUNCULACEAE

Delphinium occidentale S. Wats.

Perennial herb, reproducing by seeds (Fig. 90); *Rootstock* woody, deep, vertical; *Stems* 6–20 dm. (up to 1 m.) tall, somewhat straw-colored, especially at the base, somewhat glaucous and glabrous below; *Leaves* 1–1.5 dm. wide, divided into 3–7 rhombic divisions, these cleft below the middle, pubescent on both sides; *Racemes* usually over 15 cm. long, dense, resembling a spike or loosely paniclelike, rachis thinly to densely glandular-hairy, bracts small; *Sepals* 6–12 mm. long, narrowly egg-shaped to oblong, rounded or acute at apex, usually paler or hoary gray, with pubescence on the back, otherwise blue-purple, spur 9–12 mm. long, horizontal, straight or curved somewhat near the tip; lower petals with sinuses 1–2 mm. long; upper petals small and included; *Follicle* 9–15 mm. long, short-oblong, glabrous to glandular-pubescent; *Seed* wing-angled. July–August.

Meadows, thickets, and open woods. Native. In a distinct area in the Northwestern States.

Distribution of *Delphinium occidentale* S. Wats.

FIGURE 90.—*Delphinium occidentale* S. Wats. Duncecap larkspur. *A*, Habit—× 0.5; *B*, flower diagram—× 1.25; *C*, capsules—× 0.5; *D*, seeds—× 6.

Ranunculus acris L.

Perennial herb, reproducing by seeds (Fig. 91); *Roots* thick, fibrous; *Stems* erect, often in clusters, branched, hairy, often 5–10 dm. tall, leafy mainly below the middle; *Leaves* alternate, hairy, kidney-shapped in general outline, palmately 3-divided, the divisions sessile and parted into narrow segments, the dissection of the leaves variable; *Flowers* perfect, regular, solitary or in cymose clusters; *Calyx* mostly of 5 separate spreading sepals; *Petals* 5–7, broadly obovate, often notched at the apex 8–16 mm. long, bright-yellow, sometimes cream-colored, about twice as long as the sepals; *Stamens* numerous; *Carpels* numerous, separate, with short, recurved, persistent styles; *Achenes* numerous, in nearly globose heads, broadly obliquely obovate, 2–3 mm. long, flattened, with a prominently nearly straight beak (0.4–1 mm. long), dull, minutely pitted, dark-brown, margin often lighter. May–September.

Fields, pastures, and meadows; introduced in lawns; heavy moist soils; does not persist under cultivation. Plant contains an acrid juice that is somewhat poisonous if eaten by livestock, often blistering the mouth and intestinal tract. Introduced from Eurasia. Throughout all the United States excepting an area between central Montana and eastern Minnesota.

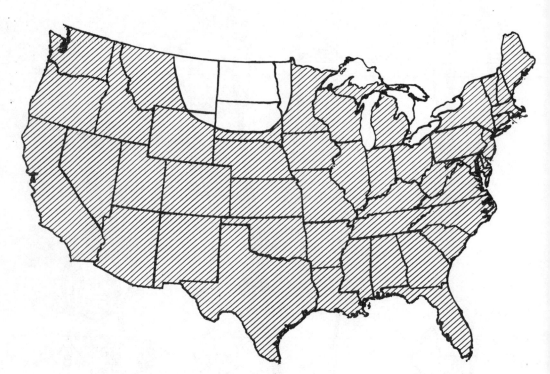

Distribution of *Ranunculus acris* L.

FIGURE 91.—*Ranunculus acris* L. Tall buttercup. *A*, Habit—× 0.5; *B*, fruiting head—× 3; *C*, achenes—× 4.

Ranunculus repens L.

Perennial herb, reproducing by seeds and runners (Fig. 92); *Stems* low, normally creeping and rooting at the nodes, rarely ascending or erect, hairy, or rarely glabrous; *Leaves* alternate, long-petioled, 3-divided or 3-lobed, the segments broadly obovate to nearly rounded in general outline, sharply toothed, hairy, dark-green or sometimes with light spots; *Flowers* perfect, regular, solitary or in corymblike clusters; *Sepals* 5, separate, green, not reflexed; *Petals* 5–7, bright glossy yellow, 8–15 mm. long, about two-thirds as wide; *Stamens* numerous, the anthers 1–2 mm. long; *Carpels* numerous, separate, with short, recurved styles;

Achenes numerous in globular heads, broadly obliquely obovate, 2.5–3.5 mm. long, sharply but narrowly margined, blackish-brown; *Beak* triangular, usually somewhat curved, 0.8–1.5 mm. long. June–August.

Fields, moist meadows, pastures, mucklands and lawns, and along ditches and roadsides. Introduced and naturalized from Europe. Throughout approximately all the northern half of the United States excepting an area between central Montana and eastern Minnesota; a distinct area in the South Central States; north into Canada from Newfoundland to Alaska.

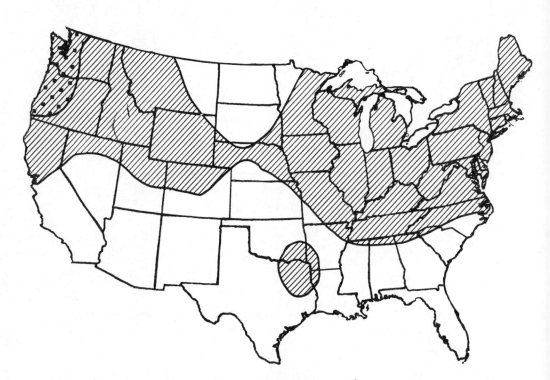

Distribution of *Ranunculus repens* L.

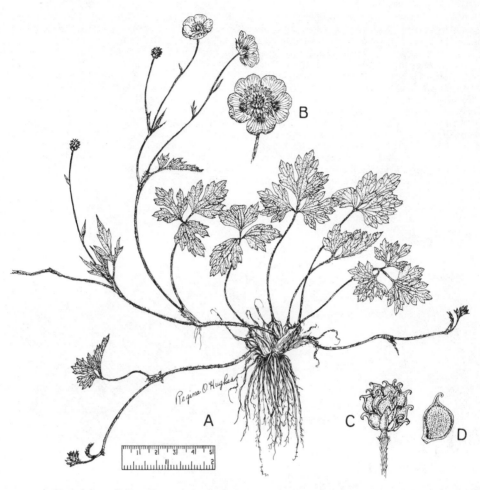

FIGURE 92.—*Ranunculus repens* L.   Creeping buttercup.   *A*, Habit—× 0.5; *B*, flower—× 1; *C*, head of achenes— × 3.5; *D*, achene—× 4.5.

CRUCIFERAE

Barbarea vulgaris R. Br.   YELLOW ROCKET

Short-lived perennial, reproducing by seeds and sometimes by new shoots from the old crowns (Fig. 93); *Taprooted*; *Stems* numerous from a crown, erect, 3–6 dm. tall, branched near the top, smooth, angular or ridged; *Leaves* 5–25 cm. long, pinnately divided (rarely simple), the basal leaves with a large terminal lobe, forming a dense rosette, the stem leaves 1–4 pairs, becoming progressively shorter, with the uppermost leaves being about 2.5 cm. long and less deeply lobed; *Flowers* in spikelike racemes at the end of each branch, bright lemon-yellow, 4-petaled, the petals narrowly obovate, 5.5–8 mm. long, 2–3 mm. broad; *Seed pod* (silique) slender-pedicelled, 2.5–5 cm. long, 1.5 mm. in diameter, nearly square in cross section, with a slender beak, 1.5–3 mm. long; *Seed* light-yellow to yellowish-brown to grayish, about 1–1.5 mm. long, wrinkled, short-oblong. April–June.

New meadows and along roadsides; rich alluvial soil; clover and alfalfa fields; seeds live several years in the soil. Introduced and naturalized from Eurasia; also native of northern North America. Throughout the northeastern area of the United States extending south as far as Arkansas; in distinct areas in the North Central States and in Washington and Oregon; north in Canada from Newfoundland to Ontario.

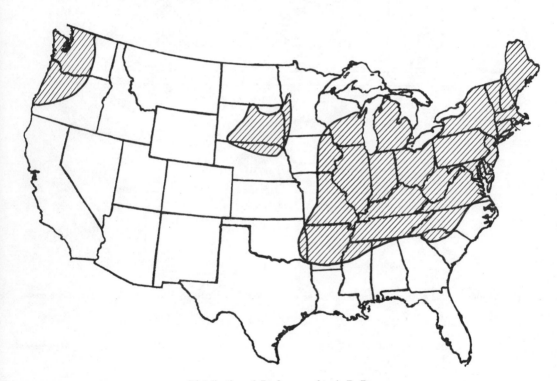

Distribution of *Barbarea vulgaris* R. Br.

FIGURE 93.—*Barbarea vulgaris* R. Br. Yellow rocket. *A*, Habit—× 0.5; *B*, flower—× 2.5; *C*, raceme of fruits—
× 0.5; *D*, silique—× 2; *E*, seeds—× 5.

CRUCIFERAE

Brassica kaber (DC.) L. C. Wheeler var. *pinnatifida* (Stokes) L. C. Wheeler

WILD MUSTARD

(*B. arvensis* (L.) Kuntze)

Annual or *winter annual*, reproducing by seeds (Fig. 94); *Stems* erect, 28 dm. tall, branched near the top, with a few bristly hairs; *Leaves* obovate in general outline, the lower ones sometimes lobed, more often merely coarsely toothed, the upper ones progressively smaller, coarsely toothed, roughly pubescent to nearly glabrous; *Flowers* in clusters at the ends of the branches, with 4 yellow petals, about 15 mm. wide, the pedicels at maturity spreading or ascending, 5–7 mm. long; *Seed pod* (silique) linear, nearly circular in cross section, ascending, glabrous or nearly so, 1–2 cm. long,

1.5–2.5 mm. wide, the beak angular, shorter than the valves, often containing 1 seed; *Seed* globular, 1–1.5 mm. in diameter, black or dark purplish-brown, smooth or minutely reticulate. May–August.

Gardens, spring grainfields (especially oats), cultivated land, and waste places; commonest mustard of grainfields in Northeastern States; seeds live in soil for many years; a serious weed in many areas. Introduced and naturalized from Europe. Throughout the United States.

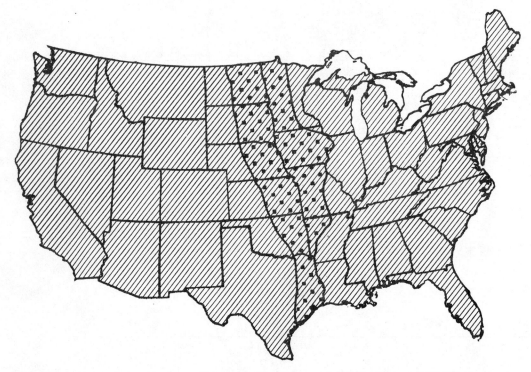

Distribution of *Brassica kaber* (DC.) L. C. Wheeler var. *pinnatifida* (Stokes) L. C. Wheeler

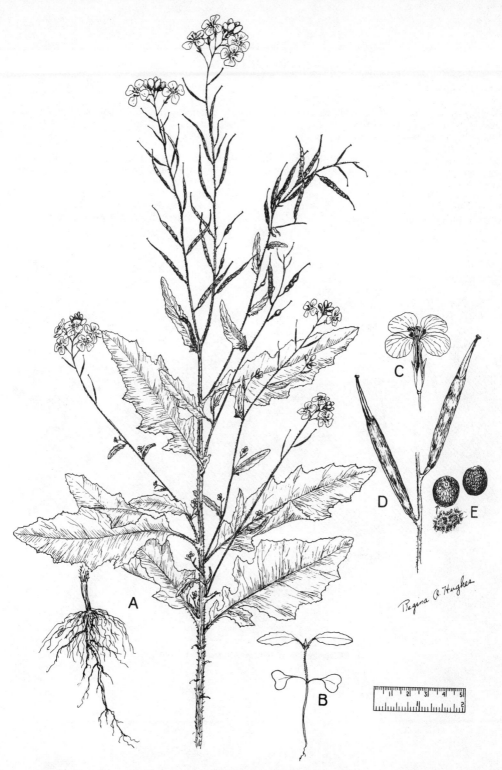

FIGURE 94.—*Brassica kaber* (DC.) L. C. Wheeler var. *pinnatifida* (Stokes) L. C. Wheeler. Wild mustard. *A,* Habit—× 0.5; *B,* seedling—× 0.5; *C,* flower—× 1.5; *D,* siliques—× 1.5; *E,* seeds—× 5.

Brassica nigra (L.) Koch

Annual or *winter annual* herb, reproducing by seeds, with taproot (Fig. 95); *Stems* erect, green, simple or branched, up to 15 dm. tall, usually bristly below, glabrous above; *Leaves* all slender-petioled, egg-shaped to obovate, the lower ones usually lobed with a large terminal lobe and a few small lateral lobes, the upper leaves merely toothed; *Flowers* 8–10 mm. wide, the pedicels at maturity erect, 3–4 mm. long; *Seed pod* (silique) erect, quadrangular, 1–2 cm.

long, smooth, the midvein nearly as strong as the sutures, the beak slender, 2.5–4 mm. long; *Seed* reddish-brown to black, 1.5–2 mm. long ellipsoidal, minutely roughly reticulate. Flowering May–July; fruiting June–October.

Neglected fields and waste places, pastures, and ditches. Principal source of table mustard. Naturalized from Eurasia. Throughout all the United States excepting an area between central Montana and eastern Minnesota.

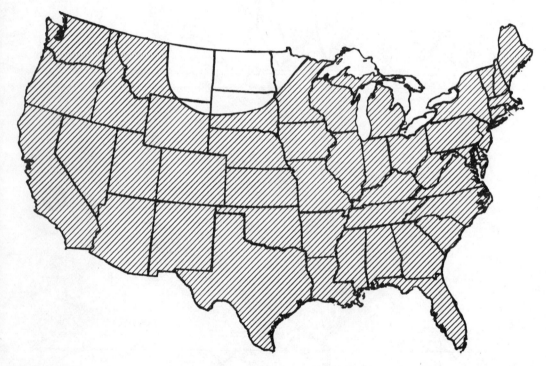

Distribution of *Brassica nigra* (L.) Koch

FIGURE 95.—*Brassica nigra* (L.) Koch. Black mustard. *A*, Habit—× 0.5; *B*, basal leaf—× 0.75; *C*, siliques—× 2.5; *D*, seeds—× 4; *E*, reticulation pattern on seed.

Camelina microcarpa Andrz.

Annual or *winter annual* herb, reproducing by seeds (Fig. 96); *Stem* 30–80 cm. tall, harsh with elongate, simple (1–2 mm. long) and branching (stellate) hairs, simple or branched above; *Leaves,* the basal and lower ones narrowly spatulate, lanceolate, entire or nearly so, more or less hirsute, the leaves arising from stems linear to lanceolate, clasping by a sagittate auriclelike base; *Flowers* in elongated raceme, the fruiting raceme often over 20 cm. long; *Sepals* erect, rounded at the end, the outer slightly sac-shaped at the base; *Petals* yellowish, spatulate, 3–4 mm. long; *Silicles* (pods) 4–7 mm. long, 4–5 mm. thick, about twice as long as the style, walls thin, egg-shaped or pear-shaped, slightly flattened parallel to the partition, somewhat keeled along the seams, narrowed to the base and a short stipe; *Seed* dark-brown, oblong, mostly less than 1 mm. long. Plants often show integration to *C. sativa.* April–September.

Roadsides, waste places, and fields, mostly in flax-growing areas. Naturalized from Europe. Throughout all the United States excepting the Mid-Atlantic Coast States and States or parts of States along the southern boundary; north into Canada from Newfoundland to British Columbia.

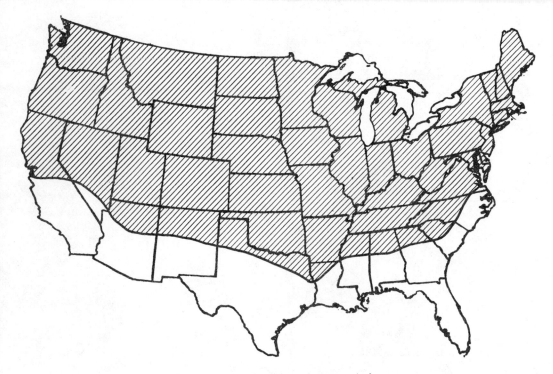

Distribution of *Camelina microcarpa* Andrz.

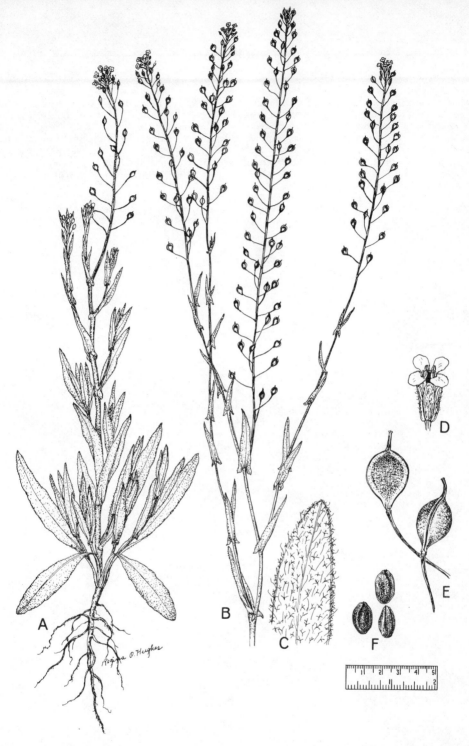

FIGURE 96.—*Camelina microcarpa* Andrz. Smallseed falseflax. *A*, Habit of young plant—× 0.5; *B*, elongated fruiting raceme of mature plant—× 0.5; *C*, enlarged portion of leaf, showing long simple and branched hairs—× 3; *D*, flower—× 4; *E*, silicles—× 3; *F*, seeds—× 7.5.

CRUCIFERAE

Capsella bursa-pastoris (L.) Medic.

Annual or *winter annual* herb, reproducing by seeds, with a branched thin taproot (Fig. 97); *Stems* erect, branched, 1–6 dm. tall, covered with gray hairs; *Leaves* alternate, simple, variously toothed or lobed, in a rosette at base, coarsely lobed, clasping the stem with pointed lobes, coarsely serrate, 5–10 cm. long, stem leaves arrow-shaped; *Flowers* small, white, 4-petaled, about 2 mm. wide, borne in elongated racemes at the ends of the branches on slender pedicels; *Seed pod* (silique) triangular, 2-parted, 5–8 mm. long; flattened at right angles to the partition, the values boat-shaped, each with several to many seeds; *Seed* small, about 1 mm. long, yellow to orangish-brown, shiny, oblong, grooved on one side. Highly variable in leaf form. March–December.

In practically all crops, gardens, and lawns, noncultivated areas, and waste grounds. Seeds long-lived in soil. Introduced and naturalized from southern Europe. A cosmopolitan weed. Common throughout North America.

Distribution of *Capsella bursa-pastoris* (L.) Medic.

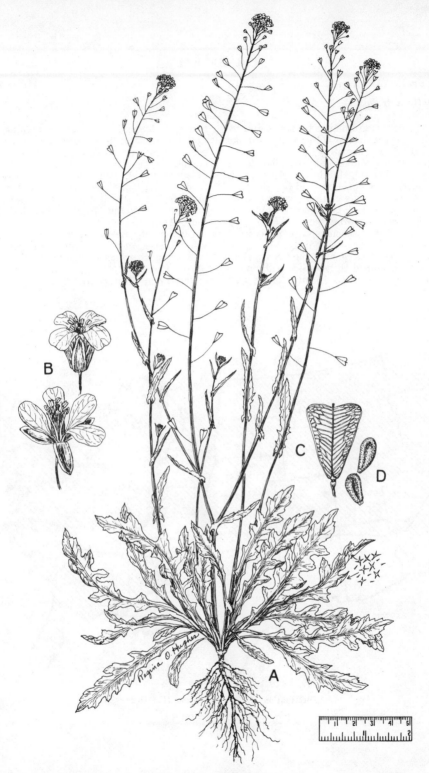

FIGURE 97.—*Capsella bursa-pastoris* (L.) Medic. Shepherdspurse. *A*, Habit—× 0.5; *B*, flowers—× 5; *C*, silicle —× 4; *D*, seeds—× 10.

Cardaria draba (L.) Desv.   HOARY CRESS

(*Lepidium draba* L.)

Perennial herb, reproducing by seeds and by horizontal creeping roots (Fig. 98); *Stems* stoutish, erect or spreading, 1–8 dm. tall, branched, sparsely pubescent to ash-colored hoary; *Leaves* alternate, simple, mostly toothed, the basal leaves 4–10 cm. long and petioled, oblanceolate to obovate, the cauline leaves sessile, 2–6.5 cm. long, oblong or tapering to the point, entire, with broad clasping bases; *Flowers* in terminal corymblike racemes; *Petals* white, clawed, 3–5 mm. long, exceeding the sepals (1.5–2 mm. long); *Ovary* glabrous; *Seed pods* (silicles) kidney-shaped to heart-shaped, on divergent slender pedicels (6–15 mm. long), gla-brous, 2–5 mm. long, often oblique and inflated, obovate to triangular-egg-shaped to egg-shaped, netted-veined, with a prominent slender persisting style (1 mm. long), barely if at all notched, dehiscent, each valve with 1 seed; *Seed* 2–4, wingless, about 2 mm. long, obovate, slightly flattened, granular, reddish-brown. Flowering April–June; fruiting late June–August.

Cultivated fields, grainfields, grasslands, waste places, meadows, and roadsides. Naturalized from Europe. Throughout all the United States excepting the area along the southern boundary in Western and South Central States.

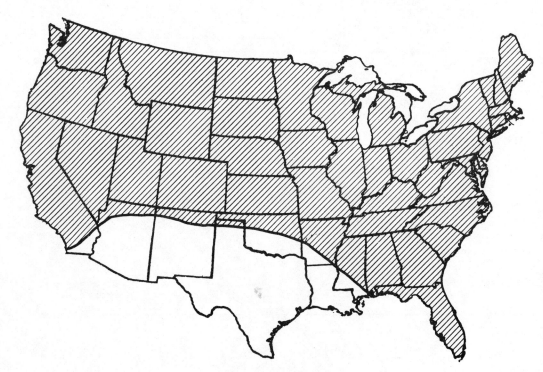

Distribution of *Cardaria draba* (L.) Desv.

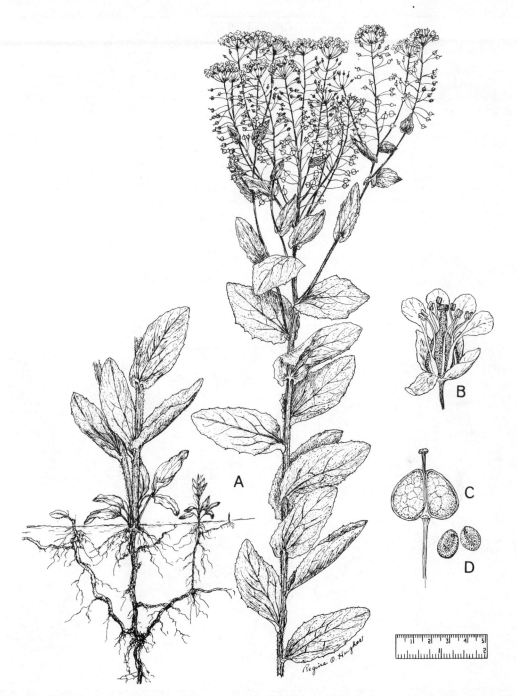

FIGURE 98.—*Cardaria draba* (L.) Desv. Hoary cress. *A,* Habit—× 0.5; *B,* flower—× 7.5; *C,* silicle—× 5; *D,* seeds—× 7.5.

CRUCIFERAE

Conringia orientalis (L.) Dum.

Annual or *winter annual* herb, reproducing by seeds (Fig. 99); *Root system* fibrous; *Stems* glabrous, glaucous, 2.5–10 dm. tall, erect, usually simple, leafy; *Leaves* alternate, sessile, entire, 4–13 cm. long, obovate, oval to elliptical, deeply cordate-clasping, very smooth, whitish, somewhat fleshy; *Flowers* in elongate racemes, perfect; *Sepals* long and narrow, nearly equal, ascending; *Petals* pale-yellow, 8 mm. long, narrow, tapering toward the point; *Style* rather long, the stigma entire or nearly so; *Pod* elongate-linear, a 2-celled capsule, 8–13 cm. long, about 2 mm. thick, ascending to erect, 4-angled, somewhat twisted or curved, the beak about 1.5 mm. long; *Seed* numerous, 2–2.5 mm. long, with 2 vertical grooves separated by a ridge, the seeds in 1 row in each cell, ellipsoid, oblong, thick, dark grayish-brown, minutely roughened, not winged. May–July.

Grainfields, roadsides, waste places, gardens, and wasteland of the plains. Native of Europe. Throughout all the United States excepting the southeastern and southwestern areas; north into southern Canada from Quebec to British Columbia.

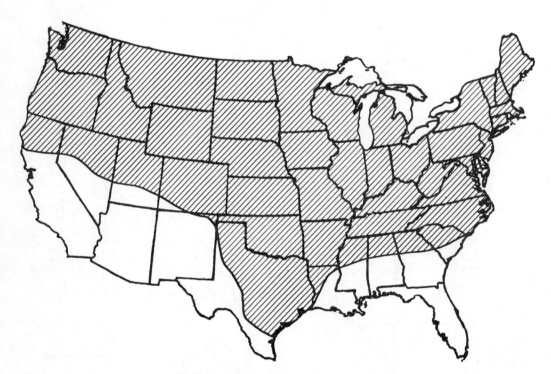

Distribution of *Conringia orientalis* (L.) Dum.

FIGURE 99.—*Conringia orientalis* (L.) Dum. Haresear mustard. *A*, Habit—× 0.5; *B*, silique—× 1.5; *C*, seeds—
× 7.5.

CRUCIFERAE

Descurainia pinnata (Walt.) Britt.

TANSYMUSTARD

Annual herb, reproducing by seeds (Fig. 100); *Stem* erect, simple or branched, 1–8 dm. tall, green, with densely hoary gray pubescence, glabrous to glandular; *Leaves* oblong, tapering toward the tip, alternate, pinnately dissected, often with grayish stellate pubescence. *Racemes* up to 3 dm. long, glandular to glabrous; *Petals* yellow or yellowish-green to nearly white, 2–4 mm. wide, nearly horizontally divergent; *Siliques* narrowly club-shaped, 5–16 mm. long, 1–2 mm. wide, on widely divergent to erect pedicels, the pedicels 0.6–1.5 cm. long; *Seed* 2-ranked in each locule, less than 1 mm. long. A variable species. March–August.

Waste places, prairies, dry or sandy soils, and open woods; especially abundant in arid and semiarid regions. Native. Widely distributed throughout the United States; north into Canada as far as the Mackenzie area; south into Mexico.

var. *pinnata*—*Leaves* with hoary gray pubescence, not glandular; *Raceme* with hoary gray pubescence, occasionally also glandular; *Siliques* spreading or ascending, 5–10 mm. long. On dry or sandy soils. Southeastern Virginia along the Coastal Plain to Flor·da and along the gulf coast to Texas.

var. *brachycarpa* (Richards.) Fern.—*Leaves* green, more or less glandular, sparse to densely beset with short, stipelike glands, otherwise glabrous or sparsely pubescent; *Flowers* slightly larger; *Siliques* erect or ascending, 6–13 mm. long. Dry ground, prairies, barrens, open upland woodlands. Quebec to Mackenzie, south to northern New England, West Virginia, Tennessee, Arkansas, and Texas, west to Montana and Colorado.

Distribution of *Descurainia pinnata* (Walt.) Britt.

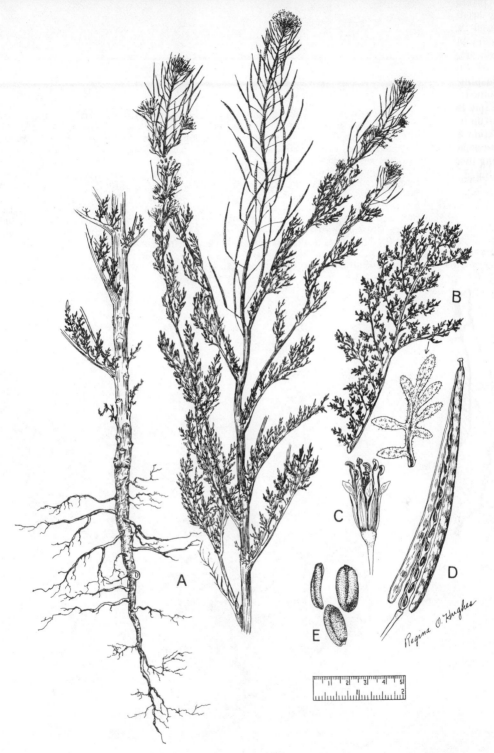

FIGURE 100.—*Descurainia pinnata* (Walt.) Britt. Tansymustard. *A*, Habit—× 0.5; *B*, enlarged cauline leaf—× 0.5; *C*, flower—× 5; *D*, silique—× 3; *E*, seeds—× 9.

CRUCIFERAE

Lepidium campestre (L.) R. Br.

Winter annual or *annual* herb, reproducing by seeds (Fig. 101); *Stems* erect, often clustered with stiff ascending branches above, hoary-pubescent, or rarely glabrous, 1.5–7 dm. tall, very leafy; *Leaves* on stem alternate, covered with soft hairs, arrow-shaped, the bases clasping the stem; the basal leaves arrow-shaped, spathulate to lanceolate, often pinnately lobed or toothed; *Flowers* inconspicuous, borne in dense racemes at the top of the plant; *Petals* 4, white or greenish, slightly exceeding the sepals; *Stamens* 6; *Seed pods* (silicles) oblong-ovate, 5–6 mm. long, 4 mm. wide, slightly winged, on short spreading pedicels, flattened at right angles to the partition, curved upward and the upper surface concave, often with small projections, dehiscent, each valve with 1 seed; *Seed* dark-brown, 2–2.5 mm. long, obovoid, 1 side flattened, coarsely granular, pointed at the tip. May–September.

Clover, alfalfa, and winter wheat fields, other grainfields, 1st-year meadows, and wastelands; locally abundant. Introduced and naturalized from Europe. Throught all the eastern half of the United States excepting the southern part; three distinct areas in Western United States; north into southern Canada from Nova Scotia to Ontario.

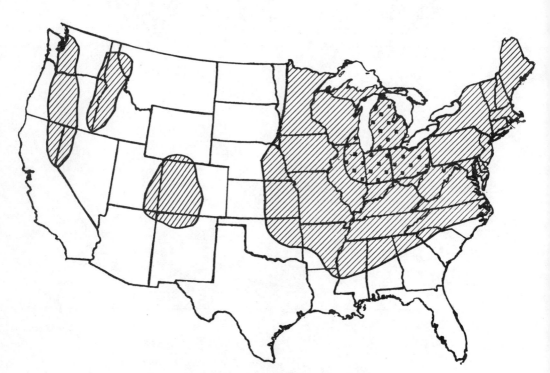

Distribution of *Lepidium compestre* (L.) R. Br.

FIGURE 101.—*Lepidium campestre* (L.) R. Br.   Field pepperweed   *A*, Habit—× 0.5; *B*, flower—× 7.5; *C*, silicles —× 4; *D*, seeds—× 5.

CRUCIFERAE

Lepidium virginicum L.

Annual or *winter annual* herb, reproducing by seeds (Fig. 102); *Stems* erect, much-branched, 2–9 dm. tall, smooth to minutely pubescent, green; *Leaves* on stem lanceolate to linear, coarsely toothed, irregularly cut or entire, usually sessile, the basal leaves obovate, irregularly cut, pinnatified or pinnate, with 1 large terminal lobe and several smaller dentate lateral ones, glabrous; *Inflorescence* in elongate racemes, that grow and flower for long periods, often with seed pods below and flowers above; *Flowers* small, with 4 white or greenish petals, the petals equaling or exceeding the sepals; *Stamens* 2 (rarely 4); *Seed pods* (silicles) nearly orbicular, 2.5–4 mm. wide, containing 2 seeds, shallow-notched at the summit; *Seed* 1.5–2 mm. long, obovate, with 1 edge straight, the other rounded, slightly winged at the apex, granular, chestnut-brown. May–November.

Fields, meadows, roadsides, and waste places; dry soils. A common weed. Native. Throughout all the United States excepting an area between eastern Montana and North Dakota and an area between southeastern California and southwestern New Mexico; north into southern Quebec.

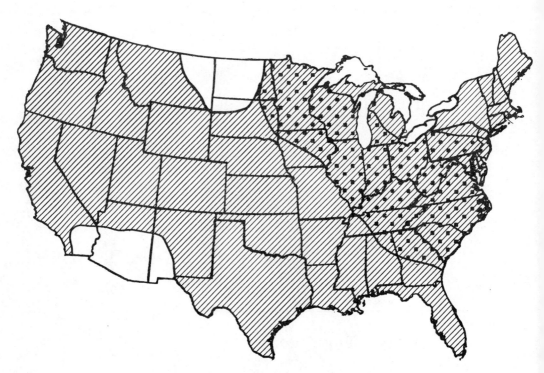

Distribution of *Lepidium virginicum* L.

FIGURE 102.—*Lepidium virginicum* L. Virginia pepperweed. *A*, Habit, upper part of plant—× 0.5; *B*, young plant, showing basal and cauline leaf forms—× 0.5 *C*, flowers—× 7.5; *D*, silicles, mature and immature—× 3; *E*, seed—× 10.

Nasturtium officinale R. Br.   WATERCRESS

Perennial aquatic or marsh herb, reproducing by seeds and rooted stems (Fig. 103); *Stems* succulent, smooth, creeping or floating, freely rooting; *Leaves* pinnate, the 3–11 leaflets roundish to oblong or elongate, somewhat fleshy, nearly entire, the terminal leaflet roundish, oval, or oblong; *Flowers* perfect, in racemes; *Sepals* equal at the base, spreading during anthesis; *Petals* white, twice the length of the calyx, without nectaries; *Seed pods* (siliques) linear-cylindric, 1–2.7 cm. long, 3 mm.

thick, somewhat curved, ascending on divergent pedicels, the convex valves nerveless or 1-nerved, the beak about 1 mm. long; *Seed* in 2 rows in each locule, small, turgid, marginless. April–October.

Brooks, rills, and springheads; often cultivated in cool waters. Native of Eurasia. Throughout all the United States excepting an area between central Montana and northeastern Minnesota; Mexico; West Indies; South America.

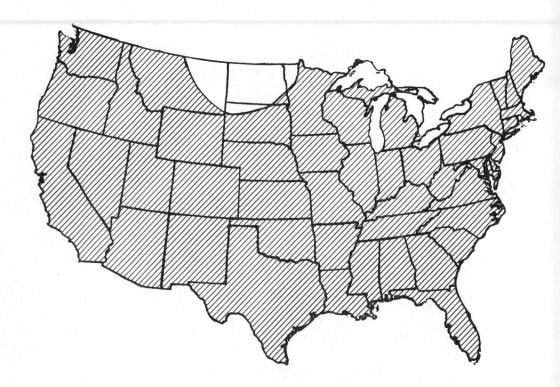

Distribution of *Nasturtium officinale* R. Br.

FIGURE 103.—*Nasturtium officinale* R. Br. Watercress. *A*, Habit—× 0.5; *B*, elongated mature plant—× 0.5; *C*, flower—× 2; *D*, silique—× 2; *E*, seeds—× 10.

Sisymbrium altissimum L.

Annual or *winter annual* herb, reproducing by seeds, with a taproot (Fig. 104); *Stem* erect, up to 6 dm. tall, bushy, branching, the stem and branches smooth above, but somewhat hairy below, pithy; *Leaves* alternate, pale-green, the lower ones large and pinnately lobed with broad, irregular, toothed lateral segments and a large terminal lobe, the upper ones with smaller narrow segments, arrowhead-shaped to lanceolate or entire; *Flowers* small, yellowish-white, 0.9–1.4 cm. in diameter, 4-petaled, in numerous but short spikelike racemes; *Seed pods* (siliques) stiff, pubescent to finely dense pubescent, awl-shaped, 1–2 cm. long, 1–1.5 mm. wide at the base, divided into 2 parts on very short pedicels, thus causing the pods to resemble stems rather than seed pods; *Seed* oblong, about 1.5 mm. long, dark reddish-brown, quite smooth. May–September.

Fields of small grain, gardens, and waste places. Naturalized from Europe. Common throughout the United States.

The stem often breaks off at maturity causing the plant to be blown about by the wind. The more common weed in most of the United States is **S. officinale var. leiocarpum DC.**, with siliques essentially glabrous and the plant greener than plants of other varieties.

Distribution of *Sisymbrium altissimum* L.

FIGURE 104.—*Sisymbrium altissimum* L. Tumble mustard. *A*, Habit—× 0.5; *B*, leaves, basal and cauline—× 1; *C*, silique—× 1; *D*, seeds—× 7.5.

Thlaspi arvense L.

Annual or *winter annual* herb, reproducing by seeds (Fig. 105); *Stem* simple to much-branched above, erect, smooth, up to 8 dm. tall; *Leaves* alternate, the lowest ones petioled, narrowly obovate, soon drooping; the middle and upper leaves membranaceous, oblong, toothed or entire, sessile, with two narrow, divergent, acute auricles 1–5 mm. long; *Flowers* in racemes; *Petals* white, 3–4 mm. long, equal, twice as long as the sepals; *Seed capsules* (silicles) orbicular to rounded-oblong, 10–18 mm. long, notched (2–3 mm.) at the top, dehiscent by 2 winged values, each with 2–8 seeds per locule; *Seed* 2–2.3 mm. long, compressed, ovoid, with 10–14 concentric granular ridges on each side, dark reddish-brown to blackish. April–August.

Waste places, fields, roadsides, grainfields, grasslands, and gardens. A troublesome weed in grainfields in the Northern and Northwestern States. Naturalized from Eurasia. Throughout the United States; north into Canada from Newfoundland to British Columbia and Alaska.

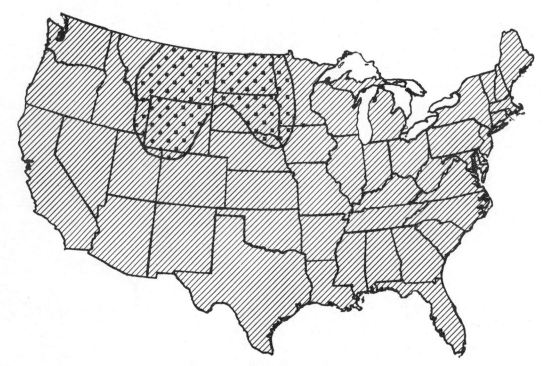

Distribution of *Thlaspi arvense* L.

FIGURE 105.—*Thlaspi arvense* L. Field pennycress. *A*, Habit—× 0.5; *B*, silicle—× 2; *C*, seeds—× 3.

Potentilla canadensis L.

COMMON CINQUEFOIL

(*P. pumila* Poir.)

Perennial herb, reproducing by seeds and runners (Fig. 106); *Rhizome* short, 0.5–2 cm. long, 4–8 mm. thick; *Stems* at flowering time, 0.1–1.5 dm. tall, soon becoming prostrate, runnerlike or threadlike, 0.3–1 mm. thick, not bearing tuberous enlargments at the tips; *Stems*, petioles, lower leaf surfaces and calyx silky soft hairs with appressed or loosely ascending soft pubescence; *Leaves* with 5 leaflets, the leaflets narrowly wedge-shaped obovate, the margins coarsely and deeply 5–15 toothed around the rounded summit, entire below the middle, the middle leaflet largest, 1.5–4 cm. long; *Stipules* of basal leaves with oblong-lanceolate, flat auricles, of the mature primary stem leaves mostly 3-cleft and 4–12 mm. long; *Flowers* 11.5 cm. broad, on long, slender peduncles 1–9 cm. long; *Bracteoles* linear or linear-lanceolate; *Petals* deep-yellow or cream-colored (**forma *ochroleuca* (Weath.) Fern.**), 10–15 mm. wide, rounded at the summit or retuse. March–June.

Dry sandy and gravelly fields and in dry woods. Native. Throughout all the eastern half of the United States excepting areas in the Southeastern Coastal States; north into Canada from western Nova Scotia to southwestern Ontario.

var. *villosissima* Fern.—Pubescence of all parts long, soft hairs, loosely spreading to reflexed; mature leaflets up to 6 cm. long. A more southern variety, Maryland to Ohio, south and southwest to Georgia, Tennessee, and Missouri; casually adventive in eastern Massachusetts.

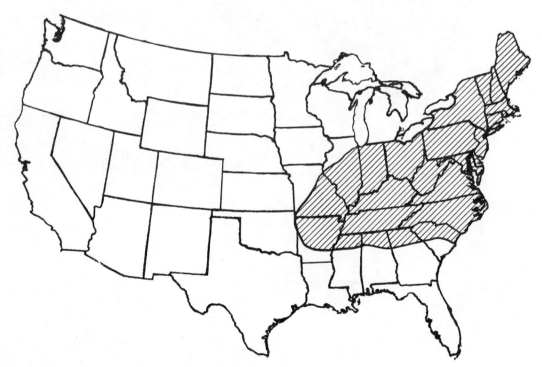

Distribution of *Potentilla canadensis* L.

FIGURE 106.—*Potentilla canadensis* L. Common cinquefoil. *A*, Habit—× 0.5; *B*, flower and calyx—× 1.5; *C*, achenes—× 10.

Potentilla norvegica L.

ROUGH CINQUEFOIL

(P. monspeliensis L.)

Biennial (rarely a short-lived *perennial*) herb, reproducing by seeds (Fig. 107); *Stems* stout and leafy, commonly branched, hairy with stiff mostly spreading hairs, semi-erect or spreading, 3–9 dm. tall; *Leaves* alternate, the lower leaves long-petioled, palmately divided, with 3 leaflets obovate to tapering toward the tip or elliptic, the margins coarsely toothed, the upper leaves sessile, with narrow leaflets, hairy, green; *Flowers* a leafy cyme at the tips of the branches; *Calyx* in fruit small, inconspicuous, enlarging to 0.8–1.7 cm. high, its bracteoles acutish, ovate-lanceolate, about equal at time of pollen shedding, the sepals enlarging with age in the fruit and up to 16 mm. long; *Petals* yellow, obovate, mostly shorter than the calyx lobes; *Stamens* 15–20; *Style* slenderly conical at base, subterminal, about equaling the mature carpel; *Achene* 0.8–1.3 mm. long, light-brown, with longitudinally curved ridges. June–October.

Fields, meadows, pastures, roadsides, waste places, and thickets. Introduced and naturalized from Eurasia; some varieties appear to be native of North America. Throughout all the United States excepting the southeastern and southwestern areas; north into Canada from Labrador to Alaska; Greenland; Mexico.

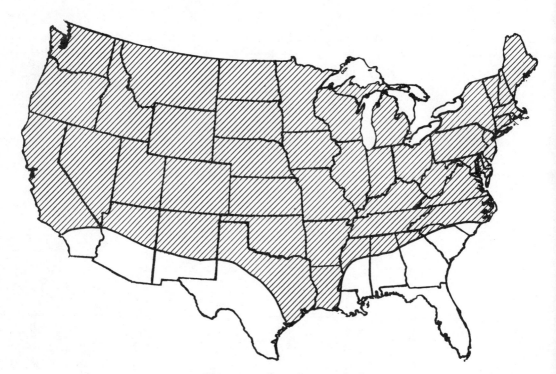

Distribution of *Potentilla norvegica* L.

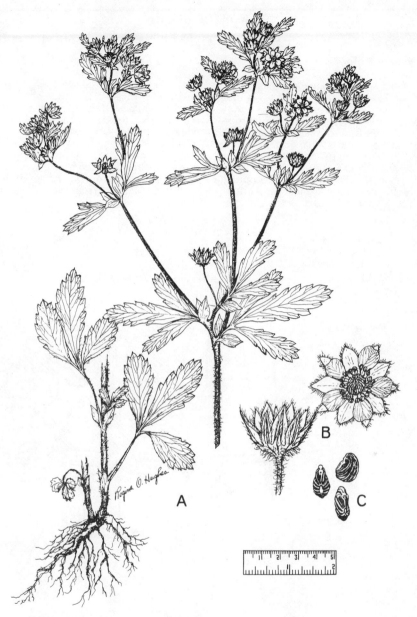

FIGURE 107.—*Potentilla norvegica* L. Rough cinquefoil. *A*, Habit—× 0.5; *B*, flower and calyx—× 2.5; *C*, achenes—× 10.

Potentilla recta L.

SULFUR CINQUEFOIL

(P. sulphurea Rydb.)

Perennial herb, reproducing by seeds (Fig. 108); *Stems* stiffly erect, very leafy, 1.5–9 dm. tall loosely hairy; *Leaves* alternate, the basal leaves on long hairy petioles, palmately divided with 5–7 leaflets, the leaflets oblanceolate, 3–14 cm. long, the margins with 7–17 prolonged triangular teeth, pale beneath, and more or less hirsute on both surfaces; *Flowers* in terminal, stiffly erect cymes; *Calyx* hairy, becoming 1–1.5 cm. high; *Corolla* conspicuous, sulfuryellow, the petals inverted heart-shaped, deeply notched at the apex, about 1 cm. long; *Stamens* mostly 30 (rarely 25); *Style* shorter than the mature carpel, filiform, terminal; *Achene* dark-brown, striate, with minute low curved ridges. Late May–August.

Dry fields, wastelands, pastures, meadows. and roadsides; troublesome in limestone regions. Naturalized from Europe. Throughout the northeastern fourth of the United States; north into Canada from Newfoundland to Ontario.

Distribution of *Potentilla recta* L.

FIGURE 108.—*Potentilla recta* L. Sulfur cinquefoil. *A*, Habit—× 0.5; *B*, base of leaf showing stipules—× 2; *C*, flower and calyx—× 1.5; *D*, achenes—× 10.

ROSACEAE

Rosa multiflora Thunb.

Perennial shrub, reproducing by seeds and sometimes rooting at the tips of the drooping side canes (Fig. 109); *Stems* up to 3 m. long, in clumps, arching or trailing, usually growing about 2 m. erect and then the tips drooping almost to the ground, beset with stiff thorns; *Leaves* pinnately compound, usually with 7 or 9 leaflets, membranaceous, deciduous, 2–4 cm. long, elliptic or obovate, obtuse to acute, nearly glabrous on the upper surface, paler and usually with short soft pubescence beneath, the petioles short-pubescent, the stipules green, membranaceous, short-pubescent and glandular hairs, the free part threadlike at the apex; *Inflorescence* a many-flowered panicle, usually pyramidal, erect, 2–4 cm. broad, mostly white, sometimes pinkish, the pedicels often with stalked glands; *Sepals* 5–8 mm. long; *Styles* glabrous; *Fruits* (hips) bright-red, often lasting until spring, about 0.8 cm. in diameter, nearly round; *Achene* enclosed in the fleshy calyx tube (hip). June–July.

Clearings, roadsides, fence rows, waysides, borders of woods, "bumper areas" along superhighways, and curves; introduced as an ornamental and used horticulturally as hardy rootstock on which to bud other ornamental varieties. Introduced and naturalized from eastern Asia. Throughout most of the United States excepting the Rocky Mountain area, the southeastern Coastal Plains, and the Nevada and California desert areas; south into Mexico.

ROSACEAE

Rosa arkansana Porter

Perennial shrub with underground rootstocks; *Stems* 3–4 dm. tall, densely prickly; *Leaves* compound, with 7–11 oval leaflets, about 2.5 cm. long; *Flowers* pink, about 4 cm. broad, fragrant; *Fruit* (hip) round, 1–1.3 cm. in diameter; *Seed* hard, hairy, brown, about 4 mm. long.

Weed in pastures, prairies, fields, roadsides, and fence rows. Native. Wisconsin, Minnesota, and North Dakota, south to Missouri, Colorado, and northeastern Oklahoma.

var. *suffulta* (Greene) Cockerell—Petioles, rachis and lower leaf surface soft hairy. Dry thickets, rocky slopes, and sands from New York to Alberta, south to the District of Columbia, Indiana, Wisconsin, Missouri, Kansas, Colorado, Texas, and New Mexico. May–August.

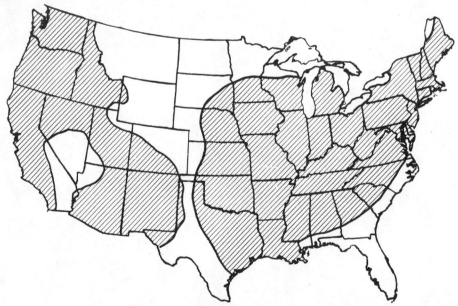

Distribution of *Rosa multiflora* Thunb.

FIGURE 109.—*Rosa multiflora* Thunb. Multiflora rose. *A*, Habit—× 0.5; *B*, leaf base—× 2; *C*, bud—× 2; *D*, styles and stamens—× 2; *E*, fruits—× 0.5; *F*, achenes—× 2.

ROSACEAE

Rubus alleghaniensis Porter

Perennial shrub, reproducing by seeds and underground runners (Fig. 110); *Stems* erect or high-arching, 1–3 m. high, armed with scattered broad-based (3–5 mm. long) lanceolate prickles, or the prickles absent; *Primocanes* often ridged or angled and finely pubescent; *Primocane leaflets* mostly 5, palmately compound, the upper 3 conspicuously stalked, the petiole and leaflet petioles prickly and pubescent and glandular, the blades typically oblong or elliptic to ovate and gradually tapering, 8–12 cm. long, 4–6 cm. broad; *Floricanes* mostly retaining strong scattered prickles, normally erect, but sometimes depressed with fruit; *Floricane leaflets* usually 3, the foliage of floral shoots of short-pointed or obtuse small leaflets; *Inflorescences* in elongated racemes, 8–25 cm. long, extending beyond the foliage, pubescent and glandular; *Flowers* 12 to 30 on long clusters, about 2 cm. in diameter, widely opening; *Petals* narrow, white, noticeably separate; *Calyx* pubescent and glandular, the lobes acute to prolonged-pointed; *Fruit* globose to thimble-shaped, compound, 2 cm. or more long, made up of 50–70 drupelets (small one-seeded fruits); *Seed* about 1 mm. long, wrinkled. A variable species with several varieties. Flowering May–June; fruiting July.

Dry places from lowlands to hills and mountains, open woodlands, roadsides, thickets, fence rows, and clearings, ubiquitous. Native. Throughout most of Northeastern United States, south in the mountains to North Carolina and Tennessee, west to Missouri and Minnesota; north into Canada from Quebec to Nova Scotia.

There are over 300 species of *Rubus*, varying from blackberries to dewberries and raspberries. *Perennials* often somewhat shrubby with semiwoody stems (canes); *Stems* trailing or upright and arching, frequently rooting at the tips, usually with thorns, or prickles or stiff soft hairs; *Canes* of two types, the primocanes that grow the 1st year and only vegetate (rarely flowering and fruiting) and these same canes becoming the floricanes the 2d year, bearing flowers and fruits, these canes then dying after the 2d year; *Leaves* petioled, palmately compound, with 3- or 5-foliolate or lobed leaflets, these varying in size and shape; *Inflorescences* terminal or axial, of few to many flowers in a cluster, the petals usually white, rarely pink or pinkish; *Fruits* compound, made up numerous small one-seeded fruits varying from dark-purple to red, yellow, or white. Various species throughout the United States, forming thickets, bramble patches, and sand dune tangles.

Distribution of *Rubus alleghaniensis* Porter

FIGURE 110.—*Rubus alleghentensis* Porter. Allegheny blackberry. *A*, Primocane habit—× 0.5; *B*, floricane habit —× 0.5; *C*, fruit showing drupelets—× 0.5; *D*, seeds—× 3.

LEGUMINOSAE

Astragalus mollissimus Torr.

Perennial herb, reproducing by seeds (Fig. 111); *Root system* deep-penetrating, woody, on which are root tubercles; *Plants* nearly stemless, the internodes few and short; *Stems* less than 10 cm. long, somewhat bushy; *Leaves* alternate, 10–20 cm. long, pinnately compound, 21–31 leaflets, 10–25 mm. long, oval, obovate to broadly elliptic, silky long soft hairs, not reduced upwards; *Flowers* bluish-purple to rose-purple, in dense racemes, almost spikelike in flower, but elongating in fruit; *Calyx* 10–15 mm. long; *Corolla* 17–21 mm. long; *Legume* (pod) 13–20 mm. long, narrowly oblong, glabrous. Flowering May–June; fruiting June–August.

Dry plains and foothills at lower elevations, east of the Continental Divide. Poisonous to stock. Native. Throughout part of the southwestern and south-central areas of the United States.

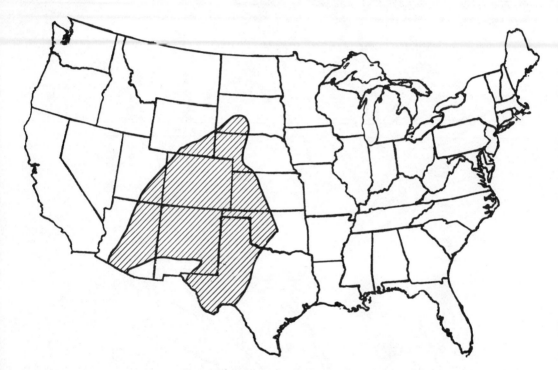

Distribution of *Astragalus mollissimus* Torr.

Figure 111.—*Astragalus mollissimus* Torr. Woolly loco. *A*, Habit— × 0.5; *B*, enlarged leaves— × 1; *C*, flower— × 1.25; *D*, pods— × 1; *E*, seeds— × 3.

LEGUMINOSAE

Daubentonia punicea (Cav.) DC.   COFFEEWEED

(*D. texana* Pierce; *D. longifolia* DC.; *Sesbania cavanillesii* Watson; *S. punicea* (Cav.) Benth.)

Perennial, herbaceous to shrub or small tree, reproducing by seeds (Fig. 112); *Stems* branching becoming bushy, up to 2.5 m. tall, usually from a clump; *Leaves* alternate, with oblong stipules, pinnate with 12–60 leaflets, the blades linear-elliptic, rounded or blunt at the apex, 1–2.5 cm. long; *Flowers* perfect, in simple axillary racemes shorter than the leaves; *Pedicels* 5–10 mm. long, curved at the apex; *Calyx* bell-shaped, the lobes acute, ciliate, much shorter than the tube, the lower lobe obtuse; *Corolla* scarlet to yellow, the standard with a blade 13–18 mm. broad, the keel petals with blades tapering into the claw; *Pods* linear-oblong, leathery, 5–8 cm. long, the stipe 1–1.5 cm. long, compressed with 4 wings arising from the margins of the valves and produced beyond the sutures, indehiscent; *Seed* several, separated from one another by transverse partitions. July–September.

Waste places, roadsides, and fence rows; in sandy soils of the Coastal Plain. Very poisonous to livestock, especially sheep. Native to tropical America. along the South Atlantic and the gulf coasts from North Carolina through Texas to Mexico.

Distribution of *Daubentonia punicea* (Cav.) DC.

FIGURE 112.—*Daubentonia punicea* (Cav.) DC. Coffeeweed. *A*, Habit, upper branches showing flowers and mature pods—× 0.5; *B*, Seed, 2 views—× 2.

Medicago lupulina L.

BLACK MEDIC

Annual, winter annual, biennial, or sometimes acting as a *perennial* herb, reproducing by seeds (Fig. 113); *Taproot* shallow; *Stems* slender, procumbent or prostrate, branched at the base, 30–60 dm. tall, sparsely pubescent, especially below; *Leaves* alternate, petioled, 3-parted, the center leaflet on a short stalk, the leaflets 5–15 mm. long, nearly orbicular to broadly obovate, sparingly hairy, the stipules ovate-lanceolate; *Peduncles* slender, hairy or glabrate; *Flowers* 3–4 mm. long, crowded in spikelike racemes (not over 12 mm. long); *Corollas* yellow, 1.5–2 mm. long, longer than the hairy calyx; *Petals* 5 (standard, 2 lateral wings and the 2 lower fused into a keel); *Calyx* 5-cleft, persistent, *Stamens* 9 fused and 1 separate; *Pistil* solitary; *Legume* nearly kidney-shaped, with a closed goove, pubescent, hairy or glabrate, net-veined, 1.5–3 mm. long, becoming black at maturity, unarmed, 1-seeded; *Seed* 1.5–2 mm. long, oval to short kidney-shaped, with a protuberance at the hilum, the sides convex, smooth, dull, yellowish-green, greenish-brown to orange-brown; *Pericarp* often persisting. March–September, sometimes to December.

Roadsides, waste places, lawns, pastures, and meadows. Grown for forage, but small-yielding; will innoculate soil for alfalfa; may be objectionable as an impurity in alsike clover fields. Naturalized from Eurasia. Widespread throughout North America.

Distribution of *Medicago lupulina* L.

FIGURE 113.—*Medicago lupulina* L. Black medic. *A*, Habit—× 0.5; *B*, flower raceme—× 6; *C*, fruiting raceme —× 3; *D*, flower—× 10; *E*, legume—× 5; *F*, seeds—× 5.

LEGUMINOSAE

Oxytropis lambertii Pursh

LAMBERT CRAZYWEED

Perennial herb, reproducing by seeds (Fig. 114); *Stem* forming a crown at the surface of the ground, from a taproot system with root tubercles; *Plant* low, 1–1.5 dm. tall, erect, stout, bushy from the top of the crown (base), densely white-pubescent (**var. sericea**), intergrading completely with the greener, less pubescent form; *Leaves* alternate, pinnately compound, 8–20 cm. long, white hairy, the leaflets 7–13, elliptic or oblong, 1–3 cm. long; *Flowers* cream to white, often tinged pink or blue, the keel frequently purple-tipped, in a peduncled, spikelike raceme, 5–10 cm. long, the raceme elongating in fruit; *Calyx teeth* 1–3 mm. long, about one-third the length of the tube; *Wings* of the *corolla* broad and deeply emarginate; *Legume* (pod) cylindric, erect, about 2 cm. long, long-tapering, nearly 2-celled; *Seed* dark-brown to blackish, about 1.5 mm. long, kidney-shaped, thinner in the scar region. A variable species, including *O. sericea* Nutt., varying in flower color, height of plant, general pubescence, and length of calyx teeth. Flowering May–August; fruiting June–October.

Mountain slopes, pasture lands, and grazing lands. Poisonous to stock, most freely eaten by cattle, sheep, and horses. Native. Throughout an area in the United States bounded by northern Idaho, northwestern Minnesota, south central Texas, and southwestern Arizona.

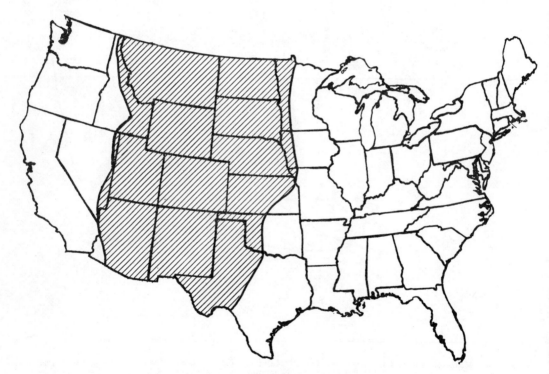

Distribution of *Oxytropis lambertii* Pursh

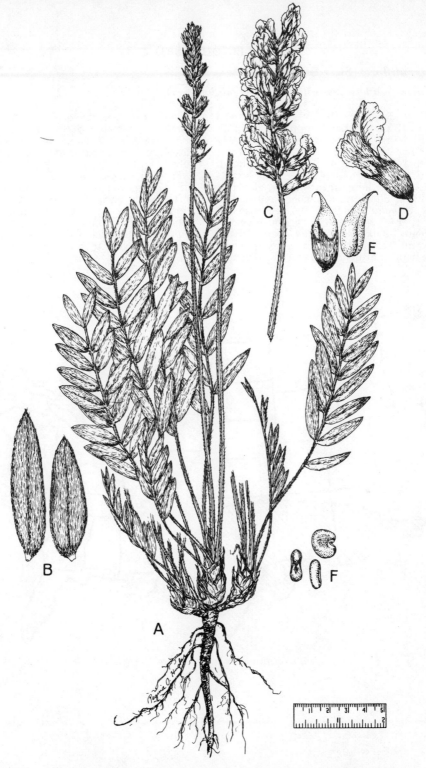

FIGURE 114.—*Oxytropis lambertii* Pursh. Lambert crazyweed. *A*, Habit—× 0.5; *B*, enlarged leaves—× 1; *C*, flower spike—× 0.5; *D*, flower—× 1; *E*, legumes—× 1; *F*, seeds—× 4.

LEGUMINOSAE

Prosopis juliflora (Sw.) DC. MESQUITE

(Neltuma juliflora (Sw.) Raf.; *Mimosa juliflora* Sw.)*

Perennial, deciduous thorny shrub or small tree, up to 12 m. tall, trunk up to 1.2 m. in diameter, bark thick, brown or blackish, shallowly fissured (Fig. 115) ; *Roots* sometimes penetrate the soil to a depth of 60 ft.; *Leaves* compound, commonly many more than 9 pairs, the leaflets mostly 5–10 mm. long, linear-oblong, glabrous, often with small hairs, commonly rounded at the apex; *Stipular* spines, if any, yellowish, often stout; *Flowers* perfect, greenish-yellow, sweet-scented, spikelike; *Corolla* deeply lobate; *Pods* several-seeded, strongly compressed when young, but thick at maturity, more or less constricted between the seeds, 10–20 cm. long, brown or yellowish; *Seed* compressed and oval or elliptic, 2.5–7 mm. long, brown, rather glossy, with a central ring on each face. May–July.

Trees or shrubs along water courses; smaller shrub on grasslands and lower mountain slopes (often with much of the trunk underground); widely spread on overgrazed grasslands. Native. Throughout most of the south-central and southwestern areas of the United States; south through Mexico to northern South America; Jamaica.

Distribution of *Prosopis juliflora* (Sw.) DC.

234

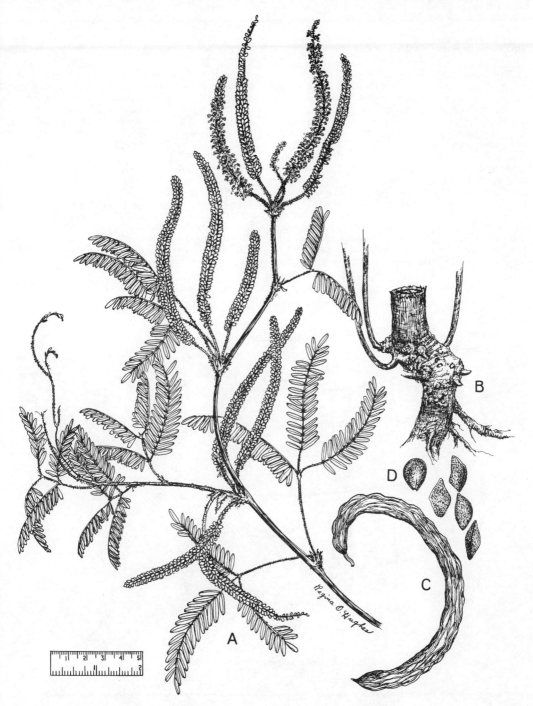

FIGURE 115.—*Prosopis juliflora* (Sw.) DC. Mesquite. *A*, Habit—× 0.5; *B*, rootstock portion × 0.5; *C*, pod—× 0.5; *D*, seeds—× 1.25.

Pueraria lobata (Willd.) Ohwi KUDZU

Perennial high-climbing vines, reproducing by seeds and from mealy tuberous roots (Fig. 116); *Stems* herbaceous to woody or ligneous, 10–30 m. long, up to 2.5 cm. thick, high-climbing and twining, the young parts pubescent; *Leaves* pinnately 3-foliolate, the leaflets entire or coarsely and palmately (2–3) lobed, broadly ovate to subrotund, up to 1.8 dm. long, pubescent beneath, the stipules herbaceous; *Racemes* simple or compound, axillary, peduncled, elongate, 1–2 dm. long, the axis and pedicels densely silky, with nonpersistent long-tipped bracts; *Flowers* reddish-purple, 2–2.5 cm. long, tufted at the nodes at the rachis; *Corolla* reddish-purple, with the fragrance of grapes; *Calyx* with the two upper lobes united, the lowest calyx lobe 8–12 mm. long; *Keel* ascending or arched at the tip, about equaling the wings, the standard yellow at the base, nearly round or obovate; *Stamens* with the filaments united, the axillary stamen free at the base; *Legume* 4–5 cm. long, flattish, continuous or with internal partitions, several-seeded, hirsute; *Seed* nearly round or transversely ovoid, compressed. Late August–September.

Borders of fields and woods and along rivers, roadsides, an embankments, often covering old dwellings and trees. Native of Japan; introduced from eastern Asia. Throughout approximately all the southeastern area of the United States. Rarely flowering north of Virginia; frequently grown as a quick-growing ornamental climber, but easily escaping and rapidly spreading.

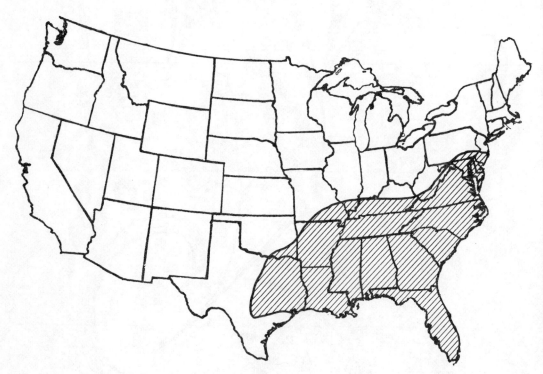

Distribution of *Pueraria lobata* (Willd.) Ohwi

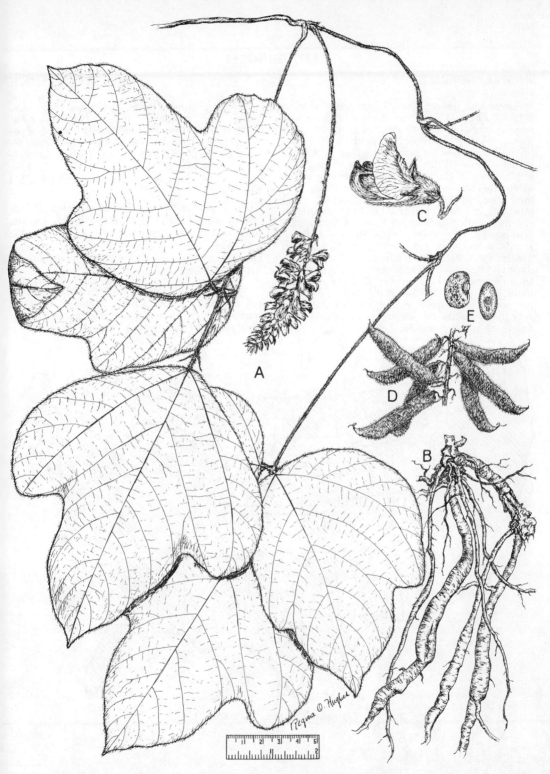

FIGURE 116.—*Pueraria lobata* (Willd.) Ohwi. Kudzu. *A*, Habit—× 0.5; *B*, root—× 0.25; *C*, flower—× 2; *D*, legumes—× 0.5; *E*, seeds—× 2.5.

LEGUMINOSAE

Vicia angustifolia L.

NARROWLEAF VETCH

Annual or *winter annual* herb, reproducing by seed (Fig. 117); *Stem* slender, glabrous or becoming glabrous, 3–9 dm. long, upright but weak, clinging to support by tendrils at the tip of the leaves; *Leaves* pinnately compound, 8–12 leaflets, those of the lower leaves oblong and blunt, those of the upper leaves linear to lance-attenuate, sharp-pointed, 1.5–3 cm. long, 1–4 mm. wide, all smooth-margined, the leaflet terminating in a branched tendril; *Inflorescence* in racemes, with 2–9 flowers; *Flowers* perfect, irregular, on very short peduncles or sessile, a few in a leaf axil, 1–1.8 cm. long; *Calyx* with nearly equal teeth, 7–11 mm. long; *Corolla* of 5 unequal purplish petals; *Stamens* 10, 9 fused by their filaments, 1 separate; *Legume* smooth, plane, 4–6 cm. long, 5–7 mm. wide; *Seed* 4–7 per pod, 3 mm. broad, round, surface dull, velvety, brown-black or olive-brown, mottled with fine black spots. June–October.

Waste grounds, fields, roadsides, waysides, slopes, and meadows; on rich gravelly soils. Cultivated for forage, but usually a wood, especially in grainfields. Naturalized from Europe. throughout the United States; north into eastern Canada to Newfoundland.

The most frequent varieties in the United States are:

var. *segetalis* (Thuill.) W. D. J. Koch—Leaflets of upper leaves oblong to oblong-obovate, blunt or notched at the tip, pointed at the apex, 2–9 mm. broad. Naturalized from Europe. throughout the range of the species, in wheatfields, roadsides, and waste places.

var. *uncinata* (Desv.) Rouy—Leaflets of upper leaves narrowly linear, blunt or abruptly narrowed, 1–2 mm. broad. Naturalized from Europe. Newfoundland to Virginia; local.

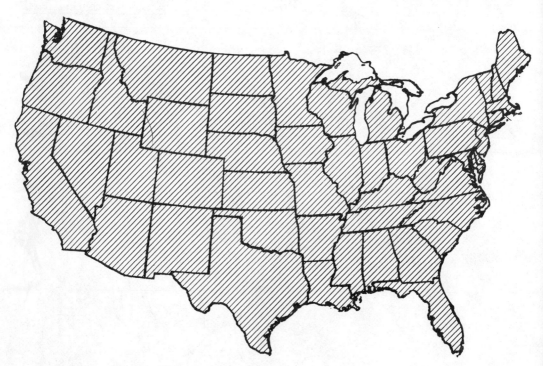

Distribution of *Vicia angustifolia* L.

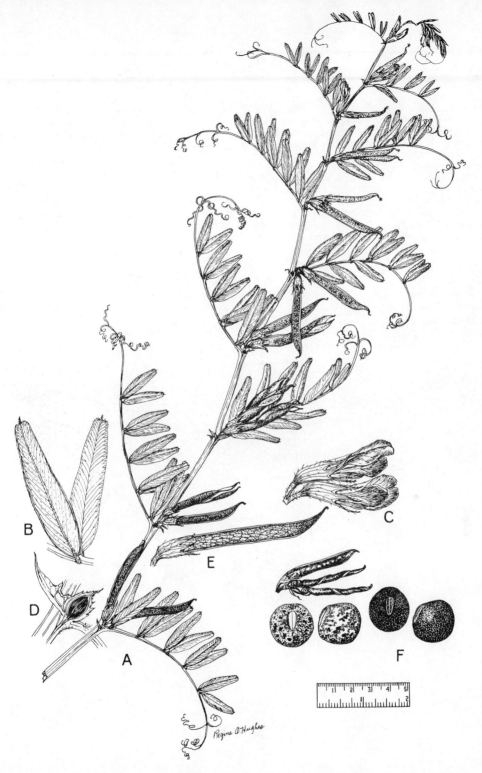

FIGURE 117.—*Vicia angustifolia* L.   Narrowleaf vetch.   *A*, Habit—× 0.5; *B*, leaves—× 1.5; *C*, flowers—× 1.5; *D*, bract, showing extra nectary—× 4; *E*, legume—× 1; *F*, seed, 4 views—× 4.

OXALIDACEAE

Oxalis stricta L.

Perennial herb, reproducing by seeds (Fig. 118); *Taproots* without subterranean stolons; *Stems* erect but weak, becoming decumbent, gray-green, 10–50 cm. tall, branching at the base, bushy, pubescent with whitish hairs, sometimes rooting at the joints; *Leaves* alternate, on long petioles, divided into 3 heart-shaped leaflets, 1–2 cm. broad, sour-tasting; *Stipules* oblong, firm, pale; *Flowers* 7–11 mm. long, with 5 yellow, rarely green petals, sometimes red at the base; *Peduncles* pubescent, mostly equaling or overtopping the leaves, umbellately 1- to 4-flowered; *Pedicels* 1–2.5 cm. long, in fruit; *Sepals* 3.5–7 mm. long; *Capsules* 1.2–2.5 cm. long, slender, cylindrical, 5-ridged, pointed, hoary pubescent; *Seed* small, 1–1.3 mm. long, flat, brown, thrown from the bursting pods. May–October.

Dry open soil, in pastures, lawns, and waste places; a troublesome weed in lawns and gardens. Throughout the United States; north into Canada from Prince Edwards Island to British Columbia; south into Mexico.

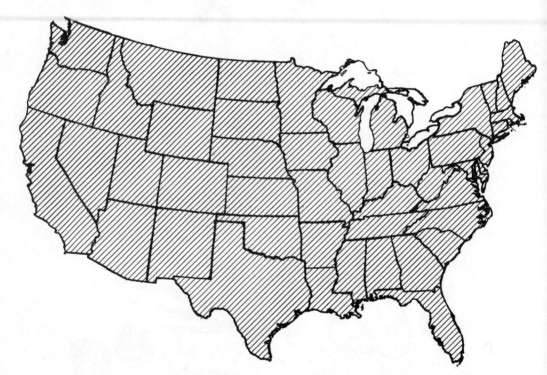

Distribution of *Oxalis stricta* L.

FIGURE 118.—*Oxalis stricta* L. Common yellow woodsorrel. *A*, Habit—× 0.5; *B*, leaves enlarged—× 1.25; *C*, flower diagrams—× 2.5; *D*, capsule—× 1.5; *E*, seeds—× 10.

ZYGOPHYLLACEAE

Tribulus terrestris L.

PUNCTUREVINE, CALTROP

Annual herb, reproducing by seeds (Fig. 119); *Root system* simple, taproot; *Stems* prostrate, branching from base to form dense mats of slender branches, 1.8–2.4 m. long, pubescent to stiff hairy; *Leaves* opposite, short-petioled, 2–6 cm. long, oblong, pubescent, divided into pinnate leaflets, the leaflets in 5–8 pairs, oblong, 5–15 mm. long; *Flowers* small, yellow, 5-petaled, 5–10 mm. wide, axillary, the peduncles 5–10 mm. long; *Seed pods* about 1 cm. thick, containing 5 burs each with 2–4 sharp, stout prickles (strong enough to puncture bicycle tires or penetrate shoe soles). June–September.

Pastures, roadsides, wastes, along railroads, ballast lots, sometimes in cultivated fields; dry waste areas and open sandy ground. A serious weed and considered a noxious weed in some states; cattle will not graze in infested areas; most common in the Southwest. Naturalized from Europe. Throughout all the United States excepting that area along most of the northern boundary; however, also in western Washington and northern Idaho.

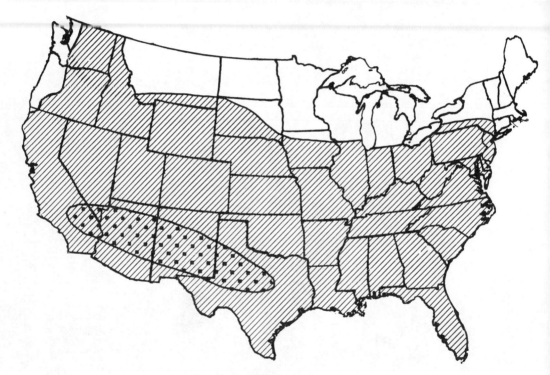

Distribution of *Tribulus terrestris* L.

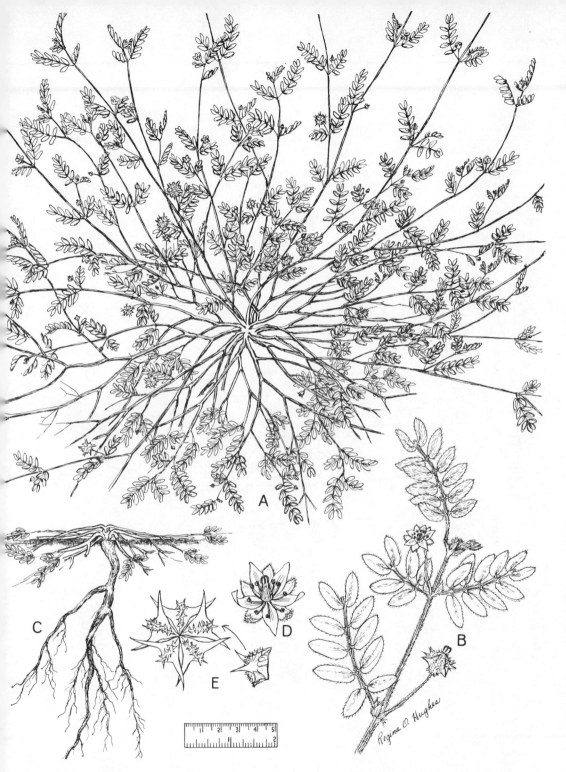

FIGURE 119.—*Tribulus terrestris* L. Puncturevine. *A*, Habit, seen from above—× 0.5; *B*, flowering branchlet— × 2; *C*, rootstock, side view—× 0.5; *D*, flower—× 5; *E*, fruits—× 2.5.

Croton capitatus Michx.

Annual herb, reproducing by seeds (Fig. 120); *Taproot* shallow; *Stems* stout, erect, up to 2 m. tall, extensively branched, densely soft-woolly with star-shaped hairs, somewhat glandular; *Leaves* usually alternate, simple, with long petioles, lanceolate-oblong to oblong or oval, entire, rounded or nearly heart-shaped at the base, 4–10 cm. long, woolly with short hairs; *Trichomes* of inflorescence brownish; *Flowers* in terminal clusters, 1–3 cm. long, surrounded by a leafy bract; *Pistillate flowers* in headlike groups, crowded at base of staminate spike; *Staminate* flowers with 5 sepals, 5 petals, 7–14 stamens; *pistillate flowers* without petals, calyx 6–12 parted, the 3 styles two or three times 2-parted; *Capsule* globose, 7–9 mm. in diameter, densely hairy, 3-sided, containing 3 seeds; *Seed* lens-shaped, nearly round, about 5 mm. long, ventrally flattened, grayish. June–October.

Waste places and overgrazed pastures; dry sandy and open soils. Native. Throughout approximately all the southeastern two-thirds of the United States excepting most of Florida.

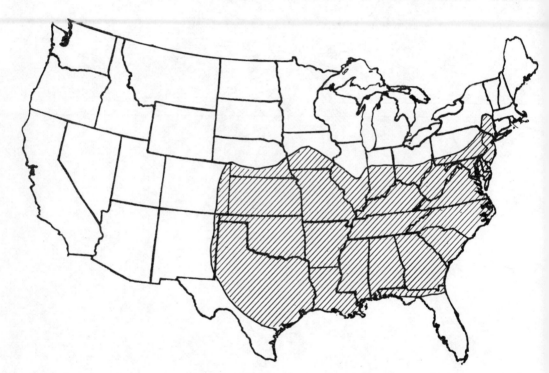

Distribution of *Croton capitatus* Michx.

FIGURE 120.—*Croton capitatus* Michx. Woolly croton. *A*, Habit—× 0.5; *B*, staminate flower—× 1.5; *C*, pistillate flower—× 1.5; *D*, fruit—× 1.5; *E*, seeds—× 2.5.

EUPHORBIACEAE

Euphorbia corollata L.

Perennial herb, reproducing by seed and by short rootstocks (Fig. 121); *Stems* single to several from a sturdy, deep root, 3–10 dm. tall, erect, light-green, glabrous, branched near the top, with a milky juice; *Leaves* oval, oblong, or linear, light-green, the lower leaves alternate, the upper leaves in whorls on the branches, firm, sessile or subsessile; *Inflorescence* umbellate, many-flowered, 3- to 7-forked and again 2- to 5-forked, the longer pedicels 7–25 cm. long; *Flowers* (cyathia) small, 1–1.5 mm. high, surrounded by 5 white petal-like bracts (7–10 mm. broad) in the form of a cup, in terminal clusters and in the axils of the upper leaves; *Capsule* on short stalks from the cuplike base, smooth, 3-lobed with 3 seeds, 3.5–4.5 mm. broad; *Seed* egg-shaped, gray or light-brown, mottled, shallowly pitted, with a dark line on one side. June–October.

Roadsides, waste places, and pastures, especially in dry and sandy areas. Native. Throughout all the eastern half of the United States excepting parts of the northernmost States and the South Central States; north into Ontario.

Distribution of *Euphorbia corollata* L.

FIGURE 121.—*Euphorbia corollata* L. Flowering spurge. *A*, Habit—× 0.5; *B*, flowering branchlet—× 2.5; *C*, capsules—× 3; *D*, seeds—× 3.

EUPHORBIACEAE

Euphorbia esula L.   LEAFY SPURGE

Perennial herb, reproducing by seeds and from extensive slender rootstocks (Fig. 122); *Roots* deep and spreading, woody, very persistent; *Stems* erect, glabrous, branched at the top, 3–9 dm. tall, with a milky juice; *Leaves* alternate, broadly linear to narrowly oblong-lanceolate or inverted lanceolate, 2–10 mm. broad, usually drooping; *Inflorescence* a terminal open umbel, the larger floral leaves kidney-shaped, 1–1.3 cm. long, yellow-green; *Flowers* (cyathia) small, 2.5–3 mm. high, greenish, the petals fused into a cuplike structure, borne just above the greenish-yellow heart-shaped floral bracts on the top of the stem; *Capsule* on short stalks from the cuplike base, 3-lobed, with 3 seeds; *Seed* elliptic-oval, about 2 mm. long, smooth, light-gray to yellow-brown, with a yellow (or white) emarginate caruncle. May–September.

Waste areas, pastures, roadsides, cultivated fields, and sandy banks; a serious weed because of its spreading nature and persistence. Naturalized from Europe. Throughout most of the northern half of the United States; north into Canada from Nova Scotia to Alberta.

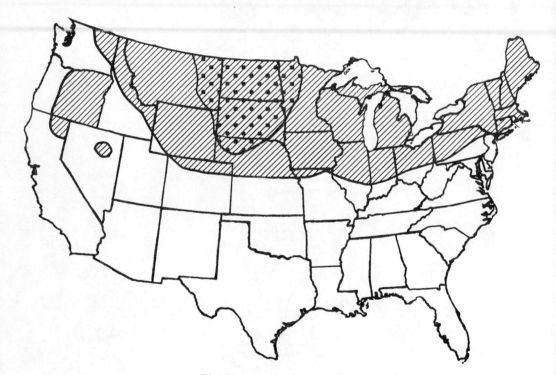

Distribution of *Euphorbia esula* L.

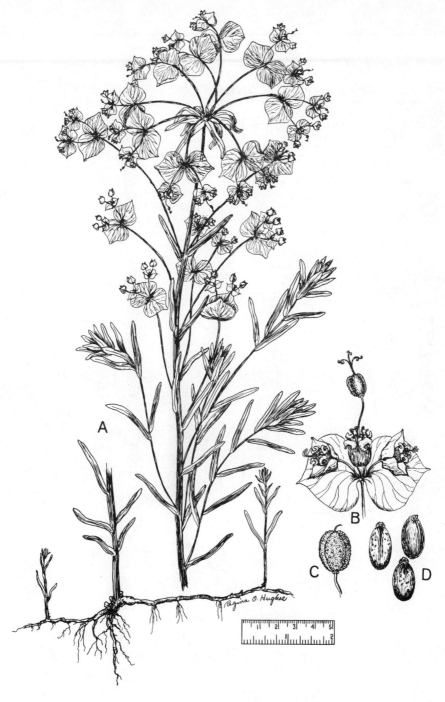

FIGURE 122.—*Euphorbia esula* L. Leafy spurge. *A*, Habit—× 0.5; *B*, flower cluster—× 2.5; *C*, capsule—× 2.5; *D*, seeds—× 6.

Euphorbia maculata L.

Annual herb, with a shallow taproot, reproducing by seeds, germinating late in the spring or early summer (Fig. 123); *Stem* simple or much-branched, erect or spreading, 0.8–1 m. tall, with a milky juice, crisp-pubescent at the young tips, soon becoming glabrous and firm; *Leaves* oblong, oblong-lanceolate or lance-falcate, 0.8–3.5 cm. long, the edges slightly toothed, borne on short petioles, with a conspicuous reddish spot or blotch; *Flowers* (cyathia) solitary or clustered, with minute petals in the form of a cup, peduncle 0.5–5 mm. long; *Invo-*

lucres 0.7–1 mm. in diameter; *Seed pods* on short stalks from the cuplike base, smooth, 3-lobed, ribbed, with 3 seeds; *Seed* 3-sided, obtusely angled, 1.1–1.6 mm. long, 0.9–1.1 mm. wide, oblong, dark-brown or black, pitted with ridged surfaces. June–October.

Gardens, cultivated fields, waste places, and roadsides; dry open soils. Native. Throughout approximately the eastern two-thirds of the United States; introduced along the Pacific coast from Washington to central California.

Distribution of *Euphorbia maculata* L.

FIGURE 123.—*Euphorbia maculata* L. Spotted spurge. *A*, Habit—× 0.5; *B*, staminate flower—× 7.5; *C*, and *D*, immature capsuies of the pistillate flower—× 7.5; *E*, mature capsule, bottom view to show deep lobes—× 5; *F*, seed, 3 views—× 7.5.

EUPHORBIACEAE

Euphorbia supina Raf. ex Boiss.

(*E. maculata,* of Amer. auth., not L. as to type)

Annual herb, reproducing by seeds (Fig. 124); *Stems* slender, prostrate or ascending, branching from near the base, forming mats 1–9 dm. in diameter, soft pubescent, often reddish, with a milky juice; *Leaves* opposite, 4–17 mm. long, elliptic-ovate to oblong, toothed to nearly entire, sparsely long fine hairs, becoming glabrous, often purple-mottled, stipules lanceolate; *Cyathia* solitary in the branch axils or in dense leafy lateral clusters, the lobes of the involucres with 4 narrow white appendaged glands, the glands transversely elongate, 0.15–0.25 mm. long, the cyathia not split down the back, the ovaries pubescent, the styles 0.4–0.7 mm. long with the upper third bifid; *Staminate flowers* 2–5; the crisp-pubescent *gynophore* barely exserted; *Capsules* stiff-haired pubescent, sharp-angled; *Seed* about 0.8–1 mm. long, 4-angled, transversely ridged, minutely pitted, gray-brown to reddish. Flowering May–October; fruiting July–November.

Dry, gravelly or sandy fields, sterile waste places, and roadsides. Native. Throughout Eastern and Central United States; introduced into the Pacific coast, with a few distinct areas in Idaho and Arizona; north into Canada in southern Quebec and southern Ontario.

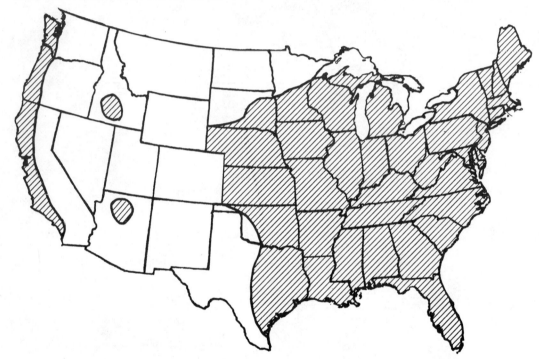

Distribution of *Euphorbia supina* Raf. ex Boiss.

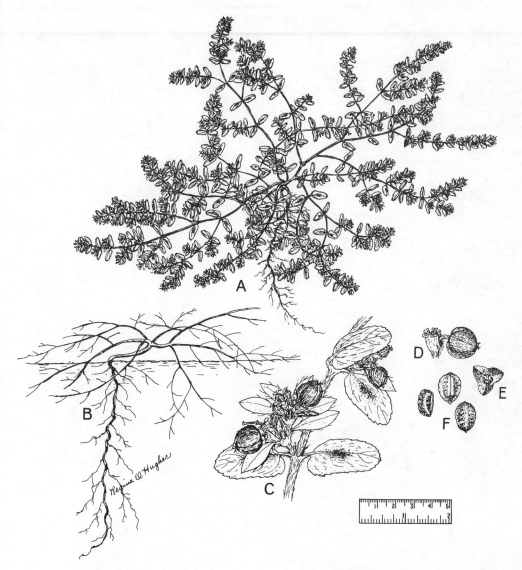

FIGURE 124.—*Euphorbia supina* Raf. ex Boiss. Prostrate spurge. *A*, Habit—× 0.5; *B*, root—× 0.5; *C*, enlarged lateral branch with cyathia—× 3.5; *D*, gynophore—× 6; *E*, capsule from top, showing subacute shape and 3-parted cleft styles—× 6; *F*, seeds—× 7.5.

ANACARDIACEAE

Rhus glabra L.   SMOOTH SUMAC

Perennial sparsely branched shrub or small tree, 0.5–6 m. tall, reproducing by seeds and rootstocks (Fig. 125); *Stems* glabrous or merely soft pubescent, glaucous, often clumped forming thickets; *Leaves* compound, odd-pinnate, the leaflets 11–31, thin, much paler beneath, sharply serrate, lanceolate to narrowly oblong, 5–10 cm. long, tapering to a point; *Flowers* in terminal dense panicles, open and up to 4.5 dm. long, the perfect or pistillate flowers dense and smaller; *Flowers* greenish-white or yellow, petals 5; *Calyx* small, 5-parted; *Sta-* mens 5, inserted under the edge or between the lobes of a flattened disk in the bottom of the calyx; *Drupes* covered with minute bright-red acrid appressed hairs (about 0.2 mm. long), indehiscent. June–July.

Dry soils, road embankments, thickets, dry wastes, upland soils, old fields, and margins of woods. Native. Throughout all the United States excepting an area in northern North Dakota and northeastern Montana; north into southern Canada from southwern Quebec to British Columbia; south into Mexico.

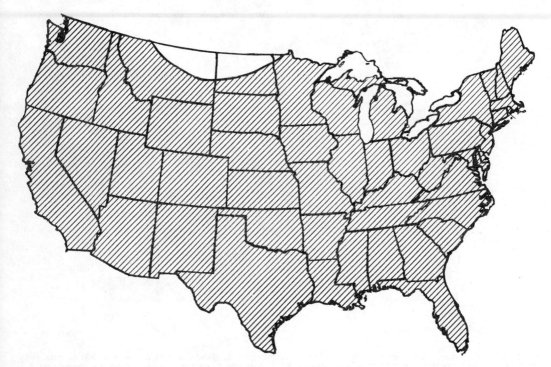

Distribution of *Rhus glabra* L.

FIGURE 125.—*Rhus glabra* L. Smooth sumac. *A*, Habit—× 0.5; *B*, flowers—× 5: *b*, diagram of flower to show disk with stamens—× 6; *C*, fruit—× 2.5; *D*, seeds—× 2.5.

ANACARDIACEAE

Rhus radicans L.

(*Toxicodendron radicans* (L.) Kuntze)

Perennial woody shrub or vine, reproducing by seeds and by creeping rootstocks from the basal stem nodes, sometimes running horizontally underground for several meters, sending up leafy shoots from their nodes (Fig. 126); *Stems* erect and shrubby or a vine climbing high into trees, on fences, the stem supported by aerial roots along the stem; *Leaves* alternate, quite variable in outline and in marginal cutting, ovate or elliptic, acute or tapering to a point, rounded to wedge-shaped at the base, entire to irregularly serrate or wavy, glabrous or thinly pubescent, compound with 3 large shiny leaflets, each 5–10 cm. long, pointed at the tip, the terminal leaflet longer petioled than the lateral leaflets; *Panicles* up to 1 dm. long, axillary or from axils of past years, ascending and divergent; *Flowers* small, yellowish-green, 5-petaled; *Drupes* small, 5–6 mm. in diameter, grayish-white, nearly globose, hard, usually glabrous, with a grayish striped, 1-seeded stone about 3–4 mm. in diameter. June–July.

Rocky fields, pastures, thickets, woods, and waste places, often climbing trees, fences, and dwellings; a ubiquitous weed. All parts of the plant contain a poisonous principle that may cause blistering of the skin. A variable species as to habit in growth, leaflet shape, rooting habit, pubescence of the leaves, petioles, and fruit, giving reason for several named varieties and forms. Native, Throughout the United States; north into southern Canada from Quebec to British Columbia; south into Mexico; West Indies.

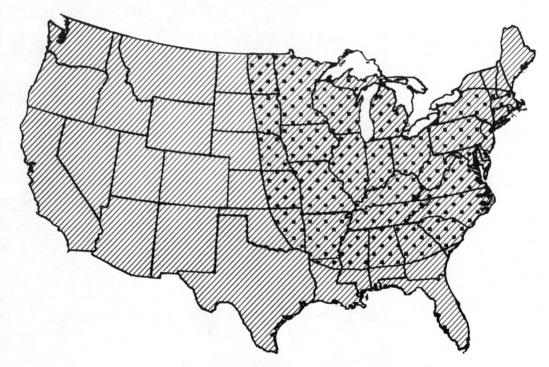

Distribution of *Rhus radicans* L.

FIGURE 126.—*Rhus radicans* L. Poison ivy. *A*, Habit— × 0.5; *B*, flower panicle— × 0.5; *C*, flowers— × 4; *D*, drupe— × 2.5; *E*, stones— × 2.5; *F*, aerial roots— × 2.5

ANACARDIACEAE

Rhus toxicodendron L. — POISON OAK

(R. quercifolia (Michx.) Steud.; Toxicodendron quercifolium Greene)

Perennial shrub, reproducing from seeds and spreading by subterranean stolons (Fig. 127); *Stems* slender, erect, woody for 0.5–6 dm., simple or with a few erect branches, not climbing, nor with aerial roots; *Leaves* 3-parted, on long erect velvety petioles, mostly near the top of the stem and often appearing falsely whorled; *Leaflets* elliptic, rhombic or obovate, hairy above, velvety beneath or eventually glabrous above, obtuse or rounded above, with 3–7 deep teeth or variously lobed, suggesting oak leaves, or unlobed (**forma *elobata* Fern.**), wedge-shaped to rounded at the base; *Fruit* (drupe) greenish to buff, about 5 mm. in diameter, pubescent or glabrous (**forma *leiocarpa* Fern.**). Flowering May–June; fruiting August–November, sometimes all winter.

Dry barrens, sandy wastes, pinewoods, and sandy woods. Native. Throughout the southeastern area of the United States from New Jersey to Florida, west to Missouri, eastern Oklahoma, and Texas.

ANACARDIACEAE

Rhus diversiloba Torr. & Gray — WESTERN POISON OAK

Perennial woody shrub or vine; *Stems* forming an upright shrub (common form), with many small woody stems rising from the ground, or attached to upright objects for support, becoming a vine, up to 8–10 m. high; *Leaves* 3-parted, very irregular as to lobing, especially the two lateral ones, the margins either even or lobed, the surface of the leaves usually glossy and uneven, thus appearing thick and leathery; *Flowers* in clusters on slender stems diverging from the axis of the leaf, greenish-white, about 2–3 mm. in diameter; *Drupes* spherical or somewhat flattened, greenish or creamy-white, with a smooth glossy surface, striped into segments, the fruits remaining on the plants fall and winter. Fruiting mid-October.

Roadsides, cultivated fields, and abandoned land. Native. Western half of Washington and Oregon; north to British Columbia; south through most of California to Baja California, Mexico.

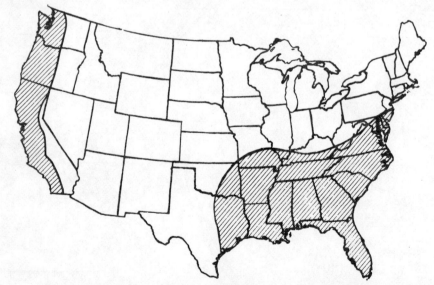

Distribution of *Rhus toxicodendron* L. (Eastern United States) and *Rhus diversiloba* Torr. & Gray (Western United States)

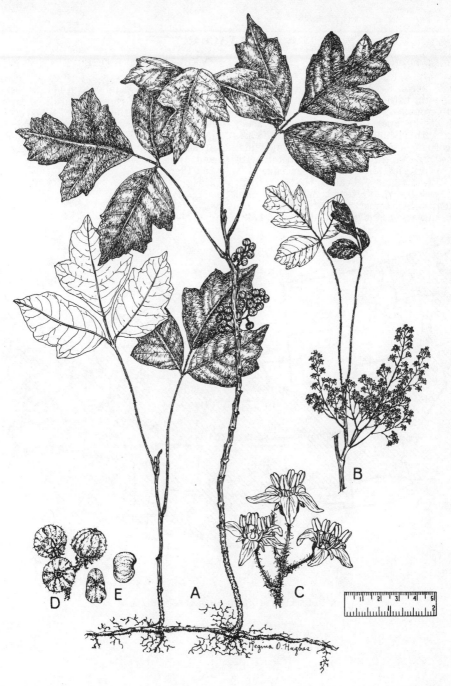

FIGURE 127.—*Rhus toxicodendron* L.   Poison oak.   *A*, Habit—× 0.5; *B*, inflorescence—× 0.5; *C*, flowers—× 5;
D, drupes—× 2; *E*, stones—× 2.

MALVACEAE

Abutilon theophrasti Medic.

Annual herb, 6–12 dm. high (Fig. 128); *Stem* smooth, with short velvety hairs; *Leaves* alternate, round to cordate at the base, taper-pointed at the apex, velvety, hairy-surfaced; *Flowers* with peduncles shorter than the petioles, corolla of 5 yellow petals, 2 cm. wide; *Seed pod* cup-shaped, 2.5 cm. in diameter, with a ring of prickles about the upper edge, the carpels 12–15, hairy, beaked, 5–15 seeded; *Seed* grayish-brown, flattened, notched, 3 mm. long. August–September.

Waste places, vacant lots, gardens, and culti-vated fields, especially corn and soybean fields, and along fence rows. Naturalized from India. Throughout all the United States excepting a large area along the northern boundary, areas in northern Wisconsin, Michigan, and Maine, areas in southwestern and south central Texas, and areas in southern Arizona, New Mexico, and Florida.

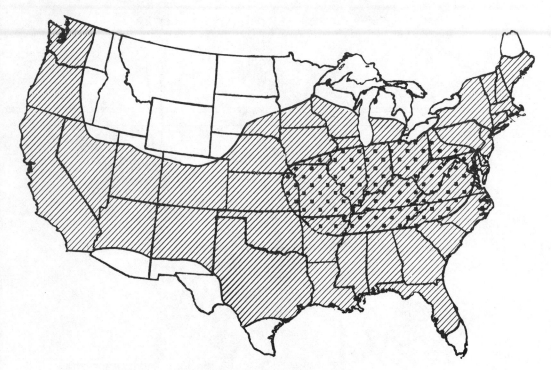

Distribution of *Abutilon theophrasti* Medic.

FIGURE 128.—*Abutilon theophrasti* Medic. Velvetleaf. *A*, Habit—× 0.5; *B*, rootstock—× 0.5; *C*, flower—× 2.25; *D*, capsule—× 1; *E*, carpels—× 1.5; *F*, seeds—× 4.5.

Malva neglecta Wallr.

Annual or *biennial* herb, reproducing by seeds, with a short straight taproot (Fig. 129); *Stems* 10–30 cm. long, procumbent or branching at the base, nearly erect, or spreading on the ground with the tips generally turned up, more or less pubescent, especially when young, often with star-shaped pubescence; *Leaves* alternate, round-heart-shaped to round-kidney-shaped, 2–6 cm. wide, simple, on very long slender petioles, toothed with 5–9 shallow rounded lobes or lobeless, more or less pubescent on both sides; *Flowers* small, with 5 whitish or pale-lilac petals, borne singly or in clusters in the axils of many leaves; *Petals* about 1 cm. long, twice as long as the calyx; *Bractlets* linear to linear-lanceolate; *Carpels* round-margined, smooth, not reticulated on the back; *Seed pod* a flattened disk, when ripe breaking up into 10–20 small, hairy, 1-seeded sections; *Seed* nearly round, flattened, reddish-brown, about 1 mm. in diameter, notched. April–October.

Cultivated fields, waste places, gardens, lawns, roadsides, and barnyards. Naturalized from Europe. Thoughout the United States.

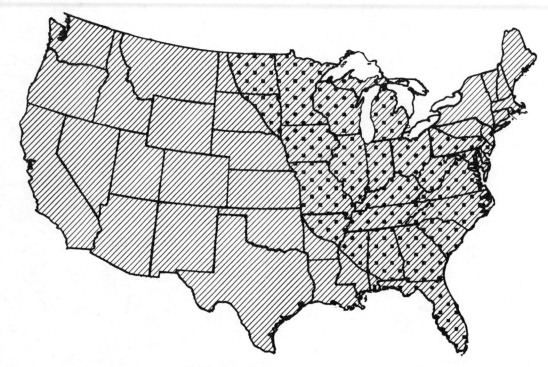

Distribution of *Malva neglecta* Wallr.

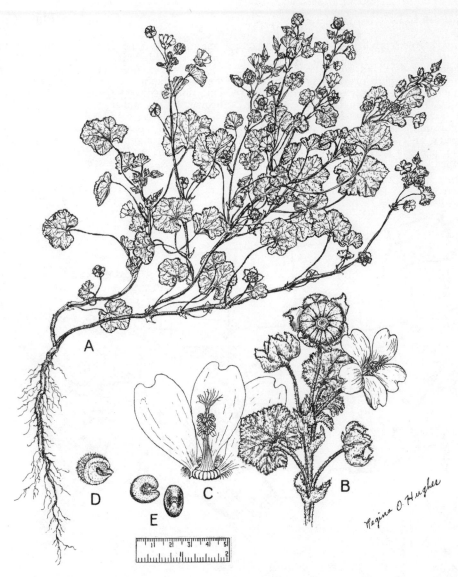

FIGURE 129.—*Malva neglecta* Wallr. Common mallow. *A*, Habit—× 0.5; *B*, enlarged branchlet—× 2; *C*, flower diagram—× 5; *D*, carpel—× 5; *E*, seeds—× 5.

MALVACEAE

Sida spinosa L.

Annual herb, reproducing by seeds (Fig. 130); *Taproot* slender, branching, rather long; *Stems* erect, 0.2–1 m. tall, softly hairy, bearing 2–3 short, blunt, spiny projections below each node, much-branched; *Leaves* alternate, simple, ovate-lanceolate or oblong, 2–4 cm. long, toothed, rather long-petioled; *Peduncles* axillary, 1-flowered, shorter than the petiole; *Flowers* solitary or clustered in the axils of the leaves, on pedicels 2–12 mm. long; *Calyx* thin, star-shaped; *Petals* 5, pale-yellow, 4–6 mm.

long; *Carpels* 5, pubescent at summit, combined into an ovoid fruit; *Seed pod* splitting at the top into 5 1-seeded sections, each with 2 sharp, spreading spines at the top; *Seed* 1–2 mm. long, 3-angled, egg-shaped, dull, dark reddish-brown. June–October.

Waste places, cultivated fields, open ground, gardens, and pastures. Naturalized from the Tropics. Throughout approximately the eastern two-thirds of the United States.

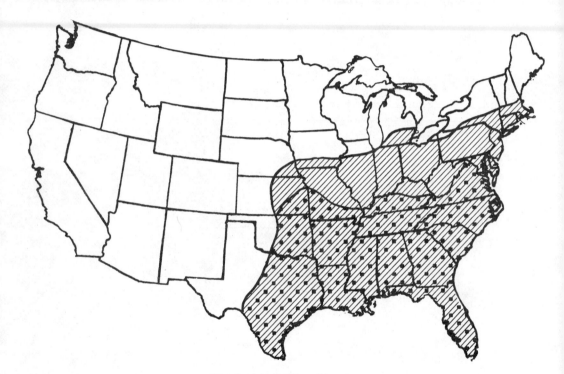

Distribution of *Sida spinosa* L.

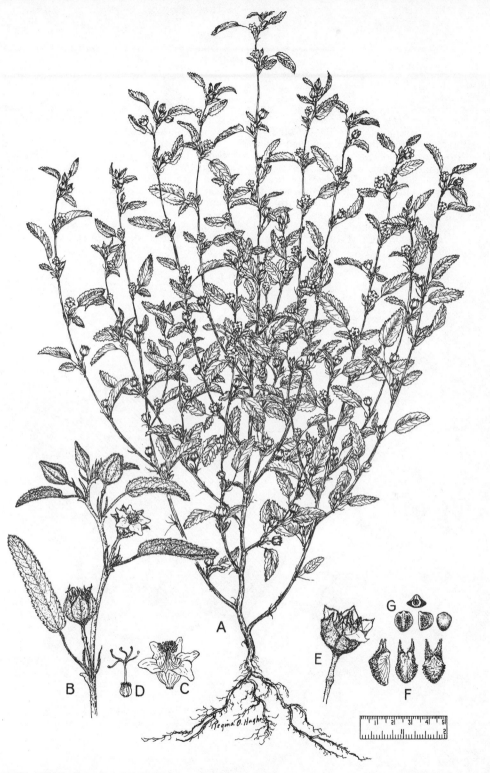

FIGURE 130.—*Sida spinosa* L. Prickly sida. *A,* Habit—× 0.5; *B,* upper part of branch, showing tubercles at base of leaves—× 3; *C,* flower, with oblique petals and united stamens—× 3; *D,* carpels with 5 styles—× 3; *E,* capsule, enclosed in the persistent calyx—× 2.5; *F,* carpels—× 3; *G,* seeds—× 3.

Hypericum perforatum L.   ST. JOHNSWORT

Perennial herb, reproducing by seeds and rootstocks (Fig. 131); *Root system* branched and extending to considerable depth, shallow short rootstocks extending out a few decimeters from the crown; *Stems* smooth, branched, erect, somewhat 2-edged, 3–9 dm. tall, woody at the base, producing leafy basal outshoots; *Leaves* opposite, elliptic to oblong, covered with small translucid dots; *Cymes* leafy, with numerous flowers; *Flowers* about 2 cm. in diameter, 5-petaled, orange-yellow with occasional black dots along the edge of the petals; *Seed pods* rounded, pointed, with 3 parts and many seeds; *Seed* about 1.5 mm. long, cylindrical, blackish, shiny with a rough, pitted, resinous surface. June–September.

Meadows, dry pastures, rangelands, and neglected fields and along roadsides. Difficult to eradicate; not relished by grazing animals; may cause skin irritation and loss of condition in livestock, especially white animals. Naturalized from Europe. Throughout approximately the eastern half of the United States; Pacific Northwest area south to northern California and central Nevada; north into southern Canada in Quebec and Ontario.

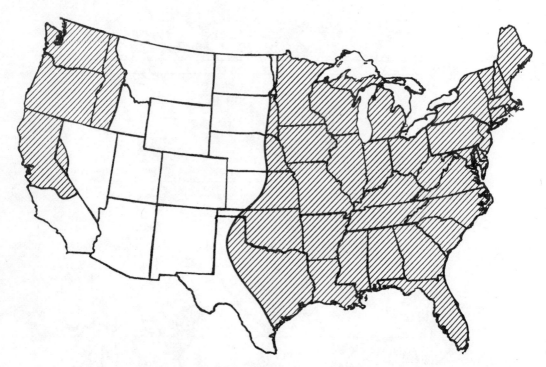

Distribution of *Hypericum perforatum* L.

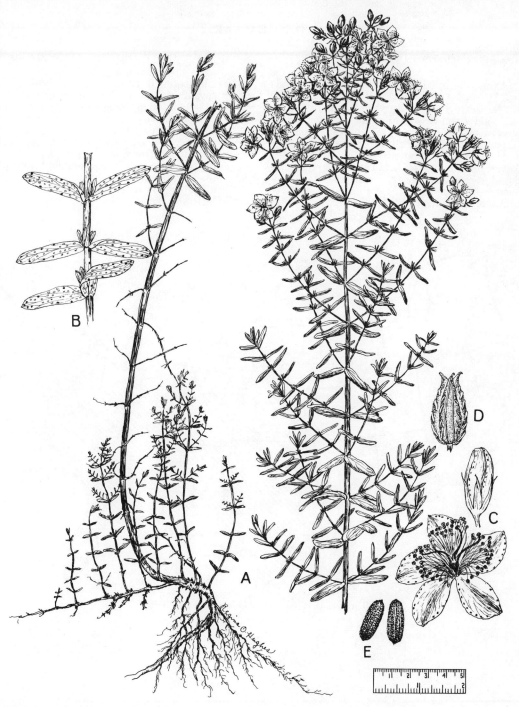

FIGURE 131.—*Hypericum perforatum* L. St. Johnswort. *A*, Habit—× 0.5; *B*, enlarged leaves—× 1.5; *C*, flower and bud—× 2; *D*, capsule—× 3; *E*, seeds—× 10.

Jussiaea decurrens (Walt.) DC.   WINGED WATERPRIMROSE

Annual herb, with clustered roots, reproducing by seeds (Fig. 132); *Stems* erect, nearly simple to freely ascending branched, up to 2 m. tall, glabrous, 4-angled, and sometimes 4-winged by the decurrent leaf bases; *Leaves* alternate, lanceolate or linear-lanceolate, nearly sessile, 5–18 cm. long, membranaceous, the leaves on the threadlike branches greatly reduced in size; *Flowers* from many axils, on pedicels 1–10 mm. long; *Hypanthium* at anthesis cone-shaped, 4-angled, 1–2 cm. long; *Calyx seg-*ments and petals 6–12 mm. long; *Capsule* slenderly pyramidal, 4-angled or narrowly 4-winged, 1–2 cm. long; *Seed* ellipsoid, free from the endocarp, 0.3–0.4 mm. long, in several rows in each locule. May–October.

Swamps, wet wastelands, ditches, and wet fields. Native. Throughout approximately all the South Atlantic and South Central States of the United States; also in areas in some North Central States; south through Mexico to tropical America.

Distribution of *Jussiaea decurrens* (Walt.) DC.

FIGURE 132.—*Jussiaea decurrens* (Walt.) DC. Winged waterprimrose. *A*, Habit—× 0.5; *B*, flower—× 1.5; *C*, capsule—× 1.5; *D*, seeds—× 16.

ONAGRACEAE

Jussiaea repens L. var. glabrescens Kuntze　　　　　Creeping Waterprimrose

Perennial herb, reproducing by seeds and spreading by stolons (Fig. 133) ; *Stems* prostrate or floating or ascending at the tips, rooting at the nodes, glabrous or very sparsely finely hairy; *Leaves* glabrous, or almost so, 3–9 cm. long, lanceolate to oblanceolate or obovate, obtuse or acute, narrowed at the base into a petiole 2–5 cm. long; *Hypanthium* at time of flowering cylindric, 7–12 mm. long, its pedicel 3–8 cm. long, smooth; *Petals* 10–15 mm. long; *Calyx segments* glabrous or slightly pubescent, about 1 cm. long; *Capsule* subcylindric, 3–5 cm. long, its pedicel 3–8 cm. long; *Seed* in one series in each locule, longer than thick with a blunt end, the true seed completely covered. June–October.

Swamps, ponds, wet areas, muddy places, and ditches. Native. Throughout approximately the south-central area of the United States; part of Georgia and Florida; southern New Jersey and most of the Delmarva Peninsula; south into Mexico.

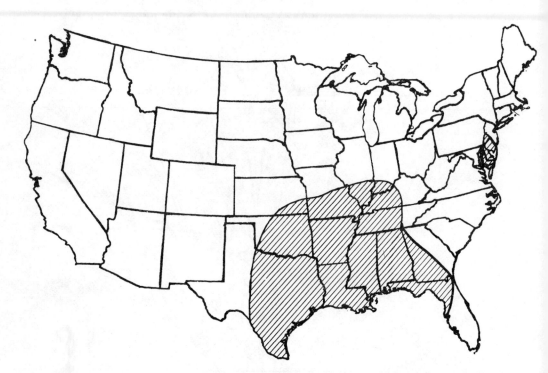

Distribution of *Jussiaea repens* L. var. *glabrescens* Kuntze

FIGURE 133.—*Jussiaea repens* L. var. *glabrescens* Kuntze.   Creeping waterprimrose.   *A*, Habit, showing bladder
on root—× 0.5; *B*, enlarged flower—× 1; *C* capsule—× 1; *D*, seeds with endocarp—× 6; *E*, seeds—× 6.

HALORAGACEAE

Myriophyllum exalbescens Fern.

Perennial aquatic herb, reproducing by seeds, running rhizomes, and fragments of the stems (Fig. 134); *Stems* simple or forking, purplish, when dry becoming white, up to 1 m. in length; *Leaves* whorled, in 3's or 4's, 1.2–3 cm. long, with 6–11 pairs of capillary flaccid or slightly stiffish divisions, the primary leaves submersed, 1–5 cm. long, 1.4 cm. broad; *Spikes* almost naked, terminal, with the flowers in whorls, the lower flowers pistillate, the upper staminate; *Bracts* persistent, rarely equaling the fruit, spatulate-obovate or oblong-shell-shaped, 0.8–1.8 mm. long, the lower serrate, the upper entire; *Bracteoles* ovate, entire, 0.7–1 mm. long; *Petals* oblong-obovate, con-cave, 2.5 mm. long; *Anthers* 1.2–1.8 mm. long; *Schizocarp* nearly globose, very slenderly 4-sulcate, 2.3–3 mm. long; *Mericarps* rounded on the back, smooth or roughened. July–September.

Lakes, ponds, pools, and quiet waters, often brackish or calcareous: especially troublesome around the edges of lakes. Native. Throughout the northern part of the United States, south to Delaware on the east coast and to the Mexican border on the west; south into northwestern Mexico; north into Canada from Newfoundland and Labrador to Alaska; Greenland. Often treated as **M. spicatum var. exalbescens (Fern.) Jepson.**

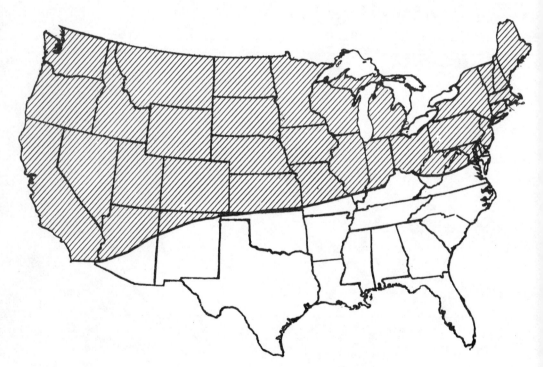

Distribution of *Myriophyllum exalbescens* Fern.

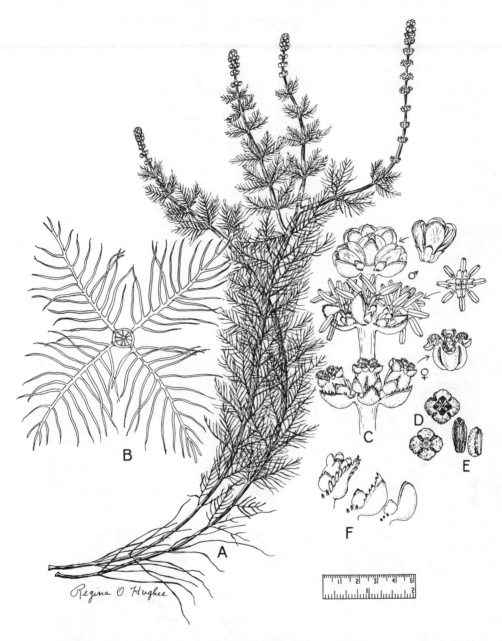

FIGURE 134.—*Myriophyllum exalbescens* Fern. Northern watermilfoil. *A*, Habit—× 0.5; *B*, whorl of leaves— × 1.5; *C*, flower spike, with male and female flowers—× 5; *D*, schizocarps—× 5; *E*, mericarps—× 5; *F*, bracts— × 5.

HALORAGACEAE

Myriophyllum heterophyllum Michx.

Perennial aquatic herbs (Fig. 135); *Stems* simple or branching, stoutish, up to 8 mm. in diameter, 6–12 dm. long, or longer; *Leaves* whorled in 4's and 6's, the submersed leaves pinnate, 2–5 cm. long with 7–10 pairs of divisions, the amphibious leaves slightly divided, the emersed leaves and bracts firm, lanceolate or lance-spatulate to elliptic, entire or serrate, 0.4–3 m. long, 1.5–5 mm. broad; *Spikes* usually above water in summer, 0.3–3.7 dm. long; *Flowers* sessile, in whorls of 4–6, chiefly in the axils of the upper leaves, both sexes together, or the lower flowers pistillate and the upper flowers staminate; *Bracts* whorled, long-persistent and eventually reflexed, lanceolate to oblong, or obovate, sharply denticulate, 4–18 mm. long; *Bracteoles* ovate, acuminate, serrate, 1–1.3 mm. long, 0.5–0.7 mm. broad; *Petals* of staminate flowers acutish, 1.5–3 mm. long; *Stamens* 4, 1–2.5 mm. long; *Schizocarp* nearly globose, 1–1.5 mm. long and wide, minutely papillose; *Mericarps* 2-ridged on the back and rounded on the sides, with conspicuous ascending beaks. June–September.

Ponds, streams, and lakes. Eastern half of the United States; most abundant toward the South; north into Ontario and southwestern Quebec.

M. hippurioides Nutt. is not too dissimilar from **M. heterophyllum** and may prove to be identical with it. *Stems* simple or branching, 3–6 dm. long; *Leaves* whorled in 4's or 5's, the emersed ones linear, about 1 mm. wide, conspicuously or obscurely serrate or the uppermost ones nearly entire, 1.5–3 mm. long, the submersed leaves pinnately dissected into capillary divisions, 1.5–3 cm. long; *Flowers* chiefly in the axils of the emersed leaves; *Petals* white, obovate; *Mericarps* 0.2 mm. long, slightly rounded on the back.

Western half of the United States.

Distribution of *Myriophyllum heterophyllum* Michx. in the eastern half of the United States and *M. hippurioides* Nutt. in the western half of the United States

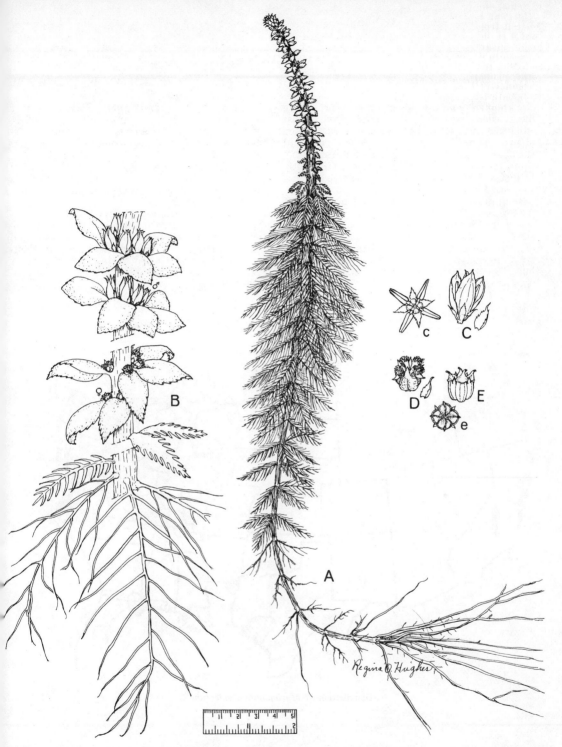

FIGURE 135.—*Myriophyllum heterophyllum* Michx. Broadleaf watermilfoil. *A*, Habit—× 0.5; *B*, leaf and flower detail—× 2.5; *C*, staminate flower and bract—× 5; *C*, diagram of staminate flower—× 5; *D*, pistillate flower and bract—× 5; *E*, mature fruits—× 5; *e*, top view of mature fruits.

HALORAGACEAE

Myriophyllum spicatum L.

Perennial aquatic-rooted herb, reproducing by seeds, but very commonly and most efficiently spreading by rhizomes, fragmented stems, and axillary buds that occur throughout the year (Fig. 136); *Stems* long and branching, often from a depth of 15 feet (most frequently to 5 ft. deep), often forming extensive mats at the surafce of the water, brick-red or olive-green in dried specimens; *Leaves* whorled in 3's or 4's, to 35 mm. long, the principal leaves of the primary stems with 14–21 pairs of rigid slenderly linear divisions; *Bracts* rhombic-obovate to elongate, the bractlets nearly round or kidney-shaped, broader than long, 0.5–0.8 long; *Spikes* terminal, 2.5–10 cm. long, often standing above the water level, after pol-lination then resubmerging; *Flowers* (after emergence) with the stigmas ripening well in advance of the stamens (favoring cross-pollination); *Petals* deciduous before ripening of the stamens; *Anthers linear*, 1.8–2.2 mm. long; *Floral bracts* longer than the fruits; *Schizocarp* 4-locular, with 4 seeds; *Mericarps* spherical, 4-angled, 2.5–3 mm. in diameter. Late July–September.

In fresh and saline waters, on muck to hard-packed sand; most common and a nuisance, especially to sportsmen. Native of Eurasia and parts of Africa. In many distinct areas in Eastern and Central United States, as far west as Wisconsin and Texas; distinct area in west central California.

Distribution of *Myriophyllum spicatum* L.

FIGURE 136.—*Myriophyllum spicatum* L. Eurasian watermilfoil. *A*, Habit—× 0.5; *B*, Whorl of leaves—× 2; *C*, part of flower spike, with pistillate flowers below and staminate flowers above—× 4; *D*, immature fruits—× 4; *E*, mature fruit—× 4.

UMBELLIFERAE

Cicuta maculata L.

Perennial herb, reproducing by seed and by fleshy roots (Fig. 137); *Roots* elongated, 3–10 cm. long, crowded or tufted; *Stems* erect, branching, stout, hollow, jointed, streaked with purple, ridged, glabrous, 1–2.2 m. tall; *Leaves* alternate or basal, petioled, the 3 major divisions nearly compound with leaflets lanceolate to oblong-lanceolate, 3–12 cm. long, pointed, deeply serrate, glabrous; *Flowers* in open spreading umbels having no involucre, but involucels of slender bractlets, pedicels of the smaller umbels very unequal; *Calyx teeth* prominent; *Corolla* white; stylopodium depressed; *Mericarps* broadly oval, about 2.5–3.5 mm. long, flat on one side, rounded with 5 light ribs on the other side, oil tubes solitary between the ridges, brown with yellow ribs. June–August.

Marshy ground, pastures, and wet meadows and along ditches and streams. Roots poisonous when eaten. Native. Throughout approximately all the eastern half of the United States excepting areas in the South Atlantic and Gulf Coast States.

Distribution of *Cicuta maculata* L.

Figure 137.—*Cicuta maculata* L. Spotted waterhemlock. *A*, Habit—× 0.5; *B*, flower—× 7.5; *C*, schizocarp—× 5; *D*, mericarp—× 5.

Conium maculatum L.   POISON HEMLOCK

Biennial herb, reproducing by seeds (Fig. 138); *Taproot* long, white, often branched; *Stems* erect, branching, stout, glabrous, purple-spotted, ridged, up to 3 m. tall; *Leaves* alternate or basal, 2–4 dm. long, petioled, broadly triangular-ovate in outline, 3–4 times pinnately compound, the leaflets lanceolate to ovate-oblong, dentate or finely cut, 4–10 mm. long; *Inflorescence* in large open compound umbels, the umbels 4–6 cm. wide, the terminal inflorescence blooming first but soon overtopped by the others; *Involucral bracts* entire; *Corolla* white; *Schizocarp* containing 2 mericarps; *Mericarps* broadly ovoid, about 2–3 mm. long, granular, with conspicuous pale-brown wavy ribs, without oil tubes but with a layer of secreting cells next to the seed, grayish-brown; face of the seed deeply and narrowly concave. June–September.

Borders of fields, pastures, meadows, roadsides, and waste places; on rich, gravelly, or loamy soils. All parts of plant notoriously poisonous, fatal (given to Socrates in ancient Greece). Introduced and naturalized from Eurasia. Throughout all the United States excepting an area between central Montana and northeastern Minnesota.

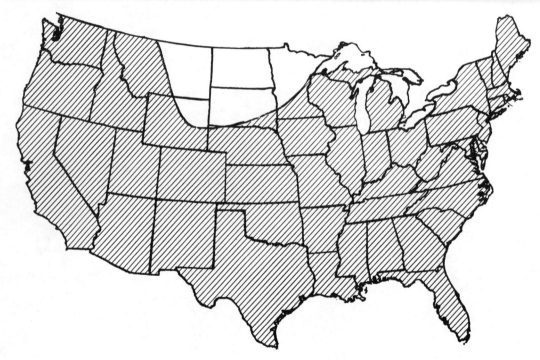

Distribution of *Conium maculatum* L.

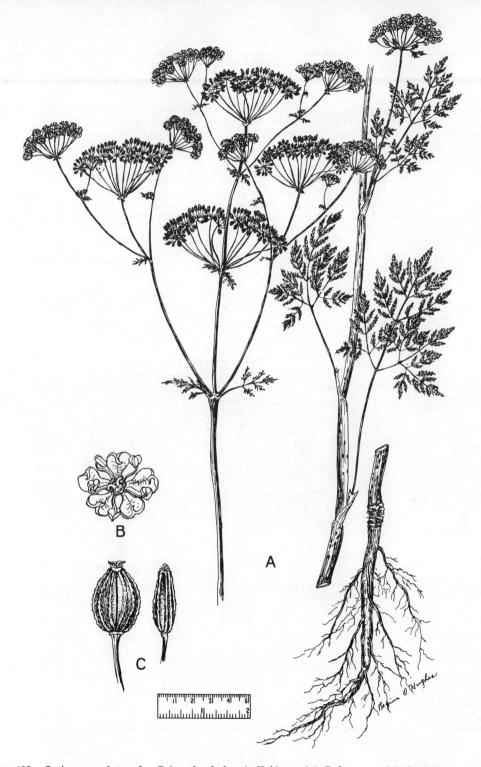

FIGURE 138.—*Conium maculatum* L. Poison hemlock. *A*, Habit—× 0.5; *B*, flower—× 7.5; *C*, schizocarps—× 7.5.

UMBELLIFERAE

Daucus carota L.

WILD CARROT, QUEEN-ANNES-LACE

Biennial herb, reproducing by seeds (Fig. 139); *Taproot* bearing a rosette of leaves the first season; *Stems* erect, branching, slender, hollow, ridged, bristly-hairy, 3–16 dm. high, bearing scattered stem leaves; *Leaves* alternate or basal, oblong in general outline, pinnately nearly compound, the ultimate segments linear, lanceolate or oblong, often lobed, somewhat hairy; stem leaves sessile, with a sheathing base; basal leaves long-petioled; *Flowers* in flat-topped umbels, which become concave as the fruits mature, 6–15 cm. broad; *Involucral*

bracts cleft or pinnatifid into narrow segments; *Corolla* white to pinkish, usually with one purple or pink flower in the center; *Mericarps* oblong, 2–4 mm. long, 1 side flattened, the other with 5 bristly primary ribs and 4 conspicuous secondary ribs that are winged and near a row of barbed prickles, oil tubes solitary under the secondary ribs and also 2 on the flat side, light grayish-brown. May–October.

Dry fields, old meadows, pastures, and waste places; a pernicious weed. Introduced from Eurasia. Throughout most of the United States.

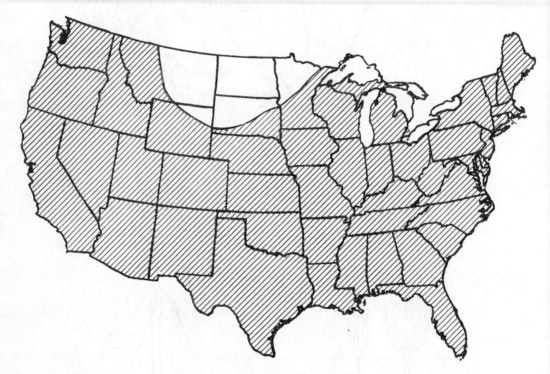

Distribution of *Daucus carota* L.

FIGURE 139.—*Daucus carota* L. Wild carrot. *A*, Habit—× 0.5; *B*, flowers—× 5; *C*, schizocarp—× 5; *D*, cross section of fruit, showing 2 mericarps—× 3.

APOCYNACEAE

Apocynum cannabinum L.

Perennial herb, reproducing by seed and long, horizontal rootstocks (Fig. 140); *Stems* erect, 3–6 dm. tall, from a woody base, exuding milky juice when broken, glabrous or nearly so; *Leaves* erect or ascending, blades 5–12 cm. long, ovate to lanceolate, smooth-edged, glabrous to sparingly pubescent beneath, petiole 2–7 mm. long to nearly sessile; *Cymes* terminal, of mostly ascending flowers with 5 greenish-white petals, 2–4 mm. long, the lobes erect; *Bracts* dry and thin, linear-attenuate, not per-sisting; *Pod* (follicle) 1.2–2 dm. long and slender, falcate; *Seed* 4–6 mm. long, thin and flat, with a tuft of soft silky hairs at one end (coma 2.5–3 cm. long). June–August.

In old fields, wastelands, dumps, thickets, borders of woods, and open ground. Native. Poisonous to cattle. Throughout all the United States excepting an area from central Montana east to northeastern Minnesota; north into Canada from western Quebec to Alberta.

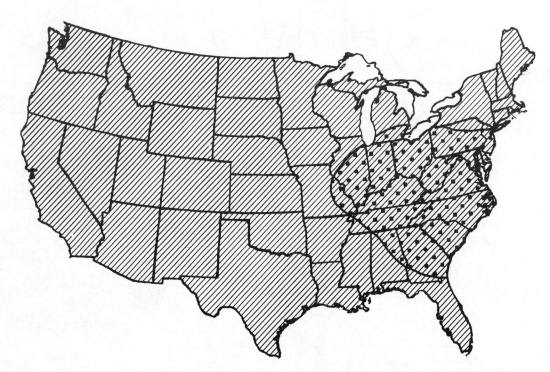

Distribution of *Apocynum cannabinum* L.

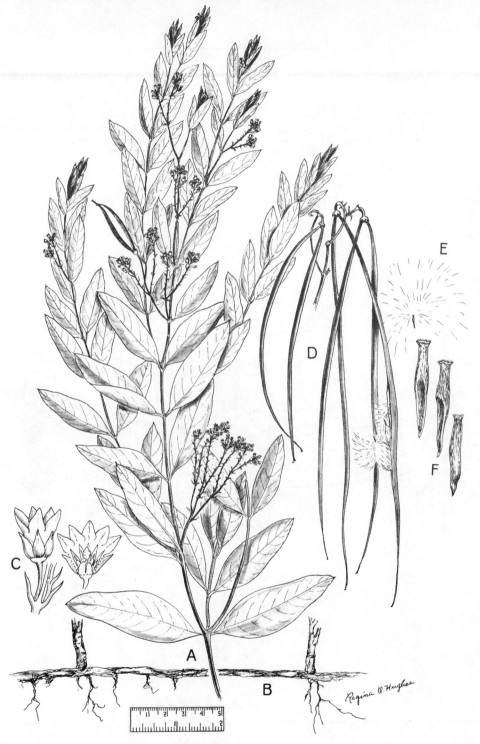

FIGURE 140.—*Apocynum cannabinum* L. Hemp dogbane. *A*, Habit—× 0.5; *B*, rootstock—× 0.5; *C*, flowers—× 5; *D*, follicles—× 0.5; *E*, seed with coma—× 1; *F*, seeds—× 5.

ASCLEPIADACEAE

Asclepias syriaca L.   COMMON MILKWEED

Perennial herb, reproducing by seeds and from long-spreading rhizomes (Fig. 141); *Stems* stout and erect, mostly simple, up to 2 m., covered with short, downy hairs, with milky juice; *Leaves* opposite, oblong, rounded, 1–2.6 dm. long, 0.4–1.8 dm. broad, with prominent veins, upper surface smooth, lower surfaces covered with short white hairs and with strong transverse nerves; *Flowers* sweet-smelling, pink to white, in large, many-flowered, bell-like clusters at the tips of the stems and in the axils of the upper leaves, corolla lobes 6–9

mm. long, hoods 3–4 mm. high; *Pod* (follicle) grayish, hairy and beset with soft spiny projections, 1–3 mm. high, slenderly ovoid, 2.5–3.5 cm. thick; *Seed* brown, flat, oval, 6 mm. long, 5 mm. wide, with a tuft of silky white hairs attached to the tip. June–August.

Dry and cultivated fields, pastures, woods, roadsides, and thickets; also on prairies in the West. Native. Throughout all the eastern half of the United States excepting States or parts of States along the gulf coast; north into Canada from New Brunswick to Saskatchewan.

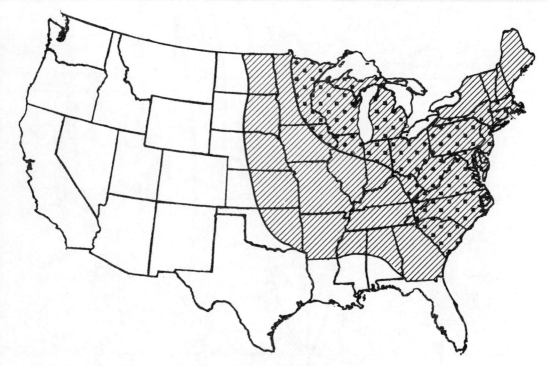

Distribution of *Asclepias syriaca* L.

FIGURE 141.—*Asclepias syriaca* L. Common milkweed. *A*, Habit—× 0.5; *B*, flower, upper view—× 3.5: side view—× 2; *C*, follicles—× 0.5; *D*, seeds with coma—× 3.

ASCLEPIADACEAE

Asclepias verticillata L.

Perennial herb, reproducing from seeds and creeping rootstocks (Fig. 142); *Stems* slender, erect, 3–9 dm. high, smooth, branching at top of plant only, with milky juice; *Leaves* linear, light-green, arranged in groups of 3 or 7, in whorls around the stem, 2–5 cm. long, 1–2 mm. wide, rolled backwards and downward; *Flowers* in umbels, borne in clusters at the top of the stem or in the axils of the upper leaves, hoods roundish-oval, peduncles 1–3 cm. long; *Petals* greenish-white, 5, ovate, 4–5 mm. long; *Pod* (follicle) erect on erect stalk, 4–5 cm. long, containing numerous seed; *Seed* flat, brown, with a tuft of fine hairs at the tip, June–August.

Meadows, pastures, barrens, and waste and sterile places; seldom in cultivated fields. Poisonous to livestock. Throughout all the eastern and central areas of the United States excepting northern New England; north into Canada from Ontario to Saskatchewan.

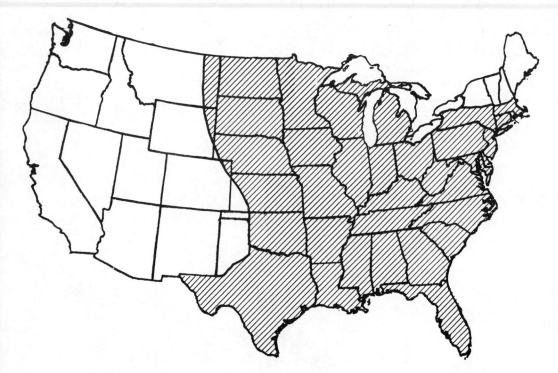

Distribution of *Asclepias verticillata* L.

FIGURE 142.—*Asclepias verticillata* L. Eastern whorled milkweed. *A*, Habit—× 0.5; *B*, enlarged leaves, showing revolute margins—× 1.5; *C*, flower—× 3.5; *D*, seed—× 4: *d*, seeds with coma—× 1.

CONVOLVULACEAE

Convolvulus arvensis L.

FIELD BINDWEED

Perennial herb, reproducing by seeds and creeping roots; *Root system* extensive, may go down 6–9 m. (Fig. 143); *Stems* glabrous to pubescent, slender, 1–3 m. long, twining or spreading over the surface of the ground; *Leaves* alternate, simple, very variable, long-petioled, entire, ovate-oblong, with hastate, cordate or sagittate bases, glabrous, up to 5 cm. long; *Flowers* perfect, regular, 1.5–2 cm. wide, usually borne singly in the axils of the leaves; *Flower stalk* with 2 bracts, 1.2–2.5 cm. below the flower; *Calyx* small, bell-shaped; *Corolla* white or pink, funnel-shaped; *Stamens* 5, attached to the corolla; *Pistil* compound with 2 threadlike stigmas, the ovary 2-celled; *Capsule* ovate, usually 2-celled, containing 4 seeds; *Seed* ovoid, dull, dark brownish-gray, ccarsely roughened, about 3–5 mm. long, with 1 rounded and 2 (or only 1) flattened sides. June–September.

All uncultivated areas and waste places, grainfields, and gardens; able to grow under most cultivated conditions; a most serious weed wherever it grows. Introduced and naturalized from Eurasia. Throughout all the United States excepting the extreme Southeast, parts of southern Texas, New Mexico, and southern Arizona; north into southern Canada from Nova Scotia to British Columbia.

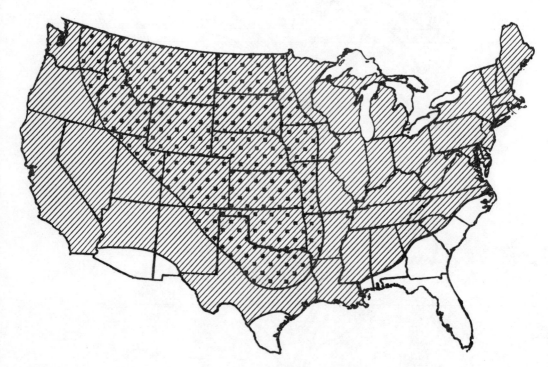

Distribution of *Convolvulus arvensis* L.

FIGURE 143.—*Convolvulus arvensis* L.   Field bindweed.   *A*, Habit—× 0.5; *B*, rootstock—× 0.5; *C*, leaf variation
—× 0.5; *D*, flower, showing 5 stamens of unequal length—× 1; *E*, capsule—× 3; *F*, seeds—× 4.

CONVOLVULACEAE

Convolvulus sepium L.

Perennial vining herb, reproducing by seeds and fleshy creeping rootstocks (Fig. 144); *Roots* extensive but relatively shallow; *Stems* coarse, glabrous to pubescent, 9–30 dm. long, twining on plants or trailing on the surface of the ground; *Leaves* alternate, simple, large, about 1 dm. long, elongated, heart-shaped, or triangular-ovate to narrowly lanceolate, usually sharp-pointed at the tip, the basal lobes large, long-petioled; *Flowers* axillary, on 4-angled, short to prolonged spreading or ascending stalks; *Bracts* paired, heart-shaped, ovate, 1.5–3.5 cm. long; *Calyx* of 5 overlapping sepals; *Corolla* bell-shaped to funnelform, white to pinkish, 4–8 cm. high, nearly or quite as broad; *Stamens* 5, 2–3.3 cm. long, attached to the corolla; *Capsule* globose, about 8–10 mm. in diameter, 2-celled, containing from 2–4 seeds, usually covered by the bracts and the calyx; *Seed* ovoid, 4–5 mm. long, slate-colored to black, dull, usually with 1 rounded and 2 flattened sides. A variable species. Mid-May–September.

Cultivated fields, fence rows, shores, thickets, waste places, and bottomlands; a serious weed, often densely covering banks and roadside shrubbery. Native of Eurasia. Throughout approximately the eastern half of the United States, extending as far west as Colorado and New Mexico; throughout parts of the Northwestern States; north into southern Canada from Newfoundland to British Columbia; New Zealand.

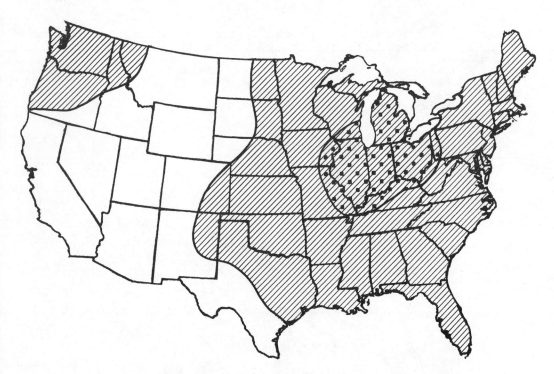

Distribution of *Convolvulus sepium* L.

FIGURE 144.—*Convolvulus sepium* L. Hedge bindweed. *A*, Habit—× 0.5; *B*, rootstock—× 0.5; *C*, diagram of flower, showing structure—× 0.25; *D*, seeds—× 2.5.

CONVOLVULACEAE

Cuscuta approximata Babington var. urceolata (Kunze) Yuncker   SMALLSEED DODDER

(C. planiflora of Amer. auth.; *C. gracilis* Rydb.; *C. anthemi* Nels.)

Annual parasitic herb, reproducing by seeds (Fig. 145); *Stems* yellow or yellowish, slender, leafless, climbing or twining on its host, with small suckers adhering to the host; *Scales* few, very minute; *Flowers* sessile, whitish, perfect, regular, 3–4 mm. long, in few- to several-flowered clusters 5–10 mm. in diameter; *Calyx* inverted cone-shaped, of 4–5 fused sepals, the lobes equaling the corolla, enclosing the corolla tube, broadly ovate to triangular-ovate, overlapping at the base, usually broader than long, slightly keeled, the tips fleshy and turgid, drying golden-yellow and shining with large prominent cells; *Corolla* of 4–5 petals, bell-shaped, soon becoming round, about the developing capsule, the lobes ovate-rounded, obtuse and bent backward, fused below, shorter than the narrow cylindrical tube; *Scales* below the stamens oblong, mostly scarcely reaching the filaments, fringed about the top; *Styles* separate; *Stigmas* filiform, about as long as the styles, recurved, reddish; *Capsule* depressed-globose, opening in a definite line near the base, capped by the persistent corolla; *Seed* usually 4, about 1 mm. long, oval to oblong, angular, finely granular and more or less scurfy, light-brown; *Hilum* short, oblong. June–October.

Commonly parasitizing cultivated legumes, clover, alfalfa, and other hosts, often doing considerable damage. Native of Eurasia and Africa introduced from southern Europe. Established in Western United States from north central Washington to eastern Montana; south as far as northern New Mexico.

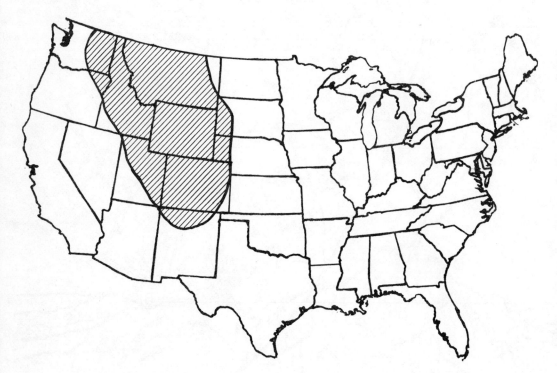

Distribution of *Cuscuta approximata* Babington var. *urceolata* (Kunze) Yuncker

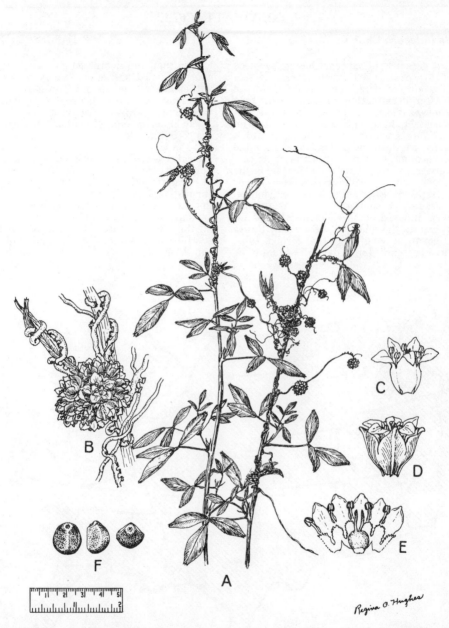

Regina O. Hughes

FIGURE 145.—*Cuscuta approximata* Babington var. *urceolata* (Kunze) Yuncker. Smallseed dodder. *A*, Habit—× 0.5; *B*, flower cluster and haustoria—× 2; *C*, corolla—× 4; *D*, calyx enclosing the corolla—× 4; *E*, corolla opened, showing fringed scales and ovary—× 4; *F*, seeds—× 8.

CONVOLVULACEAE

Cuscuta indecora Choisy

Annual parasitic herb, reproducing by seeds (Fig. 146); *Stems* relatively coarse, loosely matted, yellow, *leafless*, upon rising from the ground after germination soon adhering to a host by means of suckers developed on the surface in contact, hence climbing or twining on its host; *Flowers* whitish, parts in 5's, 2–5 mm. long, fleshy, papillose, on stalks longer than the flowers, forming rather open panicles or cymose clusters; *Calyx* much shorter than the corolla tube, with narrow triangular-ovate or acute lobes; *Corolla* 3–5 mm. long, bell-shaped, with spreading-ascending to erect triangular lobes, with inflexed acute tips; *Stamens* about half as long as the lobes of the corolla; *Scales* oblong, equal in length to the corolla tube, deeply and regularly fringed; *Styles* equal to or longer than the depressed-globose ovary; *Capsule* thickened at the summit, wrapped in the withering but persistent corolla; *Seed* 1–1.7 mm. long, globose or broader than long, somewhat scurfy, July–September.

var. *neuropetala* (Engelm.) Hitchc.—*Flowers* 2–5 mm. long; the corolla much thicker bell-shaped, the tube nearly or quite equaled by the calyx lobes; found in more southern than in northern areas.

Parasitic on a wide variety of herbs and shrubs, mainly Compositae and Leguminosae, in damp pinelands, wet bottomlands, sandy springs, and alfalfa fields. Native. Throughout all the United States excepting the northeastern fourth; south into Mexico and South America; West Indies.

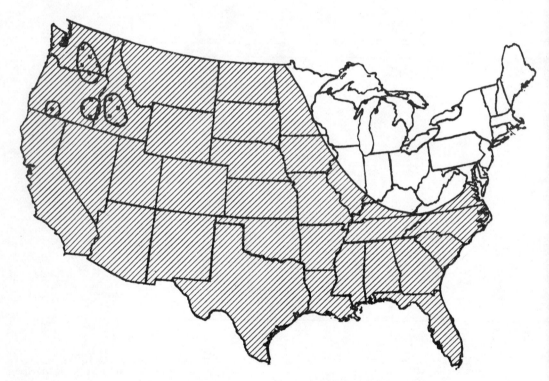

Distribution of *Cuscuta indecora* Choisy

FIGURE 146.—*Cuscuta indecora* Choisy. Largeseed dodder. *A*, Habit—× 0.5; *B*, enlarged habit—× 2.5; *C*, flower—× 5; *D*, capsule—× 5; *E*, seeds—× 5.

CONVOLVULACEAE

Cuscuta pentagona Engelm. (incl. var. *calycina* Engelm.) FIELD DODDER

(*C. arvensis*, of Manuals)

Annual parasitic herb, reproducing by seeds (Fig. 147); *Stems* pale, very slender and low; *Glomerules* globular, scattered or slightly confluent; *Flowers* whitish, parts in 5's, 1.5–2 mm. long, somewhat glandular, short-pediceled, in loose clusters; *Calyx* nearly inclosing the corolla tube, the calyx lobes obtuse to very broadly ovate or depressed, often broader than long, overlapping at the grooves; *Corolla lobes* 4–5, lance-acuminate, about equaling the broad tube, usually wide-spreading, the acute elongate tips inflexed; *Stamens* arising below the grooves, exserted in flower; *Scales* oblong, reaching slightly above the middle of the corolla tube, their longer fringe about one-fifth as long as the blades; *Stigma* with a head; *Capsule* depressed-globose, no longer than wide, not opening, protruding from the withering corolla; *Seed* 1–1.5 mm. long, one side rounded, the other flattened and often with an obtuse ridge, minutely pitted, yellow to reddish-brown; *Hilum* whitish within a smooth circular area on the flattened side. April–October.

Dry open soils, on many herbaceous and slightly ligneous hosts. Native. Widely distributed throughout all the United States. Florida to New Mexico and southern California, north to New England, excepting the northern part as far as central Montana and also the Pacific coast area; north into western Canada in Saskatchewan and Alberta.

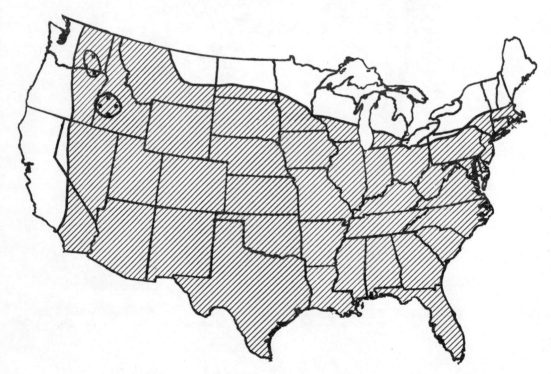

Distribution of *Cuscuta pentagona* Engelm. (incl. var. *calycina* Engelm.)

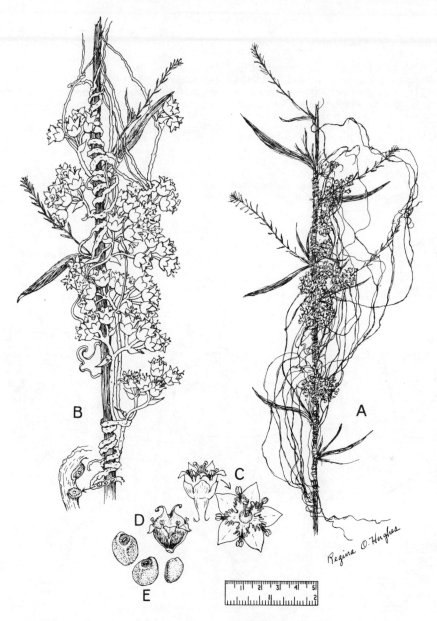

FIGURE 147.—*Cuscuta pentagona* Engelm. Field dodder. *A*, Habit—× 0.5; *B*, enlarged habit—× 2.5; *C*, flowers —× 5; *D*, capsule—× 5; *E*, seeds—× 5.

CONVOLVULACEAE

Ipomoea hederacea (L.) Jacq.

Annual herb, reproducing by seed (Fig. 148); *Stems* hairy, twining or spreading on the ground, 1–2 m. long; *Leaves* 3-lobed, occasionally 5-lobed, deeply heart-shaped with rounded basal lobes, 5–12 cm. wide and long; *Peduncles* shorter than or equaling the petioles below, bearing 1–3 flowers; *Flowers* funnel-shaped, sessile or short-pedicelled, the corolla 3–5 cm. long, pale to sky-blue when fresh, quickly changing to rose-purple, with a white tube; *Sepals* lanceolate, 15–25 mm. long, narrowed from below the middle into a slender, linear, re-curved tip, densely hairy or bristly; *Capsule* egg-shaped, partly covered by the calyx, usually with 4–6 seeds; *Seed* about 6 mm. long, dark-brown to black, with 1 rounded and 2 flattened sides. July–October.

Gardens, fields, and waste places; a troublesome weed in cultivated fields, especially in corn and soybean, where it ties the plants together before harvest. Naturalized from tropical America. Throughout all the Eastern, Southeastern, Central, and Southwestern United States; north into Ontario.

Distribution of *Ipomoea hederacea* (L.) Jacq.

FIGURE 148.—*Ipomoea hederacea* (L.) Jacq. Ivyleaf morningglory. *A*, Habit—× 0.5; *B*, sepals—× 1.5; *C*, capsule—× 2; *D*, seeds—× 5.

Ipomoea purpurea (L.) Roth
TALL MORNINGGLORY

Annual herb, reproducing by seeds (Fig. 149); *Stems* pubescent to glabrous, twining, up to 5 m. long; *Leaves* rounded-cordate to ovate-cordate, entire, or rarely 3-lobed, short, pointed, glabrous to sparsely pubescent; *Peduncles* about equaling the subtending leaves, 1- to 5-flowered; *Sepals* ovate-lanceolate to oblong, acute or acuminate, hairy below the base, 10–15 mm. long; *Corolla* blue, purple, red, white, or variegated, 4–7 cm. long; *Capsule* 10–12 mm. in diameter, globular, pointed, 4- to

6-seeded, 2- to 4-valved; *Seed* granular, pubescent, 4–5 mm. long, 3- to 4-angled, brownish-black. July–September.

Often a noxious weed, originally spread from cultivation; fields, waste places, gardens, and roadsides. Introduced and naturalized from tropical America. Throughout all the eastern half of the United States, west to the Rocky Mountains; north to Nova Scotia; also along the Pacific coast.

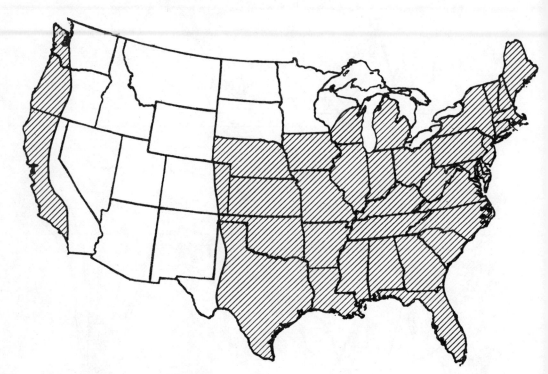

Distribution of *Ipomoea purpurea* (L.) Roth

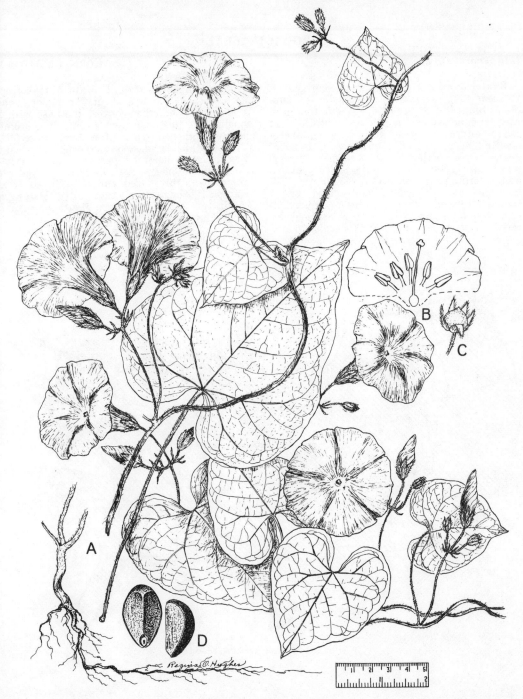

FIGURE 149.—*Ipomoea purpurea* (L.) Roth. Tall morningglory. *A*, Habit—× 0.5; *B*, flower diagram—× 0.5; *C*, capsule—× 0.5; *D*, seeds—× 3.

BORAGINACEAE

Lithospermum arvense L.

Winter annual or *biennial* herb, reproducing by seeds (Fig. 150); *Stems* erect, slender, simple or branching at the base, 2–7 dm. tall, minutely roughened and hairy, leafy at the top; *Leaves* alternate, simple, entire, sessile, lanceolate to linear, without lateral veins, 1–3 cm. long, hairy on both sides; *Flowers* perfect, regular, nearly sessile, in the axils of leafy bracts of the terminal racemes; *Calyx* 5-pointed, 5–7 mm. long, hairy; *Corolla* funnel-shaped, with 5 rounded spreading lobes, white to cream-colored, 5–7 mm. long, with 5 short stamens inserted on its tube; *Pistil* with a deeply 4-lobed ovary and a simple style; *Fruit* of 4 small erect nutlets, conical, ovoid, about 3 mm. long, one side angled, the other convex, the base with 2 small white tubercules and a scar, dull, prominently roughened, grayish-tan. April–June.

In grainfields, meadows, old gardens, and waste places; does not persist under cultivation; troublesome where winter wheat and rye are grown. Introduced and naturalized from Europe. Throughout all the United States excepting an area from eastern Montana to north central Minnesota.

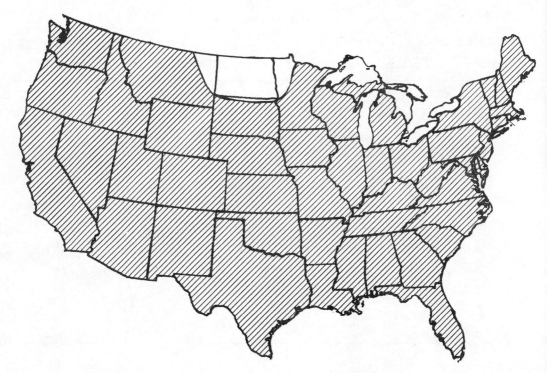

Distribution of *Lithospermum arvense* L.

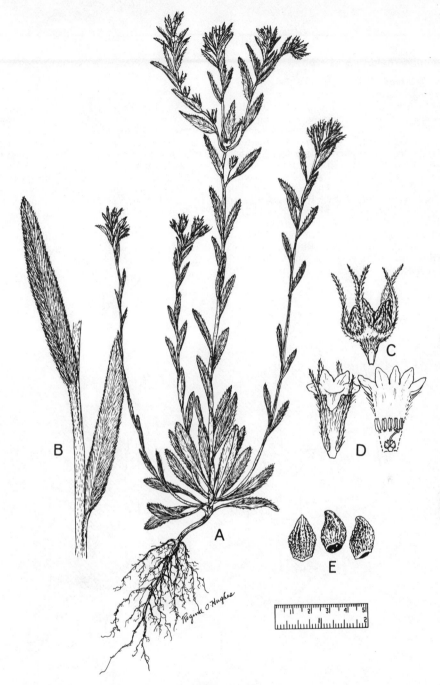

FIGURE 150.—*Lithospermum arvense* L. Corn gromwell. *A*, Habit—× 0.5; *B*, enlarged leaves—× 2.5; *C*, nutlets in calyx—× 3; *D*, flowers—× 5; *E*, nutlets—× 4.

Verbena bracteata Lag. & Rodr.

PROSTRATE VERVAIN

(V. bracteosa Michx.)

Annual herb, reproducing by seeds (Fig. 151); *Stems* diffusely branching at the base, with some spreading and some ascending branches, 1–4 dm. long, rough-hairy, somewhat 4-angled; *Leaves* opposite, simple, wedge-shaped in outline, pinnatifid and much-toothed, 1–8 cm. long, rough-hairy, short-petioled; *Flowers* perfect, sessile, in dense terminal spikes, almost hidden by the conspicuous bracts; *Bracts* stiff, hairy, longer than the calyx, 1–2 cm. long; *Calyx* short, 3–4 mm. long, hairy, tubular, 5-toothed; *Corolla* purplish-blue, irregular, tubular, 5-cleft, its limbs 2.5–3 mm. broad; *Stamens* 2 long and 2 short, included; *Ovary* 4-celled, not 4-lobed, but in fruit (schizo-carp) splitting into 4 1-seeded indehiscent nutlets; *Nutlet* linear-oblong, 2 mm. long, margin slightly winged, with 2 flattened sides and 1 rounded side, the convex surface netted above, with a white scar near the base, dark-brown. June–August.

In meadows, pastures, barnyards, sandy prairies, lawns, and waste places; rarely in cultivated fields. Native. Throughout most of the United States excepting northern New England and New York, northeastern Minnesota, and a large area of the Rocky Mountains; north into Canada from southern Ontario to British Columbia; south into Mexico.

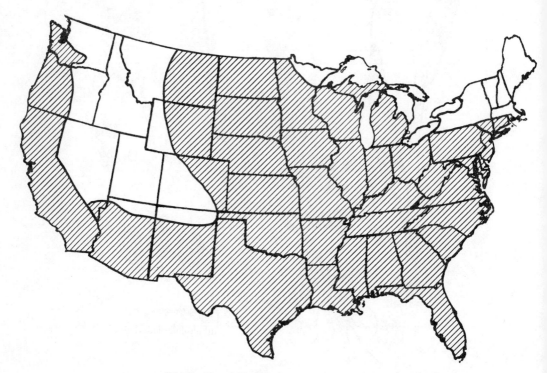

Distribution of *Verbena bracteata* Lag. & Rodr.

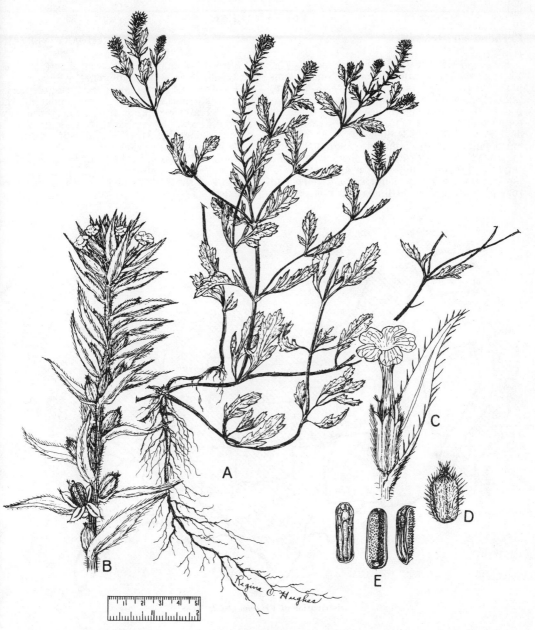

FIGURE 151.—*Verbena bracteata* Lag. & Rodr.   Prostrate vervain.   *A*, Habit—× 0.5; *B*, flowering spike, showing the long bracts—× 2; *C*, flower—× 5; *D*, schizocarp—× 5; *E*, mericarps—× 7.5.

VERBENACEAE

Verbena stricta Vent.

Perennial herb, reproducing by seeds (Fig. 152); *Stems* erect, stoutish, nearly round, simple or with a few branches above, 3–12 dm. tall, velvety with soft whitish hairs; *Leaves* opposite, simple, oblong to broadly obovate or rounded-elliptic, 2–10 cm. long, 3–6 cm. broad, doubly toothed, sessile, downy with whitish hairs, hairy beneath, pinnately veined; *Flowers* in dense spikes; *Bracts* hairy, shorter than the calyx; *Calyx* white-pilose, overlapping; *Fruiting calyces* 2.5–5 mm. long; *Corolla* purple to rosy-pink, or white, its limbs 8–9 mm. broad;

Nutlet 2.5–3 mm. long, netted above, dark or grayish-brown. June–September.

Prairies and barrenlands, pastures, old fields, and waste places. Native. Throughout all the United States excepting areas in northern New England and New York, the Southeastern States along the Atlantic and gulf coasts, an area between central Montana and central Minnesota, and an area in the West from Washington and Idaho south to the Mexican border; north into southern Ontario; south into eastern Mexico.

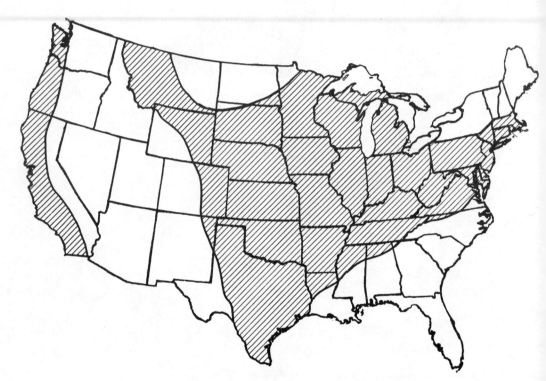

Distribution of *Verbena stricta* Vent.

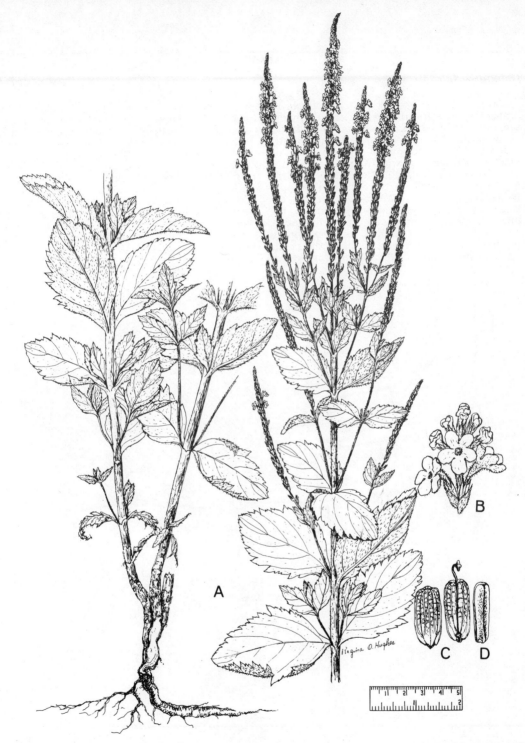

FIGURE 152.—*Verbena stricta* Vent. Hoary vervain. *A*, Habit—× 0.5; *B*, flowers—× 1.5; *C*, schizocarps—× 5; *D*, mericarp—× 5.

Galeopsis tetrahit L.   HEMPNETTLE

Annual herb (Fig. 153); *Stems* simple or branching, bristly-hairy with long, straight, somewhat reflexed hairs, 3–8 dm. tall, swollen at the nodes; *Leaves* ovate to lanceolate, mostly rounded at the base, pointed, 5–10 cm. long, on petioles 1–3 cm. long, with rounded or pointed teeth, pubescent on both sides; *Flowers* borne in 2–6 dense whorls, in the axils of the upper foliage leaves; *Calyx teeth* 7.5–11 mm. long, enlarged in fruit; *Corolla* strongly 2-lipped, the tube exceeding the calyx, the upper lip entire, erect, concave, the lower lip 3-lobed, bearing 2 protuberances (nipples) at its base, the petals white or pink suffused with purple, rarely purple completely, commonly with 2 yellow spots, about 2 cm. long, the middle lobe rarely longer than broad, usually rounded, rarely notched, the margins flat; *Nutlet* 3–4 mm. long, broadly obovate, smooth. June–September.

Waste places, roadsides, and forests; introduced as a weed of gardens and cultivated fields; abundant only northward. Naturalized from Eurasia. Throughout approximately the northeastern two-thirds of the United States; a distinct area in Washington, Idaho, and Montana; north into Canada from Newfoundland to British Columbia and Alaska.

Distribution of *Galeopsis tetrahit* L.

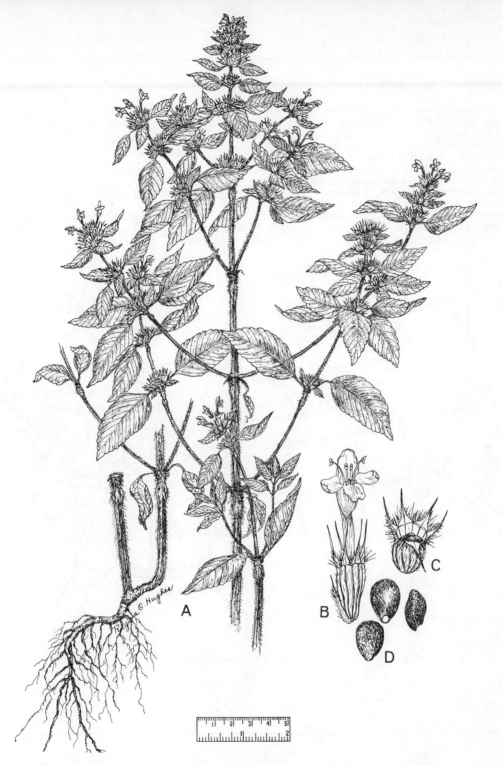

FIGURE 153.—*Galeopsis tetrahit* L. Hempnettle. *A*, Habit—× 0.5; *B*, flower—× 2.5; *C*, fruit, showing nutlets—
× 2.5; *D*, nutlets—× 4.

Glechoma hederacea L.

Perennial, reproducing by seeds and creeping stems (Fig. 154); *Roots* shallow; *Stems* 3.8–7 dm. long, creeping or trailing, rooting at the nodes, with numerous erect flowering branches, 4-angled, glabrous or nearly so; *Leaves* opposite, palmately veined, petioled, rounded kidney-shaped, round-toothed edges, bright-green, glabrous, 1–3 cm. in diameter, with a minty odor; *Flowers* small, in axillary clusters; *Calyx* tubular, with 5 equal teeth, pubescent, persistent; *Corolla* bluish-purple to purplish, 2-lipped, the upper lip erect, rather concave, 2-cleft, the lower lip 3-lobed; *Nutlet* ovoid, 1.5–2 mm. long, in 4's, flat on 2 sides and round on the 3d side, granular, dark-brown with a small whitish hilum at the base. April–June.

In lawns, gardens, orchards, damp rich and shaded areas, and waste places. Introduced from Eurasia. Throughout approximately all the eastern half of the United States excepting in parts of some Southeast and South Central States; north into Canada from Newfoundland to Ontario.

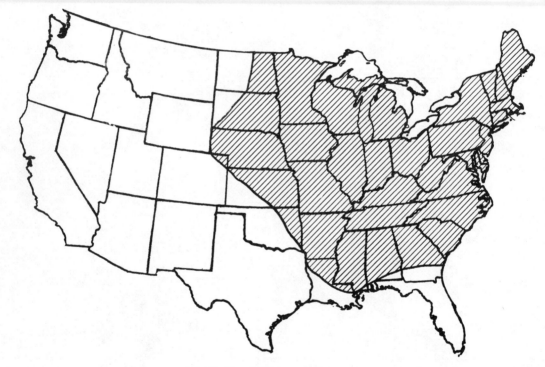

Distribution of *Glechoma hederacea* L.

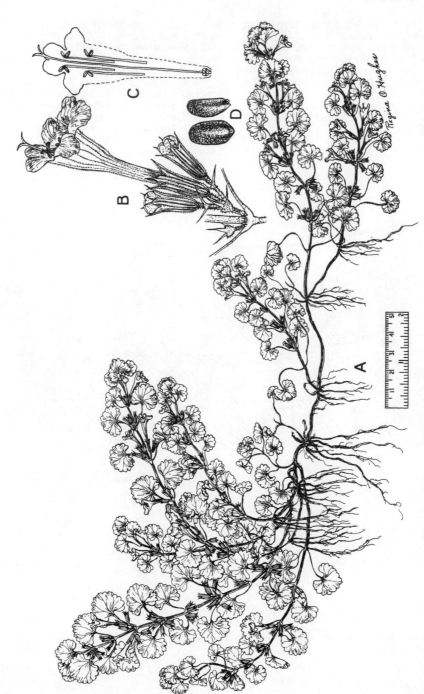

FIGURE 154.—*Glechoma hederacea* L. Ground ivy. A, Habit—× 0.5; B, flower cluster—× 2.5; C, flower diagram, showing the four ascending stamens—× 2.5; D, nutlets—× 6.

Lamium amplexicaule L.

Biennial or *winter annual* herb, reproducing by seeds and rooting systems (Fig. 155); *Roots* fibrous; *Stems* decumbent with numerous ascending branches, frequently rooting at the lower nodes, 10–40 cm. tall, slender, nearly smooth, 4-angled; *Leaves* opposite, circular, with palmate venation, hairy, with rounded teeth, the lower leaves petioled, doubly crenate-lobed, 1–2 cm. long, the upper leaves sessile and clasping the stem; *Flowers* in whorls in the axils of the upper leaves; *Corolla* tubular but 2-lipped, about 1–1.5 cm. long, pinkish to purple, surrounded at the base by the calyx (5–6.5 mm. long) with 5 sharp teeth, spotted; *Nutlets* borne 4 in a pod, sharply 3-angled, 1.5–2.4 mm. long, obovate-oblong, the apex blunt, grayish-brown speckled with silvery-gray granules. April–June; September.

Waste places, cultivated fields, and gardens, especially in rich soils. Native of Eurasia and Africa; introduced from Eurasia. Throughout all the United States excepting an area between eastern Montana and western Minnesota, extending as far south as southern Wyoming and western Nebraska; north into Canada from Newfoundland to British Columbia.

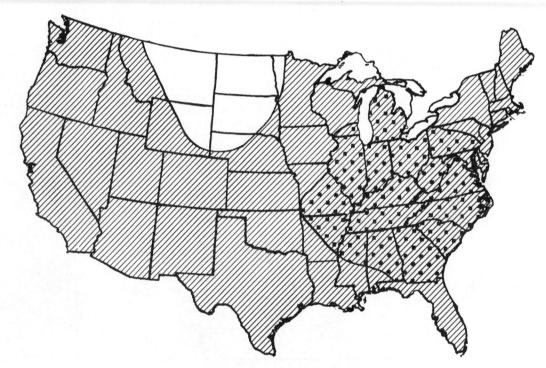

Distribution of *Lamium amplexicaule* L.

FIGURE 155.—*Lamium amplexicaule* L. Henbit. *A*, Habit—× 0.5; *B*, flower clusters, showing very short upper internodes—× 1.5; *C*, calyx surrounding nutlets—× 4; *D*, nutlets—× 7.5.

Prunella vulgaris L. HEALALL

Perennial herb, reproducing by seeds and short runners that root freely at the nodes (Fig. 156); *Stems* erect, 0.5–6 dm. tall, ascending or prostrate, mostly tufted, simple or branched, 4-angled, pubescent becoming nearly glabrous with age; *Leaves* opposite, pinnately veined, with moderately long petioles, margins entire or irregularly dentate, ovate-oblong, pubescent or glabrous, 2.5–10 cm. long; *Flowers* sessile, in a close thick spike, 3 in the axils of each rounded membranaceous bract, the bracts mostly bristly-ciliate; *Calyx* irregularly 10-nerved, 7–10 mm. long, green or purple, 2-lipped, the lips longer than the tube, the upper lip broad, shallowly 3-toothed, the lower lip deeply cleft, with two narrow segments, the teeth spinulose-tipped; *Corolla* blue or purple to white or pink, 1–2 cm. long, 2-lipped, the tube equaling or surpassing the calyx, the lips short,

the upper lip hood-shaped and entire or nearly so, the lower lip shorter and 3-lobed; *Stamens* 4, the upper pair shorter than the lower pair, exserted; *Nutlets* 4, in the persistent calyx, obovate, about 1.5 mm. long, slightly flattened on 2 sides, brown with dark vertical lines, the base tapering to a pointed white outgrowth, slightly roughened and glossy. A variable species with several named varieties. May–September.

In lawns, fields, waste places, pastures, grasslands, and roadsides. When repeatedly mowed, trampled, or grazed, the plants become densely matted, depressed, and small-leaved. Naturalized from Eurasia. Throughout all the United States excepting an area between central Montana and eastern North Dakota; north into Canada from Newfoundland to British Columbia and Alaska.

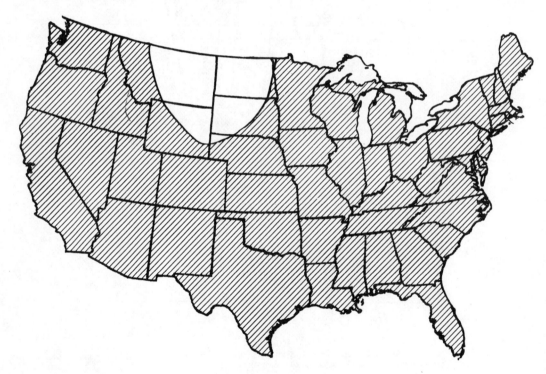

Distribution of *Prunella vulgaris* L.

FIGURE 156.—*Prunella vulgaris* L.   Healall.   *A*, Habit—× 0.5;   *B*, flower—× 2;   *C*, persistent calyx—× 2.25;   *D*, nutlets—× 4.

SOLANACEAE

Datura stramonium L.

JIMSONWEED

Annual herb, reproducing by seeds (Fig. 157); *Root* thick, shallow, extensively branched; *Stems* erect, stout, 3–15 dm. tall, with spreading branches above, glabrous, green or purple; *Leaves* alternate, simple, ovate, unevenly toothed, glabrous, dark-green above, 7–20 cm. long on stout petioles, strong-scented; *Flowers* borne singly on short stalks in the axils of the branches; *Corolla* funnel-shaped, the border with 5 teeth, white to pinkish, 5–12 cm. long; *Capsule* elongate-globular, about 2.5 cm. in diameter, erect, 4-valved, 4-locular except near the 2-locular top, covered with short, sharp spines, but sometimes unarmed; *Seed* dark-brown to black, kidney-shaped, flattened, surface irregular and pitted. July–October.

var. *stramonium*—*Stem* green, corolla white, lower prickles on fruit mostly shorter than the upper ones.

var. *tatula* (L.) Torr.—*Stem* purple or purplish; *Corolla* lavender or pale-violet; *Prickles* on fruit mostly nearly all equal.

In cultivated fields, on rich soils, old feed lots, hog pens, and waste places; a troublesome weed toward the south. Plant narcotic-poisonous. Introduced and naturalized from Eurasia and Africa. Throughout all the United States excepting a large area in northwestern and north-central parts and an area in south Texas; a distinct area in Colorado; northeast into Canada to Nova Scotia.

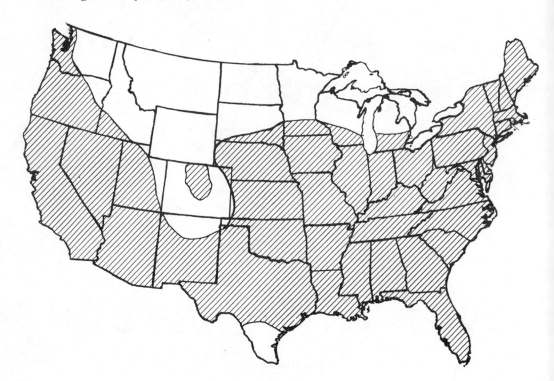

Distribution of *Datura stramonium* L.

318

FIGURE 157.—*Datura stramonium* L. Jimsonweed. *A*, Habit, upper part of plant—× 0.5; *B*, cauline leaf—× 0.5; *C*, ripe capsule—× 0.5; *D*, seeds—× 3.

Physalis heterophylla Nees

CLAMMY GROUNDCHERRY

Perennial herb, reproducing by seeds and rootstocks (Fig. 158); *Stems* erect, branched or widely spreading, 3–8 dm. tall, downy-pubescent, usually sticky or glandular, ridged; *Leaves* alternate, simple, broadly ovate, with a rounded or cordate base, sticky-pubescent, wavy or bluntly toothed, 5–7.5 cm. long; *Flowers* perfect, solitary in the axils of the leaves or branches; *Calyx* 5-cleft, reticulate and enlarging after flowering into a much-inflated balloon, inclosing the berry; *Corolla* bell-shaped to wheel-shaped, 1.5–2.2 cm. in diameter, 5-angled, 5-toothed; *Stamens* 5, inserted on the cor-olla; *Fruit* a 2-celled, many-seeded, globose, yellow berry, surrounded by the inflated papery calyx; *Seed* numerous, about 2 mm. in diameter, flattened, obovate to semicircular, dull, granular, light-orange or straw-colored. June–August.

In cultivated fields, pastures, roadsides, meadows, and gardens; on gravelly and stony soils. Native. Throughout eastern North America, west to Saskatchewan, Utah, central New Mexico, and west central Texas; distinct area in central Washington.

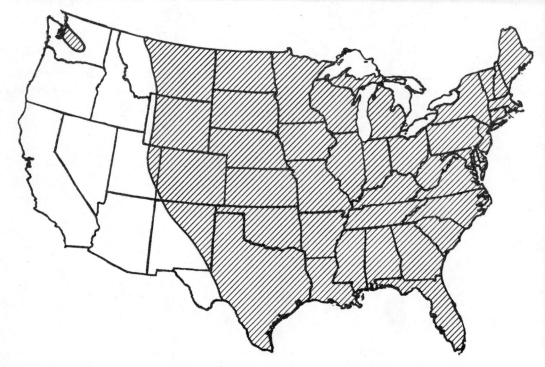

Distribution of *Physalis heterophylla* Nees

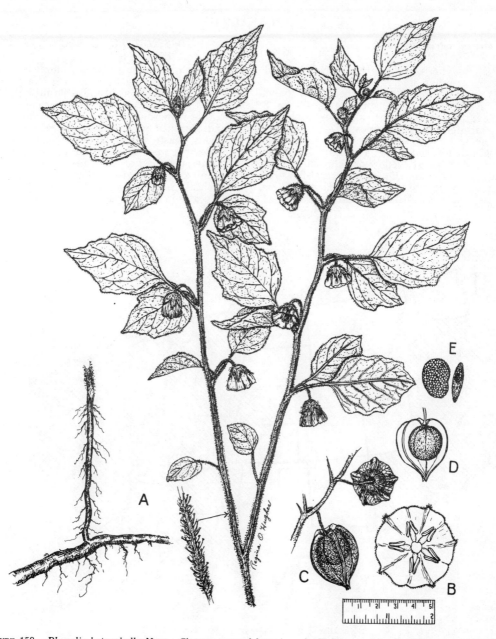

FIGURE 158.—*Physalis hetrophylla* Nees. Clammy groundcherry.   *A*, Habit—× 0.5; *B*, flower, open to show wide filaments—× 1.5; *C*, berries in transparent calyx—× 0.5; *D*, section of fruit showing berry—× 0.5; *E*, seeds—× 8.

SOLANACEAE

Solanum carolinense L.   HORSENETTLE, CAROLINA NETTLE

Perennial herb, prickly, reproducing by seeds and by creeping underground rhizomes (Fig. 159); *Stem* simple or branched, 30–120 cm. tall, hairy with star-shaped hairs (4- to 8-rayed), the slender prickles straw-shaped; *Leaves* alternate, green, mostly 7–12 cm. long and about half as wide, elliptic-oblong to oval, margin divided into lobes and coarsely toothed (2–5 teeth), rough, yellow prickles on petioles, midribs, and veins; *Racemes* several-flowered, soon becoming 1-sided; *Flowers* about 2.5 cm. across; *Calyx lobes* lance-acuminate; *Corolla* vi-olet, bluish, or white, about 2 cm. wide; *Anthers* equal, tapering to a tip; *Fruit* a yellow, juicy berry, smooth at first, becoming wrinkled late in the season, globose, 1–1.5 cm. in diameter; *Seed* numerous, about 1.5 mm. in diameter, round, flattened, yellowish. May–October.

Fields, waste places, and gardens; often a troublesome weed in sandy areas. Throughout all the eastern half of the United States excepting Maine; north into southern Ontario; also in the West from Oregon and California east to the Rockies in southern Idaho and Arizona.

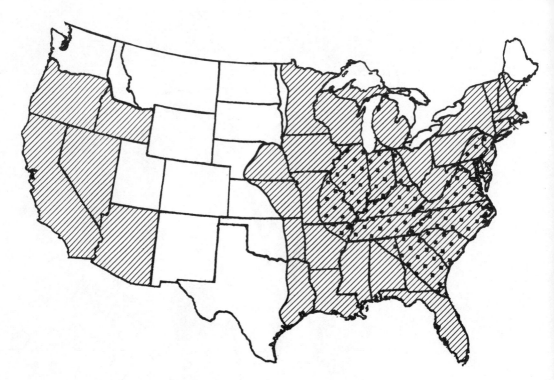

Distribution of *Solanum carolinense* L.

FIGURE 159.—*Solanum carolinense* L. Horsenettle. *A*, Habit—× 0.5; *B*, flower—× 1.5; *C*, berries—× 0.5; *D*, seeds—× 5.

SOLANACEAE

Solanum nigrum L. (incl. *S. americanum* Mill.)

BLACK NIGHTSHADE

Annual herb, without tubers, reproducing by seeds (Fig. 160); *Stems* glabrous or only sparsely or remotely pubescent, erect or spreading, 30–60 cm. tall; *Leaves* simple, bluntly lobed at the base, ovate, 2.5–7.5 cm. long, thin, membranaceous and translucent to thickish, dense or opaque to transmitted light, narrowed, the edges wavy; *Inflorescences* umbellate, or often corymbose or nearly racemose, with 5–10 flowers on pedicels; *Calyx lobes* with rounded tips; *Corolla lobes* 5–7.5 mm. long, white; *Anthers* 1.3–2.6 mm. long; *Fruit* a berry, green turning black at maturity, 5–13 mm. in diameter, lustrous to dull; *Seed* numerous, 1.2–2.3 mm. in diameter, usually without concretions, dull, pitted, yellow to dark-brown. May–November.

S. nigrum is naturalized from Europe, a weed in waste places, roadsides, disturbed and cultivated fields, and seabeaches; *S. americanum* is native, in rocky or dry open woods, thickets, shores, and openings, often spreading to cultivated or waste grounds. The unripe berries of some races are poisonous to sheep and other grazing animals. However, the ripe berries are often eaten raw or cooked for preserves or pies by humans. *S. nigrum* and *S. americanum* are very difficult to distinguish, except as races of a very polymorphic species. Throughout all the Eastern States and parts of the Central States of the United States; north into eastern Canada to Nova Scotia.

Distribution of *Solanum nigrum* L. (incl. *S. americanum* Mill.)

FIGURE 160.—*Solanum nigrum* L. Black nightshade. *A*, Habit—× 0.5; *B*, inflorescence—× 2.5; *C*, seeds—× 5.

SCROPHULARIACEAE

Linaria dalmatica (L.) Mill. (incl. var. *macedonia* Fenzl)   DALMATIAN TOADFLAX

Perennial herb, reproducing by seeds, sometimes developing horizontal or creeping rootstocks (Fig. 161); *Stems* erect, 8–12 dm. tall, robust, branched above, glabrous, more or less glaucous, from a woody branching base; *Leaves* alternate, but crowded and sometimes appearing opposite, entire, 3–8 cm. long, 1–2 cm. broad, ovate, ovate-lanceolate or even lanceolate below, sessile and cordate-clasping at the base; *Flowers* in terminal elongate racemes, short-pedicellate or nearly sessile, bright-yellow but often purplish-red at the apex in the bud; *Sepals* 5, partly united, 6–8 mm. long; *Corolla* 1.7–3.5 cm. long, exclusive of the spur (1.3–2 cm. long), strongly 2-lipped, upper lip 2-lobed, the lower one 3-lobed; *Stamens* 4, in pairs, included; *Capsule* broadly ovoid-cylindric, 7–8 mm. high, opening near the summit by pores; *Seed* numerous, irregularly wing-angled. July–September.

Roadsides and near dwellings, spreading to valleys and sagebrush flats. Native of the Mediterranean region. Established on both sides of the Cascade Mountains; scattered throughout Northern and Western United States.

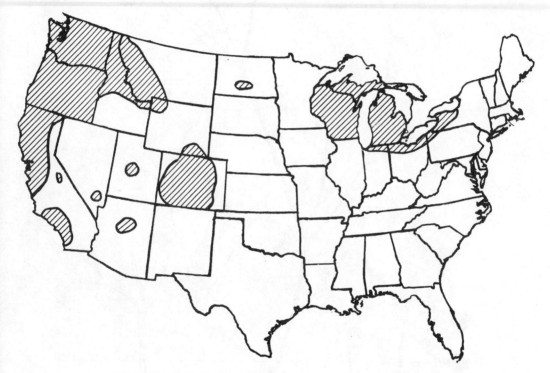

Distribution of *Linaria dalmatica* (L.) Mill. (incl. var. *macedonica* Fenzl)

FIGURE 161.—*Linaria dalmatica* (L.) Mill. Dalmation toadflax. *A*, Habit—× 0.5; *B*, flower—× 1.25; *C*, capsule—× 2; *D*, seeds—× 12.5.

SCROPHULARIACEAE

Linaria vulgaris Hill

Perennial herb, reproducing by seeds and spreading by roots and creeping rhizomes, forming colonies (Fig. 162); *Root system* well-branching; *Stems* ascending, glabrous or somewhat glandular above, up to 1.3 m. tall, sparingly branched; *Leaves* nearly opposite, but mostly alternate, simple, sessile, pale-green, 2.5 cm. long, 2–4 mm. wide, linear or linear-lanceolate, narrowed below to a petiolelike base; *Flowers* in a dense, terminal raceme, finally becoming more or less lax; *Corolla* including the awl-shaped spur 2–3 cm. long, bright-yellow, with a rounded orange palate, or the corolla whitish or creamy; *Capsule* round-ovoid, 8–12 mm. long, 2-celled, many-seeded opening by 2–3 pores or slits just below the apex; *Seed* with a nearly circular, flattened, notched wing, the body minutely warty, dark-brown or black, 1.5–2 mm. in diameter. Aberrant forms with regular flowers or with 2–5 spurs are occasionally found. Flowering May–October; fruiting August–November.

Roadsides, dry fields, grainfields, waste places, pastures, and railroad yards; frequently grown as an ornamental and escaping; mildly poisonous to stock. Naturalized from Eurasia. Throughout temperate North America; common throughout eastern North America; local on the Pacific coast.

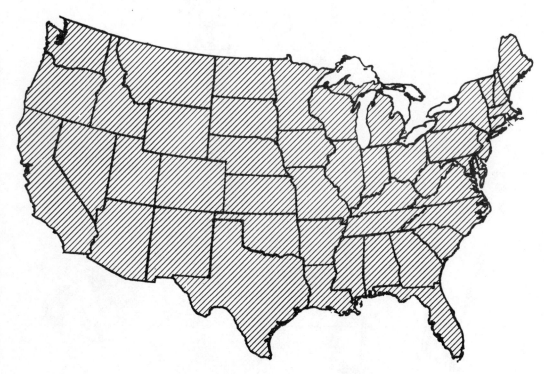

Distribution of *Linaria vulgaris* Hill

FIGURE 162.—*Linaria vulgaris* Hill. Yellow toadflax. *A*, Habit—× 0.5; *B*, flowers—× 0.75; *C*, capsules—× 1.5; *D*, seeds—× 5.

SCROPHULARIACEAE

Striga lutea Lour.   WITCHWEED

(*S. asiatica* (L.) Kuntze, Amer. auth.)

Annual herb, reproducing by seeds, parasitizing the roots of many crops (Fig. 163); *Germination* after 15–18 months' rest period, flowering and seed production continuous from July until frost (70- to 90-day cycle); *Root* watery, white, round in cross section, no root hairs, the underground portion of the stem with a series of scales placed similarly to the leaves aboveground; *Stems* above the third node on the stem square, 20–30 cm. high, rarely up to 45 cm., plants aboveground bright-green; multiple branches both near the ground and higher on the plant; *Leaves* nearly opposite, linear-lanceolate, alternating at about 90 degrees in pairs, slightly hairy, the upper and lower surfaces alike, the aerial leaf flattened with stomata more numerous on the lower side; *Flowers* small, 6–9 mm. wide, usually brick-red or scar-let, but may vary to red, yellow, or almost white, in the axils of the leaves, more flowers coming into bud, blooming and setting capsules throughout the season; *Capsules* 5-sided, each side terminating in a characteristic spur; each capsule containing about 1,350 tiny brown seeds, about 0.2 mm. in length, about three-fifths as wide as long (up to 500,000 seeds per plant), deeply reticulated, striate. Seeds may lie dormant 15–20 years. June until frost.

Pest in South Africa; native of India. Introduced and spreading in North Carolina and South Carolina. Parasitizes the roots of 60 species of grasses in 28 genera (including corn, sugarcane, sorghum, wheat, oats, barley, rice, and crabgrass), some sedges, and many broad-leaf plants.

Distribution of *Striga lutea* Lour.

FIGURE 163.—*Striga lutea* Lour. Witchweed. *A*, Habit—× 0.5; *B*, flowers—× 1.5: *b*, flower diagram, showing stamens—× 3; *C*, persistent calyx—× 2.5; *D*, capsule—× 2.5: *d*, capsule, opened, showing great number of seeds —× 3; *E*, seeds—× 60: *e*, seed, greatly enlarged, showing coarse reticulations over striae; *F*, roots—× 1.5: *f*, haustoria—× 1.5.

SCROPHULARIACEAE

Verbascum blattaria L.

Biennial herb, reproducing by seeds (Fig. 164); *Stem* erect, slender, glabrous or with glandular hairs near the top, 6–15 dm. tall, simple or sometimes branched; *Leaves* on lower part of the stem in a rosette, 2–6 dm. in diameter, dark-green, smooth or only slightly hairy, oblong, toothed or pinnately lobed, the upper leaves alternate, simple, sharp-pointed, sessile or partly clasping; *Flowers* perfect, yellow or pinkish-white, in long loose terminal racemes, on slender pedicels in the axils of bracts; *Calyx* 5-parted; *Corolla* about 2 cm. in diameter, cir-cular, 5-lobed; *Capsule* 2-celled, many-seeded, globose, 5–10 mm. in diameter; *Seed* dark-brown, blunt, 0.8 mm. long, the apex slightly rounded, with vertical rows of deep pits, those in rows next to each other alternating. June–September.

Meadows, old fields, pastures, and waste places; common on dry gravelly soils. Naturalized from Eurasia. Throughout the United States; north into southern Canada from Ontario to British Columbia.

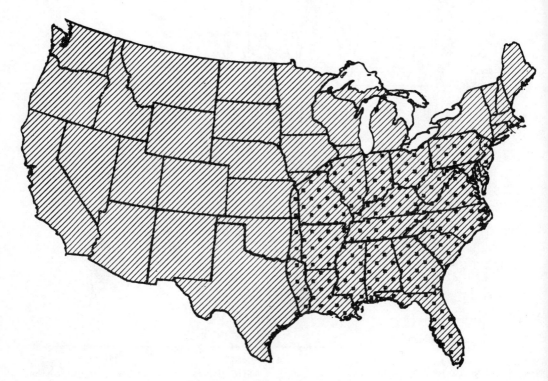

Distribution of *Verbascum blattaria* L.

FIGURE 164.—*Verbascum blattaria* L. Moth mullein. *A*, Habit—× 0.5; *B*, flower—× 0.75; *C*, capsule—× 1.5; *D*, seeds—× 20.

Verbascum thapsus L.

Biennial herb, reproducing by seeds (Fig. 165); *Stems*, 9–25 dm. tall, very stout, usually unbranched, or with a few upright branches near the top, covered with woolly hairs; *Leaves* at the base of the plant in a rosette, 2–6 dm. in diameter, the leaves 15–45 cm. long, oblong, densely woolly, the upper leaves smaller and more pointed, the bases attached to the stem and extending down it to the next leaf; *Flowers* perfect, nearly sessile in long dense terminal cylindrical spikes; *Calyx* 5-lobed and very woolly; *Corolla* 5-lobed, circular, nearly regular, sulfur-yellow, 2–3 cm. in diameter; *Capsule* globular, 2-celled, many-seeded, about 6 mm. in diameter, downy; *Seed* numerous, brown, about 0.8 mm. in diameter, wavy ridges alternating with deep grooves. June–September.

Pastures, fence rows, roadsides, old fields, and waste places; common in dry gravelly and stony soils and railroad yards. Naturalized from Eurasia. Throughout most of the United States.

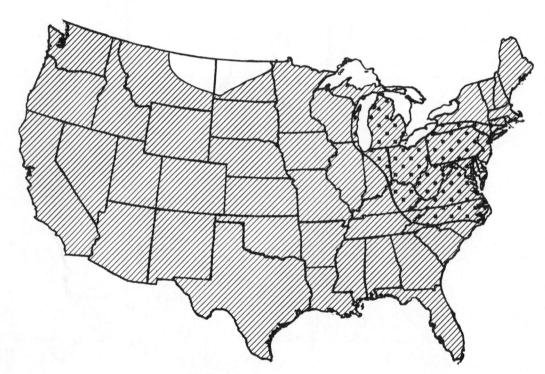

Distribution of *Verbascum thapsus* L.

FIGURE 165.—*Verbascum thapsus* L. Common mullein. *A*, Habit—× 0.5; *B*, flowers—× 2; *C*, capsules—× 2; *D*, seeds—× 12.5.

SCROPHULARIACEAE

Veronica arvensis L.

Annual herb, reproducing by seeds (Fig. 166); *Root* system fibrous; *Stems* erect or nearly so, simple to diffusely branched, with more or less long soft hairs, 0.5–4 dm. tall; *Leaves*, the lower ones rounded or ovate, obtuse, 6–12 mm. long, with 2–4 blunt teeth on each side, palmately veined, short-petioled, the upper ones smaller, sessile, lanceolate to linear; *Inflorescence* terminal racemes, constituting about two-thirds of the plant, the bracteal leaves progressively smaller upward, narrower and mostly entire; *Pedicels* up to 1.5 mm. long; *Calyx lobes* oblong or oblanceolate, very unequal, 3–5 mm. long; *Corolla* violet-blue to blue, about 2 mm. wide; *Style* about 8 mm. long, extending about as far as the summit of the capsule; *Capsule* 3–4 mm. wide, nearly as long, hairy, deeply notched. *Seed* 1 mm. long. March–August.

Weed in gardens, lawns, fields, waste open ground, rocky and sterile pastures, and woodlands. Naturalized from Eurasia. Throughout the eastern half of the United States; along the Pacific coast extending eastward to western Montana, eastern Colorado, and southeastern California; north into Canada from Newfoundland to British Columbia.

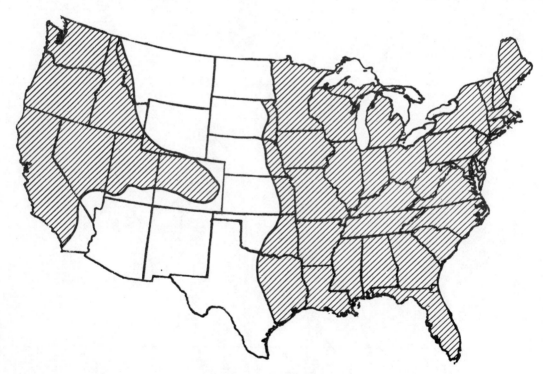

Distribution of *Veronica arvensis* L.

FIGURE 166.—*Veronica arvensis* L.   Corn speedwell.   *A*, Habit—× 0.5; *B*, enlarged branch—× 2.5; *C*, flower— × 7.5; *D*, capsules—× 3; *E*, seeds—× 5.

SCROPHULARIACEAE

Veronica officinalis L.

Perennial herb, reproducing by seeds and creeping stems (Fig. 167); *Stems* prostrate or creeping, rooting at the base, stout, pubescent; the flowering branches erect or ascending; *Leaves* opposite, simple, obovate-elliptic or oblong, obtuse, toothed, hairy or nearly rough, 2.5–6 cm. long, 1–3 cm. broad, short-petioled; *Peduncles* stout, ascending, range from shorter than the subtending leaves to longer than these leaves; *Flowers* in dense axillary racemes, the pedicels shorter than the calyx; *Calyx lobes* obtuse, nearly equal in size; *Corolla* pale-blue to lilac or lavender, or white, marked with darker lines, 5–6 mm. in diameter, with obtuse lobes; *Capsule* obovate-triangular, 3–4 mm. in diameter, about as broad as long, flattened, broadly notched, pubescent; *Seed* about 1 mm. long, oval to elliptic, flattened, minutely granular, lemon-yellow. May–July.

In pastures, open woodlands, and old fields; mostly on gravelly or stony acid soils. Native; also native to Eurasia and introduced and naturalized from Europe. Throughout approximately all the eastern half of the United States excepting the extreme South; north into Canada from Newfoundland to Ontario.

Distribution of *Veronica officinalis* L.

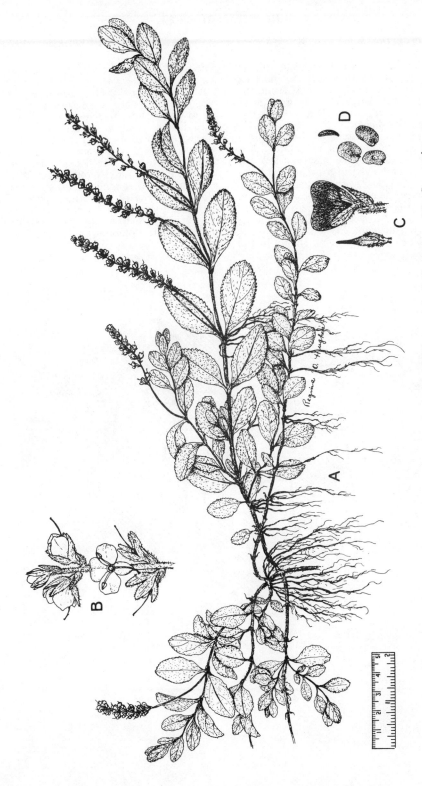

Figure 167.—*Veronica officinalis* L. Common speedwell. *A*, Habit— × 0.5; *B*, flowers— × 2.5; *C*, capsules— × 2.5; *D*, seeds— × 12.5.

SCROPHULARIACEAE

Veronica peregrina L.

Annual or *winter annual* herb, reproducing by seeds (Fig. 168); *Root* system fibrous; *Stems* erect, simple, or branching from the base, glabrous (**var. peregrina**) or glandular-puberulent (**var. xalapense (HBK.) Pennell**), 1–4 dm. tall, the lower half with opposite leaves, the upper half bearing flowers; *Leaves* simple, narrowly oblong to oblanceolate, 1.5–3 cm. long, often obtuse, entire or with a few low teeth, sessile or narrowed to a petiolelike base, the lower leaves opposite, the upper leaves alternate; *Bracteal* leaves similar to the stem leaves but progressively smaller; *Flowers* small, in axils of bracts, sessile or short-stalked; *Sepals* subequal; *Corolla* white; *Style* very short, the stigma appearing sessile in the notch of the capsule; *Capsule* flattened, heart-shaped, glabrous, 3–4 mm. long, 4–5 mm. wide, conspicuously notched; *Seed* long oval, flattened, translucent, glossy, orange-yellow, with a scar on one side. March–August.

In lawns, gardens, fertile fields, and waste places; damp open soil; a roadside weed. Considered to be native of east coast, but frequently appearing to be introduced; also introduced to the west coast of United States, West Indies, and Europe. Throughout all the eastern half of the United States excepting northern Maine; across the northern border, south to central California; a distinct area in the Central West, principally in Colorado.

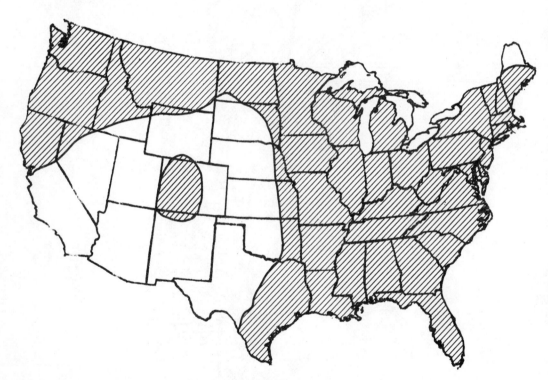

Distribution of *Veronica peregrina* L.

FIGURE 168.—*Veronica peregrina* L. Purslane speedwell. *A*, Habit—× 0.5; *B*, basal leaf—× 2; *C*, flower—× 3: *c*, corolla, showing stamens: *cc*, calyx, showing subequal sepals—× 5; *D*, capsule—× 3; *E*, seeds—× 25.

BIGNONIACEAE

Campsis radicans (L.) Seem.

Perennial vine, reproducing by seeds and vigorous running roots (Fig. 169); *Stems* glabrous, woody, vining, 6–12 m. long, or on stems 4–30 dm. long in cultivated fields; *Leaves* opposite, 20–40 cm. long, pinnately compound, with 3–13 ovate to lanceolate leaflets, 4–8 cm. long, acuminate with toothed margins, rounded at the base; *Flowers* in terminal short-stemmed corymbs; *Calyx* bell-shaped, 5-toothed, 10–15 mm. long, the lobes about 5 mm. long; *Corolla* funnel-shaped, orange to scarlet, rarely yellow, 5–8 cm. long; 5-lobed, rarely regular; *Stamens* 4, included; *Capsule* 10–15 cm. long, smooth, flattened, spindle-shaped, ridged at the edges of the 2 lengthwise halves of the pod, slightly curved; *Seed* broadly winged, about 15 mm. long, in several rows in the capsule. July–September.

In fields, yards, roadsides, waste places, and alluvial woods; on trees, posts, and old buildings; originally cultivated as an ornamental (and still is), but is an aggressive, widely distributed weed. Native. Throughout approximately all the eastern half of the United States excepting the northern areas.

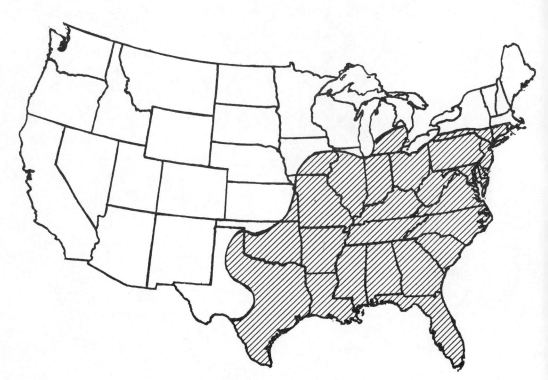

Distribution of *Campsis radicans* (L.) Seem.

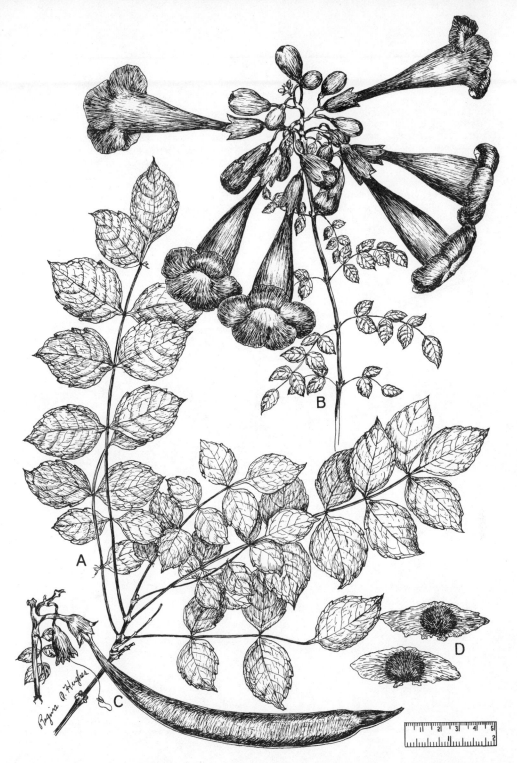

FIGURE 169.—*Campsis radicans* (L.) Seem. Trumpetcreeper. *A*, Vegetative shoot—× 0.5; *B*, flower corymb—× 0.5; *C*, capsule—× 0.5; *D*, seed (back (below) and front views)—× 1.5.

Orobanche minor J. E. Smith

Parasitic herb, reproducing by seeds (Fig. 170); *Stems* pubescent, pale yellowish-brown, 1–4.5 dm. tall; *Leaves* scalelike, the scales ovate to lanceolate, 6–20 mm. long, acute, sessile, without chlorophyll; *Spike* loosely flowered, interrupted below, continuous above, 1–2 dm. long, each purple-tinged flower in the axil of a basal bract; *Bracts* lanceolate, as long as the flowers or longer; *Calyx* pubescent, cleft before and behind almost or quite to the base, the lateral lobes often 2-cleft, lanceolate awl-shaped; *Corolla* glandular-pubescent especially along the back, irregular, the tube slightly curved, yellowish, the lips bluish with 2 rounded lobes, the upper lip erect or incurved, the lower lip spreading; *Capsule* oblong, less than 1 cm. long, 2-valved. April–July.

Parasitic on roots of clover and tobacco. Adventive and naturalized from Europe. Along the Atlantic coast from New Jersey to North Carolina.

Distribution of *Orobanche minor* J. E. Smith

FIGURE 170.—*Orobanche minor* J. E. Smith. Clover broomrape. *A*, Habit—× 0.5; *B*, enlarged flower spike—× 1.5; *C*, flower diagram—× 2.5; *D*, capsules—× 2.5; *E*, seeds—× 25.

PLANTAGINACEAE

Plantago lanceolata L.

Annual herb, becoming *perennial*, reproducing by seeds (Fig. 171, *A*); *Caudex* strong with tough slender rootlets; *Stems* erect, leafless, 10–30 cm. tall, terminating with a flower spike; *Leaves* all basal in a rosette, the blades lanceolate to lance-oblong, ascending or spreading, 5–30 cm. long, 0.6–4 cm. wide, with 3 to 5 prominent veins running lengthwise, tapering into the petiole; *Scape* tough, grooved-angled, elongating, 2–8 dm. tall, stiff-haired above; *Spikes* dense, at beginning of flowering slenderly ovoid-conic, tapering at the apex, at maturity becoming cylindric and obtuse, 1.5–10 cm. long; *Bracts* thin and papery, broadly ovate, the margin wavy; *Flowers* numerous, about 5 mm. broad, inconspicuous, the forward sepals united, 3–3.5 mm. long, the corolla lobes 2–3 mm. long; *Capsule* ellipsoid, 3–4 mm. long, 2-seeded, splitting across the middle or toward the base; *Seed* 1–2, small, 2–3 mm. long, brown or black, shining, smooth, nearly ellipsoid, deeply concave on the inner face, sticky when damp. May–October.

In lawns, meadows, pastures, and waste places; common and troublesome weed of grasslands. Naturalized from Europe. Throughout the United States.

Distribution of *Plantago lanceolata* L.

PLANTAGINACEAE

Plantago major L.

Perennial herb, sometimes an *annual*, reproducing by seeds (Fig. 171, *B*); *Leaves* alternate in rosettes, all basal, 0.5–3 dm. long, the blades thick, roughish on one or both sides when dry, with minute hairs, elliptic or lanceolate to broadly ovate, strongly ribbed, wavy or angular-toothed, the petioles broad, usually green (no purple tinge) and pubescent at the base; *Spikes* dense, obtuse, at the ends of the stems, 0.1–5 dm. long; *Flowers* sessile, the bracts glabrous, broadly ovate with a slender keel; *Sepals* glabrous, elliptic to elliptic-round, the rounded keel about as wide as the papery margins, 1.5–2 mm. long; *Corolla lobes* definitely less than 1 mm. long; *Capsule* stoutly ellipsoid, 2–4 mm. long, splitting across the upper half (near the middle), brown or purple; *Seed* 6–15, angled, net-veined, light- to dark-brown, about 1–1.7 mm. long. June–October.

In lawns, roadsides, and waste places. Native of Eurasia and probably native of northern North America; naturalized throughout the United States.

Distribution of *Plantago major* L.

PLANTAGINACEAE

Plantago rugelii Decne.

Perennial herb, reproducing by seeds (Fig. 171, *C*); *Roots* mostly fibrous; *Stems* erect, leafless, 15–30 cm. tall, teminating in the flower spike; *Leaves* alternate in rosettes, erect or spreading, all basal, blades simple, thin, broadly elliptic to oval, 5–20 cm. long, a little over half as wide, pale, glabrous or slightly hairy, usually wavy-edged, veins conspicuous, petiole margined, at base usually glabrous and tinged with purple; *Spikes* slender, dense to alternate-flowered, tapered at the apex, up to 3 dm. tall, about 5 mm. wide, rather loose, pedicels about 0.5 mm. long, bracts narrowly tri-angular-lanceolate, one-half to three-fourths as long as the calyx, tapering regularly from the

base to the apex, prominently elevated into an acute keel; *Sepals* ovate or oblong, acute, sharp keel much wider than papery margin; *Corolla* inconspicuous, lobes less than 1 mm. long, re-flexed after flowering; *Capsule* nearly cylin-drical, about 4–6 mm. long, splitting across the lower half, 4- to 9-seeded; *Seed* dark-brown or black, oval, angular, with a scar (minute hilum) near the center on one side, 1.5–2.5 mm. long, not reticulated. July–October.

Damp, rich soils; roadsides, damp shores, lawns, gardens, and waste places. Native. Throughout the eastern half of the United States, west to South Dakota, Nebraska, cen-tral Oklahoma, and central Texas.

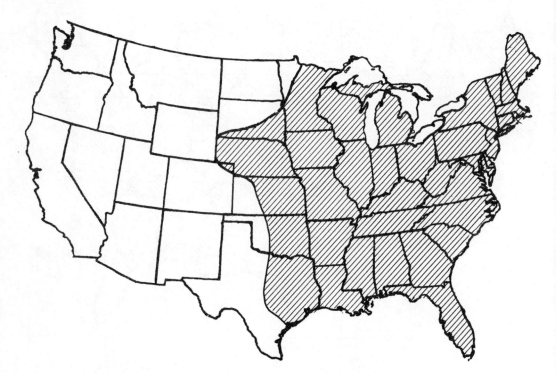

Distribution of *Plantago rugelii* Decne.

FIGURE 171.—Habit for all—× 0.5. *A*, *Plantago lanceolata* L. Buckhorn plantain. *a*, Flower—× 2.5; *b*, capsule—× 3; *c*, seed—× 5. *B*, *Plantago major* L. Broadleaf plantain. *a*, Flower—× 2.5; *b*, capsule—× 3; *c*, seeds —× 5. *C*, *Plantago rugelii* Decne. Blackseed plantain. *a*, Flower—× 2.5; *b*, capsule—× 2.5; *c*, seeds—× 3.

Diodia teres Walt.

POORJOE

Annual herbs (Fig. 172); *Roots* shallow, slender, taprooted; *Stems* hairy or minutely pubescent, branching, moderately erect to spreading, 1–8 dm. tall (or long), nearly circular; *Leaves* opposite, sessile, linear-lanceolate to elliptic, narrow, tapering to long point, edges smooth; *Stipules* fused, forming several long bristles; *Flowers* perfect, 1–3 in axils of the leaves, small; *Corolla* whitish-pink to lavender, funnel-shaped, 4–6 mm. long, with 4 short lobes; *Calyx* fused to the ovary, 4-toothed; *Stamens* 4, attached to the corolla; *Seed pods* hairy, obovoid-top-shaped, not furrowed, with the 4 short, green calyx teeth at the top, splitting when ripe into 2 or 3 indehiscent carpels; *Seed* 3–4 mm. long, hairy, oval, light-brown to grayish-brown, the inner surface indented with a forked groove. June–October.

In abandoned fields, along roadsides, and waste places; mostly on dry or sandy soils. Native. Throughout all the eastern half of the United States excepting northern New England and New York.

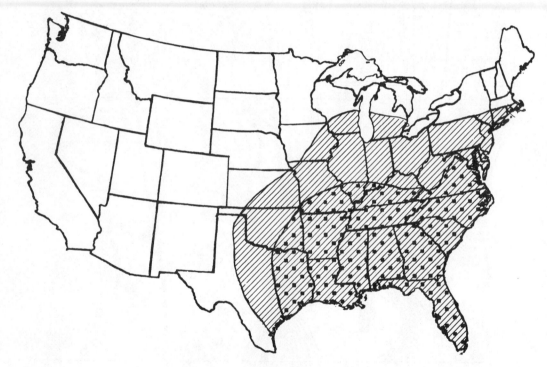

Distribution of *Diodia teres* Walt.

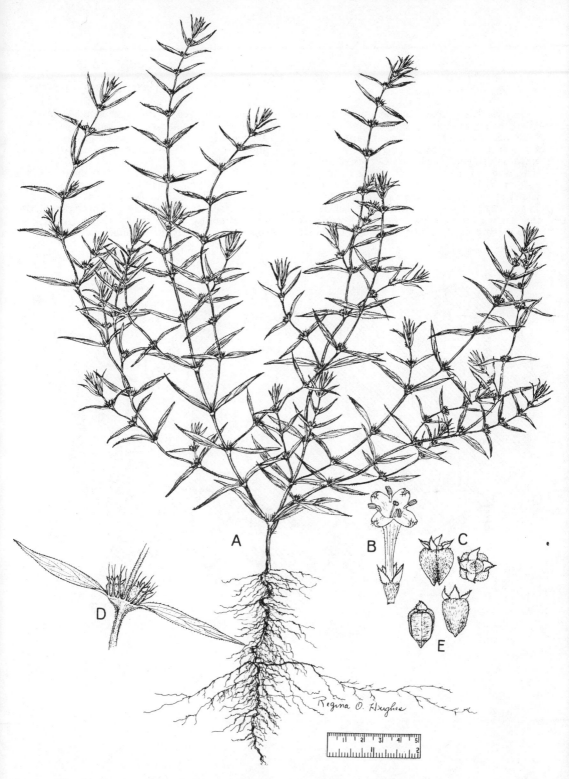

FIGURE 172.—*Diodia teres* Walt. Poorjoe. *A*, Habit—× 0.5; *B*, flower—× 2.5; *C*, fruits—× 2.5; *D*, fruits at node—× 1.25; *E*, nutlets—× 2.5.

RUBIACEAE

Galium aparine L.

Annual herb, reproducing by seeds (Fig. 173); *Roots* branching, short, shallow; *Stems* 6–15 dm. long, glabrous, weak, sprawling, 4-sided with each edge bearing a row of downward-pointing stiff bristles; *Leaves*, simple, entire, 1-veined, lanceolate, tapering at the base, 2–7 cm. long, rough, bristle-pointed, 6–8 in a whorl at each node; *Flowers* 1–3, perfect, very small, borne on slender branches in the axils of the leaves at the nodes; *Calyx* obsolete; *Corolla* with 4 white lobes; *Fruit* of 2 nearly spherical carpels, covered with stiff-hooked bristles, 1.5–4 mm. in diameter; *Seed* ball-shaped with a deep pit in 1 side, short sharp spines on the outer surface, 2–3 mm. in diameter, gray-brown. May–July.

Rich woods, thickets, seashores, waste ground, and on moist land in meadows, pastures, woodlands, and fence rows. Native and introduced from Eurasia. Throughout the United States; north into Canada from Newfoundland to British Columbia and Alaska.

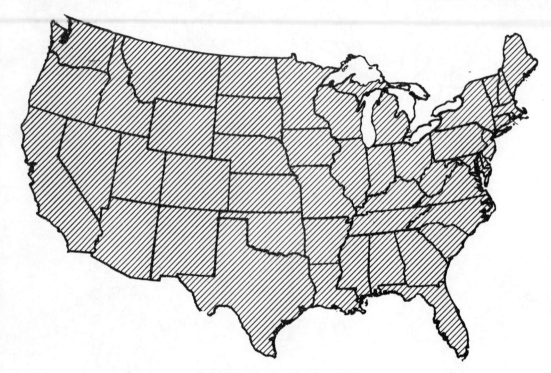

Distribution of *Galium aparine* L.

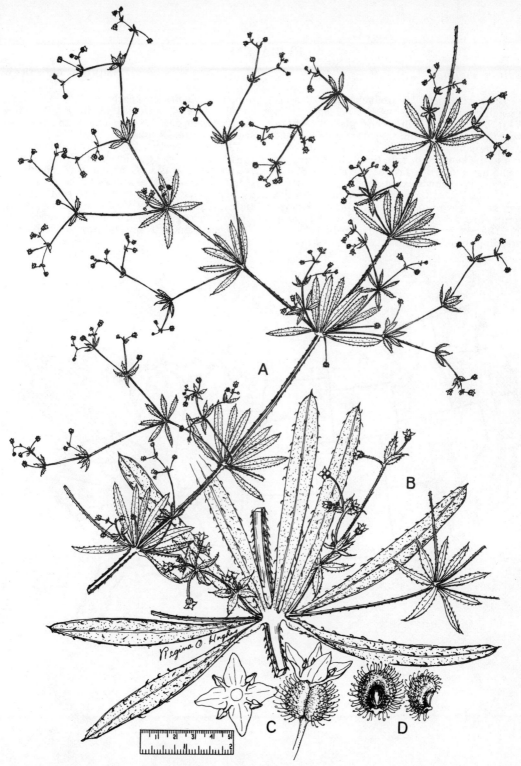

FIGURE 173.—*Galium aparine* L. Catchweed bedstraw. *A*, Habit—× 0.5; *B*, enlarged leaf whorl—× 2; *C*, flowers—× 12.5; *D*, fruits—× 10.

Galium mollugo L.

Perennial herb, reproducing by seeds, spreading or ascending, with a rhizome (Fig. 174); *Stems* diffusely branched, glabrous or pubescent, weak, 2–12 dm. tall, from a decumbent base; perennial offshoots produced from the base in the summer or fall, these short, slender, ascending, and leafy; *Leaves* whorled, 6–8 at a node, mostly oblanceolate to obovate, or almost linear, sessile, 1–3 cm. long (smaller on the branches), rough on the margins with forwardly directed prickles, 1-nerved, with a rigid tip; *Inflorescence* a terminal panicle with spreading branches, almost leafless; *Flowers* numerous, white or nearly so, 2–4 mm. wide, corollas 4-lobed, with a rigid tip; *Fruits* glabrous, roughened, 1–1.5 mm. long, with appressed segments. June–August.

Meadows, pastures, lawns, roadsides, and waste places; on gravelly or sandy loam soils. Native of Eurasia. Common throughout the North Atlantic States and as far south as Virginia and West Virginia, west to south central Indiana; along the Pacific Coast from southern Oregon through central California; north into southern Canada from Ontario to Newfoundland.

Distribution of *Galium mollugo* L.

FIGURE 174.—*Galium mollugo* L. Smooth bedstraw. *A*, Habit—× 0.5; *B*, flowers—× 5; *C*, schizocarp—× 6; *D*, mericarps—× 6.

Richardia scabra L.

Annual herb, reproducing by seeds (Fig. 175); *Stems* sparingly branched and erect, or copiously branched and diffusely spreading, round, 1–5 dm. tall, hairy; *Leaves* opposite, pubescent, the leaf blades flat, entire, oblong or elliptic to lanceolate or ovate, 2–8 cm. long, acute or acuminate, wavy-margined, narrowed into short-margined petioles or nearly sessile; *Stipules* fringed; *Flowers* mostly perfect, mostly 6-parted, in terminal clusters, the clusters depressed, the involucre of 2 unequal pairs of bracts; *Sepals* lanceolate or ovate-lanceolate, 1–1.5 mm. long, about as long as the hypan-thium, stiff-hairy; *Corolla* white, 4–6 mm. long, tube funnelform, usually 6-lobed, triangular or triangular-lanceolate, more or less hairy on the margins, much shorter than the tube; *Carpels* oblong, 3–3.5 mm. long; *Fruit* of 3–4 carpels, crowned with the sepals; *Seed* 2-grooved on the lower face. May–September.

Sandy soils. Introduced from tropical America. Mainly along the South Atlantic and Gulf Coast States, from North Carolina to Florida and west to southern Texas and Mexico; south into South America.

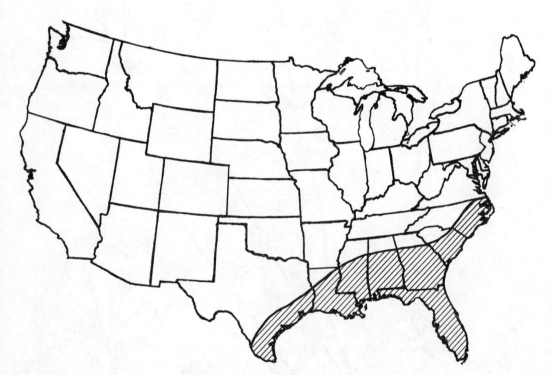

Distribution of *Richardia scabra* L.

FIGURE 175.—*Richardia scabra* L. Florida purslane. *A*, Habit—× 0.5; *B*, flower head—× 1; *C*, flower—× 6; *D*, fruit—× 3.5; *E*, cocci (lobes of the fruit)—× 3.5; *F*, cross section of fruit, showing 3 cocci—× 3.5; *G*, enlarged node, showing hairs—× 2.5.

CAPRIFOLIACEAE

Lonicera japonica Thunb. (incl. var. *chinensis* (P. W. Wats.) Baker)

Perennial high-twining, climbing or trailing shrub, reproducing by seeds and underground rhizomes, the stems freely rooting at the nodes (Fig. 176); *Stems* woody, pubescent to glabrous, long and twining, green to purplish; *Leaves* opposite, simple pubescent, mostly persistent throughout the winter especially southward, ovate or oblong, thickish, entire to variously lobed, short-petioled, green or purplish; *Bracts* leaflike, becoming smaller; *Flowers* in pairs on the summit of solitary, axillary peduncles; *Corolla* 3–4 cm. long, with 5 fused petals white to white tinged with purple, becoming yellow, sometimes carmine on the outside, very fragrant, with a pubescent tube; *Sepals* 5, fused with the ovary; *Stamens* 5, attached to the corolla; *Berries* black to purplish-black, with 2–3 seeds; *Seed* ovate to oblong, 2–3 mm. long, flattened, 3-ridged on the back, flat or concave on the inner face, dark-brown or gray-brown. Flowering late April–November; fruiting September–November.

Orchards, gardens, fence rows, thickets, borders of woods, and roadsides, a pernicious and dangerous weed, often overwhelming and strangling the native flora from Maryland south. Naturalized from Asia. Throughout all the Eastern United States excepting northern New England and northern New York, approximately southwest from Lake Michigan to southwest Texas.

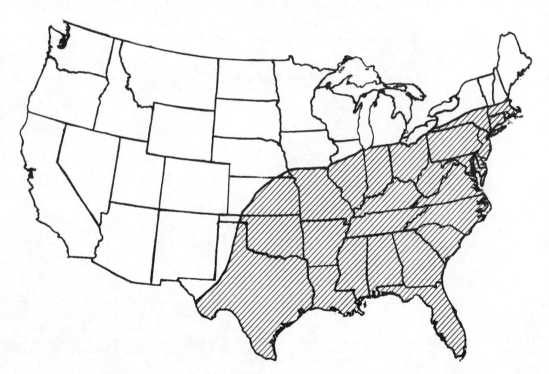

Distribution of *Lonicera japonica* Thunb. (incl. var. *chinensis* (P. W. Wats.)Baker)

FIGURE 176.—*Lonicera japonica* Thunb. Japanese honeysuckle. *A*, Habit—× 0.5; *B*, flowers—× 1; *C*, fruits—× 0.5; *D*, seeds—× 2.5.

DIPSACACEAE

Dipsacus sylvestris Huds.

Biennial herb, reproducing by seeds (Fig. 177); *Stems* the second year erect, 5–20 dm. tall, stout and coarse, prickly at the angles; *Leaves* a rosette the 1st year, the basal leaves oblanceolate and scallop-margined, 20–60 cm. long, sessile or the upper ones clasping the stem lance-oblong, toothed and often prickly on the midveins below and on the margins; the stem leaves opposite the 2d year, lanceolate, entire, sessile; *Inflorescence* in dense ovoid-ellipsoid heads, 3–10 cm. long, terminating long naked peduncles; *Involucral bracts* numerous, some of them surpassing the head, becoming stiff-hooked prickles at maturity; *Flowers* with a 4-leaved calyxlike involucel, investing the ovary and fruit (achene); *Calyx* silky, 1 mm. long; *Corolla* slender, nearly regular, 10–15 mm. long, 4-cleft, the 4 petals (tube) lilac or white, the short (1 mm.) lobes pale-purple, pubescent; *Stamens* 4, inserted on the corolla, distinct; *Achene* 2–3 mm. (rarely up to 8 mm.) long, 4-angled, ridged, hairy, grayish-brown. July–October.

Roadsides, waste grounds, old fields, and pastures and along ditches and edges of forests. Naturalized from Europe. Throughout an area extending from central Maine south to southeastern Virginia and then west to Utah; along the Pacific coast from Washington through northern California.

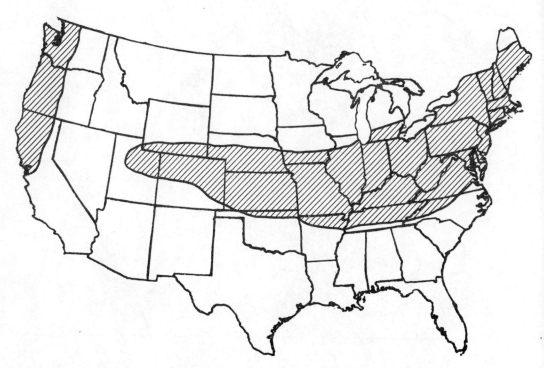

Distribution of *Dipsacus sylvestris* Huds.

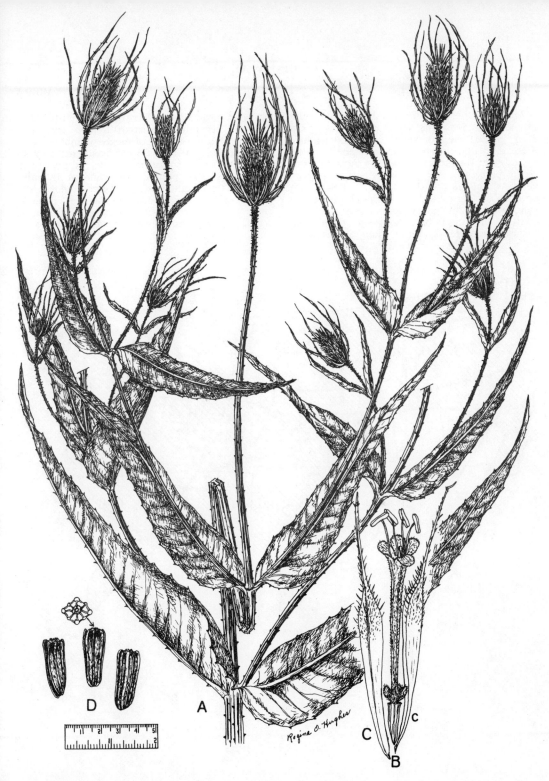

FIGURE 177.—*Dipsacus sylvestris* Huds.   Teasel.   A, Habit—× 0.5; B, flower—× 5; C, and c, bracts (chaff)—
× 5; D, achenes—× 4.

Achillea millefolium L.

Perennial herb, very variable, reproducing by seeds and underground rootstocks (Fig. 178); *Stem* simple or somewhat forked above, 3–10 dm. high, web-hairy to smooth; *Stem leaves* 8–20 (or more), smooth to loosely pubescent, dissected into fine segments; *Corymbs* very compound, flattish-topped, 0.6–3 dm. broad; *Involucre* slenderly cylindric, its scales pale, rarely dark-margined; *Ligules* usually whitish, passing to pink or deep rose-purple, short-oblong, 1.5–2.5 mm. long; *Receptacle* greatly prolonged in fruit, the mature disk flowers becoming exserted; *Achene* tiny, flat, oblong, white or gray. June–September.

Roadsides, meadows, and pastures; persists mainly on thin soil unfavorable for growth of more desirable plants; not common in cultivated fields. Plant has an offensive odor and a bitter taste. Naturalized from Europe. Throughout all the United States excepting areas in southern Texas and the Southwestern States.

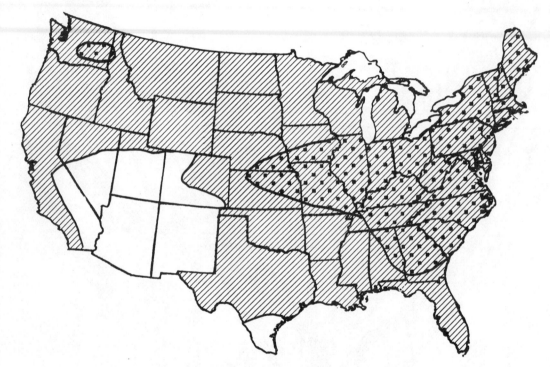

Distribution of *Achillea millefolium* L.

362

FIGURE 178.—*Achillea millefolium* L. Common yarrow. *A*, Habit—× 0.5; *B*, enlarged leaves and stem—× 5; *C*, flower head—× 4; *D*, female and male flowers—× 5; *E*, seeds—× 6.

Ambrosia artemisiifolia L.

COMMON RAGWEED

Annual herb, shallow-rooted (Fig. 179); *Stems* glabrous or hairy, erect, simple or much-branched, with one or both sexes, 0.2–2.5 m. tall; *Leaves* nearly smooth, deeply cut into many lobes, being bipinnatifid or tripinnatifid with small segments, mostly alternate, some opposite below; *Flowers* of two kinds: the male flowers in small inverted racemes at the tips of branches, slender, becoming lax; the female flowers fewer, borne at the bases of leaves and in forks of the upper branches; *Involucres* saucer-shaped, scallop-margined, glabrous or hairy, indistinctly radiate-nerved; *Achene* about 4–5 mm. long, enclosed in a woody hull, light-brown, top-shaped, pointed (the awl-shaped beak 1–2 mm. long), bearing several longitudinal ridges ending in 4–7 short, spiny projections. A variable and pernicious weed, especially **var. *elatior* (L.) Descourtils.** July–October.

Old pastures, wastelands, roadsides, vacant lots, stubble fields, cultivated lands, and sea-beaches. Abundant pollen is a hazard to hay fever sufferers. Native. Widespread throughout North America; most common in the Eastern and North Central States.

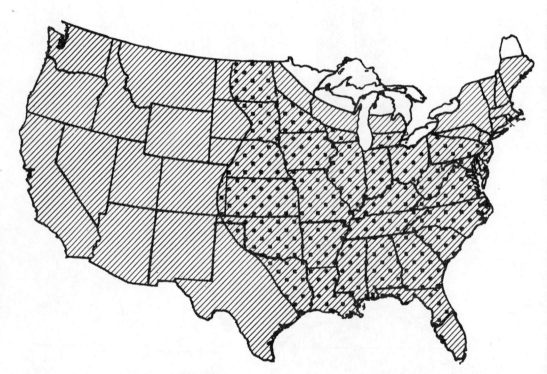

Distribution of *Ambrosia artemisiifolia* L.

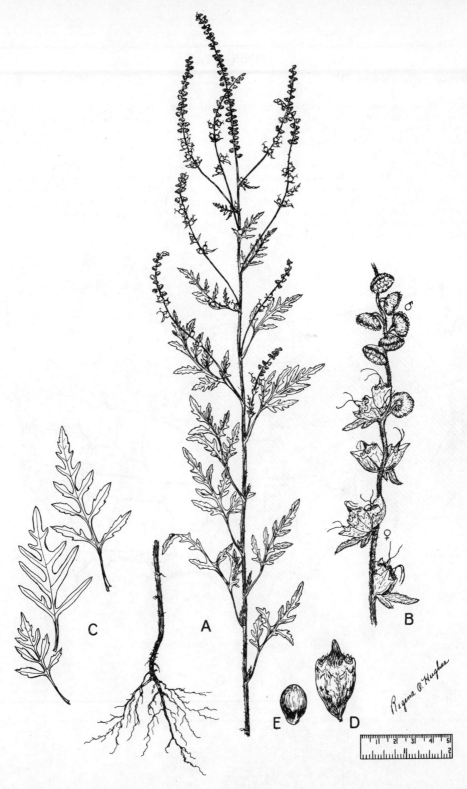

FIGURE 179.—*Ambrosia artemisiifolia* L. Common ragweed. *A*, Habit—× 0.5; *B*, raceme with male heads (*above*) and female involucres (*below*)—× 2.5; *C*, leaf variations—× 0.75; *D*, achene—× 5; *E*, seed—× 5.

Ambrosia psilostachya DC.

WESTERN RAGWEED

Perennial or *annual* herb, reproducing by creeping roots and rootstocks and seeds (Fig. 180); *Stem* erect, 0.3–2.5 m. tall, hairy, bushy, paniculately branched, often growing in dense patches; *Leaves* once-pinnatifid, with short petioles, alternate or opposite, ovate-lanceolate, with very deep lobes, sometimes compound, rough, nearly or quite sessile; *Flowers* of two kinds: the male flowers in clusters on ends of stems and branches, minutely roughened or pubescent; the female flowers few, without petals, in the axils of the upper leaves; *Achene* about 3 mm. long, obovoid, in a woody hull having a pointed tip surrounded by 4 short blunt tubercles. August–October.

Dry prairies, barrens, sands, openings, plains, and uncultivated places. Abundant pollen is a hazard to hayfever sufferers. Native. Throughout all the western half of the United States excepting an area in the Northwest; across all the northern border excepting Maine and an area in the extreme northern Great Lakes region.

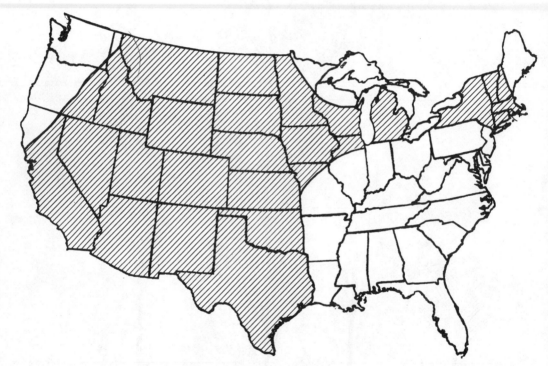

Distribution of *Ambrosia psilostachya* DC.

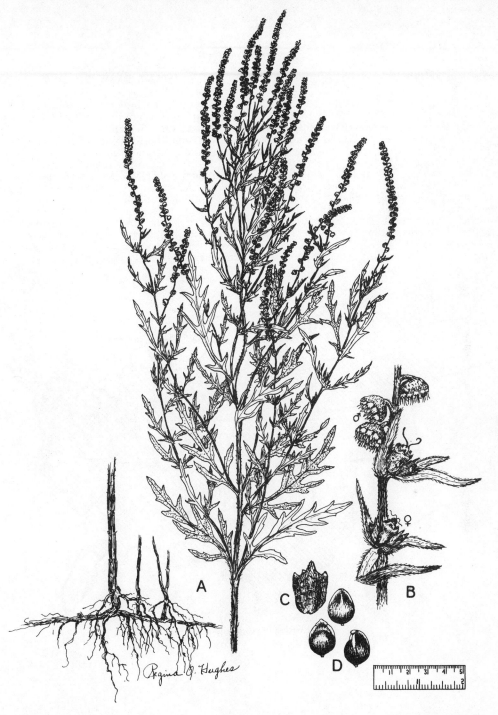

FIGURE 180.—*Ambrosia psilostachya* DC. Western ragweed. *A*, Habit—× 0.5; *B*, raceme of male heads and female involucres—× 2.5; *C*, achene—× 3; *D*, seeds—× 3.

COMPOSITAE

Ambrosia trifida L.

Annual herb, reproducing by seeds (Fig. 181); *Stems* coarse, rough-hairy, reaching a height of 4–6 m. on fertile moist soils, 1–3 m. on less fertile drier soils; *Leaves* all opposite, large, slightly hairy, entire or palmately cleft into 3 (occasionally 5) lobes, the lobes ovate-lanceolate, serrate, the petioles slightly margined; *Flowers* of two kinds and separated: the male flowers abundant in spikelike clusters (racemes) on the tips of branches and stems, the staminate involucres 3-ribbed on one side; the female flowers few, without petals, in the axils of the upper leaves, the female involucre (including the achene) 6–13 mm. long, with a woody hull, the beak acute, conical, 2–4 mm. long and 4–10 acute tubercules terminating the ribs. Late June–September.

Alluvium, bottomlands, fertile moist soils, waste places, and thickets; most serious in corn, soybeans and other cultivated crops. Abundant pollen is a hazard to hay fever sufferers. Adventive from Europe. Throughout all the United States excepting the Pacific coast area and areas in the Southwest, Florida, northern Maine, and extreme northern Great Lakes States; north into Canada from southwest Quebec to British Columbia; south into northern Mexico.

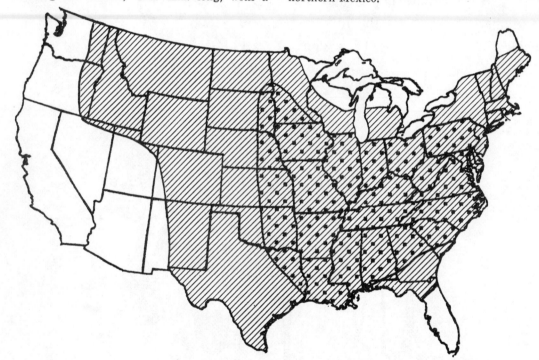

Distribution of *Ambrosia trifida* L.

FIGURE 181.—*Ambrosia trifida* L.   Giant ragweed.   A, Habit, upper portion—× 0.5; B, portion of flowering raceme—× 2.5; C, achene—× 2.

COMPOSITAE

Anthemis cotula **L.**

Annual or *winter annual* herb, with short thick taproot, reproducing only by seed (Fig. 182); *Stems* erect slender, much-branched, nearly smooth, 1–6 dm. tall; *Leaves* about 2–6 cm. long, finely divided, with narrow segments, with a strong disagreeable odor; *Flower heads* short-stalked, resembling those of the daisy, 1.3–2.5 cm. wide, borne singly at the ends of branches, ray flowers white, 5–11 mm. long, surrounding a mass of numerous small yellow disk flowers, the disk about 5–10 mm. wide, becoming ovoid to short-cylindric at maturity; *Involucre* sparsely soft hairy; *Achene* brown, oblong, 10-ribbed, with glandular tubercles; *Pappus* none. May–October.

In abandoned fields, waste places, and barnyards; a cosmopolitan weed. Native of Europe. Throughout the United States.

Distribution of *Anthemis cotula* L.

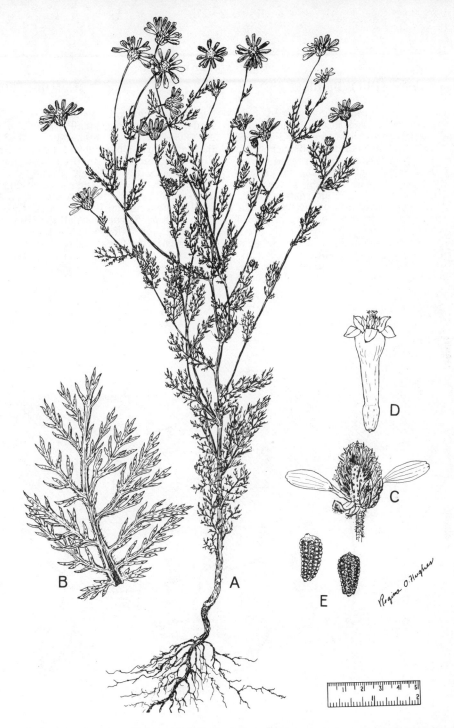

FIGURE 182.—*Anthemis cotula* L.   Mayweed.   *A*, Habit—× 0.5; *B*, enlarged leaf—× 2; *C*, flower head—× 1.5; *D*, disk flower—× 8; *E*, achenes—× 8.

COMPOSITAE

Arctium minus (Hill) Bernh.

Biennial herb, reproducing by seed only (Fig. 183); *Taproot* large, fleshy, living over 1 winter; *Stems* a crown close to the soil surface the 1st year; the 2nd year much-branched, up to 1.5 m. tall, hairy, somewhat grooved or angular; *Leaves* large, petiolate, the lower petioles hollow, the 1st year forming a dense rosette, the 2d year distributed alternately on the stem with larger leaves toward the base, the blade narrowly to very broadly ovate, up to 5 dm. long and 4 dm. wide, thinly woolly, often eventually smooth beneath, nearly glabrous above; *Inflorescence* in racemelike axillary clusters; *Flower heads* 1.5–3 cm. in diameter, short-stalked or nearly sessile, glabrous or slightly glandular to sometimes webby-woolly, made up of numerous small red-violet disk flowers, surrounded by numerous hooked bracts that later form a bur about 1.4 cm. in diameter; *Achene* rather rough, mottled dark-gray, about 0.7 cm. long. July–October.

Waste places where the soil is productive but undisturbed; neglected farmlands; not commonly found in cultivated areas. Naturalized from Europe. Throughout all the United States excepting approximately the southern border and areas in the Great Lakes States; north into Canada from Newfoundland to British Columbia.

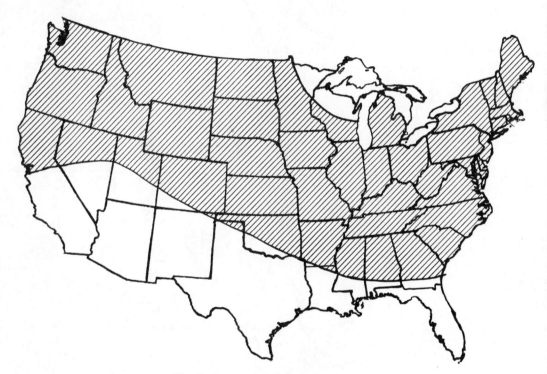

Distribution of *Arctium minus* (Hill) Bernh.

FIGURE 183.—*Arctium minus* (Hill) Bernh. Common burdock. *A*, Habit: root, leaf, upper raceme of heads—
× 0.5; *B*, flower and phyllaries—× 4; *C*, achene—× 3.

COMPOSITAE

Artemisia vulgaris L.

Perennial herb, with a short rhizome, aromatic (Fig. 184); *Stems* 0.5–1.5 m. tall, simple or branched above, glabrous or nearly so below the inflorescence; *Leaves* green, glabrous above, densely white-woolly beneath, obovate or ovate, 5–10 cm. long, 3–7 cm. wide, the principal leaves cleft nearly to the midrib into ascending, acute, unequal segments that in turn are again toothed or more deeply cleft, frequently with 1 or more pairs of stipulelike lobes at the base; *Inflorescence* generally dense and leafy; *Involucres* mostly 3.4–4.5 mm. high, more or less woolly; *Receptacle* without hairs; *Flowers* all fertile, the outer ones pistillate. July–September.

Waste places, fields, and pastures; especially on limey soils. Formerly used medicinally, but toxic properties that result from overdoses cause pain, spasms, and other disturbances. Native of Europe. Introduced and naturalized throughout the northeastern fourth of the United States; along the Pacific coast from Washington through central California; distinct areas in Washington, along the Washington–Oregon border, and in southern California; north into Canada from Ontario to Newfoundland.

Distribution of *Artemisia vulgaris* L.

FIGURE 184.—*Artemisia vulgaris* L. Mugwort. *A*, Habit—× 0.5; *B*, enlarged leaves—× 1; *C*, panicle—× 3; *D*, flower head—× 4; *E*, flowers—× 7.5; *F*, achenes—× 5.

COMPOSITAE

Bidens bipinnata L.

Annual herb, reproducing by seeds (Fig. 185); *Taproot* with numerous side branches; *Stems* erect, square, glabrous or minutely hairy, 3–17 dm. tall, branching in the upper portions; *Leaves* opposite on both stems and branches, 2–3 times pinnate, about 4–20 cm. long, the ultimate segments tending to be rounded, the petioles about 2–5 cm. long; *Heads* borne singly at the ends of long, slender, nearly leafless branches, narrow, discoid, the disk 4–6 mm. wide at anthesis, the outer involucral bracts 7–10, linear, acute, not leafy, shorter than the inner; ray flowers pale-yellow and disk flowers yellow; *Achene* linear, black or dark-brown, attenuate above, often sparsely hairy, 10–18 mm. long, the outer achenes often shorter; *Pappus* of 3–4 yellowish barbed awns. August–October.

In cultivated fields, often in sandy soil, waste places, gardens, grain stubble fields, rocky woods, and moist or wet places. Native or introduced northward. Throughout all the eastern half of the United States excepting areas in northern New England and the Great Lakes States; tropical America; a semicosmopolitan weed.

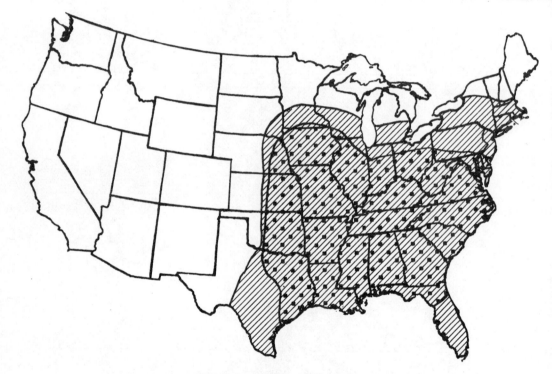

Distribution of *Bidens bipinnata* L.

FIGURE 185.—*Bidens bipinnata* L. Spanish-needles. *A,* Habit—× 0.5; *B,* enlarged leaves—× 1; *C,* flower head—× 1.5; *D,* mature achenes—× 1.5; *E,* achene—× 3.

COMPOSITAE

Bidens frondosa L.

DEVILS BEGGARTICKS

Annual herb, reproducing from seeds (Fig. 186); *Taproot* shallow, much-branched; *Stems* erect, glabrous or nearly so, 2–12 dm. (occasionally up to 1 m.) tall, somewhat 4-sided, branching near the top; *Leaves* opposite, 4-ranked, on petioles 1–6 cm. long, pinnately compound, with 3–5 lanceolate, acuminate, serrate leaflets up to 10 cm. long, 3 cm. wide, sometimes sparsely short-hairy beneath, at least the terminal one slenderly stalked; *Heads* saucer-shaped to hemispheric or nearly globose, discoid or nearly so, the ray flowers orange-yellow, neutral, sometimes absent, the disk corollas 2.5–3 mm. long, orange, equaling the disk, 5-toothed, the ligules golden-yellow, the disk up to 1 cm. wide at flowering; the outer involucral bracts 5–10 (typically 8), green and more or less leafy, usually longer than the orange disk, hairy on the margins, at least toward the base; *Achene* flat, wedge-shaped, strongly 1-nerved on each face, dark-brown or blackish, nearly glabrous or appressed-hairy, mostly 5–10 mm. long; *Pappus* of slightly divergent to erect barbed awns. June–October.

In rich, moist soils, but occasionally in dry waste places; pastures, roadsides, gardens, and damp open habitats; in cultivated ground. Native. Throughout the United States; north into Canada from eastern Quebec to western Ontario.

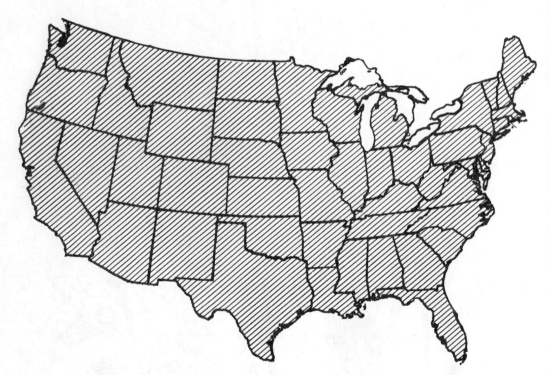

Distribution of *Bidens frondosa* L.

FIGURE 186.—*Bidens frondosa* L. Devils beggarticks. *A*, Habit—× 0.5; *B*, flower head—× 2; *C*, flower, female —× 3; *D*, achenes—× 3.

Centaurea diffusa Lam.   DIFFUSE KNAPWEED

Biennial herb, pubescent becoming glabrate, rough, with an elongated taproot (Fig. 187); *Stems* erect, 5–8 dm. tall, angled but not winged, branched near or above the base; *Leaves* alternate, the basal ones in a whorl, bipinnate to bipinnatifid, oblanceolate to oblong, up to 20 cm. long and 5 cm. wide, short-petioled, the ultimate segments narrowly oblong to elliptic, usually acute and wedge-shaped; the stem leaves sessile, the lower leaves bipinnate to bipinnatifid, the upper leaves much reduced and pinnately lobed, the uppermost leaves bractlike and entire or minutely lobed; *Flower heads* solitary, more or less clustered at the ends of the branches, 1.5 cm. long; *Involucre* narrowly ovate or oblong, about 1 cm. long, woolly becoming glabrate and granular, the phyllaries leathery, nerved, the outer and mid-dle phyllaries broadly to narrowly ovate, pale yellowish-green with a light-brown margin, the upper part narrowed into a stiff spine; the inner phyllaries lanceolate, tipped by a papery or leathery fringed appendage, spiny or spineless; *Flowers* white, pink or lavender, the outermost flowers sterile, inconspicuous, with threadlike corolla lobes; *Achene* oblong, 2.5 mm. long, dark-brown, marked with several conspicuous to faint, pale-brown or ivory lines; *Pappus* none or on the inner achenes as white chaffy scales less than 1 mm. long. June–September.

Waste grounds, fields, and roadsides; locally common. Native in southeastern Europe and western Asia. Distinct areas in the United States, with one large area along the Canadian border in the West; north into British Columbia.

Distribution of *Centaurea diffusa* Lam.

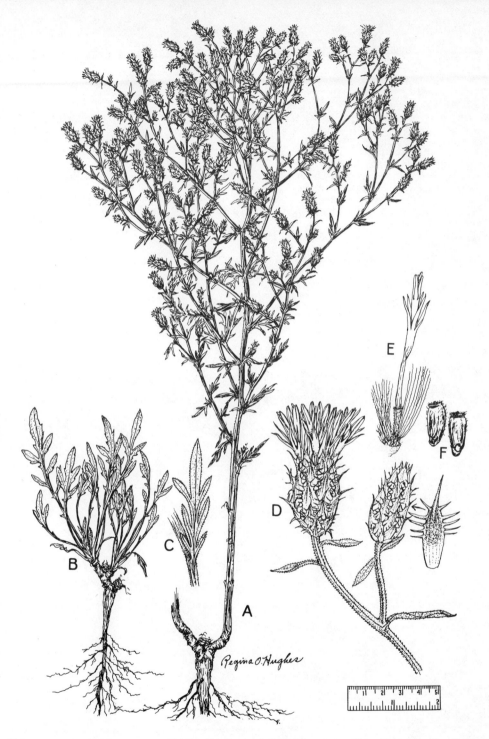

Figure 187.—*Centaurea diffusa* Lam. Diffuse knapweed. *A*, Habit—× 0.5; *B*, young rosette, showing long petioled basal leaves—× 0.5; *C*, cauline leaf, sessile—× 2.5; *D*, flower head—× 5; *E*, flower—× 5; *F*, achenes—× 5.

COMPOSITAE

Centaurea maculosa Lam.

Biennial herb, reproducing by seeds (Fig. 188); *Stems* erect or ascending, with slender wiry branches, rough-pubescent, 3–10 dm. high; *Leaves* alternate, pinnatifid, with narrow divisions, rough-pubescent, the upper leaves often linear; *Flower heads* terminal and axillary, numerous and clustered, 1.5–2.5 cm. in diameter, many-flowered; *Involucre* pale, 1–1.4 cm. high, its smooth strongly ribbed outer and median ovate phyllaries with firm points and 5–7 pairs of cilia, the dark tip 1–2 mm. long, the innermost phyllaries entire or fringed; *Receptacle* bristly, flat; *Flowers* all tubular, whitish to pink or purple, perfect, the marginal flowers enlarged, falsely radiate, neutral; *Achene* brownish, about 2 mm. long, notched on one side of the base; *Pappus* with a short tuft of bristles at tip end, 1–2 mm. long, persistent. August–September.

Dry sterile, gravelly, or sandy pastures, old fields, and roadsides. Introduced and naturalized from Europe. Throughout all the eastern half of the United States excepting the Southern States; along the Pacific coast from southern California into British Columbia and east to central Montana; north in the east to Quebec.

Distribution of *Centaurea maculosa* Lam.

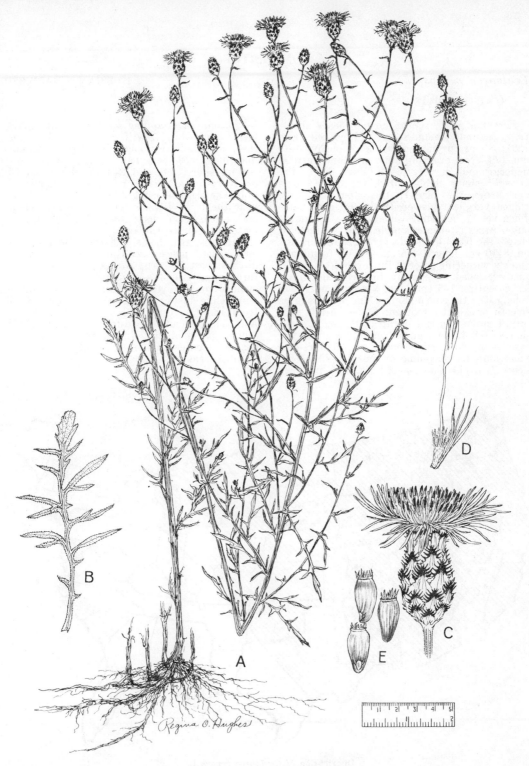

FIGURE 188.—*Centaurea maculosa* Lam. Spotted knapweed. *A*, Habit—× 0.5; *B*, enlarged leaf—× 1; *C*, flower head—× 2; *D*, disk flower—× 3.5; *E*, achenes—× 4.

COMPOSITAE

Centaurea repens L.

RUSSIAN KNAPWEED

(C. picris Pall.)

Perennial herb, reproducing by leafy shoots from the underground stems and by seed (Fig. 189); *Stems* corymbose-branched, bushy, 3–10 dm. tall, from creeping horizontal and vertical underground stems (6–12 dm. deep, the younger stems light-colored, the older stems dark-brown or black), the stem wingless, ridged, very leafy, covered with soft gray hairs when young, becoming velvety to nearly glabrous; *Leaves* alternate, simple, firm, variable in shape, the basal leaves deeply lobed or pinnatifid, 5–10 cm. long, 1–2.5 cm. broad, forming a quickly withering rosette; the lower stem leaves smaller, lobed or sharply toothed; the upper leaves entire, 1–3 cm. long, linear to narrowly oblong, the tip sharp-pointed and the margins smooth or slightly toothed; *Flower heads* solitary, terminating leafy branchlets, small, cone-shaped, 0.8–1.3 cm. in diameter just above the base, many-flowered; *Flowers* all tubular, lavender-blue to rose-pink or purple; *Involucre* slenderly ovoid, pale, about 1 cm. high, phyllaries in many overlapping series, the outer phyllaries rounded-ovate with clear entire margins, the inner phyllaries oblong-acuminate and cut-margined, with very hairy, long, taillike tips; *Achene* shortly obovoid, 2–3 mm. long, grayish or ivory-colored, smooth with inconspicuous lines, the basal scar not oblique and not notched near the base; *Pappus* whitish, threadlike, in one series, deciduous (dropping off by achene maturity). June–October.

Pastures, grainfields, cultivated fields, meadows, waste places, roadsides, and irrigation ditches; pest in corn, alfalfa, sugarbeets, and forage-seed crops. A noxious perennial weed, avoided by all livestock because of the bitter quininelike taste. Introduced and naturalized from the Caucasus in southern Russia and Asia. Throughout the western and much of the central parts of the United States, with the boundary extending from Michigan to south central Texas.

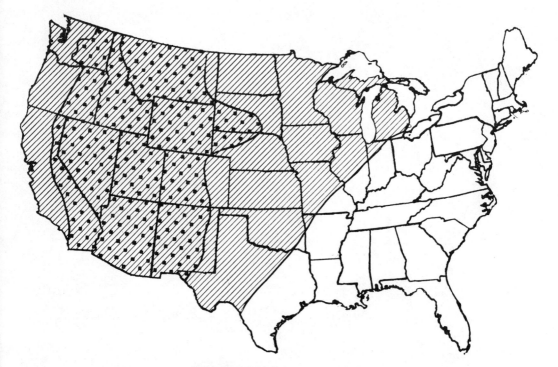

Distribution of *Centaurea repens* L.

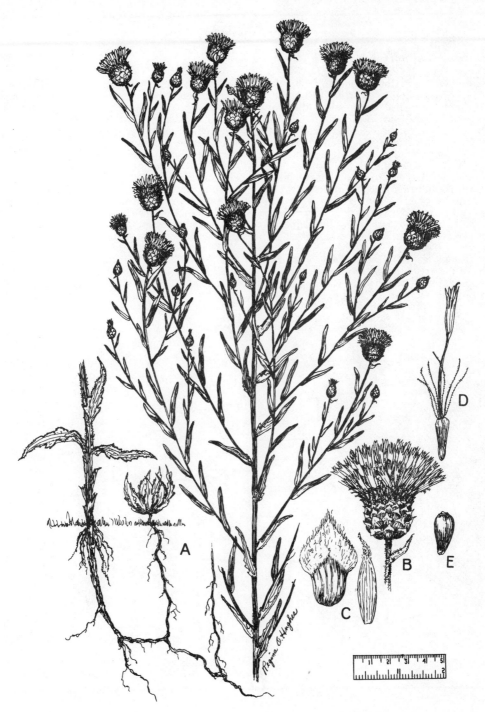

FIGURE 189.—*Centaurea repens* L. Russian knapweed. *A,* Habit—× 0.5; *B,* head—× 1.5; *C,* bracts, outer and inner—× 4.5; *D,* flower × 2.5; *E,* achene—× 5.

Centaurea solstitialis L.   YELLOW STARTHISTLE

Annual herb, sometimes biennial, from a tap-root, reproducing only by seed (Fig. 190); *Stems* rigid, branched from near the base, bushy, woolly, grayish, 1.5–7.5 dm. tall, with narrow green wings; *Leaves* alternate, cottony-hairy; the basal leaves clustered on the ground, 5–15 cm. long, usually petioled, deeply lobed with a much larger lobe at the tip; the stem leaves entire, stalked, narrow, sharp-pointed and lobeless, margins smooth, often wavy, the bases continuing down the stem as wings; the upper leaves greatly reduced; *Flower heads* terminal, urn-shaped with many inconspicuous bright-yellow, tubular flowers stiffly spreading above the narrow tip, the whole 1.8–2.5 cm. high, without leafy bracts; *Involucre* globose, woolly; *Involucral bracts* numerous, closely overlapping, stiff and papery, the middle bracts ending in a stout, rigid, unbranched yellow spine, 1.2–2.5 cm. long, with 1 or 2 pairs of very short spines at its base; *Re-ceptacle* bristly, flat; *Achene* smooth, light-colored, often darker mottled, or dark-brown, 2–3 mm. long, oblong, notched on one side just above the base; *Pappus* of many white, thin bristlelike scales of unequal length, 3–5 mm. long, these lacking on the outermost seeds, persistent or deciduous. May or June to frost.

In cultivated and fallow fields, pastures, rangelands, and waste places; mostly at low elevations, but sometimes up to 8,200 feet. A noxious weed in some areas; in fields of alfalfa and small cereals (wheat, oats, barley, and rice); a rangeland weed in Western States; an injurious pest because of the vicious spines. Native in the Mediterranean region; also in western and central Asia. Throughout all the extreme western part of the United States excepting northern Washington; distinct areas scattered throughout the rest of the United States; north into Canada from Ontario to British Columbia.

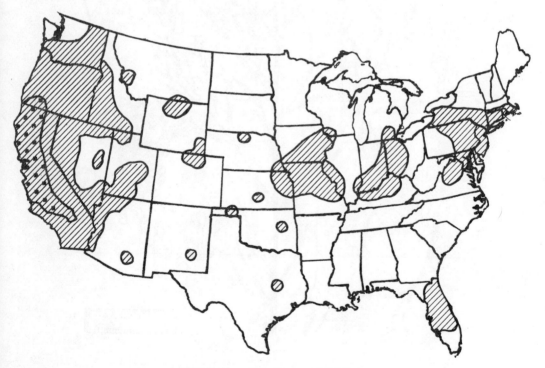

Distribution of *Centaurea solstitialis* L.

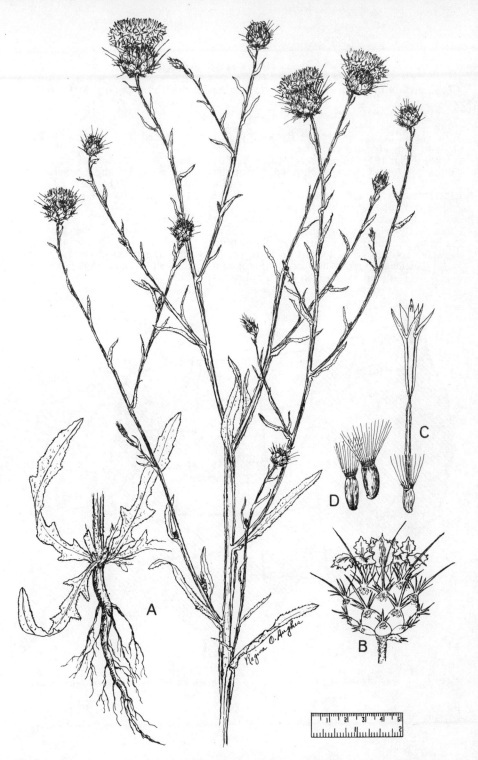

FIGURE 190.—*Centaurea solstitialis* L.   Yellow starthistle.   *A*, Habit—× 0.5; *B*, involucre—× 1.5; *C*, flower—× 3; *D*, achenes—× 6.

COMPOSITAE

Chrysanthemum leucanthemum L. var. *pinnatifidum* Lecoq & Lamotte

FIELD OXEYE-DAISY

Perennial herb, reproducing by seed and by short to wide creeping rhizomes, often forming patches (Fig. 191); *Stems* erect, 0.3–1 m. tall, simple or forked toward the top, glabrous; *Basal leaves* in rosettes, pinnatifid, subpinnatifid or coarsely and irregularly toothed; the middle and upper *stem leaves* alternate, simple, sessile, tooth-margined, narrowly oblong or oblanceolate, conspicuously nearly pinnatifid at the base, glabrous; *Heads* terminal, 2–6 cm. in diameter, solitary at the tops of the stem and of long branches, many-flowered; *Involucral bracts* overlapping, numerous, narrow, brown-margined; *Ray flowers* 20–30, white, pistillate, 10–15 mm. long; *Disk flowers* numerous, yellow, perfect; *Achene* narrowly obovate, 1–1.5 mm. long, bearing a tubercle at the apex, black with 8–10 light-gray ribs; *Pappus* wanting. (**var. *laciniatum* Vis.**, published same year as var. *pinnatifidum*, and may be earlier.) June–August.

Fields, wastes, meadows, and roadsides; a pernicious weed. Naturalized from Europe. Throughout most of the United States; north into southern Canada from Labrador to British Columbia.

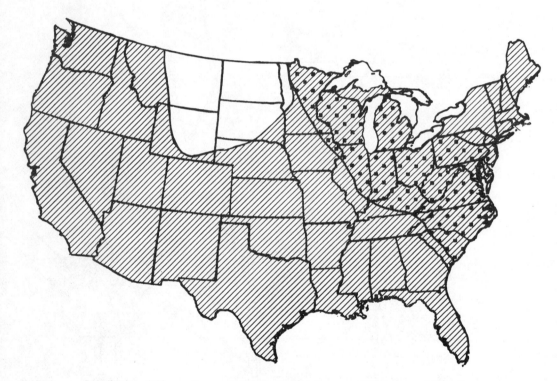

Distribution of *Chrysanthemum leucanthemum* L. var. *pinnatifidum* Lecoq & Lamotte

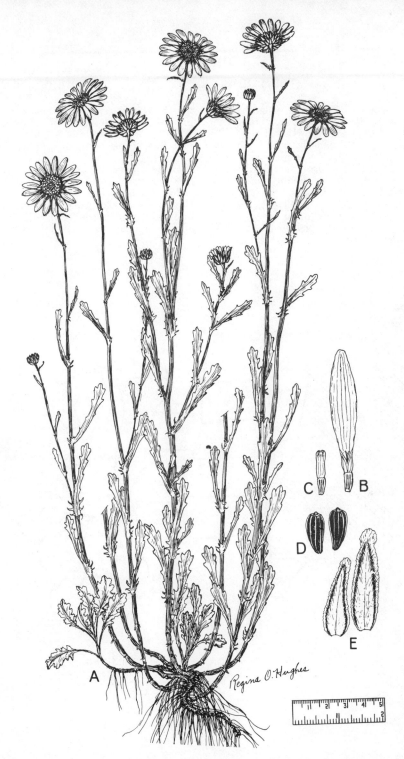

FIGURE 191.—*Chrysanthemum leucanthemum* L. var. *prinnatifidum* Lecoq & Lamotte. Field oxeye-daisy. *A*, Habit —× 0.5; *B*, ray flower—× 2.5; *C*, disk flower—× 2.5; *D*, achenes—× 7.5; *E*, involucral bracts—× 5.

Chrysothamnus nauseosus (Pall.) Britt.

Perennial shrub, 3–20 dm. tall, usually with several fibrous-barked main stems from the base, these much-branched, the twigs ill-scented, erect, usually densely leafy, clothed with a persistent feltlike gray, white, or greenish wool (Fig. 192); *Leaves* variable, linear-filiform to narrowly linear-oblanceolate, 2–7 cm. long, 0.5–4 mm. wide, 1- to 3-nerved, woolly to nearly glabrous, not much twisted; *Flower heads* in terminal rounded cymose clusters; *Involucre* 6–13. mm. high, the phyllaries (20–25) usually 3- or 4-seriate, strongly graduate, mostly lanceolate or linear-lanceolate, not green-tipped, usually with resinous-thickened midrib; *Flowers* usually 5, yellow; *Corolla* 7–12 mm. long; *Pappus* copious, dull-white. August–October.

In dry, open places, in valleys, plains, and foothills; also in mountains. Native. Throughout approximately all the western third of the United States excepting the Pacific coast; north into Canada from southern British Columbia to Saskatchewan; south into northern Mexico.

Distribution of *Chrysothamnus nauseosus* (Pall.) Britt.

FIGURE 192.—*Chrysothamnus nauseosus* (Pall.) Britt. Rubber rabbitbrush. *A*, Habit—× 0.5; *B*, inflorescence—× 3; *C*, flower—× 6; *D*, enlarged leaves—× 1.5; *E*, achene—× 5.

COMPOSITAE

Chrysothamnus viscidiflorus (Hook.) Nutt.

DOUGLAS RABBITBRUSH

Perennial shrub, rounded, many upright branches, white-barked, up to 1 m. tall, with brittle twigs, glabrous or minutely velvety with rather stiff spreading hairs (Fig. 193); *Leaves* linear to linear-lanceolate, flat or twisted, erect, spreading or reflexed, 1–6 cm. long, 0.5–10 mm. wide, 1- to 5-nerved, glabrous or puberulent, sticky, sometimes with punctate glands ventrally; *Flower heads* about 5-flowered, in terminal broad cymes; *Involucre* 5–8 mm. high,

the phyllaries (about 15) linear-oblong to lanceolate, obtuse to acute, not keeled, strongly graduate but in obscure vertical ranks, papery; *Achene* densely hairy; *Pappus* brownish-white. A very polymorphic species, with several subspecies or varieties. July–September.

Dry open places in valleys, plains, and foothills. Native. Throughout approximately all the the Pacific coast; north into southern British Columbia.

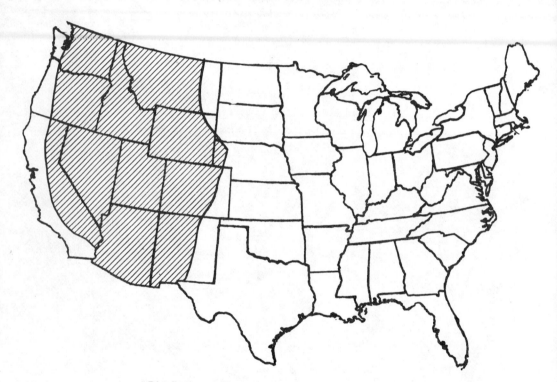

Distribution of *Chrysothamnus viscidiflorus* (Hook.) Nutt.

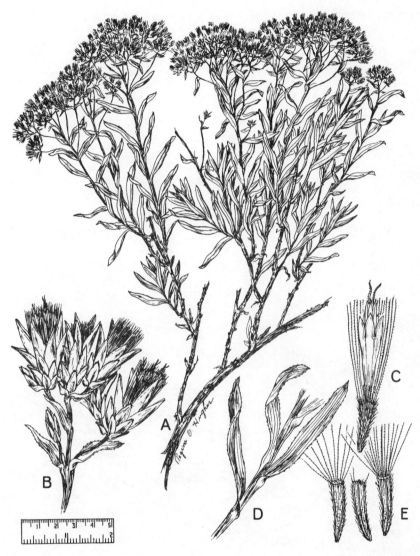

FIGURE 193.—*Chrysothamnus viscidiflorus* (Hook.) Nutt. Douglas rabbitbrush. *A*, Habit (a branch)—× 0.5; *B*, inflorescence—× 4; *C*, flower—× 6; *D*, enlarged leaves—× 1.5; *E*, achenes—× 5.

COMPOSITAE

Cichorium intybus L.

Perennial herb, reproducing by seeds and from roots below the crown (Fig. 194); *Tap-root* long, deep, branched, with a milky sap; *Stems* hollow, 3–24 dm. tall, often rough-hairy, becoming woody and reddish, the branches rigid, stiffly spreading; *Leaves* alternate, mainly clustered near the base, or forming a rosette at the ground, long-petioled, 1–2 dm. long, up to 12 cm. broad, irregularly toothed to deeply lobed, glabrous to rough-hairy; *Upper leaves* entire and dentate, oblong-lanceolate, greatly reduced (3–7 cm. long), sessile, clasping the stem, the base extended into a pair of earlike projections; *Flower heads* numerous, 2.5–3 cm. in diameter, axillary, 1–4 together in sessile clusters along the rigid, nearly glabrous branches or at the tip of short, stiff branches that often have gland-tipped hairs; *Flowers* perfect, all strap-shaped ray flowers, sky-blue, sometimes white or rarely pink; *Bracts* surrounding the flower heads in 2 rows, the outer 5 about half as long as the 8–10 inner, thick-

ened and yellowish at the base, sometimes with gland-tipped hairs, the margins minutely spiny; *Achene* 2–3 mm. long, obovate, light-brown and darker mottled, finely granular, obscurely 4- to 5-angled, the tip blunt, beakless; *Pappus* a minute fringed crown of tiny bristlelike scales. June–October, as early as March in the South and in the Pacific Northwest.

Along roadsides, grasslands, fence rows, and waste ground, preferring neutral or limestone (where most troublesome) soils; in lawns, fields of small grain and pastures; does not survive in cultivated land. Roots used for a coffee substitute; roots eaten boiled; leaves cooked for greens or in salads; relished by all livestock; gives bitter taste to milk and butter. Native of the Mediterranean region, cultivated in Europe. Throughout most of the Eastern and Central States; along the Pacific Coast; distinct areas scattered throughout the rest of the United States; north into southern Canada from Nova Scotia to British Columbia.

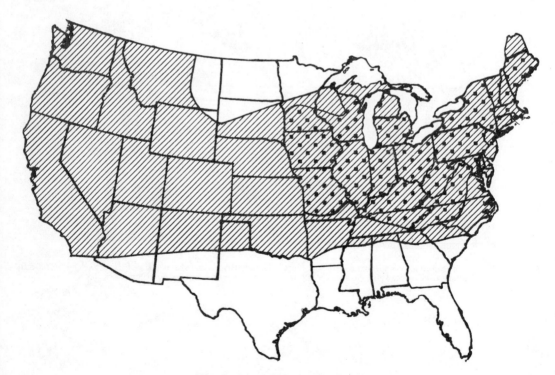

Distribution of *Cichorium intybus* L.

FIGURE 194.—*Cichorium intybus* L. Chicory. *A,* Habit—× 0.5; *B,* terminal portion of inflorescence; *C,* involucre—× 2.5; *D,* flower—× 2.5; *E,* achenes—× 7.5.

COMPOSITAE

Cirsium arvense (L.) Scop.   CANADA THISTLE

Perennial herb, reproducing by seeds and horizontal roots (Fig. 195); *Roots* extending several feet into the soil or extensively creeping horizontally; *Stems* erect, 4–12 dm. tall, grooved, branching only at the top, nearly glabrous or slightly hairy when young, increasingly hairy with maturity; *Leaves alternate*, oblong or lanceolate, usually with crinkled edges and spiny margins, somewhat lobed, hairy beneath or often glabrous or nearly so at maturity, the upper leaves sessile and only slightly decurrent; *Flower* heads dioecious (male and female flowers usually in separate heads and borne on different plants), numerous, compact in corymbose clusters, terminal and axillary, 2–2.5 cm. in diameter, with lavender, rose-purple, or white disk flowers only; *Involucre* 1–2 cm. high, the bracts numerous, overlapping, spineless; *Receptacle* bristly, chaffy; *Achene* light- to dark-brown, smooth oblong, 2.5–3.5 mm. long, flattened, curved or straight, apex blunt with a tubercle in the center; *Pappus* tannish-brown, plumose, about 2 mm. long, deciduous. July–October.

In all crops, pastures, meadows, and waste places; in rich, heavy soils; a noxious weed. Introduced and naturalized from Eurasia; not native of Canada. Throughout the northern half of the United States; north into Canada from Quebec to British Columbia.

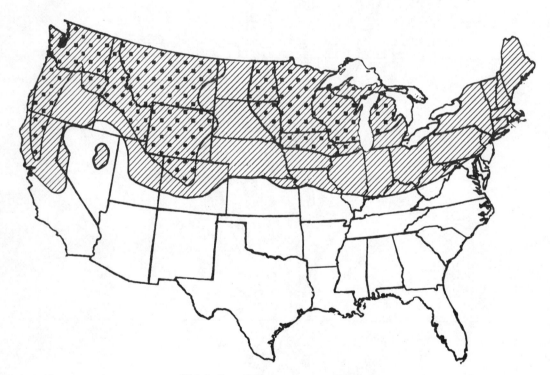

Distribution of *Cirsium arvense* (L.) Scop.

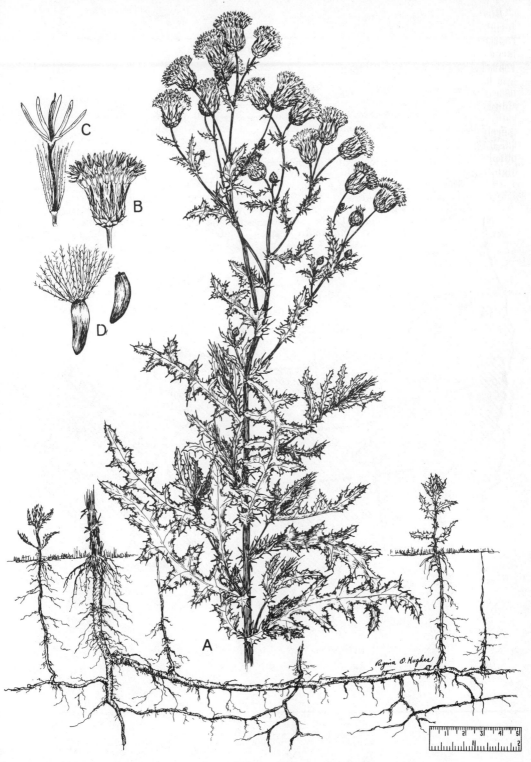

FIGURE 195.—*Cirsium arvense* (L.) Scop. Canada thistle. *A*, Habit—× 0.5; *B*, head—× 1; *C*, flower—× 2.5; *D*, achenes—× 3.

Cirsium vulgare (Savi) Tenore

(C. lanceolatum Hill)

BULL THISTLE

Biennial herb, reproducing by seeds, plants forming 1st year oblanceolate to elliptic coarsely toothed leaves in a rosette, from a large fleshy taproot (Fig. 196); *Stems* erect 2d year, 1–2 m. tall, stout, often branched, more or less hairy, spiny-winged by the decurrent leaf bases; *Leaves* alternate lanceolate, pinnatifid, spiny with long needle-pointed tips, rough-spiny above, thinly white-woolly to green and merely hairy beneath; *Flower heads* compact, 2.5–5 cm. in diameter, composed of many deep-purple or rose disk flowers; *Involucre* 2.5–4 cm. high, its numerous bracts spine-tipped, without any well-developed sticky dorsal ridges; *Receptacle* flat, bristly; *Achene* straw-colored, striped with brown or black, ridged around one end, tipped with down, less than 4 mm. long; *Pappus* plumose, about 2 mm. long; deciduous. June–October.

Fields, pastures, 1st-year meadows, and wastelands. An aggressive and bad weed, but will not survive in cultivated fields. Introduced and naturalized from Eurasia. Throughout the United States; north into Canada from Newfoundland to British Columbia.

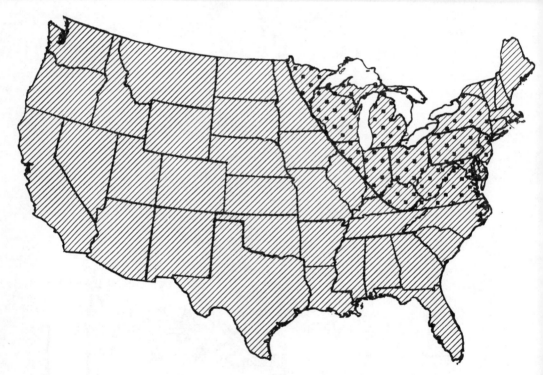

Distribution of *Cirsium vulgare* (Savi) Tenore

FIGURE 196.—*Cirsium vulgare* (Savi) Tenore. Bull thistle. *A*, Habit—× 0.5; *B*, flower—× 5; *C*, immature fruit—× 1.75; *D*, achenes—× 3.5.

Conyza canadensis (L.) Cronq.

(Erigeron canadensis L.)

HORSEWEED

Annual herb, reproducing by seeds (Fig. 197); *Stems* erect, stout, unbranched at base, up to 1.5–2 m. tall, with bristly hairs; *Leaves* alternate, simple, numerous, without petioles, dark-green, with scattered coarse white bristles; the lowest oblanceolate or spatulate, toothed or entire, tapering to petioles, 3–13 mm. broad; the abundant stem leaves narrowly oblanceolate to linear, mostly entire and sessile; *Flower heads* numerous, racemose or cymose on the branches, forming elongate panicles; *Involucres* slenderly saucer-shaped, 2.5–5 mm. long, the linear-tapering phyllaries with pale tips; *Ray flowers* greenish-white to lavender, inconspicuous, over 100 per head; *Disk flowers* numerous, perfect, yellow; *Receptacle* flat, 1.2–2.5 mm. broad when bare; *Seed* about 1 mm. long with numerous slender white bristles at one end. July–November.

In pastures, roadsides, wastelands, cultivated fields, and gardens; mostly on rather dry soils. A semicosmopolitan weed. Native; also introduced in some localities. Common throughout the United States and North America.

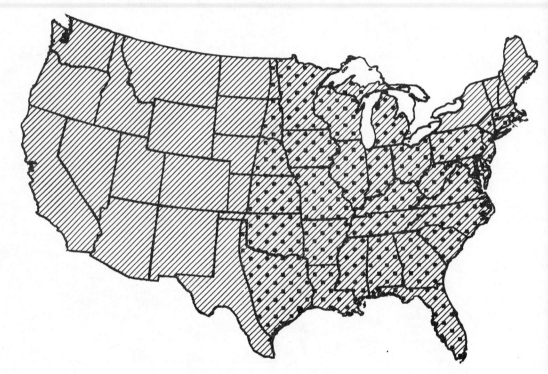

Distribution of *Conyza canadensis* (L.) Cronq.

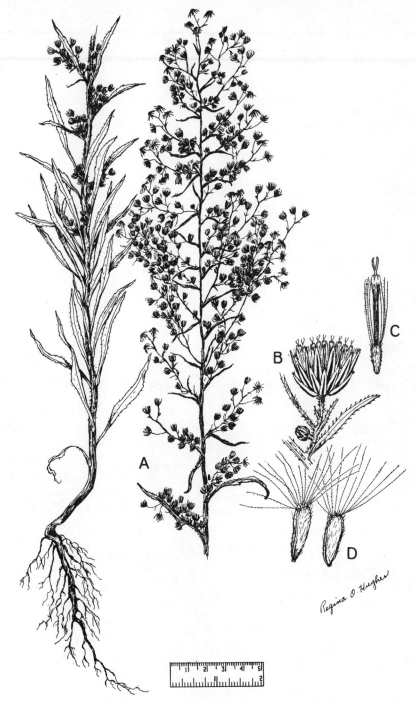

FIGURE 197.—*Conyza canadensis* (L.) Cronq. Horseweed. *A*, Habit—× 0.5; *B*, flower head—× 5; *C*, disk flower —× 10; *D*, achenes—× 10.

COMPOSITAE

Erigeron annuus (L.) Pers.

ANNUAL FLEABANE

Annual or *biennial* herb, reproducing by seeds (Fig. 198); *Stems* erect, branched above, 3–15 dm. tall, glabrous or with scattered spreading stiff hairs; *Leaves* alternate, simple, coarsely and sharply dentate, membranaceous, nearly glabrous, the lower leaves ovate, tapering into margined petioles, the upper leaves lanceolate, acute and entire at both ends, mostly sessile, the uppermost leaves often entire, linear; *Flower heads* in a corymbose cluster, numerous, 1.5–2 cm. in diameter, many-flowered, on naked peduncles; *Involucral bracts* in 1- to 2-series, narrow, equal, slightly hairy; *Ray flowers* about 50–75, white or tinged purple or lavender, much longer than the disk flowers, 1 mm. wide, pistillate; *Disk flowers* numerous,

yellow, perfect; *Achene* about 1 mm. long, obovate, flattened, with minute appressed hairs, straw-colored; *Pappus* double, the outer a crown of short scales, the inner of deciduous bristly hairs, usually absent in the ray flowers. May–November.

Fields, meadows, pastures, and waste places; a cosmopolitan weed. Native. Used in domestic medicine as an astringent, tonic, and diuretic. Throughout approximately all the eastern half of the United States excepting the extreme southeastern part; along the Pacific coast from southern California north to the Canadian border and east to central Montana; north into southern Canada from Nova Scotia to Manitoba.

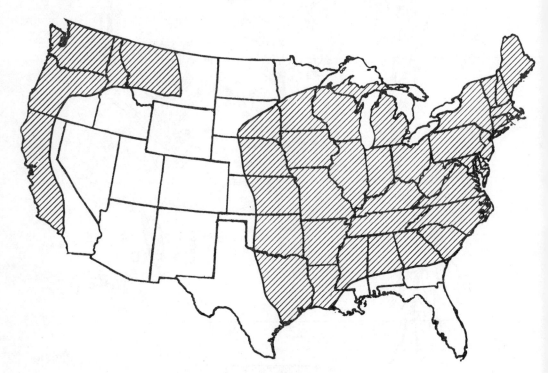

Distribution of *Erigeron annuus* (L.) Pers.

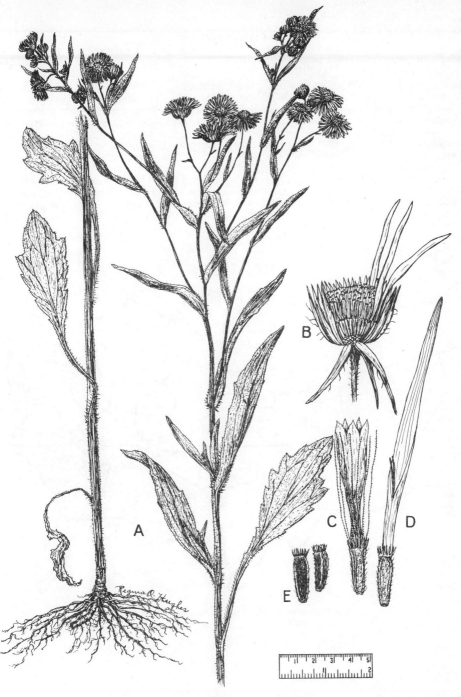

FIGURE 198.—*Erigeron annuus* (L.) Pers. Annual fleabane. *A*, Habit—× 0.5; *B*, flower head—× 5; *C*, disk flower—× 13; *D*, ray flower—× 1; *E*, achenes—× 10.

Eupatorium capillifolium (Lam.) Small

Annual herb (Fig. 199); Stems slender, several from a stout woody caudex, 5–30 dm. tall, downy or smooth below, much-branched; Leaves once or twice pinnately divided or dissected into fine, linear divisions, those of the inflorescence mostly simple, glandular-punctate, glabrous, the lowermost leaves opposite, the others alternate, mostly 2–10 cm. long, often with axillary clusters; Flower heads green to bronze, very numerous in an elongate, much-branched panicle, the lower or outer heads blooming first; Involucre 2–3.5 mm. high, the inner bracts much longer than the outer ones, usually with a sharp tip or abruptly pointed; Flowers 3–6 in each head, corolla greenish-white, 1.5–3 mm. long; Achene glabrous. September–October.

Borders of woods and old fields and pastures; in wet or dry soil in open places; aggressive and weedy. Native. Along the Atlantic coast from Massachusetts south; throughout the southern third of the United States.

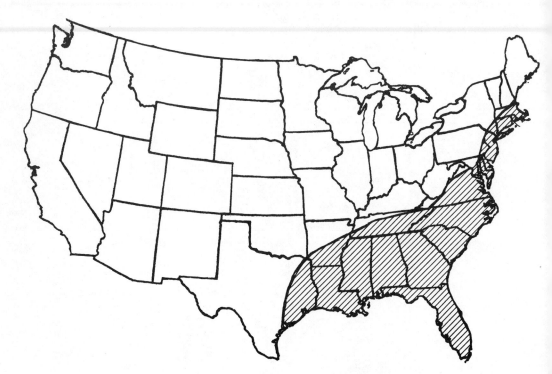

Distribution of Eupatorium capillifolium (Lam.) Small

FIGURE 199.—*Eupatorium capillifolium* (Lam.) Small. Dogfennel. *A*, Habit—× 0.5; *B*, flower panicle—× 5; *C*, enlarged leaves—× 5; *D*, disk flower—× 15; *E*, achenes—× 10.

Eupatorium rugosum Houtt.

(*E. urticaefolium* Reichard)

Perennial herb, reproducing by seeds and from the rhizome (Fig. 200); *Rhizome* rough, knotty, fibrous-rooted; *Stems* erect, firm, solitary or clustered, simple or branching above, 0.2–1.5 m. tall, glabrous; *Leaves* opposite, simple, long-petioled, 3–nerved, glabrous, broadly ovate, the larger ones membranaceous flat blades, 5–18 cm. long, 3–11 cm. broad, coarsely and often sharply 9- to 25-toothed on each margin, gradually tapering from above the base to a long tapering tip, often rounded or heart-shaped bases, the upper leaves gradually smaller; *Heads* in dense compound corymbs with 8–30 perfect disk flowers, in well-developed plants the corymbs open with loosely ascending branches from the upper axils, in smaller plants more compact and terminal;

Involucral bracts (phyllaries) subequal, usually in 1 row, green, tapering to obtuse scarcely overlapping, 4–6 mm. long, glabrous or short-hairy; *Flowers* 5–7 mm. in diameter, with bright white petals 3–4 mm. long; *Receptacle* flat and naked; *Achene* 2–2.5 mm. long, linear, black or dark-brown, glabrous or nearly so. Late July–October.

Woodlands, thickets, clearings, damp and shady pastures, and fields; chiefly on gravelly and calcareous soils. Native. Poisonous to livestock; the poison transmissible to man in milk. Throughout all the eastern half of the United States excepting areas in the extreme South; north into southern Canada from New Brunswick west to southeastern Saskatchewan.

Distribution of *Eupatorium rugosum* Houtt.

FIGURE 200.—*Eupatorium rugosum* Houtt. White snakeroot. *A*, habit—× 0.5; *B*, branch of corymb—× 3.5; *C*, achenes—× 6.5.

COMPOSITAE

Franseria discolor Nutt.

SKELETONLEAF BURSAGE, BUR-RAGWEED,
SILVERLEAF, POVERTYWEED

Perennial herb, reproducing by seeds and by deep creeping rootstocks (Fig. 201); *Stems* erect or ascending, 2–6 dm. tall, bushy, branching from the base, white-woolly to sparingly pubescent; *Leaves* alternate, mostly bipinnately lobed, white tomentose on the underside, green or grayish rough-haired to smooth above, 5–12 cm. long, the lobes narrow, irregularly cut on the margin, petiole winged; *Flowers* small, male and female borne separately but on the same plant; the staminate heads with spathulate, 1–nerved chaff shorter than the corollas, in small drooping heads along the tips of the branches, solitary or in several terminal racemes; the pistillate flowers 1–2, in the axils of the upper leaves; *Burs* (mature involucres) 4–6 mm. long, rough-haired, with 2 beaks, with 8–12 spines, about 1–1.5 mm. long, conical; *Achene* 1–3 per bur, 4–6 mm. long. July–September.

Meadows, in moist cultivated fields, waste places, pastures, and irrigated fields, especially if poorly drained; also in dry regions and plains. Native. Throughout an area of the United States bounded by Wyoming and South Dakota on the north, east to central Kansas and west to eastern Nevada; south to the Mexican border.

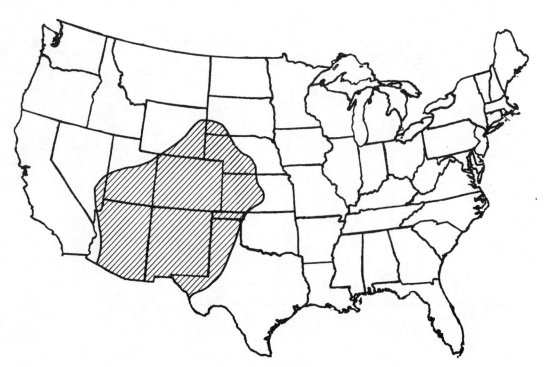

Distribution of *Franseria discolor* Nutt.

FIGURE 201.—*Franseria discolor* Nutt. Skeletonleaf bursage. *A*, Habit— × 0.5; *B*, enlarged raceme, with staminate (*a*) and pistillate (*b*) flowers— × 2.5; *C*, fruit (burlike)—× 4.

Galinsoga parviflora Cav.

Annual herb, reproducing by seeds (Fig. 202); *Stems* erect or spreading, much branched, slender, 3–7 dm. tall, glabrous or sparsely pubescent; *Leaves* opposite, ovate to lance-ovate, pointed at the tip, thin, 2–7 cm. long, 1–4 cm. wide, serrulate or crenulate, glabrous or sparsely appressed-hairy; *Flower heads* small, numerous, scattered at the ends of the branches, in leafy cymes; *Ray flowers* very small, white, 4–5 in number, surrounding the small yellow disk flowers; *Pappus* of the disk flowers without awns, equaling or longer than the corolla; *Achene* about 1:5 mm. long, wedge-shaped, 4-sided, dark-brown to black, with a fringe of tiny scales at one end, or glabrous. June–November.

Weedy gardens, dooryards, lowland fields, and waste places, especially in damp areas with rich soil. A cosmopolitan weed. Naturalized from Mexico and South America. Throughout all the United States excepting areas along the northern border and along the central Atlantic coast.

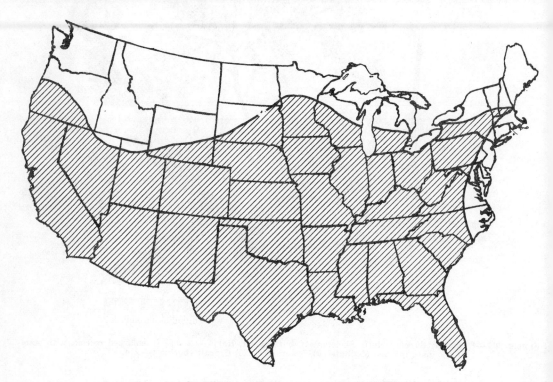

Distribution of *Galinsoga parviflora* Cav.

FIGURE 202.—*Galinsoga parviflora* Cav. Smallflower galinsoga.   *A*, Habit—× 0.5; *B*, enlarged flowering branch—
× 2; *C*, flower head—× 4; *D*, ray flower—× 7.5; *E*, disk flower—× 7.5; *F*, achene with pappus—× 5.

COMPOSITAE

Gutierrezia dracunculoides (DC.) Blake   COMMON BROOMWEED

(Brachyris dracunculoides DC.; *Amphiachyris dracunculoides* DC.;
Xanthocephalum dracunculoides (DC.) Shinners)

Annual herb, reproducing by seeds (Fig. 203); *Stems* 3–10 dm. tall, simple at the base, effusely branching above, paniculate; *Leaves* alternate, entire, blades of the upper leaves narrowly linear or thread-shaped, with a tendency to fall away early leaving the plant naked and wiry; *Flower heads* numerous, small with few yellow flowers; *Involucres* about 3 mm. thick and 3 mm. long; *Ray flowers* fertile, their pappus crownlike, of extremely minute, irregular, hyaline teeth in layers; *Disk flowers* abortive their pappus a short papery cup, tipped with about 5 coarse, white or straw-colored fine bristles; *Achene* elongated, but never strongly flattened. August–October.

Dry upland prairies, rocky open limestone barrens, roadsides, and fallow fields and along railroads. Native. Throughout approximately all of the area of the United States bounded by extreme southern Iowa in the north, east to southwestern Illinois and west through most of New Mexico, south to the Mexican border; distinct area in southwestern Alabama; south into Mexico.

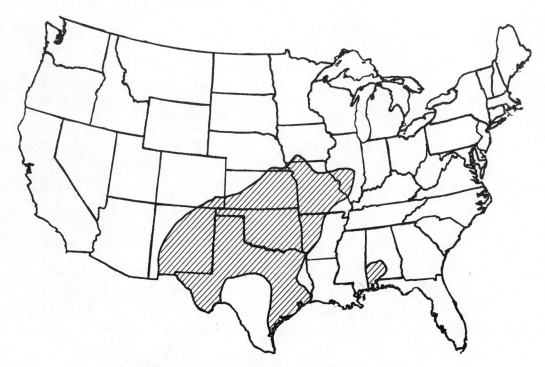

Distribution of *Gutierrezia dracunculoides* (DC.) Blake

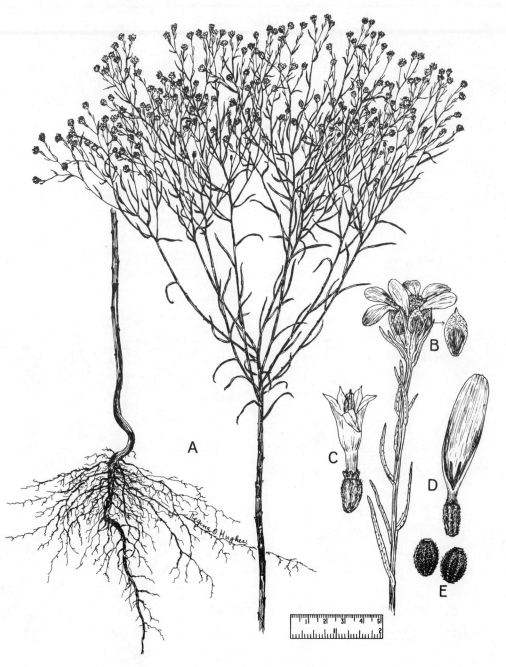

FIGURE 203.—*Gutierrezia dracunculoides* (DC.) Blake. Common broomweed. *A*, Habit—× 0.5; *B*, flower head—× 5; *C*, disk flower—× 7.5; *D*, ray flower—× 7.5; *E*, achenes—× 5.

COMPOSITAE

Haplopappus tenuisectus (Greene) Blake ex Benson BURROWEED

Perennial, woody half-shrub, 0.5–1 m. in diameter and 0.5–1 m. tall (Fig. 204); *Taproot* up to 18 ft. deep, with a few shorter lateral roots; *Stems* densely branched at the base, 5–7 dm. tall (rarely taller), gray-green to brighter green above, forming a nearly spherical bush; *Leaves* pinnatifid, glandular, resinous and sticky, 20–35 mm. long, about 1 mm. broad, oblong or spathulate-oblong with narrow (2–22 mm. long by 1 mm. wide) linear lobes extending from each side; *Flower heads* discoid, with 8–12 flowers; each *involucral bract* with a thickened green warty apical spot, this with minute resin glands, the apical portion of the involucre at fruiting time 3–4 mm. in diameter; *Flowers* yellow, borne in small dense heads, the corolla lobes acute, not more than 1 mm. long; *Style* appendages triangular, shorter than the stigmatic region; *Achene* with simple pappus of 30–60 bristles. September–October.

On alluvial plains of desert and in semidesert grasslands; invades depleted rangelands. Poisonous to cattle and to humans through the milk of cows. Southwestern United States along the Mexican border from eastern Arizona to central Texas; south into Mexico.

Distribution of *Haplopappus tenuisectus* (Greene) Blake ex Benson

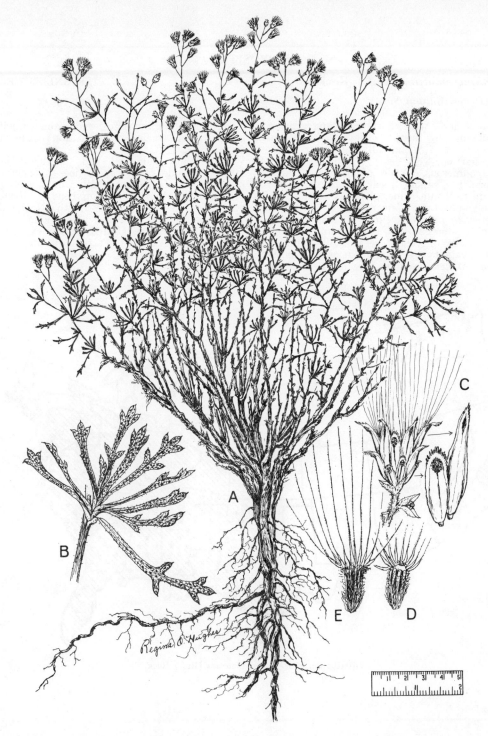

FIGURE 204.—*Haplopappus tenuisectus* (Greene) Blake ex Benson. Burroweed. *A,* Habit—× 0.5; *B,* fascicle of leaves—× 2.5; *C,* flower head—× 5; *D,* disk flower—× 7.5; *E,* achene—× 7.5.

COMPOSITAE

Helenium amarum (Raf.) Rock   BITTER SNEEZEWEED

(H. tenuifolium Nutt.)

Annual herb, with short branching taproot, reproducing by seeds (Fig. 205); *Stems* smooth, erect, 1–8 dm. tall, branching in the upper portion, very leafy; *Leaves* alternate, simple, numerous, crowded along the main stem and branches, sessile, linear-filiform, 1.5–8 cm. long, up to 2 mm. wide, glabrous and densely glandular-punctate; *Flower heads* 1.5–2 cm. in diameter; *Ray flowers* yellow, pistillate and fertile, with 3-toothed tips, surrounding a dome-shaped mass of yellow perfect disk flowers; *Pappus* ovate, long-awned, about as long as the achene; *Achene* reddish-brown, 1–1.5 mm.

long, hairy along the edges, wedge-shaped, with bristle-tipped scales at the top. August–October.

Wastelands, old feed lots, pastures, idle lands, roadsides, and yards; does not persist under cultivation. Causes bitter unmarketable milk produced by cows grazing heavily infested pastures, especially in the South. Native to Southeastern United States. Throughout the eastern half of the United States excepting areas in the north; distinct areas in north central California.

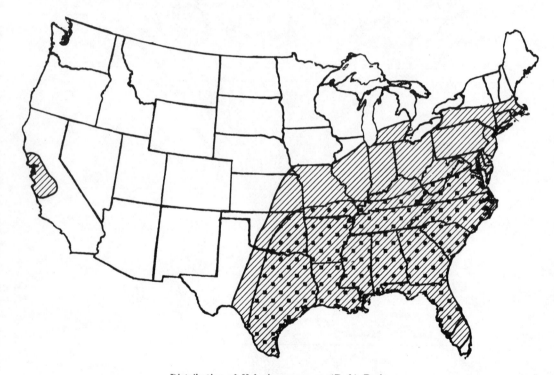

Distribution of *Helenium amarum* (Raf.) Rock

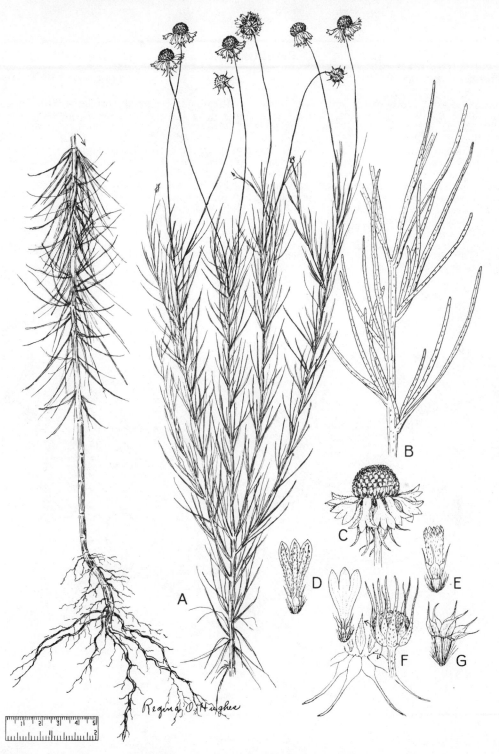

FIGURE 205.—*Helenium amarum* (Raf.) Rock. Bitter sneezeweed. *A*, Habit—× 1; *B*, leaf detail—× 1.5; *C*, flower head—× 2.5; *D*, ray flower, back and face—× 5; *E*, disk flower—× 5; *F*, involucre—× 2.5; *G*, achene—× 7.5.

Helianthus annuus L.

Annual herb, reproducing only by seeds (Fig. 206); *Root system* fibrous; *Stems* erect, usually branching above, stout, coarse, rough and pubescent, 0.5–3 m. or more high; *Leaves* mostly alternate, simple, petioled, with 3 main veins, the blade 0.2–3 dm. or more wide, ovate or the lower ones cordate, rough on both surfaces, the margins serrate; *Heads* solitary and terminal, or also axillary, 6–12.5 cm. in diameter; *Involucral bracts* overlapping, oblong-lanceolate to oval or broadly ovate, long-ciliate, with pubescent to glabrescent backs and tapering tips; *Receptacle* nearly flat, chaffy, 4 cm. or more in diameter; *Ray flowers* mostly neutral, bright-yellow; *Disk flowers* numerous, perfect,

with tubular brownish corolla; *Achene* about 9 mm. long by 4–8 mm. broad, glabrous except for the sparsely hairy summit, ovate to wedge-shaped, slightly 4–angled and flattened, white, gray, or dark-brown with light stripes or gray mottled; *Pappus* of 2 thin scales, chaffy, deciduous. July–November.

Plains, in cultivated fields, waste places, grainfields, pastures, fence rows, roadsides, and ballast lots. Throughout the United States, being native from Minnesota to Saskatchewan, south to Missouri and Texas; introduced eastward to Nova Scotia, New Brunswick, and the Atlantic States; also introduced westward.

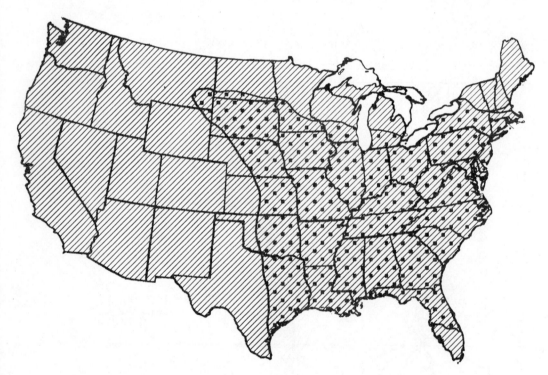

Distribution of *Helianthus annuus* L.

FIGURE 206.—*Helianthus annuus* L.   Sunflower.   *A*, Habit—× 0.5; *B*, ray flower—× 2; *C*, disk flower—× 2.5; *D*, achenes, 2 views—× 1.5.

COMPOSITAE

Hymenoxys odorata DC. BITTER RUBBERWEED

Annual herb, reproducing by seeds (Fig. 207); *Stems* low, spreading, many-branched, varying from 3–60 cm. tall, the foliage with a bitter taste and an aromatic odor when crushed; *Leaves* somewhat fleshy, sparingly hairy to almost glabrous, divided into 3–13 very narrow segments about 1.6 mm. broad, the surface covered by minute depressed glandular pits; a basal rosette of leaves 2.5–10 cm. long formed first, soon withering, the stem leaves alternate, numerous, 1.8–7 cm. long; *Flower heads* yellow, solitary at the tips of the stiff leafless stalks, 2.5–15 cm. long, small, 0.8–3.3 cm. wide, including the 8–13 golden-yellow ray flowers and the many tubular disk flowers in the center, (as many as 3,000 heads per plant); *Involucral bracts* surrounding each head in 2 rows, erect, greenish-yellow, somewhat glandular, the outer 8–10 bracts 0.3–0.5 cm. long, united and thickened at the base, the tips pointed, the inner bracts not united, free at the base, slightly longer than outer bracts and pressed inward in fruit; *Achene* numerous, 50–75 per head, narrowly cone-shaped, 1.6–2.2 mm. long, indistinctly 4–angled and covered with silky grayish hairs; *Pappus* of 5 (rarely 6) dry, colorless or tawny scales, sharp-pointed or tipped with a short bristle, the scales about the same length as the achenes. Flowering March–June, beginning in January in warmer areas.

Plains and drainage areas, barren disturbed soil around watering areas, and overgrazed rangelands and pastures; abundant where water collects along roadsides, lake beds, and bottomlands near rivers. Native. Heavy infestations may cause death to sheep and occasionally to cattle. Southwestern United States along the Mexican border from eastern California through Texas, north to east central Colorado; south into northern Mexico.

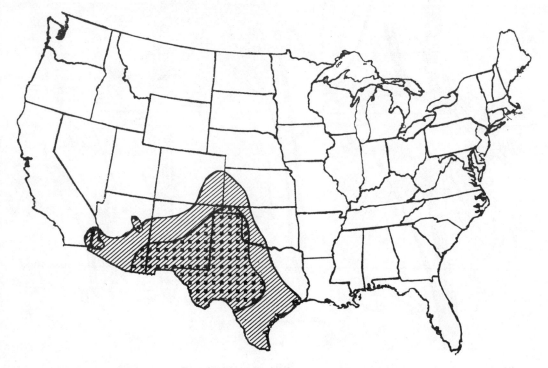

Distribution of *Hymenoxys odorata* DC.

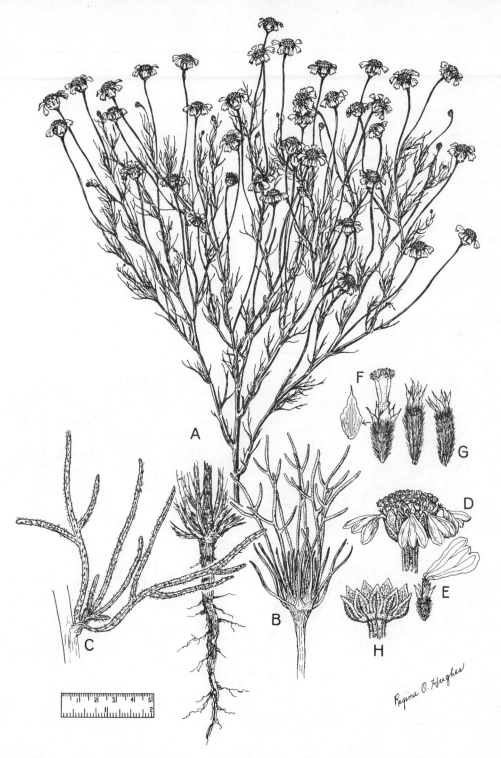

FIGURE 207.—*Hymenoxys odorata* DC. Bitter rubberweed. *A*, Habit—× 0.5; *B*, young plant—× 0.5; *C*, enlarged leaf detail—× 3; *D*, flower head—× 2.5; *E*, ray flower—× 0.75; *F*, disk flower—× 5; *G*, achenes—× 5; *H*, involucre—× 2.5.

COMPOSITAE

Iva xanthifolia Nutt.

Annual herb, with a taproot, reproducing by seeds (Fig. 208); *Stems* 4–24 dm. tall, coarse branching, grayish-green, glabrous below, becoming viscid-villous in the inflorescences; *Leaves* broad, mostly opposite, light grayish-green, ovate, covered with short hairs, 5–20 cm. long and 2.5–15 cm. wide, coarsely and often doubly serrate; *Inflorescence* large, in panicle shape; *Flower heads* small, numerous, nearly sessile, drooping in panicles at the top of the stem and in the axils of the upper leaves; *Flowers* either male or female, but borne in the same head, without petals, greenish-yellow; *Involucre* viscid-hairy or nearly glabrous, about 1.5–3 mm. high, the 5 outer bracts larger than the 5 inner ones; *Achene* gray to black, triangular, somewhat flattened with a ridged surface, about 3 mm. long, abundant. August–October.

Bottomlands, along roadsides, ditches, pastures, and farmyards; infrequent in cultivated fields. Native in an area extending from central Washington east to eastern Minnesota and south as far as New Mexico and central Texas and north into Manitoba; adventive in the northeast from New Jersey north through Maine and into Quebec and New Brunswick.

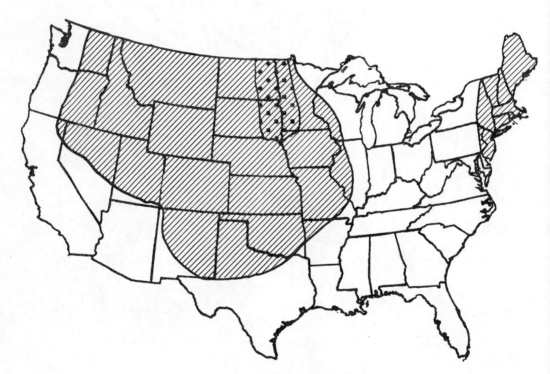

Distribution of *Iva xanthifolia* Nutt.

FIGURE 208.—*Iva xanthifolia* Nutt. Marshelder. *A*, Habit—× 0.5; *B*, inflorescence, showing staminate and pistillate flowers in same head—× 2; *C*, achenes—× 5.

COMPOSITAE

Lactuca pulchella (Pursh) DC.   BLUE LETTUCE

Perennial herb, reproducing by seeds and from a deep taproot or spreading horizontal roots that produce new shoots (Fig. 209); *Stem* 3–9 (rarely 12) dm. tall, very leafy up to the flowering portion, the lower stem not spiny; *Leaves* alternate, thickish, all stalkless, or the lower leaves more or less narrowed into a winged stalk; the principal leaves 5–15 (occasionally to 20) cm. long, slightly smaller upward, all unlobed or divided into 2 to many backward-pointing projections, these varying from mere notches to segments 2.5 cm. or more long, the upper half of the leaf usually undivided; the upper leaves numerous, narrow lance-shaped, mostly unlobed; *Flowers heads* few, 2–3, cm. in diameter in flower, their stalks with minute scaly bracts; *Flowers* all ray flowers, petallike, blue or purple, drying whitish, much longer than the surrounding bracts; *Bracts* surrounding the flower heads 13–20 mm. high, often purplish; *Achene* dark red-brown or sometimes slate-gray, 2–3 mm. long, tapering above into a short firm beak, 0.5–3 mm. long, which bears a tuft of white hairs (pappus) at the top, with 3–7 lengthwise ribs on each side. Usually July–September; June–October in the Pacific States.

Native of the grassland and sagebrush plains, alkali flats, wet meadows, and stream and river valleys; along roadsides, railroads, and ditches; irrigated pastures, cultivated lands, and grainfields. Common throughout an area extending from central Washington east to the Great Lakes, south as far as the Mexican border in New Mexico; distinct in Oklahoma; rare in Northeastern States.

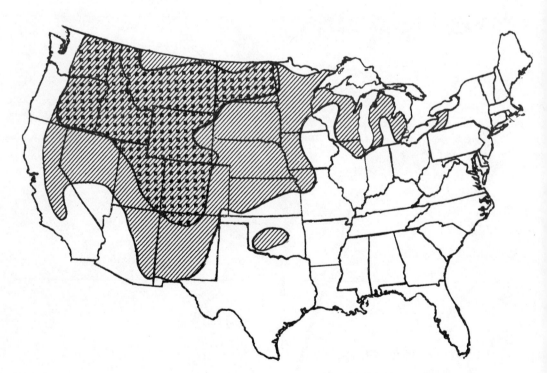

Distribution of *Lactuca pulchella* (Pursh) DC.

FIGURE 209.—*Lactuca pulchella* (Pursh) DC. Blue lettuce. *A*, Habit—× 0.5; *B*, involucre and flowers—× 1.5; *C*, achene—× 5.

COMPOSITAE

Lactuca serriola L.

Annual, winter annual, or *biennial* herb, with milky juice, from a large deep taproot, reproducing also by seeds (Fig. 210); *Stems* pale-green or straw-colored, 4.5–18 dm. tall, the lower stem often prickly; *Leaves* alternate, bluish-green, the edges prickly toothed, stalkless, clasping the stem, the base extended into a pair of arrowhead-shaped projections; the lower leaves 5–30 cm. long, 2.5–10 cm. wide, the midrib usually with short spines on the underside; the principal leaves with 1 to several irregular lobes along each side, or the leaves unlobed and merely prickly toothed (in the very common **var. integrata Gren. & Godr.**); *Flower heads* small, only 8–10 mm. in diameter in flower, with very narrow buds, numerous in the large many-branched flowering part; *Flowers* all strap-shaped, petallike ray flowers pale-yellow, often drying blue; *Bracts* surrounding the flower heads in 3 or 4 lengths, 9–16 mm. high; *Achene* flattish, pale-brown to gray, 3–3.5 mm. long, with 5–7 lengthwise ribs on each side, these and the 2 margined edges short-bristly near the summit, oblong, broader above, the tip sharp-pointed, from which arises a very slender, white, once-bent beak, slightly longer than the achene body, and bearing a parachutelike tuft of white hairs (pappus). July–September.

Dry soils; along roadsides, railroads, and sidewalks; vacant lots, dumps, fence rows, run-down pastures; cultivated fields, orchards, and vineyards. Native of Eurasia to the Himalayas; introduced from Europe. In Wyoming pulmonary emphysema develops in cattle feeding exclusively on this weed. Throughout all the United States excepting areas in extreme northern Maine and in extreme southern Florida.

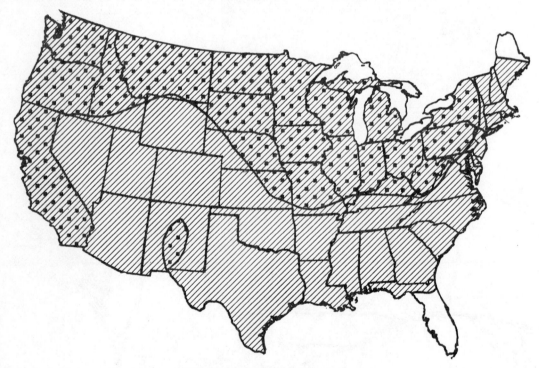

Distribution of *Lactuca serriola* L.

Regina O. Hughes

FIGURE 210.—*Lactuca serriola* L.   Prickly lettuce.   *A*, Habit—× 0.5: *a*, upper part of plant--× 0.5: *b*, lobed lower
leaves— × 0.5: *c*, linear upper leaves—× 1.5:*d*, root—× 1.5 *B*, flower heads—× 3; *C*, achenes— × 8.

COMPOSITAE

Senecio jacobaea L.

Biennial herb, or a rather short-lived *perennial* (Fig. 211); *Taproot* poorly developed to well-developed; *Stems* solitary or several, erect, simple up to the inflorescence, 2–10 dm. tall, pubescence floccose-tomentose, usually absent by flowering time; *Leaves* alternate, mostly 4–20 cm. long, 2–6 cm. wide, mostly 2- to 3-times pinnatifid, the lower leaves stalked and often deciduous, the upper leaves becoming sessile; *Flower heads* several or rather numerous, in a short broad inflorescence; *Disk* usually 7–10 mm. wide; *Involucre* about 4 mm. high, its bracts about 13, over 1 mm. wide, generally dark-tipped; *Rays* commonly about 13, mostly 4–10 mm. long; *Disk flowers* perfect and fertile; *Ray flowers* pistillate and fertile; *Achene* of the disk flowers minutely pubescent, achene of the ray flowers glabrous. July–September.

Pastures and disturbed situations. Native of Europe. Newly established along the Pacific Coast from Washington to northern California; along the Atlantic Coast from Maine to Rhode Island; Canada.

Distribution of *Senecio jacobaea* L.

FIGURE 211.—*Senecio jacobaea* L.   Tansy ragwort.   *A*, Habit—× 0.5; *B*, flower head—× 3; *C*, ray flower—× 4;
D, disk flower—× 4; *E*, achenes, ray flower—× 4; *F*, achenes, disk flower—× 4.

Solidago canadensis L.

Perennial herbs, reproducing from seed and from creeping rhizomes, without any well-developed caudex (Fig. 212); *Stems* clustered or solitary, about 3–15 dm. tall, glabrous at base, more or less puberulent above the middle; *Leaves* alternate, thin, sharply serrate to nearly entire, glabrous or slightly roughened above, glabrous to puberulent on the midrib and main veins beneath; the basal leaves lacking, or similar to the lower stem leaves, reduced and soon deciduous, the other leaves numerous and crowded, being gradually reduced upwards, lance-linear to narrowly lance-elliptic, long acuminate, tapering to the sessile base, 3-nerved, the larger leaves 6–13 cm. long, 5–18 mm. wide; *Inflorescence* a terminal, broadly pyramidlike panicle, 5–40 cm. high, with conspicuously recurved branches; *Involucres* about 2–3 mm. high, their bracts (phyllaries) overlapping in 3- to 4-series, thin and slender, acute or acuminate, yellowish to yellowish-green, without well-defined green tips; *Ray flowers* mostly 10–17, sometimes only 7, minute, about 1–1.5 mm long; *Disk flowers* fewer, thin corollas, 2.4–2.8 mm. long; *Achene* short-hairy. July–October.

Open places, both moist and dry. Native. Throughout approximately the northeastern and north central parts of the United States; north into Canada from Newfoundland to Manitoba.

About 100 species of goldenrod are known, mainly from North America. In addition to *Solidago canadensis*, species known to be weedy and of economic importance are:

S. gigantea Ait.—Damp thickets. Prince Edward Island to British Columbia south to New England, Florida, Mississippi, Louisiana, Texas, and New Mexico. Late July–October.

S. graminifolia (L.) Salisb, and var. *nuttallii* (Greene) Fern.—Damp or dry thickets and shores. Newfoundland to Minnesota, south to New England, North Carolina, Kentucky, and Missouri. August–October.

S. missouriensis Nutt.—Dry prairies, gravels, and rocky slopes. Southern British Columbia to Wisconsin, south to Arizona, Oklahoma and Missouri; also in northwestern Indiana, eastern Tennessee, and New Jersey. July–September.

S. nemoralis Ait.—Dry sterile open soils and thin woods. Florida to Texas, north to southern Canada, Minnesota, and South Dakota. Late June–December.

S. occidentalis Nutt.—Moist ground. Alberta to British Columbia, south to New Mexico and California. August–October.

S. rigida L.—Dry or gravelly open woods, thickets, and prairies. Massachusetts to Saskatchewan and Alberta, south to Georgia, Louisiana, New Mexico, and Texas. August–October.

S. rugosa Mill.—Damp open soil, thickets, and borders of woods and streams. Newfoundland to Ontario, south to New England and Florida, west to Michigan, Missouri, and Texas. August–October.

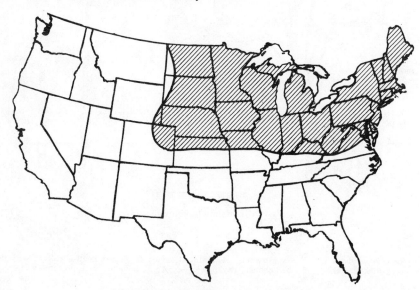

Distribution of *Solidago canadensis* L.

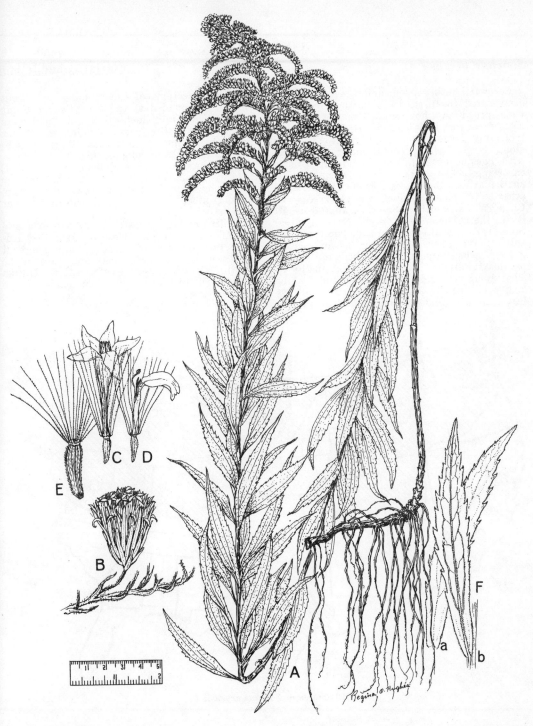

FIGURE 212.—*Solidago canadensis* L. Canada goldenrod. *A*, Habit—× 0.5; *B*, flower head—× 5; *C*, disk flower —× 12.5; *D*, ray flower—× 12.5; *E*, achene—× 12.5; *F*, leaves—× 1; *a*, upper surface; *b*, lower surface.

Sonchus arvensis L.

Perennial herb, reproducing by seeds or from deep-seated (5–10 ft. deep) vertical roots and wide-spreading, horizontal, plant-producing roots from root buds nearly 2 ft. deep, thus establishing large colonies (Fig. 213); *Stems* stout, large, hollow, containing milky juice, with conspicuous, stalked, gland-tipped hairs occurring on the upper stems, flowering stalks, particularly on the bracts surrounding the flowerheads (glands lacking in **var. glabrescens G. G. & W.**, also called **Sonchus uliginosus M. Bieb.**, the common form in the North Central States); *Leaves* alternate, crowded on the lower half of the stem, the upper leaves scarce, greatly reduced and often unlobed; the principal leaves divided into 2–5 (occasionally 7) lobes along each side, usually with the tip lobe longer or broadly triangular; or with all the leaves mostly unlobed or merely toothed; the earlike projections of the clasping leaf bases small and rounded at the tips; *Flower heads* large, 3–5 cm. in diameter in flower, the flowers orange-yellow; *Bracts* surrounding the flower heads 14–25 mm. high; *Achene* dark reddish-brown, 2–3.5 mm. long at maturity, oblong, slightly narrowed at each end, 5–7 distinct, lengthwise ribs on each side, the ribs strongly cross-ridged, but not the furrows in between. June–October, as early as April in warmer regions.

Cultivated lands, wastelands, oak woods, and grainfields. Native of western Asia and Europe. Locally frequent to occasional throughout Northern United States, becoming rare in the South, Central, and Southwestern United States. Distinct areas in other parts of the United States.

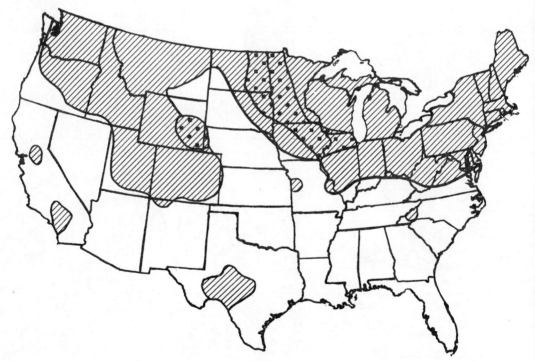

Distribution of *Sonchus arvensis* L.

FIGURE 213.—*Sonchus arvensis* L. Perennial sowthistle. *A*, Habit—× 0.5; *B*, achene—× 7.5.

Sonchus asper (L.) Hill

SPINY SOWTHISTLE

Annual herb, rarely *biennial*, reproducing by seeds only (Fig. 214); *Taproot* short; *Stem* erect, often reddish, very leafy up to the flowering part, gland-tipped hairs lacking or abundant (in the more common **forma glandulosus Beckh.**) on the upper stems and flower stalks; *Leaves* alternate, crowded along the stem, but progressively smaller and fewer lobes above; the main leaves many-lobed (5–11 lobes per side), usually with the tip lobe not longer or broadly triangular, to forms being scarcely lobed, margins with very long and stiff spines; the earlike projections at the leaf bases rounded; *Flower heads* small, 1.2–2.5 cm. in diameter in flower, the flowers pale-yellow; *Bracts* surrounding the flower heads only 9–16 mm. high; *Achene* at maturity orange-brown, 2–3 mm. long, thin and flat, broad through the center, the edges thinner than the body and winglike, usually with 3 distinct central ribs on each side (rarely 4 or 5), not cross-ridged, but the edges sometimes minutely serrate or cross-marked. Late June to frost; flowering year around in Florida, Texas, and California.

Winter vegetable crops, orchards, grainfields, alfalfa, and lawns. Native of western Asia, northern Africa, and Europe. Throughout the United States.

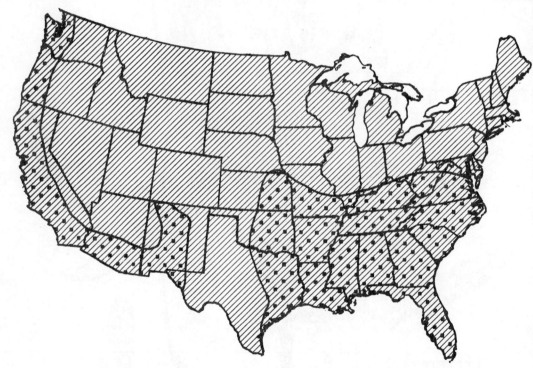

Distribution of *Sonchus asper* (L.) Hill

FIGURE 214.—*Sonchus asper* (L.) Hill. Spiny sowthistle. *A*, Habit—× 0.5; *B*, flower head—× 1.5; *C*, single flower—× 3; *D*, achenes—× 5.

Sonchus oleraceus L.

Annual herb, rarely *biennial*, reproducing by seeds (Fig. 215); *Stems* from a taproot, erect, branched, stout, glabrous and glaucous, 3–20 dm. tall, with a milky juice; *Leaves* alternate, crowded on the lower stem, fewer on the upper stem, often some of the principal leaves, as well as the basal leaves, stalked, the principal leaves deeply cut into 1–3 lobes along each side, with the tip lobe broadly triangular or rounded and cut nearly to the midvein; or the leaves sometimes with just 1 large lobe at the tip and a long winged stalk; or the leaves many-lobed with the tip lobe not enlarged; earlike projections of clasping leaf bases not rounded, but sharp-pointed or tapering to a point; the margins with weak prickly teeth; *Flower heads* 2–3 cm. broad, the ligulate flowers pale-yellow, the hairs (when present) on the bracts surrounding the flower heads, not gland-tipped; *Achene* 2.3–3 mm. long, broadest toward the top, tapering to a narrow base, the 5–7 lengthwise ribs not prominent and distinct, often running together, the ribs not strongly cross-ridged. July–September.

Cultivated fields, lawns, gardens, vineyards, orchards, roadsides, waste lots, railroad yards, beaches, grainfields, and ditchbanks. Native of North Africa, western Asia, and Europe. Widely distributed in the United States; most common in the Pacific States.

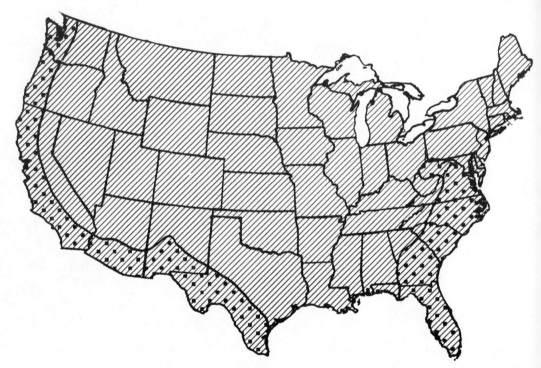

Distribution of *Sonchus oleraceus* L.

FIGURE 215.—*Sonchus oleraceus* L. Annual sowthistle. *A*, Habit—× 0.5; *B*, flower head—× 2; *C*, ray flower—× 6; *D*, achenes with pappus—× 7.5.

Taraxacum officinale Weber

(*T. vulgare* Lam.)

Perennial herb, from a thick taproot, often several feet deep, with many-branched crowns, with a milky juice, reproducing by seeds and by new shoots from the root crowns (Fig. 216); *Stems* very short and wholly underground, producing a rosette of leaves at the ground surface; *Leaves* 5–40 cm. long, variable in shape from lobeless or entire to being divided into many shallow to deep-cut lobes with long soft points and intermediate small teeth, a larger lobe at the tip, or the edges merely toothed, narrowed at the base into a short hollow petiole, usually pubescent; *Flower heads* 2–5 cm. in diameter in flower, solitary at the end of a naked hollow stalk 5–75 cm. long; *Receptacle* flat or convex, naked; *Flowers* all strap-shaped ray flowers, golden-yellow, 5-notched at the tip, 100–300 per head; *Bracts* (phyllaries) green to brownish, surrounding the flower heads in 2 rows, the outer row hanging down and one-third to one-half as long as the inner, erect row; *Achene* yellowish to greenish-brown, 3–4 mm. long, 5- to 8-ribbed on each side with minute curved spines on the rib margins of the upper half of the seed; *Beak* threadlike, 2–4 times longer than the body of the seed, topped by a tuft of whitish hairs (pappus), 3–4 mm. long, persistent. Flowering and fruiting from March to frost, or throughout the year in warmer areas.

Nearly a ubiquitous weed in waste areas, lawns, overgrazed pastures and meadows, open fields, and roadsides from sea level up to about 12,000-ft. elevation. Mainly a lawn pest, but also in hayfields and pastures; often an impurity in Kentucky bluegrass and forage grass seeds. Introduced and naturalized from Eurasia: perhaps also native of northern North America. Throughout most of the United States.

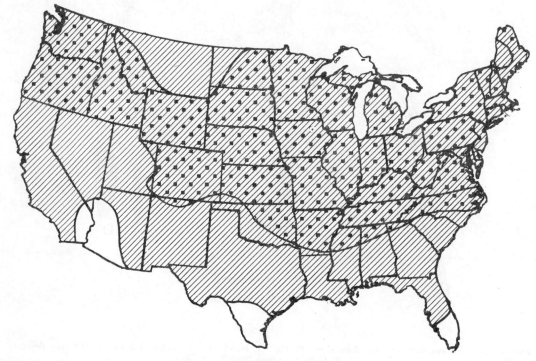

Distribution of *Taraxacum officinale* Weber

FIGURE 216.—*Taraxacum officinale* Weber. Dandelion. *A*, Habit—× 0.5; *B*, flower—× 3; *C*, achenes—× 7.5; *D*, achenes with pappus—× 1.

Vernonia altissima Nutt.

Perennial herb, reproducing by seeds and rhizomes (Fig. 217); *Roots* strong, fibrous; *Stem* 1–2 m. tall, widely branched in the upper region; *Leaves* alternate, loosely ascending to spreading, lance-oblong, or narrowly ovate, sharply toothed, mostly 3–8 cm. broad, the lower surface minutely pubescent, rarely dotted, with cottony hairs along the midrib; *Flowers* in cymes, 1–5 dm. broad, open, rarely dense; *Heads* saucer-shaped, 13- to 30-flowered; *Invo-*

lucres 4–6 mm. high, their flattened ovate phyllaries obtuse, acute, or short-pointed; *Disk flowers* reddish-purple; *Achene* oblong, with rough bristly hairs along the ribs. August–October.

Damp rich soils, meadows, pastures, and wastelands. Native. Throughout all the eastern half of the United States excepting areas along the northern border.

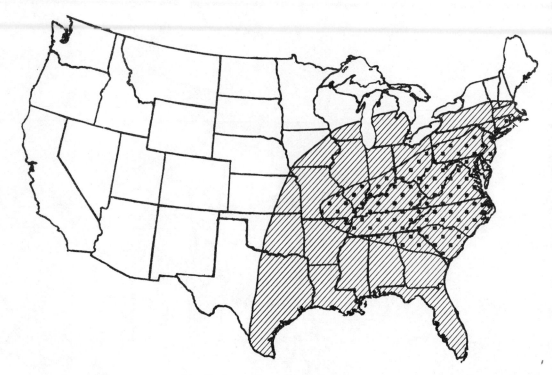

Distribution of *Vernonia altissima* Nutt.

FIGURE 217.—*Vernonia altissima* Nutt. Tall ironweed. *A*, Habit—× 0.5; *B*, flower head, showing the involucre—× 3; *C*, flower—× 3; *D*, achene—× 5.

Vernonia baldwinii Torr.

Perennial herb (Fig. 218); *Stems* 6–20 dm. tall, velvety; *Leaves* alternate, oblong or ovate-lanceolate, acute or acuminate, sharply cut on the margins, rough-bristly above, velvety beneath, 1–2 dm. long; *Heads* 18-to 34-flowered; *Involucre* 6–8 mm. broad, thick-cylindric to saucer-shaped, its tapering to awl-shaped phyllaries (bracts) spreading in all directions or recurving at the tip, pubescent within and their midribs prominent; *Inflorescence* corymblike to paniclelike; *Receptacle* flat; *Achene* about 3 mm. long. July–September.

Prairies, pastures, open ground, and woods. Native. Throughout approximately the central area of the United States extending west as far as Colorado and New Mexico and east as far as West Virginia and Virginia.

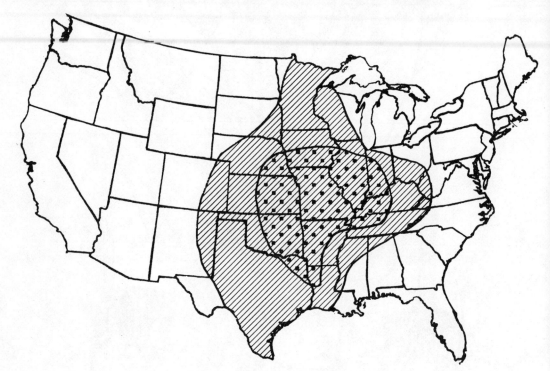

Distribution of *Vernonia baldwinii* Torr.

442

FIGURE 218.—*Vernonia baldwinii* Torr. Western ironweed. *A*, Habit—× 0.5; *B*, tomentose underside of leaf, enlarged; *C*, flower head—× 3; *D*, single flower—× 6; *E*, achenes—× 6.

Xanthium pensylvanicum Wallr.

Annual herb, robust, reproducing by seeds (Fig. 219); *Taproot* rather woody, stout; *Stems* erect, normally bushy, 2–9 dm. tall, ridged, rough-hairy, often purple-spotted; *Leaves* alternate, simple, heart-shaped to truncate, triangular-ovate or broadly wedge-shaped, toothed or lobed, with petioles about as long as the blades, rough on both sides; *Leaf axils* without spines; *Flowers* small, male and female separate in clusters, the staminate flowers in short terminal spikes, dropping soon after shedding the pollen, the pistillate flowers in axillary clusters; *Staminate involucre* top-shaped, with 7–12 separate bracts; *Pistillate involucre* ovoid, tough, closed, hairy and spiny, bearing 2 pistillate flowers, developing into a hard, woody bur; *Bur* oval to oblong, light-brown, about 1–2 cm. long, glabrous or nearly glabrous, with numerous crowded prickles 3–6 mm. long, these hooked at the summit, glandular-pubescent and sometimes very sparsely spiny near the base; *Beaks* 2, stout, incurved; *Achene* 1–1.5 cm. long, 2 in each bur, dark-brown, oblong, flattened, with pointed apex. Late August–October.

In cultivated fields, abandoned land, poor pastures, roadsides, bottomlands, waste places, and vacant lots. Native of Eurasia, Central America, and the Mississippi Valley. Widespread from southern Canada throughout most of the United States to Mexico. A variable species, having several similar forms based on variations of the shape, hairiness, and spininess of the mature burs. These forms are classified under **X. strumarium** L. and **X. orientale** L. by various authors, including **X. canadense Mill.** and **X. commune Britton.** The seedling is the most poisonous stage.

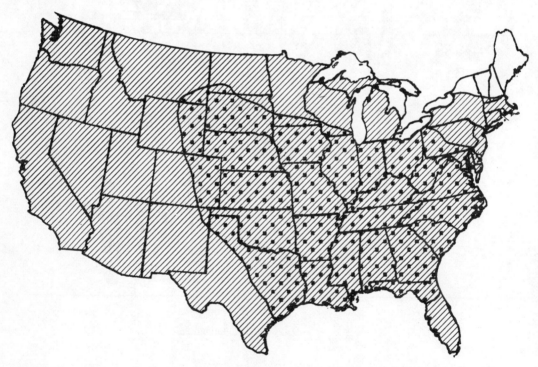

Distribution of *Xanthium pensylvanicum* Wallr.

FIGURE 219.—*Xanthium pensylvanicum* Wallr. Common cocklebur. *A*, Habit—× 0.5; *B*, seedling—× 0.5; *C*, bur—× 1.25; *D*, seed—× 1.5.

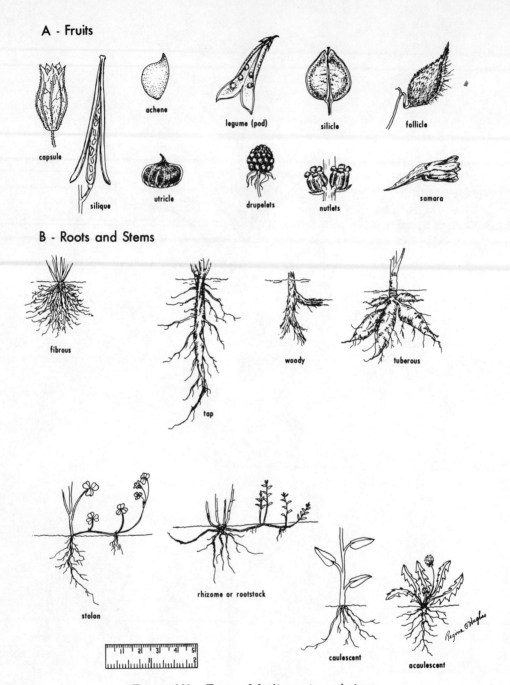

A - Fruits

capsule

silique

achene

utricle

legume (pod)

drupelets

silicle

nutlets

follicle

samara

B - Roots and Stems

fibrous

tap

woody

tuberous

stolon

rhizome or rootstock

caulescent

acaulescent

FIGURE 220.—Types of fruits, roots, and stems.

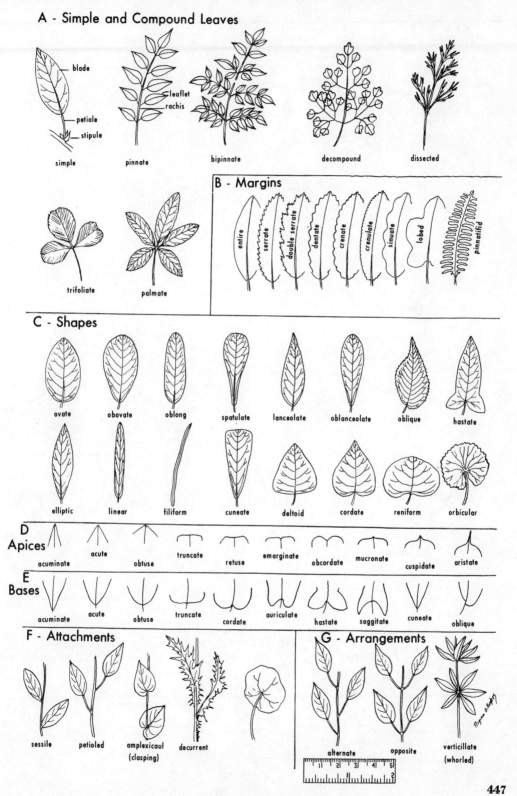

A - Simple and Compound Leaves

blade
petiole
stipule

simple

leaflet
rachis

pinnate

bipinnate

decompound

dissected

trifoliate

palmate

B - Margins

entire · serrate · double serrate · dentate · crenate · crenulate · sinuate · lobed · pinnatifid

C - Shapes

ovate · obovate · oblong · spatulate · lanceolate · oblanceolate · oblique · hastate

elliptic · linear · filiform · cuneate · deltoid · cordate · reniform · orbicular

D - Apices

acuminate · acute · obtuse · truncate · retuse · emarginate · obcordate · mucronate · cuspidate · aristate

E - Bases

acuminate · acute · obtuse · truncate · cordate · auriculate · hastate · saggitate · cuneate · oblique

F - Attachments

sessile · petioled · amplexicaul (clasping) · decurrent

G - Arrangements

alternate · opposite · verticillate (whorled)

447

FIGURE 221.—Leaf characters.

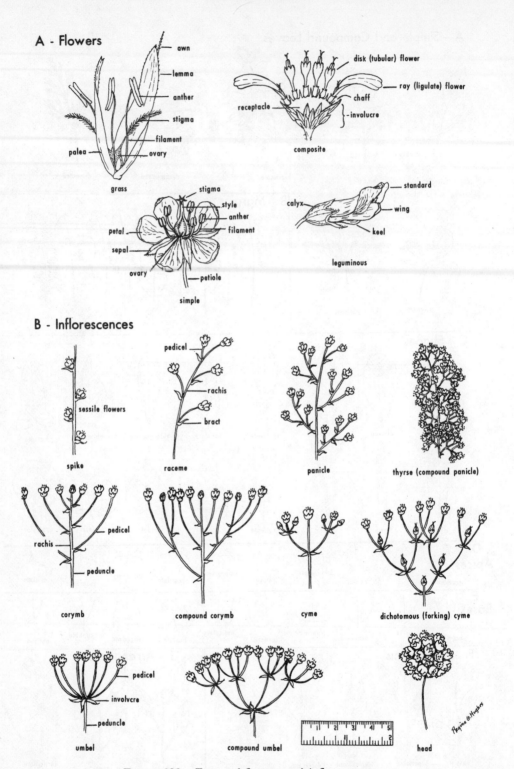

FIGURE 222.—Types of flowers and inflorescences.

GLOSSARY

Acaulescent – Stemless, or nearly so.

Achene – A dry indehiscent, one-seeded fruit, formed from a single carpel, the seed distinct from the fruit, as in Compositae.

Acuminate – Tapering gradually to the apex or tip.

Acute – Sharp-pointed.

Adnate – Attached to.

Alternate – With a single leaf or other structure at each node.

Amplexicaul – Said of a sessile leaf with its base clasping the stem horizontally.

Annual – Living one growing season.

Anthesis – The opening of the flower bud.

Areola (pl. -ae) – Small pits, usually surrounded by a ridge.

Aristate – Having awns, or awn-shaped.

Articulate – Jointed; breaking into distinct pieces without tearing at maturity.

Attenuate – Narrowed, tapered; elongated.

Auricle – Ear-shaped appendages, usually on leaves, petals, or stamens.

Auriculate – Having ear-shaped appendages.

Awn – A bristle on the flowering glumes of grasses.

Axil – The angle between the leaf or branch and the main axis.

Biennial – Living two growing seasons.

Bipinnate – Twice pinnately compound.

Blade – The expanded part of a leaf or floral part.

Bract – A small, rudimentary or imperfectly developed leaf.

Bulb – A bud with fleshy bracts or scales, usually subterranean.

Caducous – Nonpersistent; falling away readily.

Calyx – The outer set of sterile, floral leaves; the sepals considered collectively.

Campanulate – Bell-shaped.

Canescent – Becoming gray or grayish.

Capitate – Arranged in a head, as the flowers in Compositae.

Capitellate – Small-headed, as the flower heads in Compositate.

Capsule – A dry fruit of two or more carpels, usually dehiscent by valves.

Carpel – A portion of the ovary or female portion of the flower.

Caruncle – An outgrowth near the micropyle and hilum of the seed, as in Euphorbiaceae.

Caryopsis – "Seed" of grasses, a fruit, a grain; an achene in which the pericarp layers are fused.

Caudex – A trunk or stock.

Caulescent – Having a stem.

Cauline – On the stem, as stem leaves, as opposed to rosette or basal.

Cilia – Fine hairs or projections.

Ciliate – Having fine hairs or projections, usually as marginal hairs.

Ciliolate – Minutely ciliate.

Circumscissile – Opening all around by a transverse split.

Cleistogamy, Cleistogamous – Pollination and fertilization before the flower has opened.

Cochleiform – Shell-shaped.

Coma – A tuft of hairs attached to the testa of a seed.

Compound – Composed of several parts or divisions.

Contiguous – Touching but not united.

Cordate – Heart-shaped.

Corolla – The inner set of sterile, usually colored, floral leaves; the petals considered collectively.

Corymb – A raceme with the lower flower stalks longer than those above, so that all the flowers are at the same level.

Crenate – With roundish teeth or lobes.

Crenulate – Minutely crenate.

GLOSSARY—Continued

Culm – The stem of a grass or sedge.
Cuneate – Wedge-shaped.
Cuspidate – Having a rigid point.
Cyathium (pl. -ia) – An inflorescence reduced to look like a single flower.
Cyme – An inflorescence; a convex or flat flower cluster, the central flowers unfolding first.
Cymos – Having cymes, or cyme-like.

Deciduous – Dying back; seasonal shedding of leaves or other structures; falling off.
Decompound – Several times compounded or divided, as in leaves of carrot.
Decumbent – Lying flat, or being prostrate, but with the tip growing upwards.
Decurrent – Applied to an organ extending along the sides of another, as the leaf blade extending as wings down the petiole on the stem.
Deltoid – Triangular.
Dentate – Toothed, with outwardly projecting teeth.
Denticulate – Finely toothed.
Diffuse – Loosely spreading.
Digitate – Diverging like the spread fingers.
Dioecious – Only one sex in a plant; with male or female flowers only.
Disk (disc) – A flattened enlargement of the receptable of a flower of inflorescence; the head of tubular flowers, as in sunflower.
Dissected – Divided into many segments.
Divaricate – Widely spreading; forked.
Drupe – A fruit with a fleshy or pulpy outer part and a bone-like inner part; a single-seeded fleshy fruit.
Drupelet – A small drupe, as one section of a blackberry.

Eciliate – Without cilia or hairs.
Elliptic – Oval.
Emarginate – Lacking a distinct margin; with a notched apex.
Emersed – Amphibious; protruding upwards out of the water.
Endocarp – The inner layer of a fruit wall (pericarp); it is usually woody.
Entire – Without teeth, serrations, or lobes, as leaf margins.
Evanescent – Disappearing early; not permanent; or as veins fading away toward the margins of a leaf.

Falcate – Sickle-shaped.
Fascicled – A tuft of leaves or other structures crowded on a short stem, as the flowers in *Cuscuta*.
Fibrous – A mass of adventitious fine roots.
Filiform – Threadlike.
Flaccid – Limp or flabby.
Floccose – Cottony.
Follicle – A many-seeded dry fruit, derived from a single carpel, and splitting longitudinally down one side.
Fruit – The ripened ovary or ovaries with the attached parts.
Fugacious – Lasting for a short time; soon falling away.
Fuscous – Dingy-brown.
Fusiform – Elongated and tapering towards each end.

Glabrate – Nearly without hairs.
Glabrescent – Very thinly covered with hairs; becoming hairless as it matures.
Glabrous – Smooth or hairless.
Glaucous – Covered with a bluish or white bloom.
Glomerules – Cluster of short-stalked flowers, as in *Cuscuta*.
Glume – One of a pair of dry bracts, at the base of and enclosing the spikelet of grasses.
Gynophore – Said of a style that arises near the base of the carpels or ovary lobes, as in Euphorbiaceae.

Hastate – Arrow-shaped with the basal lobes spreading.
Head – A dense inflorescence of sessile or nearly sessile flowers, as in Compositae.

Hilum – Scar on a seed where it is attached to the fruit.
Hirsute – Having rather coarse, stiff hairs.
Hispid – With rough, bristly hairs.
Hyaline – Clear and translucent.
Hypanthium – An enlargement of the axis of a flower under the calyx, as in Euphorbiaceae.

Imbricate – Overlapping.
Incised – Cut into sharp lobes.
Indehiscent – Not opening at maturity.
Indusium (pl. -ia) – Covering of the sorus in a fern.
Inflorescence – The arrangement of the several flowers on the flowering shoot, as a spike, panicle, head, cyme, umbel, raceme.
Internode – The stem between two successive nodes.
Involucre – Any leaflike structure protecting the reproducing structure, as in flower heads of Compositae and Euphorbiaceae.

Keel – A projecting ridge, as in the flowers of Leguminosae.

Laciniate – Cut into narrow segments or lobes; fringed.
Lacuna (pl. -ae) – A large multicellular cavity, or a cavity anywhere in a plant.
Lanceolate – Flattened, two or three times as long as broad, widest in the middle and tapering to a pointed apex; lance-shaped.
Leaf sheath – The lower part of a leaf, which envelops the stem, as in grasses.
Leaflet – One of the divisions of a compound leaf.
Legume – A dry fruit consisting of one carpel, splitting by two longitudinal sutures with a row of seeds on the inner side of the central suture; pod, as in Leguminosae.
Lemma – The outer bract of a grass flower.
Lenticular – Bean-shaped; shaped like a double convex lens.
Ligule – A membrane at the junction of the leaf sheath and leaf base of many grasses.
Linear – A long and narrow organ with the sides nearly parallel.
Lobed – Divided to about the middle or less.
Locule – A compartment divided by a septa.
Lyrate – Pinnatified with the terminal lobe the largest.

Membranaceous – Thin and rather soft, often papery.
Mericarp – A one-seeded portion of a fruit that splits up at maturity.
Midrib – The central rib of a leaf or other organ; midvein.
Monadelphous – Said of stamens whose filaments are united in bundles or to form a tube.
Moniliform – Like a string of beads.
Monoecious – Both sexes in the same flower or on the same plant.
Mucronate – With a sharp, abrupt point.
Muricate – Having a surface roughened by short, sharp points.

Nerved – Veined or veiny.
Node – The part of a stem where the leaf, leaves, or secondary branches emerge.
Nutlet – A one-seeded portion of a fruit that fragments at maturity.

Obcordate – Inversely heart-shaped.
Oblanceolate – Inversely lanceolate.
Oblique – With part not opposite, but slightly uneven.
Oblong – Elliptical, blunt at each end, having nearly parallel sides, two to four times as long as broad.
Obovate – Inversely ovate.
Obtuse – Blunt or rounded.
Ocrea (pl. -ae) – A thin, sheathing stipule or a united pair of stipules.
Ocreolae – Stipular sheaths on the secondary stems, as in Polygonaceae.
Orbicular – Nearly circular in outline.
Ovate – Egg-shaped.

Palea or **Palet** – The inner bract of a grass floret.
Palmate – Diverging like the fingers of a hand.

GLOSSARY—Continued

Panicle – An inflorescence, a branched raceme, with each branch bearing a raceme of flowers, usually of pyramidal form.
Paniculate – Borne in panicles; resembling a panicle.
Pappus – A ring of fine hairs developed from the calyx, covering the fruit, as in Compositae; acting as a parachute for wind-dispersal, as in dandelion.
Pedicel or **Peduncle** – A short stalk.
Pedicelled – Having a short stalk, as a flower or fruit.
Peltate – More or less flattened, attached at the center on the underside.
Perennial – Growing many years or seasons.
Perfect – A flower having both stemens and carpels.
Perfoliate – Leaves clasping the stem, forming cups, as in *Dipsacus*.
Perianth – The calyx and corolla together; a floral envelop.
Pericarp – The body of a fruit developed from the ovary wall and enclosing the seeds.
Perigynium (pl. -ia) – The perianth in Cyperaceae, consisting of scales, bristles, or an inflated sac, as in *Carex*.
Persistent – Remaining attached after the growing season.
Petal – One of the modified leaves of the corolla; usually the colorful part of a flower.
Petiole – The unexpanded portion of a leaf; the stalk of a leaf.
Phyllary – An involucral bract in Compositae.
Pilose – Having scattered, simple, moderately stiff hairs.
Pinnate – Leaves divided into leaflects or segments along a common axis; a compound leaf.
Pinnatifid – Pinnately cleft to the middle or beyond.
Pistillate – Female-flowered, with pistils only.
Polymorphic – With many forms or variations, as in leaves; variable.
Prickle – A stiff, sharp-pointed outgrowth from the epidermis, as in *Solanum*.
Procumbent – Lying on the ground.
Puberulent – With very short hairs; woolly.
Pubescent – Covered with fine, soft hairs.
Punctate – With translucent dots or glands.

Raceme – An inflorescence, with the main axis bearing stalked flowers, these opening from the base upward.
Racemose – Like a raceme or in a raceme.
Rachilla – The axis in the center of a grass spikelet.
Rachis – The axis of a pinnately compound leaf; the axis of inflorescence; the portion of a fern frond to which the pinnae are attached.
Ray – A marginal flower with a strap-shaped corolla, as in Compositae.
Receptacle – The end of the flower stalk, bearing the parts of the flower.
Reniform – Kidney-shaped.
Reticulate – Netted, as veins in leaves; with a network of fine upstanding ridges, as on the surface of spores.
Retrorse – Pointing backwards and downward.
Retuse – Having a bluntly rounded apex with a central notch.
Rhizome – An elongated underground stem, as in ferns.
Rootstock – An elongated underground stem, usually in higher plants.
Rosette – A cluster of leaves, usually basal, as in dandelion.

Sagittate – Arrowhead-shaped.
Samara – A single-seeded, indehiscent fruit, having a winglike extension of the pericarp.
Scaberuluos – Slightly scabrous.
Scabrous – Having a surface covered with small wartlike projections; scurfy or rough.
Scale – A highly modified, dry leaf, usually for protection.
Scape – A leafless or nearly leafless stem, coming from an underground part and bearing a flower or flower cluster, as in *Allium*.
Scarious – Dry, thin, and with a dried-up appearance, usually at the tips and edges.
Schizocarp – A fruit that splits up at maturity into mericarps.
Scurfy – Covered with minute, membranous scales, as in *Chenopodium*.
Segment – A division of a compound leaf or of a perianth.
Sepal – One of the members of the calyx.
Serrate – With teeth projecting forward.

Serrulate – Finely serrate.
Sessile – Lacking a petiole or stalk.
Sigmoid – S-shaped.
Silicle – Similar to a silique, but short and broad, never more than four times as long as broad.
Silique – A dry elongated fruit divided by a partition between the two carpels into two sections.
Sinuate – With long, wavy margins.
Sinus – A depression or notch in a margin between two lobes.
Sorus – The fruiting structure in ferns, usually on the underside of the frond.
Spatulate – Widened at the top like a spatula.
Spike – An elongated inflorescence with sessile or nearly sessile flowers.
Spikelet – A small spike; the ultimate flower cluster of the inflorescence of grasses and sedges.
Spine – A short, thornlike organ.
Spinose – With spines, or spinelike.
Spinule – Small spine, giving a prickly effect.
Spinulose – With small, sharp spines.
Spreading – Diverging from the root and nearly prostrate, as the growth habit of *Mollugo*.
Stamen – The organ in the flower which produces pollen grains.
Staminate – Male-flowered, with stamens only.
Standard – The large petal that stands up at the back of the flower in Leguminosae.
Stellate – Star-shaped.
Stipule – Appendage at the base of a leaf, petal, or other plant part.
Stolon – A basal branch rooting at the nodes.
Stramineous – Straw-colored.
Striate – Marked with fine, longitudinal, parallel lines, as grooves or ridges.
Strigose – Bearing stiff, appressed, or ascending hairs.
Subcaulescent – Nearly treelike, or having a short stumplike stem.
Subinvolute – Parts rolled inward and under, as leaves, sepals, or petals.
Submersed or **Submerged** – Growing under water.
Subulate – Awl-shaped.

Taproot – A root system with a prominent main root, bearing smaller lateral roots.
Tendril – A slender, coiling structure.
Terete – Circular in cross section.
Ternate – Three-parted.
Thyrse – A densely branched inflorescence, with the main branching racemose but the lateral branching cymose; a compound panicle.
Tomentose – Covered with dense, woollike hairs.
Toothed – Dentate.
Trifoliate – A compound leaf with three leaflets, as in legumes.
Trigonous or **Trigonal** – Three-angled, as the stems of sedges.
Truncate – Terminating bluntly.
Tuber – A modified branch, usually underground and for storage of food.
Tuberous – Thickening and forming tubers.

Ubiquitous – Everywhere; in all types of habitats.
Umbel – A raceme in which the axis has not elongated, so the flower stalks arise at the same point, as in Umbelliferae.
Undulate – Wavy, as the margins of leaves.

Veins – The vascular portions of leaves, as in *Galium*, or flowers, as in *Potamogeton*.
Villosulous – Nearly villous.
Villous – Covered with short, soft hairs; nappy.
Viscid – Sticky.

Whorled – Three or more structures at a node, as leaves, branches, or floral parts.

INDEX [2]

[2] In the index, only synonyms will appear in italic.

457

462

A CATALOGUE OF SELECTED DOVER BOOKS
IN ALL FIELDS OF INTEREST

A CATALOGUE OF SELECTED DOVER BOOKS
IN ALL FIELDS OF INTEREST

THE NOTEBOOKS OF LEONARDO DA VINCI, edited by J.P. Richter. Extracts from manuscripts reveal great genius; on painting, sculpture, anatomy, sciences, geography, etc. Both Italian and English. 186 ms. pages reproduced, plus 500 additional drawings, including studies for Last Supper, Sforza monument, etc. 860pp. 7⅞ x 10¾.   USO 22572-0, 22573-9 Pa., Two vol. set $12.00

ART NOUVEAU DESIGNS IN COLOR, Alphonse Mucha, Maurice Verneuil, Georges Auriol. Full-color reproduction of Combinaisons ornamentales (c. 1900) by Art Nouveau masters. Floral, animal, geometric, interlacings, swashes — borders, frames, spots — all incredibly beautiful. 60 plates, hundreds of designs. 9⅜ x 8¹/₁₆ .   22885-1 Pa. $4.00

GRAPHIC WORKS OF ODILON REDON. All great fantastic lithographs, etchings, engravings, drawings, 209 in all. Monsters, Huysmans, still life work, etc. Introduction by Alfred Werner. 209pp. 9⅛ x 12¼.   21996-8 Pa. $6.00

EXOTIC FLORAL PATTERNS IN COLOR, E.-A. Seguy. Incredibly beautiful full-color pochoir work by great French designer of 20's. Complete Bouquets et frondaisons, Suggestions pour étoffes. Richness must be seen to be believed. 40 plates containing 120 patterns. 80pp. 9⅜ x 12¼.   23041-4 Pa. $6.00

SELECTED ETCHINGS OF JAMES A. McN. WHISTLER, James A. McN. Whistler. 149 outstanding etchings by the great American artist, including selections from the Thames set and two Venice sets, the complete French set, and many individual prints. Introduction and explanatory note on each print by Maria Naylor. 157pp. 9⅜ x 12¼.   23194-1 Pa. $5.00

VISUAL ILLUSIONS: THEIR CAUSES, CHARACTERISTICS, AND APPLICATIONS, Matthew Luckiesh. Thorough description, discussion; shape and size, color, motion; natural illusion. Uses in art and industry. 100 illustrations. 252pp.
21530-X Pa. $2.50

TEN BOOKS ON ARCHITECTURE, Vitruvius. The most important book ever written on architecture. Early Roman aesthetics, technology, classical orders, site selection, all other aspects. Stands behind everything since. Morgan translation. 331pp.
20645-9 Pa. $3.50

THE CODEX NUTTALL. A PICTURE MANUSCRIPT FROM ANCIENT MEXICO, as first edited by Zelia Nuttall. Only inexpensive edition, in full color, of a pre-Columbian Mexican (Mixtec) book. 88 color plates show kings, gods, heroes, temples, sacrifices. New explanatory, historical introduction by Arthur G. Miller. 96pp. 11³/₈ x 8½.   23168-2 Pa. $7.50

EAST O' THE SUN AND WEST O' THE MOON, George W. Dasent. Considered the best of all translations of these Norwegian folk tales, this collection has been enjoyed by generations of children (and folklorists too). Includes True and Untrue, Why the Sea is Salt, East O' the Sun and West O' the Moon, Why the Bear is Stumpy-Tailed, Boots and the Troll, The Cock and the Hen, Rich Peter the Pedlar, and 52 more. The only edition with all 59 tales. 77 illustrations by Erik Werenskiold and Theodor Kittelsen. xv + 418pp. 22521-6 Paperbound **$4.00**

GOOPS AND HOW TO BE THEM, Gelett Burgess. Classic of tongue-in-cheek humor, masquerading as etiquette book. 87 verses, twice as many cartoons, show mischievous Goops as they demonstrate to children virtues of table manners, neatness, courtesy, etc. Favorite for generations. viii + 88pp. 6½ x 9¼.
22233-0 Paperbound **$2.00**

ALICE'S ADVENTURES UNDER GROUND, Lewis Carroll. The first version, quite different from the final *Alice in Wonderland,* printed out by Carroll himself with his own illustrations. Complete facsimile of the "million dollar" manuscript Carroll gave to Alice Liddell in 1864. Introduction by Martin Gardner. viii + 96pp. Title and dedication pages in color. 21482-6 Paperbound **$1.50**

THE BROWNIES, THEIR BOOK, Palmer Cox. Small as mice, cunning as foxes, exuberant and full of mischief, the Brownies go to the zoo, toy shop, seashore, circus, etc., in 24 verse adventures and 266 illustrations. Long a favorite, since their first appearance in St. Nicholas Magazine. xi + 144pp. 6⅝ x 9¼.
21265-3 Paperbound **$2.50**

SONGS OF CHILDHOOD, Walter De La Mare. Published (under the pseudonym Walter Ramal) when De La Mare was only 29, this charming collection has long been a favorite children's book. A facsimile of the first edition in paper, the 47 poems capture the simplicity of the nursery rhyme and the ballad, including such lyrics as I Met Eve, Tartary, The Silver Penny. vii + 106pp. (USO) 21972-0 Paperbound
$2.00

THE COMPLETE NONSENSE OF EDWARD LEAR, Edward Lear. The finest 19th-century humorist-cartoonist in full: all nonsense limericks, zany alphabets, Owl and Pussycat, songs, nonsense botany, and more than 500 illustrations by Lear himself. Edited by Holbrook Jackson. xxix + 287pp. (USO) 20167-8 Paperbound **$3.00**

BILLY WHISKERS: THE AUTOBIOGRAPHY OF A GOAT, Frances Trego Montgomery. A favorite of children since the early 20th century, here are the escapades of that rambunctious, irresistible and mischievous goat—Billy Whiskers. Much in the spirit of *Peck's Bad Boy,* this is a book that children never tire of reading or hearing. All the original familiar illustrations by W. H. Fry are included: 6 color plates, 18 black and white drawings. 159pp. 22345-0 Paperbound **$2.75**

MOTHER GOOSE MELODIES. Faithful republication of the fabulously rare Munroe and Francis "copyright 1833" Boston edition—the most important Mother Goose collection, usually referred to as the "original." Familiar rhymes plus many rare ones, with wonderful old woodcut illustrations. Edited by E. F. Bleiler. 128pp. 4½ x 6⅜. 22577-1 Paperbound **$1.50**

HOW TO SOLVE CHESS PROBLEMS, Kenneth S. Howard. Practical suggestions on problem solving for very beginners. 58 two-move problems, 46 3-movers, 8 4-movers for practice, plus hints. 171pp. 20748-X Pa. $2.00

A GUIDE TO FAIRY CHESS, Anthony Dickins. 3-D chess, 4-D chess, chess on a cylindrical board, reflecting pieces that bounce off edges, cooperative chess, retrograde chess, maximummers, much more. Most based on work of great Dawson. Full handbook, 100 problems. 66pp. 7⅞ x 10¾. 22687-5 Pa. $2.00

WIN AT BACKGAMMON, Millard Hopper. Best opening moves, running game, blocking game, back game, tables of odds, etc. Hopper makes the game clear enough for anyone to play, and win. 43 diagrams. 111pp. 22894-0 Pa. $1.50

BIDDING A BRIDGE HAND, Terence Reese. Master player "thinks out loud" the binding of 75 hands that defy point count systems. Organized by bidding problem—no-fit situations, overbidding, underbidding, cueing your defense, etc. 254pp. EBE 22830-4 Pa. $3.00

THE PRECISION BIDDING SYSTEM IN BRIDGE, C.C. Wei, edited by Alan Truscott. Inventor of precision bidding presents average hands and hands from actual play, including games from 1969 Bermuda Bowl where system emerged. 114 exercises. 116pp. 21171-1 Pa. $1.75

LEARN MAGIC, Henry Hay. 20 simple, easy-to-follow lessons on magic for the new magician: illusions, card tricks, silks, sleights of hand, coin manipulations, escapes, and more —all with a minimum amount of equipment. Final chapter explains the great stage illusions. 92 illustrations. 285pp. 21238-6 Pa. $2.95

THE NEW MAGICIAN'S MANUAL, Walter B. Gibson. Step-by-step instructions and clear illustrations guide the novice in mastering 36 tricks; much equipment supplied on 16 pages of cut-out materials. 36 additional tricks. 64 illustrations. 159pp. 6⅝ x 10. 23113-5 Pa. $3.00

PROFESSIONAL MAGIC FOR AMATEURS, Walter B. Gibson. 50 easy, effective tricks used by professionals —cards, string, tumblers, handkerchiefs, mental magic, etc. 63 illustrations. 223pp. 23012-0 Pa. $2.50

CARD MANIPULATIONS, Jean Hugard. Very rich collection of manipulations; has taught thousands of fine magicians tricks that are really workable, eye-catching. Easily followed, serious work. Over 200 illustrations. 163pp. 20539-8 Pa. $2.00

ABBOTT'S ENCYCLOPEDIA OF ROPE TRICKS FOR MAGICIANS, Stewart James. Complete reference book for amateur and professional magicians containing more than 150 tricks involving knots, penetrations, cut and restored rope, etc. 510 illustrations. Reprint of 3rd edition. 400pp. 23206-9 Pa. $3.50

THE SECRETS OF HOUDINI, J.C. Cannell. Classic study of Houdini's incredible magic, exposing closely-kept professional secrets and revealing, in general terms, the whole art of stage magic. 67 illustrations. 279pp. 22913-0 Pa. $2.50

MODERN CHESS STRATEGY, Ludek Pachman. The use of the queen, the active king, exchanges, pawn play, the center, weak squares, etc. Section on rook alone worth price of the book. Stress on the moderns. Often considered the most important book on strategy. 314pp. 20290-9 Pa. $3.50

CHESS STRATEGY, Edward Lasker. One of half-dozen great theoretical works in chess, shows principles of action above and beyond moves. Acclaimed by Capablanca, Keres, etc. 282pp. USO 20528-2 Pa. $3.00

CHESS PRAXIS, THE PRAXIS OF MY SYSTEM, Aron Nimzovich. Founder of hypermodern chess explains his profound, influential theories that have dominated much of 20th century chess. 109 illustrative games. 369pp. 20296-8 Pa. $3.50

HOW TO PLAY THE CHESS OPENINGS, Eugene Znosko-Borovsky. Clear, profound examinations of just what each opening is intended to do and how opponent can counter. Many sample games, questions and answers. 147pp. 22795-2 Pa. $2.00

THE ART OF CHESS COMBINATION, Eugene Znosko-Borovsky. Modern explanation of principles, varieties, techniques and ideas behind them, illustrated with many examples from great players. 212pp. 20583-5 Pa. $2.50

COMBINATIONS: THE HEART OF CHESS, Irving Chernev. Step-by-step explanation of intricacies of combinative play. 356 combinations by Tarrasch, Botvinnik, Keres, Steinitz, Anderssen, Morphy, Marshall, Capablanca, others, all annotated. 245 pp. 21744-2 Pa. $3.00

HOW TO PLAY CHESS ENDINGS, Eugene Znosko-Borovsky. Thorough instruction manual by fine teacher analyzes each piece individually; many common endgame situations. Examines games by Steinitz, Alekhine, Lasker, others. Emphasis on understanding. 288pp. 21170-3 Pa. $2.75

MORPHY'S GAMES OF CHESS, Philip W. Sergeant. Romantic history, 54 games of greatest player of all time against Anderssen, Bird, Paulsen, Harrwitz; 52 games at odds; 52 blindfold; 100 consultation, informal, other games. Analyses by Anderssen, Steinitz, Morphy himself. 352pp. 20386-7 Pa. $4.00

500 MASTER GAMES OF CHESS, S. Tartakower, J. du Mont. Vast collection of great chess games from 1798-1938, with much material nowhere else readily available. Fully annotated, arranged by opening for easier study. 665pp. 23208-5 Pa. $6.00

THE SOVIET SCHOOL OF CHESS, Alexander Kotov and M. Yudovich. Authoritative work on modern Russian chess. History, conceptual background. 128 fully annotated games (most unavailable elsewhere) by Botvinnik, Keres, Smyslov, Tal, Petrosian, Spassky, more. 390pp. 20026-4 Pa. $3.95

WONDERS AND CURIOSITIES OF CHESS, Irving Chernev. A lifetime's accumulation of such wonders and curiosities as the longest won game, shortest game, chess problem with mate in 1220 moves, and much more unusual material — 356 items in all, over 160 complete games. 146 diagrams. 203pp. 23007-4 Pa. $3.50

MANUAL OF THE TREES OF NORTH AMERICA, Charles S. Sargent. The basic survey of every native tree and tree-like shrub, 717 species in all. Extremely full descriptions, information on habitat, growth, locales, economics, etc. Necessary to every serious tree lover. Over 100 finding keys. 783 illustrations. Total of 986pp.
20277-1, 20278-X Pa., Two vol. set $9.00

BIRDS OF THE NEW YORK AREA, John Bull. Indispensable guide to more than 400 species within a hundred-mile radius of Manhattan. Information on range, status, breeding, migration, distribution trends, etc. Foreword by Roger Tory Peterson. 17 drawings; maps. 540pp.
23222-0 Pa. $6.00

THE SEA-BEACH AT EBB-TIDE, Augusta Foote Arnold. Identify hundreds of marine plants and animals: algae, seaweeds, squids, crabs, corals, etc. Descriptions cover food, life cycle, size, shape, habitat. Over 600 drawings. 490pp.
21949-6 Pa. $5.00

THE MOTH BOOK, William J. Holland. Identify more than 2,000 moths of North America. General information, precise species descriptions. 623 illustrations plus 48 color plates show almost all species, full size. 1968 edition. Still the basic book. Total of 551pp. 6½ x 9¼.
21948-8 Pa. $6.00

AN INTRODUCTION TO THE REPTILES AND AMPHIBIANS OF THE UNITED STATES, Percy A. Morris. All lizards, crocodiles, turtles, snakes, toads, frogs; life history, identification, habits, suitability as pets, etc. Non-technical, but sound and broad. 130 photos. 253pp.
22982-3 Pa. $3.00

OLD NEW YORK IN EARLY PHOTOGRAPHS, edited by Mary Black. Your only chance to see New York City as it was 1853-1906, through 196 wonderful photographs from N.Y. Historical Society. Great Blizzard, Lincoln's funeral procession, great buildings. 228pp. 9 x 12.
22907-6 Pa. $6.00

THE AMERICAN REVOLUTION, A PICTURE SOURCEBOOK, John Grafton. Wonderful Bicentennial picture source, with 411 illustrations (contemporary and 19th century) showing battles, personalities, maps, events, flags, posters, soldier's life, ships, etc. all captioned and explained. A wonderful browsing book, supplement to other historical reading. 160pp. 9 x 12.
23226-3 Pa. $4.00

PERSONAL NARRATIVE OF A PILGRIMAGE TO AL-MADINAH AND MECCAH, Richard Burton. Great travel classic by remarkably colorful personality. Burton, disguised as a Moroccan, visited sacred shrines of Islam, narrowly escaping death. Wonderful observations of Islamic life, customs, personalities. 47 illustrations. Total of 959pp.
21217-3, 21218-1 Pa., Two vol. set $10.00

INCIDENTS OF TRAVEL IN CENTRAL AMERICA, CHIAPAS, AND YUCATAN, John L. Stephens. Almost single-handed discovery of Maya culture; exploration of ruined cities, monuments, temples; customs of Indians. 115 drawings. 892pp.
22404-X, 22405-8 Pa., Two vol. set $8.00

EGYPTIAN MAGIC, E.A. Wallis Budge. Foremost Egyptologist, curator at British Museum, on charms, curses, amulets, doll magic, transformations, control of demons, deific appearances, feats of great magicians. Many texts cited. 19 illustrations. 234pp. USO 22681-6 Pa. $2.50

THE LEYDEN PAPYRUS: AN EGYPTIAN MAGICAL BOOK, edited by F. Ll. Griffith, Herbert Thompson. Egyptian sorcerer's manual contains scores of spells: sex magic of various sorts, occult information, evoking visions, removing evil magic, etc. Transliteration faces translation. 207pp. 22994-7 Pa. $2.50

THE MALLEUS MALEFICARUM OF KRAMER AND SPRENGER, translated, edited by Montague Summers. Full text of most important witchhunter's "Bible," used by both Catholics and Protestants. Theory of witches, manifestations, remedies, etc. Indispensable to serious student. 278pp. 6⅝ x 10. USO 22802-9 Pa. $3.95

LOST CONTINENTS, L. Sprague de Camp. Great science-fiction author, finest, fullest study: Atlantis, Lemuria, Mu, Hyperborea, etc. Lost Tribes, Irish in pre-Columbian America, root races; in history, literature, art, occultism. Necessary to everyone concerned with theme. 17 illustrations. 348pp. 22668-9 Pa. $3.50

THE COMPLETE BOOKS OF CHARLES FORT, Charles Fort. Book of the Damned, Lo!, Wild Talents, New Lands. Greatest compilation of data: celestial appearances, flying saucers, falls of frogs, strange disappearances, inexplicable data not recognized by science. Inexhaustible, painstakingly documented. Do not confuse with modern charlatanry. Introduction by Damon Knight. Total of 1126pp.
23094-5 Clothbd. $15.00

FADS AND FALLACIES IN THE NAME OF SCIENCE, Martin Gardner. Fair, witty appraisal of cranks and quacks of science: Atlantis, Lemuria, flat earth, Velikovsky, orgone energy, Bridey Murphy, medical fads, etc. 373pp. 20394-8 Pa. $3.50

HOAXES, Curtis D. MacDougall. Unbelievably rich account of great hoaxes: Locke's moon hoax, Shakespearean forgeries, Loch Ness monster, Disumbrationist school of art, dozens more; also psychology of hoaxing. 54 illustrations. 338pp. 20465-0 Pa. $3.50

THE GENTLE ART OF MAKING ENEMIES, James A.M. Whistler. Greatest wit of his day deflates Wilde, Ruskin, Swinburne; strikes back at inane critics, exhibitions. Highly readable classic of impressionist revolution by great painter. Introduction by Alfred Werner. 334pp. 21875-9 Pa. $4.00

THE BOOK OF TEA, Kakuzo Okakura. Minor classic of the Orient: entertaining, charming explanation, interpretation of traditional Japanese culture in terms of tea ceremony. Edited by E.F. Bleiler. Total of 94pp. 20070-1 Pa. $1.25

Prices subject to change without notice.
Available at your book dealer or write for free catalogue to Dept. GI, Dover Publications, Inc., 180 Varick St., N.Y., N.Y. 10014. Dover publishes more than 150 books each year on science, elementary and advanced mathematics, biology, music, art, literary history, social sciences and other areas.